Japan's Postwar Peace Settlements

By the same author

CHINA PAKISTAN AND BANGLADESH : BASIC DOCUMENTS,
   1950-1976

DETENTE IN EUROPE : IMPLICATIONS FOR ASIA

CHINA AND JAPAN, 1949-1976

JAPAN'S POSTWAR PEACE SETTLEMENTS

SOVIET-SOUTH ASIAN RELATIONS, 1947-1977
A DOCUMENTARY STUDY (in two volumes)

PARTY POLITICS IN CHINA, 1945-1977
A DOCUMENTARY HISTORY OF PARTY CONGRESSES AND PARTY
   CONSTITUTIONS (forthcoming)

JAPAN'S POSTWAR PEACE SETTLEMENTS

R K JAIN

HUMANITIES PRESS
ATLANTIC HIGHLANDS, N.J.

First Published 1978 in the United States of America by
Humanities Press
Atlantic Highlands
N.J. 07716

Printed in India.

Library of Congress Cataloging in Publication Data

Jain, Rajendra Kumar.
    Japan's postwar peace settlements.

    Bibliography: p.
    Includes index
    1. Japan—Foreign relations—1945- 2. Japan—
    Foreign relations—Treaties. I. Title.
JX1577.J34   1978   327.52   78-4992
ISBN 0-391-00869-2

CONTENTS

45414

CONTENTS

LIST OF DOCUMENTS

UNITED KINGDOM

SOVIET UNION

INDIA

Southeast Asia

BURMA

PHILIPPINES

INDONESIA

CAMBODIA

LAOS

SOUTH VIETNAM

NORTH VIETNAM

THAILAND

NORTH KOREA

SOUTH KOREA

JAPAN

ABBREVIATIONS

ACC   — Allied Council for Japan
CFM   — Council of Foreign Ministers
EROA   — Economic Rehabilitation of Occupied Areas
FEC   — Far Eastern Commission
GARIOA   — Government and Relief in Occupied Areas
IMTFE   — International Military Tribunal for the Far East
POW   — Prisoner-of-War
SANACC   — State-Army-Navy-Air Force Coordinating
           Committee (successor of SWNCC)
SCAP   — Supreme Commander, Allied Powers, Japan
SWNCC   — State-War-Navy Coordinating Committee
UNRRA   — United Nations Relief and Rehabilitation
           Administration

xvi   JAPAN'S POSTWAR PEACE SETTLEMENTS

PREFACE

The San Francisco Peace Treaty of 8 September 1951, though signed by 48 nations, did not represent an over-all peace settlement with Japan. The Soviet Union, Poland and Czechoslovakia refused to sign it; Philippines refused to ratify it until satisfactory settlement had been reached about its reparations claims; Indonesia failed to ratify it even after the reparations problem had been solved and preferred to sign yet another Treaty of Peace (bilateral Treaty) in January 1958; both China and Taiwan were not invited to sign it; while India, Burma and Yugoslavia chose to dissociate themselves with it and concluded their separate bilateral peace arrangements.

The Soviet Union and other socialist countries of Europe normalized their relations with Japan in 1956 but a peace treaty has not been concluded so far between the Soviet Union and Japan because of the territorial dispute over the Kurile Islands. Japan's relations with China were normalized only in September 1972 when the Japan-Taiwan Peace Treaty of April 1952 was declared null and void. An accomodation was reached between Japan and South Vietnam in 1959 but relations with North Vietnam could be normalized only in October 1975 when Japan extended an aid grant of yen 8500 million. Japan established normal relations with South Korea in 1965 but relations with North Korea still await normalization. Thus, even after thirty long years, Japan cannot be said to have finalized its peace settlements with all the countries of the world.

Never before had a defeated nation to engage itself in such protracted, piece-meal and separate peace-making processes extending over a period of three decades, thus making Japan's case unique in the history of peace-making in the world.

The present study examines the attitudes of the United States, Britain, the Soviet Union, India, Southeast Asian countries and others towards peace-making with Japan and the reaction of the Japanese Government and political parties to various peace settlements. It also contains 98 basic documents (some of them translations from the French and Chinese languages), which include all the peace treaties, bilateral as well as multi-lateral, and various protocols, declarations, reparations and economic cooperation agreements and joint communiques on termination of state of war and normalizalion of relations.

New Delhi

R.K. JAIN

Chapter 1

UNITED STATES OF AMERICA

Although 49 nations signed the San Francisco Peace Treaty in 1951, it was primarily a peace settlement entered into and effected by the Western Powers, rather the two Anglo-Saxon countries, Britain and the United States, with Japan, with the US playing a dominant part. Most of the countries which signed the treaty were either allies of the USA or sympathetic to the American viewpoint. The treaty was, therefore, basically an American document which reflected Cold War considerations and American interests. Accordingly, it did not immediately establish peace between Japan and its immediate neighbours, particularly the Soviet Union and China, and with nonaligned Asian countries like Burma, India and Indonesia.

When Japan surrendered in 1945 nobody would have thought that within a few years international circumstances would compel the US, the principal occupying Power, to think of the defeated enemy as a potentially against the Soviet Union, the principal collaborator in the war against Japan. In the changed circumstances, many of the injunctions of the wartime agreements and the initial policy directives after the surrender were either modified or revised, if not completely set aside or ignored.

The change in American occupation policy towards Japan was not sudden. In the first phase of the occupation, from 1945 to 1947, the US set out in right earnest to implement the provisions of the Potsdam Declaration[1] and the terms of the Initial Post-Surrender Policy[2] which emphasized demilitarisation and democratisation of Japan and deconcentration of its economic base. Thus the Japanese Constitution of 1946 fundamentally changed the basic political philosophy of the country's government and incorporated a provision (Article 9) by which the Japanese renounced war as a national right as well as the threat or use of force to settle international disputes. This article also specified that land, sea and air forces would "never be maintained" by Japan.

The US occupation authorities carried out a broad programme of socio-economic reforms including agrarian relations, industrial labour and the Zaibatsu, besides the police system and education. Of the various American-inspired reforms under the Occupation two were outstandingly important. These were the new constitution and land reform, which served as protective shields, the first against reaction and the second against revolution. If the new constitution provided a firm foundation for parliamentary rule, land reform, by abolishing the tenancy system which had impoverished farmers in prewar years, removed a dangerous source of unrest and turned potential revolutionaries into cautious supporters of the conservative factions which have governed the country for the last 25 years.[3]

To ensure that Japan would not menace world peace and security again it was stripped of its colonial possessions and imperial pretensions, and completely disarmed and demilitarised, while steps were taken to establish a democratic and peace-loving government and to see that it did not regain power economically to make war. One method of reducing Japan's war potential was "exaction of just reparations in kind," another to forbid industries which would enable Japan to re-build its war machine.

A sweeping directive that General Douglas MacArthur, head of the Occupation administration, issued on 24 August 1946, ordered the Japanese Government to set aside as potential war reparations, and to maintain in good condition until their transfer, 505 of Japan's largest and most modern plants in eight basic branches of industry. These plants produced at their wartime peak 95 per cent of Japan's pig iron, 88 per cent of steel ingots, 50 per cent of machine tools, 90 per cent of ball and roller bearings, and 87 per cent of ship building facilities.

The Zaibatsu owned most of these concerns, and the list included 273 munitions plants, 90 machine tool factories, 22 iron and steel mills, 20 electric power stations, 25 shipyards, five large naval bases (including Yokosuka and Kure which the Americans and the British had occupied respectively), and 43 plants producing basic chemicals. The directive was based on a report that Edwin Pauley, President Truman's representative in the Far East, had prepared after detailed study and presented recommendations to the President and the Foreign Relations Committee of the US Senate on Japanese reparations.[4]

The US Government issued subsequently, in April 1947, an interim directive to the Supreme Commander of the Allied Powers authorising him to make available as reparations 30 per cent of the surplus industrial facilities in specified primary and secondary war industries. China was to receive half of these facilities and the Philippine Republic, Britain (for Burma and Malaya) and the Netherlands (for Netherlands East Indies) were each to receive one-sixth, that is five per pent.[5] Transfers under this interim programme did not begin until the third year of the Occupation and were the only reparations paid (some $160 million) by Japan on the authority of the Far Eastern Commission. In determining the shares of the countries concerned due account seems to have been taken to the scope of material and human destruction each claimant country had suffered as a result of Japanese aggression and of its contribution to Japan's defeat, including the extent and duration of its resistance to aggression.[6]

Apart from prescribing demilitarisation, disarmament and deconcentration of economic powers, the Potsdam Declaration and the Basic Post-Surrender Policy for Japan also stipulated that stern justice should be meted out to all war criminals. An International Military Tribunal for the Far East was accordingly instituted, and it tried some 28 major war criminals who were given severe punishment in the trial judgement officially pronounced in November 1948.

A change in the direction of US occupation policy was evident from 1948 onwards, when the emphasis shifted from retribution and reform to rehabilitation and rearmament. This change was due primarily to events outside Japan, and the increasing tensions of the Cold War in Europe in 1947-48

played a crucial part in it. The desirability of having a strong
and friendly Japan increased still more when the future of
Nationalist China became increasingly doubtful. Instead of
looking to China as a base for US Far Eastern policy in the
struggle against the Soviet Union, policymakers in Washington
began to look to Japan as the northern anchor of its defence
system. Thus the US decided to utilise Japan's geographical
position, manpower and industrial potential in its global efforts
to check alleged Soviet expansion.

The desire to reduce the economic burden of Japan on the
US taxpayer[7] was a minor factor contributing to this policy
switch. The decisive factor was however Washington's desire
to re-evaluate the international balance of forces and Japan's
relation to it. As early as May 1947, Under Secretary of State
Dean Acheson spoke of Germany and Japan as the "two great
workshops of Europe and Asia" and stressed the need to spur
their economic recovery.[8] In August 1947, John P. Davies, Jr.
of the Policy Planning Staff spoke of "a stable Japan, integrated
into the Pacific economy, friendly to the U.S. and in case of
need, a ready and dependable ally of the U.S."[9] The US
representative McCoy's statement before the Far Eastern
Commission in January 1948 urged the early revival of the
Japanese economy on a peaceful, self-supporting basis.[10]

Even Frederick S. Dunn, who seeks to picture the reversal
of economic and social policies by the Occupation authorities
in Japan as due primarily to the economic distress of that
country, rather than to considerations of US global strategy,
concedes that the changes effected were consistent with that
strategy and certainly received some impetus from the architects
of the policy of containment. He further says : "Although
the immediate purpose of SCAP's (Supreme Command, Allied
Powers) shift of policy with regard to the Zaibatsu and the
unions was also economic rehabilitation a definite political
objective always hovered in the background."

The change in the direction of American policy towards
Japan had been a gradual process. But "if any one event is to
be designated as the turning point in America's postwar policy
toward Japan," Dunn says, it was the National Security
Council decision of November 1948. The decision laid stress
on strengthening Japan economically and socially so that it

could remain stable and friendly to the United States, even after the termination of occupation, and suggested the creation of 150,000 man national police force.[11]

As the direction of US occupation policy in Japan changed from retribution and reform to rehabilitation and rearmament the pattern of pro-American and anti-American forces in Japan was neatly reversed. By the spring of 1952, when the occupation ended, the most influential sections of the Japanese intelligentsia and at least a substantial segment of the urban working population, who had earlier been greatly impressed by MacArthur's reforms and his purge of some tens of thousands of public figures and officials, had become disenchanted and suspicious of US intentions in regard to East Asia and Japan. On the other hand most of the original "purgees" had been "depurged" by early 1952, and many of them were back in public life. The far Left now suffered in some degree from an American-inspired governmental purge.[12]

Thus restrictions were placed on labour unions and the early directive, which had referred to "ultranationalistic territoristic or secret patriotic societies," was used to institute a drive against suspected Communists. In the changed circumstances resurgent big business, depurged politicians and bureaucrats paraded sentiments strongly pro-American while the Left bitterly attacked the Japanese *zaikai* (business world) for its subservience to "American monopoly capital."[13]

The changed American outlook on Japan led Washington to think of rearming Japan and retaining US military forces in Japan even after the occupation ended. It also manifested itself in pressing for the early revival of Japan's foreign trade and industry. An important offshoot of this policy was a reversal of the US position on reparations. The Johnston report of 26 April 1948 not only favoured economic aid instead of relief to rebuild Japanese industry and an enlarged merchant marine but also considered "authoritative action" on reparations "imperative" because this would affect the success of the entire recovery programme. So long as uncertainty prevailed about what constituted reparations, the Johnston report argued, it was impossible to plan intelligently to rehabilitate Japan's industry. It accordingly recommended an end to reparations.[14]

In his statement before the Far Eastern Commission on

12 May 1949 McCoy pointed to the persisting stalemate within
the Commission on the question of reparation shares,[15] the deficit Japanese economy, the need for economic stability, and to
the fact that Japan had already paid substantial reparations
through expropriation of its former overseas assets and in
smaller degree under the Advance Transfer Programme. He then
announced the decision of the US Government to rescind its
interim directive of 4 April 1947, thereby ending the programme. He also informed the Commission of Washington's
withdrawal of its proposal of 6 November 1947 on reparations
and made it quite plain that the US Government had no intention of taking further unilateral action under its interim directive powers to make more reparations removals possible. Japan,
McCoy said must be allowed to develop its non-military
industries without limit. "The problem facing us," he declared,
"is not one of limitation of Japan's peaceful industries but of
reviving these industries to provide the people's barest
wants."[16]

The first attempt at peacemaking with Japan was launched
on 11 July 1947 when the US proposed discussions on the
draft of a treaty with Japan in an 11-Power conference and
suggested a tentative date of 19 August 1947 for the convening
of a Japanese peace conference. The members of the proposed
conference would be the states represented on the Far Eastern
Commission, but the conference would be outside the commission. Decision at the conference would be taken by a simple
two-thirds majority.[17] A conference outside the framework of
the Commission was deliberately proposed to obviate the
necessity of following the voting method of the Commission,
which required the concurring votes of the Big Four in any
decision.

The Soviet proposal of 22 July 1947 that the Council of
Foreign Ministers of Britain, China, the Soviet Union and the
US should provisionally examine the question of a Japanese
peace treaty was not acceptable to Washington,[18] because this
would have given a power of veto to the Kremlin. It is significant to recall here that after examining the statements, contained in the joint declaration by United Nations of 1 January
1942,[19] the communique of the Moscow Conference of Four
Nations on General Security of 30 October 1943,[20] the Tehran

Declaration of 1 December 1943[21] and Part IX of the Crimea
Conference report of 11 February 1945,[22] the Legal Adviser to
the US Under-Secretary of State came to the conclusion that
those statements comprised political undertakings by the
Powers concerned to act in concert after the war, with respect
to the negotiation of peace treaties as well as other matters in
the organisation of peace. "But direct commitments regardless
of circumstances to make treaties of peace only jointly are not
found in the statements." No rules of international law, he
asserted, prevented the employment of separate peace-procedure
by a number less than all of the victorious belligerents in a war.[23]

Although the voting procedure Moscow suggested was not
acceptable to the US the idea of a punitive or restrictive treaty
was not completely abandoned. In 1946, US Secretary of State
James Byrnes had proposed a four-Power Draft Treaty on
Disarmament and Demilitarisation of Japan, to be enforced for
25 years by a quadripartite Commission of Control, acting by
majority vote. The system of inspection as provided in the
control concept was considered the most effective method of
assuring continued peace in Asia.[24] This concept was embodied in the Draft Treaty of peace with Japan prepared in the
US Department of State in early 1947. The Byrnes proposal
was welcomed in principle by Chinese and British Governments
but went unacknowledged by the Soviet Union. It was dropped
subsequently by the United States in view of its growing realization of Soviet threat and its changed policy in the matter. If
Russia continued to present "the same sort of threat to world
security that it presented today," George F. Kennan remarked
in his top secret report of 25 March 1948, "either we must not
have the [peace] treaty at all and retain allied troops in Japan
or we must permit Japan to rearm to the extent that it would
no longer constitute an open invitation to military aggression."[25]

The treaty draft, drawn up by the Hugh Borton group in
the US Department of State in March 1947, and the revised
drafts of August 1947 and January 1948 reflected the general
idea that all precautions must be taken against Japan's military
renaissance, which was considered "Asia's greatest menace."[26]
Accordingly the Japanese were to be permitted no military
forces, restrictions were to remain in force for 25 years, and
stringent reparations were to be imposed. The drafts envisaged

certain formal Allied controls over Japan lasting into the post-
treaty period, contained no provisions for the country's post-
treaty security, and made no mention of granting bases or other
military advantages to the US.[27]

In a memorandum concerning drafts of Chapter V (Interim
Controls) and Chapter VI (Disarmament and Demilitarisation)
of a Treaty of Peace with Japan in Process of Preparation by
the State Department, and Draft of Treaty on the Disarmament and Demilitarisation of Japan, General MacArthur
remarked, as early as 21 March 1947, that proposals in the
drafts about continuing military occupation of Japan even after
the signing of a Treaty of Peace and keeping existing control
machinery in slightly modified form "could not fail to be chal-
lenged as imperialistic in concept, in purpose, and in form."
The proposal for a later four Power control, to the exclusion
of other nations actively engaged in the war against Japan, he
pointed out, would be "highly offensive to the latter nations
and most unwarranted.[28]

The Policy Planning Staff of the State Department, headed
by George F. Kennan, one of the chief architects of the containment policy, did not agree with the Borton proposal for an early
peace settlement. It favoured a security pact against communism which would necessitate the retention of US forces in Japan.
In the opinion of this group the drafts seemed to have been
prepared in a policy vacuum or in the context of pre-Cold War
policy.[29] The Policy Planning Staff questioned whether it would
be preferable to pursue Washington's maximum objective—
Japan as an ally providing bases and industrial resources in the
struggle against the Soviet Union—or to settle for a peace which
left Japan neutral—and neutered—in the Cold War. George F.
Kennan shared the belief of many ranking officials that Japan's
strategic position, human resources and industrial potential must
somehow be denied to the Soviet Union.[30] When Kennan met
General Douglas MacArthur in Japan, he found the General
"unalterably opposed" to rearming Japan; to do so would be
costly, ineffective and contradictory to Occupation policies and
Washington's pledges to its allies.[31] Yet Kennan recognized the
potential value of a naval base at Yokosuka and concurred in
Army Department estimates of Okinawa's worth.[32] His views
very strongly influenced the definition of a new Japan policy,

embodied in NSC-13.[33]   That document, Roger Dingman observes, postponed peace, proposed winding down Occupation
reforms, and left open the door for American retention of bases
in Japan and Okinawa and for establishment of Japanese police
and coast guard forces which could serve as the nucleus for a
reconstituted, rearmed Japanese military.[34]

George F. Kennan laid much stress on the serious problem
of defending Japan against Russian domination. Soviet forces,
he said, were stationed in the Kurile Islands and South Sakhalin,
only a few miles away from Japan.   They also had a powerful
base at Vladivostok and it would probably not be many months
before they had overrun the whole Korean peninsula. This was
stated by Kennan in his conversations with officials of the
Canadian Department for External Affairs as early as June 1948.
"If a peace treaty were to be signed now and the Japanese cast
adrift," Mr. Kennan felt, it was obvious that the Russians would
exercise a good deal of military pressure against demilitarised
Japan.   The United States did not intend to permit that and it
was largely for this reason to quite an extent that they proposed
to prolong the occupation period. Certain responsibilities, however, had to be taken over by the Japanese themselves. Kennan
referred to the fact that the police force and the local gendarmerie were inadequate in numbers and had only one pistol for
every fourth man. The most urgent need at present, Kennan
observed, was for a coast guard to prevent the Russians from
infiltrating agents into Japan. Numbers of them, he added, were
already landing on Kyushu.[35]

Keeping in mind the defenceless state of Japan, the US Army
and Navy Departments considered the unrestricted use of bases
by the US and freedom to move men anywhere in the Japanese
islands, or throughout Asia from Japan, to be the basic essentials
of any plan to protect the country in the face of continued
Soviet hostility. They believed that a security pact or a contrac-
tual arrangement with Japan would confine US forces to particular bases which might be vulnerable to pinpoint attack. The
occupation was on the other hand more advantageous as it had
converted the whole of Japan into a vast American military base
which enabled the US to deploy its troops without any inter-
ference from the Japanese government anywhere in Japan and
other parts of Asia. The military preferred to drop the idea of

a peace treaty altogether and to prolong the occupation indefinitely.[36]

The defence of Japan, the *New York Times* observed on 27 May 1950, required more than one American base in Okinawa and a couple of airfields on the main islands. If Japan was to be defended against Soviet aggression "all of Japan has to be a base militarily and economically." In the opinion of this newspaper that would not mean the permanent US occupation of Japan but would signify a firm commitment on the part of Japan. The alternative was simply turning over the whole of East Asia to the Soviet Union. "What that would do to our Alaskan position," the paper commented, "is enough to give us pause." The paper desired that the problem of peace for Japan be approached "in the light of these grim realities."[37]

In pursuance of the policy decision taken in November 1948 on the recommendations of the National Security Council (Policy Paper NSC 13/2), which were based on Kennan's report of 25 March 1948,[38] the peacemaking efforts were officially shelved for the next two years.[39] Not only did occupation policy undergo vital changes in this period but also momentous events took place in the world arena. They included the Czechoslovak coup in 1948, the formation of the North Atlantic Treaty Organisation, the Communist victory in China, and subsequently war in Korea. These developments had an important bearing on making peace with Japan.

In the changed international context Japan was no longer considered an enemy but a potentially useful ally, and the idea of a punitive and restrictive settlement was accordingly given up. Reconciliation and lenience became Washington's watchwords. The buildup of Japan's economic and military strength no longer caused anxiety to the US. On the contrary, it was considered an asset to the global strategy against communism. The advancing course of the Cold War and the growing determination of the US that Japan should keep on the side of the Western nations, Dunn observes, made it increasingly clear that the Council of Foreign Ministers, with its principle of unanimity, could find no basis for agreement on a treaty.[40]

The idea of "positive neutrality" put forward by the Japanese Socialist leaders of Japan (Inejiro Asanuma and Masaburo Suzuki among others) with a view to avoiding involvement in the Cold War and the proposals to withdraw US forces and bases and keep Japan totally unarmed were regarded as lacking "practical understanding of the world situation and of the complexities in negotiating formal peace with Japan."[41] Thus the US decided to negotiate a separate peace treaty with Japan.

The question of a peace settlement was taken up with a sense of urgency in 1949-50 because the deleterious effects of an indefinite occupation were too obvious. The Japanese people were becoming restive about the prolonged presence of American troops and the Korean War had made an early peace with Japan imperative. To pacify the Japanese and get their willing cooperation for US military strategy in the Far East, Washington decided to proceed with restoring a formal status of independence to Japan.

It was believed that a free Japan under a friendly and conservative government would be a better ally of the US than one condemned to continued foreign rule. Japan had already proved a useful ally in the Korean crisis. It was apparent, however, that unless the country was given real independence in the foreseeable future it could not be expected to recognise its responsibilities in connection with the fight against communism waged under the flag of the United Nations in Korea.

The US decided to remove all restrictions on the Japanese Government and on industry, establish close links with the ruling conservative leadership to whom the reins of government were to be transferred, keep Tokyo permanently aligned with Washington, and retain its troops and bases on Japanese territory, in short to restore Japan's sovereignty in every respect except security and to grant Tokyo "autonomy in a divided world" as Borton put it.[42]

This bore at least some resemblance to the idea of a "half-treaty" Under Secretary of the Army Voorhees proposed in March 1950. That ingenious proposal would nominally have restored sovereignty and allowed the Japanese to exercise authority in civil matters, but retained SCAP and the occupation troops. By retaining SCAP the Voorhees proposal seemed to solve the problem of the legal right of a nonsignatory Soviet Union to send troops to Japan. But a conditional and qualified grant of sovereignty did not really signify an end of the occupation and conferred only a status of protectorate or "an

American puppet state" on Japan.[43]

The failure of US policy to help build China as a strong democratic nation closely allied with Washington and exercising a stabilising influence in Asia led American policymakers to devote increasing attention to Japan. In a speech before the National Press Club in Washington on 12 January 1950 Secretary of State Acheson stressed the need to assume the military defence of Japan and specifically included it in the defence perimeter of the US, which was said to run along the Aleutians to Japan and then to the Ryukyus, in the interests of maintaining security in the entire Pacific area.[44]

The Korean War and the Chinese intervention in it further enhanced the value of Japan as an indispensable military base and source of military supply for the UN forces in Korea. Japan, Korea, Okinawa, Formosa and the Philippines were seen as forming a defence ring against Communist expansion.

It was against this background that soon after the outbreak of the Korean War MacArthur authorised in July 1950 the formation of a 75,000-man Japanese National Police Reserve force,[45] and the US Government decided to give prominence to Japanese security arrangements and accelerate efforts for a peace settlement.[46]

Although the treaty draft of 13 October 1949, prepared by the State Department contained no security provisions, as these were to be inserted after consultations with the Defence Department, it embodied "the cardinal principle of protecting Japan against aggression, and in particular against Soviet aggression." This was the first draft, Dunn observes, written with full awareness of the Cold War, the policy of containment and the National Security Council decision of November 1948. The draft contained a few restrictions on Japanese sovereignty, prescribed no control or inspection agency after the occupation ended, required Japan to preserve a democratic form of government but made no specific mention of agrarian, labour and deconcentration reforms. These were left to the discretion of the Japanese themselves.

Though Japan was required to pay reparations no reference was made to the stocks of gold in Japan and those owned by Japan and held in neutral countries. The treaty draft thereby exempted Japan from paying war indemnities from that stock.

Japan was obliged to repay all GARIOA (Government and Relief in Occupied Areas)[47] and EROA (Economic Rehabilitation of Occupied Areas) grants from the US, and their repayment had priority over all reparations. The intent of this clause was to give the US control over the volume of reparations exacted by other nations. The primary motivation of this draft, in many respects similar to the treaty finally signed at San Francisco in September 1951, was "to align Japan with the United States in world affairs" by not subjecting it to severe restrictions and humiliating terms.[48]

John Foster Dulles was assigned the task of peacemaking with Japan on 18 May 1950. The first memorandum on Japan he issued on 6 June 1950 reflected his deep conviction that in the post-World War II era the greatest threat to peace was the communist movement and that it was not desirable to impose harsh, retaliatory terms on Japan if it was to be prevented from falling a prey to communism and used in the service of anti-communism.

The memorandum contained provision for a progressive withdrawal of their military occupation, establishment of a strong police force to deal with subversion, a security guarantee for Japan resting primarily on the US though not excluding the Soviet Union and other countries, admission of Japan to the UN, avoidance of any post-treaty control machinery and dropping all reparations or economic restrictions.

On the question of procedure, the 6 June memorandum not only envisaged an exchange of ideas with the non-communist members of the Far Eastern Commission before a preliminary conference was called of countries represented on the Commission plus Indonesia, Ceylon, South Korea and Indochina but also contained a novel suggestion for representing China at the conference. Both Nationalist China and Communist China would be invited, and each would be given one vote in case of disagreement, but only one vote between them on any issue they agreed upon. All procedural matters in preliminary conference would be decided by a majority vote while the terms of the treaty would be settled by a two-third vote.[49]

President Truman announced on 14 September 1950 that further discussions about a peace treaty for Japan would be undertaken with members of the Far Eastern Commission. By that time the US had decided not to place any restrictions on Japanese rearmament. It was quite apparent, however, that a peace settlement which failed to restrict Japanese rearmament was not likely to be adopted in an open conference composed of members of the Far Eastern Commission. Dulles therefore devised a new procedure of negotiating a treaty with Japan, through a series of bilateral negotiations or consultations with the nations concerned.

In October 1950 the US circulated a seven-point memorandum to the members of the Far Eastern Commission on the suggested content of the treaty.[50] It left no doubt that the US was prepared to make peace with Japan without the Soviet Union. The memorandum envisaged, among other things, Japanese membership of the UN, retention of US "and perhaps other" forces in Japan and adherence by Japan to the multilateral treaties dealing with narcotics, fishing and international trade. It also contained provisions regarding mutual waiver of claims and reference of disputes to the International Court of Justice. But it said nothing about limits on rearmament.

On territorial questions the memorandum called for Japanese recognition of the independence of Korea, renunciation of special rights and interests in China, and acceptance of the future decisions of the Big Four on the status of Formosa, the Pescadores, South Sakhalin and the Kuriles. If no decision was taken within a year the UN General Assembly would decide. Moreover Japan was required to "agree to United Nations trusteeship, with the United States as administering authority, of the Ryukyu and Bonin Islands." In the earlier version, Japan had been asked to "accept any decision of the United Nations which extends the trustee system to all or part of the Ryukyu and Bonin Islands."[51]

Replying to questions raised in a Soviet aide memoire of 20 November 1950, Washington said that it would not allow any single Power to hold up a peace settlement with Japan indefinitely. It defended its proposal to place Ryukyu and Bonin Islands under UN trusteeship and considered it reasonable for Japan to participate with the US and other nations in arrangements for individual and collective self-defence under Article 51 of the UN Charter. It was also made clear that the US did not favour limitations on the Japanese peacetime economy or denial of access to sources of raw materials or participation in world trade.[52] In addition Dulles stated that the US did not propose restrictions on rearming Japan.[53]

Before starting on a trip to Japan, the Philippines and Australia to hold bilateral discussions with their government, Dulles spoke of his desire to put the future relations of the US with Japan "on a long-term friendly basis" and to make the Japanese "worthy members of the free world," sharing honourably its opportunities, its responsibilities, and the common purpose of surmounting its dangers.[54]

In his public statements in Japan, Dulles justified Japan's right to protect itself against indirect aggression and to "share collective protection against direct aggression." In that connection he offered on behalf of the US to "sympathetically consider the retention of United States armed forces in and about Japan."[55] Dulles discussed "provisional security arrangements" between the US and Japan so as not to leave a power vacuum when the treaty came into force. He wanted Japan, to become "a useful member of the free world community" and therefore favoured a treaty which did not place heavy economic or financial burdens or major commercial disabilities on Japan.[56]

In the Philippines Dulles faced the difficult task of convincing his hosts about the waiver of reparations. Not only was he presented with a reparations claim of $8 billion but he also noticed that the Philippine mood was like that of the French at the end of World War I. He, therefore, sought to impress upon the Philippine Government the necessity of meeting the communist threat to the free world and of not repeating the errors of the Treaty of Versailles.[57]

Dulles argued that the US had already paid $2 billion after the Japanese surrender for imports of food and raw materials to make up the current deficits in Japan. It seemed ridiculous to think of extracting more from Japan in the form of reparations when it was already unable to pay for its essential imports.[58] Either the US would have to pay the reparations bill, which Dulles categorically stated it was not prepared to do, or Japan would default in its payments. Widespread starvation and unemployment in Japan would assure the communist conquest of Japan.[59] Despite this forceful pleading the countries the Japanese had occupied in the war continued to insist on reparations. Thus the discussions proved inconclusive.

The main issue Dulles discussed in Australia and New Zealand was how to prevent a possible recurrence of Japanese aggression. Dulles saw for himself the devastation and scars of Japanese bombing in the Philippines as well as Australia. This led him to remark : "In that part of the world, the threat of Russian and Chinese Communist invasion seemed rather remote, while the possibility of another Japanese invasion seemed a reality to those who had recently experienced that danger at first hand." But he insisted on the analogy of the Versailles Treaty that the surest way to induce rearmament was to forbid it.[60]

A solution was ultimately arrived at by concluding treaties with these countries (a bilateral Mutual Defence Treaty with the Philippines on 30 August 1951 and a tripartite Security Treaty with Australia and New Zealand on 11 September 1951) assuring them of US assistance in the event of attack by a remilitarised Japan.

Asked whether these Pacific security arrangements (then at the negotiating stage) were for defence against communism or due to fear of resurgent Japanese militarism, Dulles observed on 19 April 1951 that from the point of view of the US the proposed security arrangements were "primarily concerned with the danger from the Communist-controlled areas on the mainland" and that he did not envisage any danger from the Japanese side "unless by some mischance," which he did not foresee, Japan fell under Communist domination. He considered it natural however for countries like Australia which had suffered from Japanese invasion to still entertain fears from that side.[61]

A peace settlement with Japan, Dulles emphasised in a broadcast over the Colombia Broadcasting System on 1 March 1951, should restore Japan as an equal in the society of nations, give it a chance to earn its way in the world and become self-sustaining, encourage close cultural relations between it and the West, and provide it with a reasonable degree of security.[62]

In an address in Los Angeles on 31 March 1951 Dulles set out the principles underlying a treaty with Japan. He spoke of "a peace of reconciliation" restoring Japan to "a position of dignity and equality among the nations" and envisaged "provisional security measures" including retention of US armed forces in and about Japan for its protection. Any validation of Russia's title to South Sakhalin and the Kurile Islands in the treaty would be "dependent upon Russia's becoming a party to that treaty."

Dulles said Soviet participation in a Japanese peace settlement was not indispensable because Japan, unlike Germany and Austria, was not divided into zones of occupation. He denied Moscow had legal power to veto a settlement. In his opinion, the Soviet Union did not have even any "moral due bills, for its vast takings in Manchuria, Port Arthur, Dairen, Sakhalin, and the Kuriles repay it a thousand fold for its six days of nominal belligerency." Commenting on the uncooperative attitude of the Soviet Union in regard to a settlement, Dulles remarked : "When peace is far off, the Russian leaders speak lovingly of peace. But when peace comes near, they shun peace like the plauge."[63]

Dulles did not think it advisable to impose continuing burdens and restrictions on Japan. He did not favour extracting reparations "other than in terms of the Japanese assets already received from Japan or within the territory of the Allied powers." But the US had not closed its mind on the subject and was "actively exchanging views with countries which were most grievously damaged by Japanese aggression."[64]

The draft of the Japanese Peace Treaty prepared by Dulles was confidentially handed over by the US on 29 March 1951 to the representatives of some 15 countries which had been very actively engaged in the Pacific war. As the draft found its way into the press Washington deemed it necessary to clarify that it was "a tentative and suggestive draft of a peace treaty," a working paper subject to alteration and changes which the US itself might want to propose and "of course subject to considerations advanced by other governments." That "first tentative draft" was described as reflecting "in general substance" the type of treaty Dulles had proposed in considerable detail in his Los Angeles address.

A US Government press release of 6 April 1951 stated that in details and concrete language the draft did not "necessarily reflect the final views of the United States," much less those of other governments whose comments were awaited.[65] For instance, while the draft provided that reparations claims would be deemed satisfied out of assets in Allied countries a note appended to it stated that no final decision had been taken and that negotiations on the subject would be conducted with the nations concerned. Even though Dulles noticed an increasing area of understanding on the economic limitations on Japan's capacity to pay reparations he found no indication "as yet that the Philippines have abandoned its reparations claims."[66]

Addressing a meeting of the United Nations Association of Japan in Tokyo on 23 April 1951, Dulles spoke of a "prompt peace," a "just peace" and a "secure peace" which would be insured by the deterrent of collective power. He envisaged collective security arrangements for Japan and indicated that the US would continue to maintain its armed forces in Okinawa. He accused the Soviet leaders of ambitions for world conquest and observed that those who advocated a so-called overall peace with Japan were in effect advocating no peace at all. In the opinion of Dulles neutrality offered no protection of security, rather "it encourages aggression."[67] The Soviet desire to see Japan totally disarmed forever and without any security pact with any other nation had ulterior motives.[68]

In a memorandum of 19 May 1951 to the Soviet Union the US analysed Soviet comments on the draft treaty and replied in detail to Moscow's objections to procedure and to the proposed treatment of Formosa and the Pescadores, the Ryukyu and Bonin Islands and Japan's future security in the treaty.[69] The points the Soviet Union raised in a memorandum of 10 July 1951 were replied to by the US on 9 July 1951. It stated that the Soviet Union was not justified in denying Japan the right to enter into collective security arrangements—a right the UN Charter recognised as "inherent"—and that the terms of the treaty would recognise and protect equally the legitimate interests of every state which took part in the Japanese war.[70]

In his capacity as consultant to the US Secretary of State, Dulles replied on 3 September 1951 to the principal charges of the Soviet Union concerning the preparation and content of the Treaty. He admitted that a "total" peace without the participation of a Chinese government which was peacefully disposed and which had both legitimacy and power to bind all China by its ratification was not possible, but he saw no point in any suggestion to delay "giving Japan the very large measure of peace" which was possible. As regards Formosa the differences of opinion were such that it could not be definitely dealt with by a peace treaty to which the Allied Powers were as a whole parties. The treaty merely took Japan formally out of the Formosa picture, leaving the position otherwise unchanged. To Dulles, the proposed arrangement for collective security, the retention of US troops in Japan under the bilateral security pact, constituted "an exercise of sovereignty, not a derogation of sovereignty."[71]

While the US was not prepared to offer any special concession to buy Soviet participation since the basic issue of Japan's role as a member of the Western alliance offered no opportunity for compromise, Washington was inclined to obtain the consensus of its Cold War allies, particularly Britain. The US appeared keen, for reasons of prestige among others, to have Britain as a co-sponsor of the draft. Accordingly, in the course of a visit to London in June 1951, Dulles conceded some points the British raised, resisted other points which he considered placed undue restrictions on the Japanese economy or limited in any way the legitimate activities of Japanese industrialists, traders and ocean carriers, while in the case of some others a compromise was reached. Thus a joint draft of a peace treaty was hammered out. The communique issued on Dulles' talks with British Foreign Secretary Herbert Morrison spoke of "full agreement" between the two countries "on all main problems outstanding," though "this provisional agreement" was said to be subject to final approval by both sides.[72]

In his report to President Truman on his visit to Britain Dulles stated that although there had been initially considerable differences of opinion on important matters, they had all been cleared away as a result of "better understanding of facts and that reasoning which underlay the attitudes of the two governments." The agreement reached did not require any compromise of principle by anybody but represented "a fair agreement based upon mutual understanding and community of purpose."[73]

Dulles visited Paris in June 1951 and discussed the treaty with Alexander Parodi, Secretary-General of the French Ministry of Foreign Affairs. The French raised three demands: that Japan should pay France $2 billion in reparations; that it should conclude a commercial agreement protecting French trading interests in Indochina against "dumping"; and that the three associated states of Indochina—Laos, Cambodia and Vietnam—should participate in negotiating and signing the treaty. Dulles explained the reasons for the treaty provisions on these points, and it was agreed that further discussions would be carried on through regular diplomatic channels. The French case on the third point was eventually recognised, and the three associated states of Indochina were allowed to sign the final treaty as independent sovereign entities.[74]

The joint Anglo-American draft of the treaty, with which France was also said to be in accord, was circulated to the Allied Powers on 3 July 1951 and published on 12 July 1951. Dulles felt particularly happy about the British sponsorship of the draft (of the 15 nations principally concerned Dulles said seven were members of the British Commonwealth) and what he called "the striking evidence of unity as between our three great democracies"—the US, Britain and France. Describing certain features of the joint draft, Dulles proudly asserted that the proposed treaty did not put Japan under any permanent restrictions or disabilities, not even regarding rearmament or research on atomic weapons. Imposition of treaty limitations or discriminatory restrictions were rarely enforced and often provoked the very result sought to be avoided. The bilateral US-Japan security treaty, he added, would make it "materially impossible for Japan to wage a war of revenge."[75]

After further consultations and exchanges in July-August 1951 the 3 July 1951 joint draft, which was believed to combine and reconcile, "as far as practicable," the point of view of all the Allied Powers at war with Japan, was further modified and a "final text" prepared and circulated on 13 August 1951. According to Dulles, "no less than 30 additional changes" were made in this text compared with the revised 3 July draft, and the final version comprised 27 articles and two accompanying declarations against 22 articles in the 29 March draft.[76]

In addition to amendments on legal points, clauses dealing with the sovereignty of the Japanese people, with the repatriation of prisoners of war, and with reparations were inserted or substantially rephrased to meet the wishes of a number of countries in the text of the 13 August draft, which was declared to be final and not open for change or amendment.

The San Francisco Conference, it was specifically stated in the invitations Washington issued on 20 July 1951 to all governments at war with Japan (except China) to attend it, was not a conference to re-open negotiations on the terms of peace but "a conference for conclusion and signature of the treaty of peace with Japan on the terms of that text."[77]   A series of identical bilateral treaties could have been signed and a general conference avoided altogether. Signature of the treaty was preceded by a conference because a number of "allied powers had expressed a desire that they should have an opportunity to make statements regarding the treaty prior to the actual signing."[78] It was also believed that the re-entry of Japan into the international community would be given far greater significance if it were marked by an impressive public ceremony in which a large number of states recorded their agreement.[79]

Dulles considered the Final Text of the peace treaty to be "the most broadly based peace treaty in all history" although the disunity among the members of the Far Eastern Commission seemed to dilute, if not totally disprove, the validity of this claim. Commenting on "the most difficult problem" of reparations, he observed that if the treaty validated all just claims against Japan it would be submerged by liabilities of more than 100 billion dollars. On the other hand it was realised that the treaty could not ignore the principle of reparations for damage and suffering Japan had caused in the war. A via media was found whereby the devastated countries could export to Japan the raw materials many of them had in abundance while the Japanese could process them with their industrially trained workforce and industrial equipment, both of which were partly unemployed, free of charge and provide "appreciable reparations." Such arrangements, Dulles stated, could cover not merely consumer goods but machinery and capital goods to enable the underdeveloped countries to speed up the development of their own industry.[80]

The question of fisheries also engaged the attention of the US. The operations of long-range Japanese fishing vessels before the war were a cause of concern not only to fishing interests on the Pacific coast of the US and Canada but also to Australia, South Korea, the Philippines and Indonesia.

Besides considering them a threat to the fishing interests of these maritime states, Japanese fishermen were also viewed as a possible cover for espionage, smuggling and illegal immigration. After the war the fishing fleet of Japan, the biggest fishing nation with a catch of 8.6 billion pounds in 1951, had more than doubled—from 526,000 gross registered tons in 1934-1939 to 1.2 million in 1951.

To meet the wishes of those states which felt concerned at the far-ranging and ably organised Japanese fishing operations fleets Dulles had secured in February 1951 a letter from Prime Minister Yoshida expressing his government's intention to prohibit Japanese resident nationals and vessels from fishing in conserved fisheries where they had not operated in 1940. Specifically mentioned as subject to this protection were salmon, halibut, herring, sardine and tuna fisheries in the eastern Pacific and the Bering Sea. On 13 July 1951, at the prompting of the US, the Japanese Cabinet made a public announcement that this intention extended to conserved areas anywhere. American and Canadian interests were protected by the specific mention of fisheries in the eastern Pacific and the Bering Sea, but other nations did not feel satisfied with the arrangement. It was therefore not surprising that both the Netherlands and Indonesia singled out the fisheries article of the final text (Article 9) as the one needing amendment.[81] This Article merely required Japan to "enter promptly into negotiations with the Allied Powers so desiring for the conclusion of bilateral and multilateral agreements providing for the regulation or limitation of fishing and the conservation and development of fisheries on the high seas." The US, Canada and Japan signed the North Pacific Fisheries Convention on 9 May 1952 and it came into effect on 12 June 1953.

In his detailed statement before the San Francisco Conference on 5 September 1951, Dulles analysed in depth the significance of the various provisions of the treaty and explained why certain obligations such as human rights and fair trade practices were put in its preamble rather than written into the treaty in the form of legal obligations. He said Japan could enter into collective security arrangements even before the treaty came into force, thereby avoiding the physical removal of the occupation elements before they could serve as collective security forces. To insist otherwise, he observed, would be "a burdensome requirement and a risky one for it would for a time leave Japan wholly defenceless, in close proximity to proved aggressors possessed of great military strength." To avoid that danger, provision had been made in Article 6 for the continued stay of the occupation elements in Japan for its defence if the Japanese Government desired.

Dulles regretted that the Sino-Japanese War could not be formally ended on that occasion. But by Article 21 China without need of signature, "gets the sweeping renunciation by Japan (Article 10) of all Japan's special rights and interests in China." Also China "receives automatically and without need of signature, the benefit of Article 14 (a) 2 which validates the seizure of Japanese property subject to its jurisdiction." The treaty, Dulles emphasized "preserves in full the right of China as one of the Allied victors in this war." He concluded his statement by saying that although the treaty text contained imperfections, and nobody was completely satisfied with it, it was a "good treaty," it did not contain the seeds of another war and was "truly a treaty of peace."[82]

A statement Dulles made to the conference on 7 September 1951 was concerned with Soviet proposals, which, as Dunn points out, were aimed at removing all influence of the US in Japanese affairs and eliminating American military power in the whole area as well as a rigorous limitation on any Japanese rearmament.[83] If Japan was to be allowed only a token defence force and denied the benefit of collective security Japan would stand exposed to external aggression, Dulles argued. He said Soviet proposal No. 13, which stated that La Perouse (Soya), Nemoru, Tsugaru and Tsushima Straits might be used only by the navies of such countries as were based on the Sea of Japan, meant that only the Soviet naval force based on Vladivostok could use them. The Soviet Navy could patrol the waters in and about Japan, cut Japan in two and divide it from Korea, so that not even a UN force could operate in the straits between Korea and Japan.[84] Thus acceptance of the Soviet proposal would have given Moscow the means to control Japan from the north.

The Soviet representative was not the only delegate at San Francisco to express his dissatisfaction with the Anglo-

American text of the treaty. The Polish and Czech representatives fully supported Andrei Gromyko in his criticism of it. The Philippine and Indonesian delegates expressed their serious reservations about the reparations clauses. The French representative, Maurice Schuman, while accepting the treaty, referred to its imperfections and risks. The Netherlands delegate, Dirk Stikker, complained that the treaty did not satisfy the Dutch in respect of reparations and spoke of the sufferings of Dutch military prisoners and civilian internees at the hands of the Japanese. The Egyptian representative, Kamil Rahim, while announcing his intention to sign the treaty, objected to the continuance of American troops and bases in Japan after the occupation ended. He also expressed the opinion that the final disposition of the Ryukyu and Bonin Islands should have been left to the UN General Assembly.[85]

Despite the divergent views expressed at the conference, the final text of the treaty was signed on 8 September 1951 by 49 nations, including Japan, out of the 52 nations represented. Only the Soviet Union, Poland and Czechoslovakia refused to sign. On the same day, the US Secretary of State and the Japanese Prime Minister exchanged letters confirming on the Japanese side that if and when the forces of a member or members of the UN were engaged in any UN action in the Far East after the treaty came into force "Japan will permit and facilitate the support in and about Japan, by the member or members, of the forces engaged in such United Nations action."[86]

Signing the San Francisco Peace Treaty and the bilateral US-Japan Security Treaty on 8 September 1951 was considered a severe diplomatic defeat for the Soviet Union, "a great setback" for Soviet diplomacy and a corresponding gain for the US as the principal sponsor of these instruments.[87] The peace treaty was accompanied by a declaration in which the Japanese Government announced its intention to resume its rights and obligations under a number of multilateral agreements to which Japan had been a party at the time of the outbreak of the European War in 1939. The Government also signified its intention of adhering to several similar agreements to which it was not a party. After the necessary ratifications had been exchanged the peace treaty came into force on 28 April 1952.

45414

The administrative Agreement signed on 28 February 1952 in pursuance of Article 3 of the security treaty provided that after the peace treaty came into force the US Government could bring into Japan whatever armed forces were needed, together with their dependants and attached civilians, to implement the provisions of the bilateral pact. No limit was placed on the size or type of such forces. Japan would grant all facilities to the US forces in respect of ports, airfields and other requirements, and the US authorities would retain criminal jurisdiction over their service personnel and their dependents.[88]

The ratification of the San Francisco Treaty by El Salvador on 6 May 1952 was accompanied with the following declaration :

I.   El Salvador neither accepts nor ratifies engagements which other states may have contracted with respect to the transfer or the final disposal of the territories enumerated in Article 2 of the Treaty of Peace with Japan, in all cases in which the will of the populations affected, freely expressed, has not been consulted and respected. This reserve applies to the transfer of the Kurile Islands or a part of Sakhalin Islands and to all other analogous cases, including in addition any engagement regarding the island of Formosa; and

II. The provisions of Article 14 of the Treaty of Peace with Japan, which authorises the confiscation of the property of Japanese natural or juridical persons shall be of no effect in El Salvador, as being contrary to the political constitution of the country.[89]

The final treaty with Japan, signed on 8 September, "reflected an almost complete reversal of national viewpoint towards the Japanese on the part of the United States and many of its allies," US Ambassador William Sebald remarked. The initial vengefulness had yielded eventually to cooperation, and fear of resurgent Japan disappeared behind the realities of the Cold War.[90] With a view "to translate Japan from a defeated enemy into a positive contributor to collective security in the Pacific as against the new menace of aggression,"[91] the US deemed it necessary to offer a peace of reconciliation to Japan which did not impose any economic or military limitations.

It was believed that reparation liabilities, if enforced, would have permanently depressed Japanese standards of living to a dangerous level.[92] Insistence on payment in any proportion commensurate with the claims of the injured countries and their nationals, a report of the US Senate Committee on Foreign Relations said, would wreck Japan's economy, destroy the initiative of its people and create misery and chaos in which the seeds of discontent and communism would flourish. A free, prosperous and democratic Japan could on the other hand exert an important stabilising influence in the Far East.[93]

The Committee on Foreign Relations also explored in its hearings the question of the "belligerent rights" of USSR and Communist China in Japan after the treaty came into effect. The Potsdam surrender terms of 26 July 1945, to which USSR later adhered, it was stated, provided for a single Allied occupation—not for separate and independent Allied occupations—which was to end with the achievement of certain stated objectives. Signature of the treaty by 49 nations was considered conclusive evidence that these objectives had been attained. Accordingly, the exercise of belligerent rights by any single Power was stated to be a unilateral action in direct violation of Potsdam.[94]

In considering the treaty in February 1952, the Foreign Relations Committee of the US Senate attached a two-part reservation which provided that nothing in the treaty diminished or prejudiced Japanese or Allied rights in the Kuriles and southern Sakhalin or implied US recognition of Soviet territorial gains attributable to the Yalta Agreement.[95] A State Department aide memoire of 7 September 1956 supported Japan's claims to the Kuriles and described the Yalta Agreement as "simply a statement of common purpose" rather than a final determination of the islands' status. The ultimate disposition of the Kuriles and other territories to which Japan had renounced all claims could only be decided by future "international solvents."[96]

Chapter 2

UNITED KINGDOM

While Britain had generally shown understanding of the US
standpoint on the Japanese peace settlement it was not unmindful of its own interests. As early as May 1947 Foreign Secretary Ernest Bevin said that the problems of the British trade in
textiles had been raised by several members of Parliament. In
that connection he referred to the enactment on labour conditions "recently made in Japan, incorporating a wage plan and
enforcing wage standards for the textile industry." The fair
wage clause also covered child labour and meant that children
below the age of 15 would not be employed in Japanese mills.
Bevin considered this "a very important law" so far as Japan
was concerned and expressed his conviction that "it will certainly have an effect." He observed at the same time : "We cannot save the Lancashire and Yorkshire textile trade by imposing
restrictions on other countries."[1] In June 1947, the British
Government expressed its disappointment at what it called "the
ungenerous treatment" by the US Government in proposing a
smaller percentage of 8 per cent for the United Kingdom share
of reparations from Japan.[2]

The Canberra conference of Commonwealth countries held
in August-September 1947 stressed, among other things, the
observance of fundamental human rights, trade unionism and
the removal of causes of low living standards, and desired that
the Japanese Government should accept minimum international
standards of industrial conduct.[3]

The US took decisive measures in 1948-49 to promote the
revival of Japanese trade and industry, relaxed controls on the

Zaibatsu and imposed restrictions on labour unions. As these measures posed a serious commercial competition for Britain the British Government voiced its concern. As early as May 1947 British MPs had expressed their anxiety about the revival of the Japanese textile industry, because of the effect it would have on Lancashire, and about reparations, of which the US was claiming 30 per cent for itself and 45 per cent for China. Anthony Eden admitted the need to revive the Japanese textile industry because if Japan's heavy industries, which formed the basis of its war-making capacity, were to be eliminated or reduced its only hope of survival was through its textile trade. Nobody denied that Japan must live, but clearly the revival of its textile trade to its pre-war standard would be a serious matter for Lancashire, he said. Britain would feel less concerned about this "if we were satisfied that at least decent rates of wages were paid and proper hours of work maintained in Japan." The influence of the trade unions could do a great deal in that regard.[4]

The Secretary of State for Overseas Trade, Bottomley, recognised the need to make Japan's economy viable and give the Japanese a reasonable standard of living, but he desired at the same time that Japan should be prevented "from being the aggressive power [it was] before and violently undercutting prices."[5] Britain rejected the American suggestion about according most-favoured-nation treatment to Japanese goods, saying that the British Government did not "at present contemplate entering into any such arrangements."[6]

When one MP sought an assurance about inserting specific provisions in the Japanese Peace Treaty to prevent the textile industry from again flooding British markets with goods produced by cheap sweated labour Bottomley replied that in negotiations for a treaty the British Government "will endeavour to ensure that Japan undertakes to conform to the provisions of international conventions" such as the Havana Charter for an International Trade Organisation, "which provide a common standard of international commercial conduct, and to abstain from dumping and the kind of unfair practices familiar before the war."[7]

The most difficult problem, the British Minister of State Younger said on 28 March 1950, was on the one hand to ensure

that Japan "can stand on its own feet and offer a reasonable
livelihood to its people," and on the other hand "to allay the
anxieties of other nations about the impact of unfair Japanese
competition based upon low living standards." That was
obviously a matter which required very close study.[8]

Britain, the *Economist* pointed out, remembered Japan from
the decade before the war as "an alarmingly powerful competitor in world markets," and the same danger was seen "as a
new Frankenstein monster in Manchester." In this connection,
this British weekly recalled that Japan was already exporting
about 1000 million square yards of cloth yearly compared with
2700 million in the 1930s. It recognised the great importance
of Japan, the most industrialised country in Asia after the
USSR, for the Western Powers. Describing Japan as "the key
to eastern and southern Asia," the *Economist* remarked : "If it
is held against communism, there is great hope of containing
the Sino-Soviet bloc on its pre ent line and perhaps eventually
of detaching China from Russia." But if Japan was lost the
effect would be "catastrophic, militarily, industrially and
psychologically, from the western Pacific to the Indian Ocean."[9]

It was apparent to Britain that it could hope to secure protection against unfair Japanese competition in matters of trade
only by working in close cooperation with the US or by placing
its "own views and those of the other Commonwealth governments...at the disposal of the United States," to quote Bevin.
The task of peacemaking with Japan, Bevin said, was "a matter
in which we cannot move without the United States." The
Americans were "the prime factor in the whole business."[10]
The Americans, Younger remarked a month later, bore "the
greatest responsibility" in the matter. The Japanese settlement
was "more a matter for the United States" than for Britain,
which 'really cannot move unilaterally in the matter."[11]

Partly because Britain was aligned with the US in the so-called
free world contest against communism, and partly because
it realised it could safeguard its own interests only by working
closely with Washington, London deemed it necessary to support the American viewpoint on the important issue of Japanese
peacemaking. Britain repeatedly endorsed the US on the
procedure to be followed in preparing a peace settlement. For
instance, in a note of 12 December 1947 to the USSR, the

British Government, after stating that in its opinion there was nothing in the protocol of the Berlin Conference of 1945, which established the Council of Foreign Ministers, confirming the study of a settlement to that body, declared that "all those countries which are specially concerned in the settlement with Japan, by reason not only of their contributions to the defeat of Japan, but also of the degree to which they suffered from Japanese aggression, and of their vital interests in the future peaceful development of the Pacific area, are entitled to be represented as parties principal in that settlement." It also expressed its belief that "any voting procedure involving the right of the veto could only delay the conclusion of an early settlement and would conflict with the principle of equitable representation of the interests of all the principal combatants."[12]

Bevin described the Soviet proposal to refer the treaty to the Council of Foreign Ministers as "not a very encouraging prospect" and found it very difficult to agree to it.[13] Commenting on 21 February 1949 on the differences among the Powers as to the composition and voting procedure of a Japanese peace conference, Minister of State McNeil observed that the countries which had carried the burden of the combat against the Japanese, and in particular the Commonwealth countries and Burma, should rank equally with the Great Powers in drafting the treaty.[14] Bevin said emphatically later that Britain was not prepared to accept the Soviet view that drafting the treaty should be confined to the Council of Foreign Ministers.[15]

Bevin also expressed his understanding of the US decision of May 1949 stopping further removal of reparations from Japan under the Advance Transfer Reparations Programme. He did not think it was possible for Japan to pay "any further substantial reparations and at the same time to pay her own way in the world." While refusing to give any formal commitment about Britain not demanding further reparations Bevin said that in view of Japan's adverse balance of payments the Americans had "a good case" for not allowing further reparation removal from Japan.[16]

In September 1949 Bevin and the Under-Secretary for the Far East, Sir Ester Denning, visited Washington with a view to establishing rapport between the two countries on the fundamentals of a peace treaty. Bevin not only agreed that a liberal, non-punitive treaty was necessary to draw Japan into the Western alliance but also expressed his willingness to act as an intermediary between the US and the Commonwealth countries in working out the terms of peace.

Shortly after the Korean War had broken out, Younger observed : "We have to consider not only defence against possible Japanese aggressiveness but also now, more recently, defence of Japan which has in its new constitution agreed not to maintain armed forces." In the delicate and dangerous state of security in that region,[17] he considered it impossible "to contemplate leaving a power vacuum." In the absence of Soviet and Chinese participation in a peace treaty, Japan would still be in a state of war with them and some provision had therefore to be made for Japanese security. Otherwise Japan would be "at the mercy of forces whom we should not like to see in charge of Japan." It would be too much to ask the US to defend Japan indefinitely with American troops. He did not rule out rearming Japan.[18]

While Britain endorsed Dulles' stand that the USSR would not be permitted to hold up peacemaking indefinitely it could not favour completely unrestrained revival of Japanese commerce and industry. Speaking in the House of Commons on 19 March 1951, Harold Wilson, President of the Board of Trade, said the British Government wished to see Japan recover its economic health. But to protect Britain's vital economic interests and maintain full employment London must note the special characteristics of the competition from Japan, with damaging effects on employment in British industries before the war. The British Government wanted to have a free hand in dealing with that problem and therefore decided not to conclude any formal most-favoured-nation agreement with Japan.[19] Thus Britain continued to think in terms of economic restrictions and controls.

In April 1951, the British Government produced its own draft of a peace treaty and communicated it on 9 April to the governments of the other Commonwealth countries, the United States, France and the Netherlands. This preliminary working paper, Britain's Acting Political Representative in Japan observed, incorporated "the views of His Majesty's Government in the United Kingdom as expressed at the various Commonwealth conferences"[20] The differences in the British and American attitudes towards a settlement with Japan, as reflected in their respective drafts of April 1951 and 29 March 1951 respectively, were :

(1) The preamble of the British draft listed China as one of "allied and associated powers," and Article 23 specifically referred to the Central People's Government of China. The United States, which then recognised Taipeh, rejected any suggestion that the Peking regime should participate in the peace settlement. A compromise solution of this difficult question provided that neither the Chiang Kai-shek nor Mao regimes would be mentioned by name in the final text of the treaty.

(2) The preamble referred to Japan's militant regime and its "share of responsibility for the war." This was not acceptable to the US.

(3) According to Article 4 of the draft Japan was to cede Formosa and the Pescadores to China, whereas the Americans merely called for renouncing Japanese sovereignty over these islands. The American viewpoint prevailed.

(4) In regard to the Ryukyu and Bonin Islands, the British draft was somewhat harder on Japan as it called upon Tokyo to renounce sovereignty over these islands and took note of the US intention to negotiate with the UN its trusteeship agreement in regard to them. The American draft had merely stated that the US might propose trusteeship for these islands and that Japan would concur.

(5) The British draft required Japan to renounce all future as well as present claims to any interest in the Antarctic area. Australia, New Zealand, and South Africa joined in urging this exclusion apparently on security grounds. The US accepted the demand that Japan should surrender existing, but not future claims in Antarctica.

(6) Article 9 called for suppression of undesirable societies in Japan and provided a long definition of "undesirable." In the next article Japan was to undertake not to molest Japanese sympathizers with the Allied and Associated Powers. Neither of these provisions reached the final text.

(7) The draft required Japan to renounce its rights under

various treaties and to recognise the validity of the treaties of peace with Italy, Romania, Bulgaria, Hungary, and Finland, and of the prospective treaties with Austria and Germany. These clauses seemed unnecessary to the American negotiators but as there was no firm opposition they survived.

(8) As regards reparations it was recognised that nothing further should be taken from industrial equipment in Japan, and that payments from current production would be incompatible with a tolerable standard of living. Yet Article 23 of the British draft earmarked Japanese gold stocks for reparations, while Article 28 proposed the transfer of Japanese property in neutral or former enemy countries to Allied representatives there. Article 27 of the British draft asked the Japanese Government to compensate its nationals for property seized by the Allied and Associated Powers in their territories.

Of these three points, only the second survived US objections, and then with the qualification that the property should be handed over to the International Committee of the Red Cross for distribution to Allied prisoners of war who had been ill-treated in Japanese prison camps.

(9) Articles 30 and 31 of the draft required Japan to acknowledge that the war had not absolved it of the obligation to pay pre-war debts and to affirm its liability for the external state debt. These acknowledgements were accepted and became Article 18 in the final text.

(10) Article 35 of the draft called upon Japan to negotiate a Far Eastern fisheries convention and, pending its conclusion, to prohibit Japanese nationals from fishing in conservation areas. This was an effort to satisfy Australian demands. The US draft had not limited the proposed fisheries agreements to the Far East but had spoken of "high seas fisheries" and had omitted any interim prohibition. The US draft prevailed so far as the text was concerned, though Japan was required to give informal assurances to the Allies along the lines contemplated in the British text.[21]

The British document was much longer than the US draft because it set out in greater detail claims to property and damages. This precision was in many cases useful and, with some abridgment the British drafting on such matters found its way into the final treaty. This draft also solved some of the drafting problems of the US. For instance the US draft contained nothing about the withdrawal of troops since no way had been found to combine the departure of occupation forces with the maintenance in Japan of enough strength to guarantee the country's security against Soviet domination.[22] After stipulating that all occupation forces of the Allied Powers should be withdrawn 90 days after the treaty came into force the British draft stated : "Nothing in this provision shall, however, prevent the stationing or retention of foreign armed forces in Japanese territory under or in consequence of any bilateral or multilateral agreements which have been or may be made between one or more of the Allied Powers, on the one hand, and Japan on the other." This became Article 6(a) of the final draft.

On Dulles' visit to London in June 1951 "full agreement" was reached "on all main problems outstanding," though the provisional agreement was said to be subject to final approval on both sides. The communique issued on the Dulles-Morrison talks also recorded "the deep essential unity of purpose of the two countries."[23] Thus the two governments were able to agree on the joint draft of 3 July 1951, which was released to the press on 12 July. The agreement reached was a compromise. The US agreed that neither Japan should be obliged to apply for membership of the UN nor the Allied Powers to support such an application. Washington even weakened on an economic issue when it consented to 100 per cent compensation for damage to Allied property in Japan.[24] Britain also won a point when Japan was made to renounce its rights under the Congo Basin Treaties of 1919, which by stipulating equality of treatment for the commerce of all nations had made it possible for Japan to capture the Congo market for cheap textiles. The revision of these treaties was designed to benefit the spinning and weaving industries of Lancashire by preventing fresh Japanese inroads into British markets in the Congo.

It was also agreed that Japanese property in neutral and former enemy countries should be transferred to the International Red Cross for the benefit of former prisoners of war and their families.

The British were not very successful on a number of other counts. They had insisted on Japan's renouncing its director-

ship of the Bank of International Settlements. By arranging
the disposal of 19,770 of the 200,000 shares, worth about
$7 million, owned by Japanese financial houses, the institution
was sought to be brought under exclusive Western control. The
US was inclined to accept this proposal in May. It was
omitted from the revised joint draft of 3 July and the final 13
August text of the treaty, presumably because since they did
not belong to Japan but to Japanese institutions they would not
be affected unless explicitly mentioned.[25]

As late as March 1951 the British Government had also
desired Japanese shipbuilding capacity above an agreed tonnage
should be destroyed. This was not acceptable to the US, and
the British dropped the proposal in their draft of April in order
to "allay the restiveness on the American side over what was
regarded as a somewhat niggardly response of Britain to
America's willingness to compromise." The British proposal
that, as part of the national treatment stipulated in the peace
treaty, Allied shipping should be admitted to the Japanese
coastal trade was also not acceptable to the US, which viewed
this as an invasion of a domain customarily reserved to nationals. But the special British preoccupation with shipping
won a point when it was agreed that unless an Allied Power
was discriminating against Japanese shipping or its essential
security interests were at stake Japan must grant the shipping
of that Power national treatment (Article 12(d) of the San
Francisco Peace Treaty).[26]

The British fear of renewed Japanese competition, the prospect of flooding world markets with the products of cheap
labour, led Britain to insist on treaty clauses that would impose
levels of wages and conditions of labour in Japan together with
a code of international commercial ethics. In the end a compromise was reached by which Japan was asked to declare in
the preamble of the treaty its intention of promoting human
rights, to create within Japan conditions of stability and well-
being as laid down in Articles 53 and 56 of the UN Charter,
and to observe "in public and private trade and commerce . . .
internationally accepted fair practices." The President of the
British Board of Trade attached "special importance" to the
intention Japan expressed of observing internationally accepted
fair practices in public and private trade and commerce.[27]

As to imposing on Japan the obligation to grant most-favoured-nation or national treatment to Allied nationals the US desired this obligation should apply only to countries granting similar treatment to Japanese interests. The West Europeans were however unwilling to bind themselves not to discriminate against Japanese trade. They feared a resumption of dumping and of other practices such as concealing the origin of goods which had helped to make Japanese competition so formidable before the war. If these tactics were again resorted to, Dunn points out, they wished to be at liberty to impose discriminatory restrictions on Japanese goods. France at one time proposed that for an initial period after the treaty Japan should be bound to grant most-favoured-nation treatment without any condition of reciprocity. Britain insisted on retaining freedom of retaliation.[28]

The Allies retained complete freedom in the final text of the treaty to treat Japanese commerce as they chose. But they failed to secure the right of most-favoured-nation treatment or national treatment from Japan unless they themselves accorded similar treatment to Japan. Japan was on the other hand bound to accord for four years from the date the treaty came into force—that is up to 28 April 1956—most-favoured-nation treatment to each Allied Power and its interests in respect of certain matters relating to trade, business and navigation provided it received similar treatment.

In addition Japan agreed to conduct its trade on an individual competitive basis and to make all external purchases and sales of Japan state enterprises solely on a commercial basis for four years. It also declared its readiness to negotiate promptly on treaties with each of the Allied Powers, placing trade, maritime and other commercial relations on a stable and friendly basis. "These are important commitments," the report of the US Senate Committee on Foreign Relations observed, "if one recalls that Japan was making substantial inroads upon British and American trade in the pre-World War II period."[29]

The threat of future Japanese competition, the President of the British Board of Trade remarked, was "great and grave." He said, "we have a powerful, industrious people, deprived of their normal markets, with a large, cheap labour force and notable assistance from the United States," with no particular obligation to rearm but compelled by the very facts of life to export goods. He therefore considered it very important that Britain should not be obliged to extend most-favoured nation treatment to Japan. Britain was "free to impose quotas, to put on tariffs or to discriminate against Japanese trade" coming into Britain.[30]

After Britain joined the US as a co-sponsor of the joint draft of the peace treaty London not only defended the compromise settlement reached with Dulles on points of interest to Britain but also supported the treaty provisions in general. Foreign Secretary Morrison took pride in the "liberal, non-punitive and non-restrictive nature" of the treaty, justified the reparations clauses and supported both rearmament of Japan and what he called "the voluntary conclusion by Japan of a defence pact with the United States of America." Japan, had been deprived of important sources of raw materials and would not be able in the foreseeable future to rearm to the extent of becoming a potential aggressor. He regretted China had not signed the multilateral treaty but felt satisfied that the rights and interests of China had been safeguarded. He also referred to the anxieties of Lancashire, Yorkshire and the Midlands, which were particularly concerned with the effects of Japanese competition on the textile and pottery interests and observed : "For practical purposes . . . it is useless—indeed I think it is impossible—to write into the treaty effective restrictions."[31]

The Joint Secretary of State for Foreign Affairs, Anthony Nutting, pointed out that Great Britain was not in a position to dictate the industrial and commercial articles of the treaty. Even if restrictions had been imposed on Japanese industry and production there was no means of enforcing their observance on an independent and sovereign Japan.[32] Minister of State Younger said Britain could not be wholly saved from Japanese competition. Keeping in view the "long past history of unfair practices, Britain had deemed it necessary to keep its hands free on the question of according most-favoured-nation treatment[33] "to protect our economy if necessary against abnormal and injurious competition."[34] Britain retained its freedom to take appropriate action whenever it felt that its "own economic well-being is gravely imperilled."[35]

As regards unfair practices, particularly that of copying, Younger pointed out that the Japanese Government declaration attached to the treaty covered two international conventions, the International Convention for the Protection of Industrial Property and the Berne Copyright Convention, and that Japan would become subject to the obligations of those conventions.[36]

In a statement before the San Francisco Conference Younger stoutly defended the procedure and the provisions of the treaty. Even the anxieties of the Indian Government about certain treaty terms were described as "unfounded." He linked a solution of the Formosa problem with settlement of the Korean question.[37] He contrasted the territorial clauses pertaining to the Ryukyu and Kurile Islands. Japan's rearmament did not at all bother him. On the contrary, he stated that the "problem today" was not of Japan's disarmament but its defence against aggression. Younger also pointed out that in spite of the widespread anxiety sincerely felt in Britain about "the risk to our own economy from a revival of Japanese competition," no restrictions had been imposed upon Japanese industry or commerce. Further, he justified the reparations provisions of the treaty and explained the significance of the protocol attached to it.[38]

The British misgivings about unfair Japanese competition with British industries persisted. Thus when a bill was introduced in the British Parliament to ratify the treaty, Ellis Smith a Labour member, moved for its rejection. He emphasized that the industrial north, and particularly the pottery and cotton industries, "remembered the past to their cost." He said they were greatly alarmed at the prospect of renewed unfair Japanese competition and called for steps to safeguard British industry against "economic aggression of the worst type."[39]

The Labour motion was defeated by 382 votes to 33 and the bill passed through the remaining stages in both Houses of Parliament and became an act on 7 December 1951. Speaking on that day in the House of Commons, Parliamentary Under-Secretary for Foreign Affairs, Nutting, observed that his Majesty's Government attached the greatest importance to fostering healthy and democratic trade unions in Japan and looked forward after the treaty was enforced to a progressive development in Japan of sound labour practices such as freedom of association, collective bargaining and satisfactory working conditions.[40]

Chapter 3

SOVIET UNION AND EASTERN EUROPE

The Soviet Union

The Soviet Union and the United States emerged as strong Powers in East Asia. After World War II, the pre-war struggle for political predominance in this region between Japan and USSR was replaced by American-Soviet rivalry. As a result of the secret understanding reached by Britain, the US and USSR at Yalta on 11 February 1945, the Russians agreed to enter the war against Japan on the side of the Allies on condition that southern Sakhalin and the Kurile Islands would be given to them.[1] Moscow accordingly occupied these territories in 1945.

The Kremlin also desired that the northern half of the adjoining Japanese island of Hokkaido should be occupied by its troops. In a secret message on 16 August 1945 to President Truman, Stalin proposed that Hokkaido should be divided into northern and southern sectors by a "line running from the town of Kushiro on the East coast of the island to the town of Rumoi on the West coast of the island" and that Soviet troops should occupy the northern sector by accepting the surrender of Japanese forces in it.[2]

Washington rejected the Soviet suggestion, but Moscow indicated that it was not inclined to give Washington complete control over the destiny of Japan. In 1946 the Russians argued that the new Japanese Constitution must receive the positive approval of the Far Eastern Commission established in Washington to exercise substantial control over the overall direction of the occupation and in which the Big Four enjoyed the power of veto. Although the Soviet proposal was in line with the Moscow Agreement of Big Four Foreign Ministers in December 1945 it was not acceptable to the US.

While the Soviet Union desired to obtain a substantial share in the control and administration of occupied Japan, Washington was not inclined to tolerate any obstruction or challenge to its administering authority. The Soviet Union desired a control commission for Japan similar to those for Germany and Austria, but the US did not allow the Allied Council for Japan to become a control council. Washington also retained the power to issue interim directives through the Supreme Commander. This official was obliged to consult the Allied Council in advance before issuing orders on matters of substance, "the exigencies of the situation permitting." The phrase within quotes was not deleted although USSR wanted this done.

When the US raised the question of a peace treaty in July 1947 USSR insisted that the task of drawing one up should be assigned to the Council of Foreign Ministers of the Big Four where the Russians would enjoy the right of veto.[3] The US on the other hand proposed that the governments represented on the Far Eastern Commission (FEC) should examine the question and decide by two-third majority without requiring the concurring votes of the Big Four.[4] While the US conceded the competence of the Council of Foreign Ministers to negotiate peace with Germany it did not think that peace with Japan was a matter for this body to undertake.

The composition of the FEC[5] was such that it was not difficult for the US to obtain a two-thirds majority. The suggested American procedure for peace making was a modification of the voting method of FEC—a majority could decide provided the Big Four concurred—which had earlier ensured that the commission could adopt only those policies of which the US approved. The modified version of that procedure in peace-making deprived Moscow of its veto power and thus worked to its disadvantage. The Russians argued their case on the basis of Potsdam and other wartime Allied agreements while the Americans endeavoured to refute those arguments.[6]

Disagreement between the two super Powers on procedural questions pertaining to a Japanese peace was only a symptom and not really the cause of the conflict. It highlighted the importance of Japan in the worldwide struggle for power between the super Powers. In the emerging conditions of Cold War the *New York Times* called for an early peace settlement with Japan, with or without the Soviet Union, as early as 16 August 1947.[7]

The Chinese Government proposal of 17 November 1947, based on the recognition of special interests of the Big Four and requiring their consent in all decisions on a peace settlement with Japan but contemplating the convening of a special preliminary conference of FEC members,[8] was not acceptable to the USSR. Moscow insisted that the preparation of a peace settlement should be considered at a special session of the Council of Foreign Ministers. It proposed that the session should be convened in China in January 1948.[9]

The subsequent exchange of notes between the Chinese and Soviet Governments hardly made any difference to the Soviet stand. Moscow believed the Chinese view that the functions of FEC were directly related to the peace conference for Japan was not quite justified because the Commission was specifically debarred from trying to settle territorial problems, which evidently constituted "one of the important component parts of the future peace settlement for Japan." The participation of FEC members, other than the Big Four, who had made their contribution to the cause of the common victory over Japan, in the preparatory work of the Council of Foreign Ministers, could be arranged by enlisting their cooperation in the work of the committees, the corresponding subcommittees and the information and consultative conference, the Russians argued. This participation would safeguard "in the necessary degree the interests of those powers in the period preceding the peace conference."[10]

When the US shelved a Japanese peace settlement in 1948, the USSR urged a treaty, presumably because it considered the speedy termination of the US occupation of Japan desirable from the point of Soviet interests. Throughout 1948 the Soviet leaders repeatedly urged that negotiations be initiated with Japan. In May 1949, at a meeting of the Council of Foreign Ministers in Paris, it proposed that the Council should draft a settlement with Japan at an early date. In February 1950 the Soviet Union and China pledged themselves to work for peace in the shortest possible time.

The reforms the American occupation authorities instituted in the first phase (1945-47) aimed at democratising Japan, had enjoyed tacit Soviet support. But as the Cold War intensified, Washington embarked upon a policy of economic rehabilitation of its former enemy with a view to cultivating Japan as a potential ally against communism. Moscow became critical of the actions of the Supreme Commander of the Allied Powers. Thus, in his statement of 28 October 1948, the Soviet representative on the Far Eastern Commission referred to the American press reports about secret military conferences with General MacArthur about increasing US occupation forces in Japan and converting former Japanese naval base in Yokosuka into a modern naval base, capable of serving large naval forces. These activities were stated to be in contradiction to the Cairo and the Potsdam Declarations as well as to the decisions of the Far Eastern Commission. In the US reply, the military conferences of General MacArthur with high US military officers were described as "purely routine matters of sole concern to this [US] Government" while the allegation about Yokosuka being converted into a modern naval base was declared to be "not true," notwithstanding the fact that the use of the base by US naval forces for supporting the objectives of the occupation was regarded as "both necessary and proper."[11]

On 11 June 1949 the Soviet member on the Allied Council for Japan, Derevyanko, wrote to Gen. MacArthur and protested formally against the suppression of the legal activities of Japanese trade unions and other democratic organisations. He referred in particular to the brutal suppression by the Japanese police of the peaceful demonstrations of representatives of trade unions and students staged in Tokyo on 30 and 31 May and the killing of a worker named Hashimoto. He described such anti-labour measures as a flagrant violation of the Potsdam Declaration and the policies of the Far Eastern Commission in regard to democratisation of Japan.

MacArthur dismissed Derevyanko's protest as "routine Soviet propaganda" which completely unmasked "the Soviet role as an incitor of disorder and violence in an otherwise orderly Japanese society." He accused the Soviet Union of creating confusion, unrest and bewilderment in the ranks of the law-abiding Japanese masses. He also denounced Moscow for its failure to abide by the requirements of international law and specific Potsdam commitments on the return of over 400,000 Japanese citizens, whom the Russians had held captive for long, to their homeland. When the Soviet Union was following totalitarian concepts and ruthlessly suppressed individual liberty and personal dignity MacArthur said it looked hypocritical on the part of the Russians to speak of derogation of labour in Japan and of "democratic rights."[12]

On 23 June 1949 the Soviet member of the FEC criticised the manner in which MacArthur and the Japanese Government were handling labour problems in Japan. He specifically denounced the revision of labour laws enacted at the last session of the Diet and the manner in which the Japanese authorities had handled the recent labour demonstration in Tokyo and Hiroshima. The US member of the Commission, McCoy, denied the charges as propaganda in a statement on 13 July. Revision of the labour laws had strengthened the democratic character of the Japanese trade unions, he contended. The participants in the demonstrations referred to had sought to provoke the authorities into acts of force, which would then be denounced as "repressive measures" and "police brutality." In these cases of mob violence, he saw a "centrally directed campaign to create fear, social unrest, confusion and disorder" intended to undermine the authority of the government in the hope of creating conditions favourable to seizing political power. He said the central issue was whether the legitimate rights and interests of the Japanese people should be protected by duly constituted authority or to be placed at the mercy of a lawless few.[13]

Moscow challanged circular No. 5, entitled Clemency for War Criminals, issued on 7 March 1950 by MacArthur, on the ground that it violated the Charter of the International Military Tribunal and a FEC decision of 3 April 1946.[14] The US reply to a Soviet protest note of 11 May 1950 justified the action of the Supreme Commander by saying that he had not reduced or altered the sentences the tribunal had imposed. A parole, Washington contended, was in no sense an alteration of a sentence but permission by the appropriate authority for a convicted person to serve part of his sentence outside prison under certain conditions and controls and subject to returning to prison to serve the remainder of his sentence if the conditions of parole were violated. This method of dealing with convicted criminals was described as "in accordance with the practice in enlightened and democratic countries."[15]

MacArthur directed the Japanese Government on 5 June 1950 to "remove and exclude" from public office the 24 members of the Central Committee of the Japanese Communist Party. Two days later he imposed a similar ban on 17 members of the staff of the Communist Party newspaper *Akahata* (*Red Star*) which had denounced the earlier ban on the Central Committee as a violation of the Potsdam Agreement and had called for a general strike. The Soviet member of the Allied Control Council in Tokyo protested against what he called the "anti-democratic" measures taken by the Japanese Government in pursuance of American directives and described them as a "gross violation" of the Potsdam Agreement and a "danger to the existence of all democratic organisations in Japan." The Soviet protests went unheeded and on the outbreak of the Korean War MacArthur ordered indefinite suspension of the entire Communist press in Japan. An extensive purge of Communists and sympathisers on the staff of newspapers and broadcasting stations started at the end of July 1950.[16]

In retaliation Soviet commentator V. Kudriavtsev bitterly attacked US policy on Japan and Japanese "reactionary" forces headed by the Yoshida Government, which was seen as "readily joining in all the criminal plans and designs of American imperialism." The purpose of the policy US ruling circles pursued towards Japan throughout the postwar period was "to convert Japan into a military base of American imperialism in the Far East and to revive the Japanese army as a shock troop of the aggressive forces of US imperialism in Asia." American armed intervention in Korea had completely exposed the aims of the US in Japan while Yoshida's article in *Foreign Affairs* of January 1951 was sufficient proof of the fact that the Japanese Government had "irrevocably" thrown in its lot with US imperialism, he said. He criticised Japanese rearmament, the wholesale exemption of war criminals, and the alleged persecution of democratic organisations.[17]

Echoing Kudriavtsev, a Communist member of the Lower

House of the Japanese Diet, Kawakami, said Japan had been turned into an operational base and arsenal of the US interventionists in Korea. He characterised the rearmament of Japan as a plot to make the Japanese the slaves of the imperialists and demanded withdrawal of all the occupation troops as speedily as possible. Kawakami denounced the government's "aggressive policy to conclude a separate peace in the interests of the imperialists, to convert the country into a military base of international imperialism and to utilise the Japanese as cannon foddar in the war against Japan's neighbours."[18]

As the US decided to initiate discussions on a peace treaty with Japan in the fall of 1950 Moscow submitted an aide-memoire on 20 November 1950 in which it sought clarification of a number of points in the US memorandum of 26 October containing a brief general statement of the kind of treaty Washington wanted. The statement discussed the justification of a separate peace treaty, restoration of Formosa and the Pescadores to China, fulfilment of the terms of the Yalta Agreement, proposed trusteeship arrangements for the Ryukyu and Bonin Islands, withdrawal of the occupation forces from Japan after the conclusion of a treaty, rearmament of Japan, maintenance of US military bases after the development of a peacetime economy in Japan, and the steps taken to ascertain the views of China, which was said to have a special interest in a treaty.[19]

It was apparent that Moscow wanted the treaty to be approved first by the four chief Allied Powers and that China should be represented by the Peking regime. In Soviet eyes the suggested trusteeship arrangement for the Ryukyus smacked of territorial expansion on the part of the US. Moscow emphasised the need to prevent Japanese rearmament. In a statement issued on 3 March 1951 Soviet Deputy Foreign Minister Jacob Malik said that he had not talked with Dulles on a treaty and that Dulles statement at a press conference about a message from Malik to him on this subject as well as Malik's willingness to resume negotiations was "absolutely groundless."[20]

In response to Malik's statement in New York, the State Department issued a press release on 5 March 1951 drawing attention to Dulles' discussions with Malik on 16 October 1950 and 13 January 1951 and the exchange of notes between the two governments.[21] On 10 June 1951, the Soviet Government declared that Moscow had not at any time conducted any negotiations with the US on a draft peace treaty and that the "personal meetings" between Dulles and Malik did not fall within the purview of such negotiations.[22]

In a detailed study of the US draft the Soviet Government criticised the procedure Washington had adopted in regard to a separate peace excluding USSR, China and other countries. The study referred to the protracted, hard-fought war China had waged against Japanese imperialism and the great sacrifices it had made in that process. Moscow asserted that a real, peaceful settlement in the Far East was "not possible" without the participation of the People's Republic of China.

On questions of substance, Moscow stressed the restoration of Formosa and the Pescadores to China. It considered "wresting away" the Ryukyu and Bonin Islands from Japan and placing them under UN trusteeship with the US as the sole administering authority wholly unjustified. It expressed deep concern over the future rebirth of Japanese militarism. Moscow also criticised the draft for not laying down a time limit for the withdrawal of occupation troops and for permitting American military bases in Japan even after the conclusion of a treaty.

The Soviet Government proposed convening a session of the Council of Foreign Ministers in June or July 1951 to prepare a treaty. Such a treaty should be drafted on the basis of the Cairo and Potsdam Declarations and the Yalta Agreement and governed by the following basic aims and considerations :

1. Japan should become a peaceloving, democratic, independent state.

2. The democratic rights of the Japanese people should be guaranteed.

3. Restrictions should be imposed on the size of the Japanese armed forces.

4. No limitations should be placed on developing a peaceful Japanese economy.

5. All limitations in Japan's trade with other nations should be removed.

6. Japan should not enter any coalition directed against any power which had participated in the war against it.

7. All occupation troops should withdraw from Japan within one year, and no foreign power should be allowed to station troops or hold military bases in it.[23]

Moscow considered the US memorandum of 19 May 1951 containing answers to the Soviet "remarks" of 7 May wholly unsatisfactory and reiterated its views in a long memorandum on 10 June. It referred to the FEC directives in support of its position that the rebirth of Japanese militarism should be prevented. It said the American draft contained no guarantee of the future security of countries which had suffered from Japanese aggression. In the opinion of Moscow the military agreement between the US and Japan had "an obvious aggressive character" and was most likely to push Japan even more towards militarism. Stationing foreign troops in Japan after the conclusion of treaty, under whatever pretext, contradicted the Potsdam Declaration and signified "camouflaged prolongation of the occupation of Japan for an indefinite, protracted period," thereby allowing Washington to remain "the real master in Japan" for a long time. The Russians further contended that Japan should not be deprived of the opportunity of engaging in normal trade with the neighbouring states.[24]

The note also sought to refute what it called the "slanderous attacks" on the Soviet Union in the US memorandum of 19 May about Soviet acquisition of zones of interest in Manchuria, its delay in repatriating about 200,000 Japanese soldiers to their homeland, and about its role in the defeat of Japanese militarism. The note criticised the US for imposing a separate peace treaty and for concluding a military agreement with Japan in order to transform it into a "shameful weapon for carrying out the aggressive plans of the United States in the Far East." The note concluded by stressing the need for an overall peace settlement with Japan on the basis of Cairo, Potsdam and Yalta and proposing that a peace conference of representatives of all the states which participatad with their armed forces in the war against Japan should be called in July or August 1951 to consider the available drafts for a treaty.[25]

At the San Francisco Conference the Soviet delegate Andrei Gromyko raised the question of Chinese participation in the conference, but he was ruled out of order by the Chairman of the conference, Dean Acheson. The Chairman's ruling, when put to the vote, was approved by a vote of 35 in favour and three against. Fourteen states did not participate in the voting. The attempts of the Polish delegate to have a thorough discussion of the rules of procedure were also frustrated by the majority. The conference was thus conducted under rules of procedure so framed that the participants were allowed only to record their view without discussing any possible modification of the terms of the treaty.

In a statement on 5 September 1951 Gromyko declared that the proposed peace settlement contained insufficient guarantees against a revival of Japanese militarism, no assurance on the democratisation of Japan and the suppression of "fascist tendencies" in it, and that it made no provision for the withdrawal of the occupation forces. The Soviet delegate took strong exception to the fact that the joint Anglo-American draft did not prevent Japan from participating in "aggressive blocs" in the Far East created under the aegis of the US.

Gromyko criticised the territorial clauses of the draft treaty for their gross violation of the indisputable rights of both China and the Soviet Union and for its "arbitrary and illegal" arrangements in regard to the Ryukyu and Bonin Islands. The economic provisions of the treaty safeguarded the economic privileges the American monopolies had obtained under the occupation and placed the Japanese economy "in a slavery-like dependence" on those foreign monopolies. Gromyko was not satisfied with the reparations clauses in the draft because they ignored the legitimate claims of nations which had suffered from Japanese occupation in World War II. The provision for redeeming losses direct through the labour of the Japanese population imposed "a slavery-like form of reparations" on Japan. Gromyko summed up his long statement by asserting that the American-British draft was "not a treaty of peace but a treaty for the preparation of a new war in the Far East."[26]

Since the rules of procedure of the San Francisco Conference forbade the presentation of amendments to the Anglo-American draft Gromyko put forward amendments on behalf of his government as part of his statement. When the Chairman asked whether the Soviet delegate was proposing to move amendments Gromyko replied that he was making a "declaration" and was defending his position. The amendments reflected the well-known Soviet position in a more detailed and precise manner. If they had been accepted they would have transformed the very nature and purpose of the treaty as the US had conceived it.

By these amendments, 13 in number, the Soviet Government sought Japanese recognition of the sovereignty of the Chinese People's Republic over Manchuria, Formosa, the Pescadores and various other groups off the China coast such as the Paracels and Spratlys which are now the subject of dispute; recognition of full Soviet sovereignty over southern Sakhalin and the Kuriles; recognition of Japanese sovereignty not only over the four main islands of Japan but also to the islands of Ryukyu, Bonin and other clusters which formed part of Japan prior to 7 December 1941 and which were administered by the US; withdrawal of all Allied forces from Japan within 90 days of the coming into force of the treaty, after which no foreign Power was to be allowed to maintain troops or military bases on Japanese territory; an undertaking by Japan to remove all obstacles to the revival and strengthening of "democratic tendencies"; and undertaking not to permit the resurgence of fascist or militaristic organisations and a further undertaking not to enter into any coalitions or military alliances directed against any Power which had taken up arms against Japan.[27]

The Soviet Government sought an undertaking from Japan to pay compensation for damage caused by its military operations, the amount and the sources of such payment being settled at a conference of interested states, including those which had been subjected to Japanese occupation, namely, Burma, China, Indonesia and the Philippines. The amendments restricted the size of the Japanese forces and armaments. The army should be limited to 150,000 men, the navy to 25,000 men and a total of 75,000 tons, and the air force, including the naval air arm, to 200 fighter and reconnaisance planes and 150 transport and training air craft, with a total manpower of 20,000. Japan was not to have bombers and its medium and heavy tanks were not to exceed 200. It was also prohibited from possessing, constructing or experimenting with any atomic weapon or other means of mass destruction, including bacteriological and chemical weapons, self-propelled or guided missiles, guns with a range of more than 20 kilometres, sea mines or torpedoes of the non-contact type or manned torpedoes.

The amendments imposed no restrictions on developing Japan's peaceful industries or its trade with other states or access to raw materials necessary for a peaceful economy. The Straits of Japan along its entire coasts were to be demilitarised and open to merchant ships of all countries, while warships belonging only to Powers adjacent to the Sea of Japan had the right of passage through those waters. The treaty should come into force only after a majority of certain specified states, including the US, the Soviet Union, China and Britain, had deposited their instruments of ratification.[28]

In his subsequent statement at the San Francisco Conference on 7 September 1951, Gromyko criticised its procedure, which did not allow discussion or vote on the Soviet amendments. He also reiterated the Soviet position in regard to turning Japan into an American military base, the rebirth of Japanese militarism and the limitation of armed forces. He said the Soviet proposals and amendments would be liked and accepted in China, India, Burma, even perhaps in Ceylon, and in all those countries which had suffered at the hands of the Japanese. Gromyko concluded by saying that the Anglo-American draft treaty was "not a peace treaty at all" but exclusively "a plan for the preparation of a new war in the Far East."[29]

When Gromyko insisted that his amendments should be considered and voted upon he was ruled out of order by the chair, and this ruling was upheld by a vote of 46 to three—the dissidents being the Soviet Union, Poland and Czechoslovakia. The representatives of these three countries staged a five-minute walkout in protest. Speaking at a press conference after the signing ceremony, Gromyko denounced the treaty as an "aggressive" pact aimed at Russia and China, declared that no peace was possible in the Far East without the participation of those countries, and described the treaty as calculated to "sow the seeds of new war in the Far East."[30]

A *Pravda* commentary entitled "Treaty for the Preparation of War" by F. Orekhov said that "under the dictate of US ruling circles" a deal between "American imperialism and Japanese irredentism" had been struck. Real peace, the com-

mentator pointed out, could be attained in Asia only if the
peace settlement prevented the rebirth of Japanese militarism,
if it provided security to other Asian countries, if it satisfied
the just demands of the victims of Japanese aggression, and if
it ensured the conversion of Japan into a peace-loving independent, democratic state. The treaty did not satisfy any of these
conditions. A real settlement of any Asian question was in-
conceivable when it lacked the participation of the Asian
countries, particularly the big ones. Orekhov asked : "Can a
document pertaining to the basic problems of Asia be considered effective if it lacked the signature of India...the second
largest and the most important state in Asia ?"[31] It might be
recalled here that even the London *Times* considered a Far
Eastern settlement which excluded Soviet Russia, the Chinese
People's Republic, India and Burma "conspicuously incom-
plete."[32]

When the treaty came into force on 28 April 1952 the US
announced that the Allied Control Council in Tokyo and the
Far Eastern Commission in Washington ceased to exist. The
Soviet representatives on both these bodies protested against
the "illegality" of the treaty. A.S. Panyuskin, the Soviet
spokesman in the 14-nation FEC, denounced in a memorandum
to the US representative and chairman of the Commission on
28 April the dissolution of the Commission as "another illegal
act on the part of the Government of the United States." In
carrying out the occupation of Japan the American authorities
had, instead of fulfilling the decisions on democratisation,
helped to establish arbitrary police rule against democratic
organisations and leaders. He recalled in particular the mass
police reprisals against democratic organisations in Japan on
21-22 February 1952. He contended that Japan still remained
an occupied country because of the retention of US troops
under the so-called security pact—a pact directed towards "the
preparation of another war in the Far East." The conclusion
of a separate peace treaty showed how far the US Government
had gone in its policy of converting Japan into "a military
bridgehead of the United States in the Far East."[33]

On 30 May 1952 Yukihisa Tamura, Chief of the Protocol
Section of the Japanese Foreign Office, delivered a verbal notification to the Soviet mission that it had lost its official status

in Japan by virtue of the termination of the Allied Council for Japan when the treaty became effective on 28 April 1952. The Soviet Government responded in a note to the Japanese Foreign Minister on 11 June 1952, which asserted that the effectuation of the treaty could not serve as "a legal basis" for Tamura's statement because the Allied Council had been established in accordance with a decision of the Moscow Conference of Foreign Ministers of USSR, USA and Britain and subsequently adhered to by China. The Council, the note observed, had been dissolved by the US Government "in a unilateral manner in connection with the illegal separate peace treaty with Japan, concluded in violation of the existing international agreements of powers on Japan."[34] A Japanese Foreign Office statement of 12 June reiterated the view that with the dissolution of the Council from the date the treaty came into force the office of the Soviet member of the Council did not exist from that time onward and the assertions of the Soviet side had "no foundation."[35]

Although the Soviet Union had occupied the Kuriles and southern Sakhalin at the end of the war, Soviet sovereignty over them was not recognised in the San Francisco Peace Treaty. Japan was made to renounce all title to those territories ; the Soviet Union was not named as the beneficiary of Japan's renunciation. It appeared that their final status had still to be decided. This created problems in Soviet-Japanese relations. The Japanese commitment to a military alliance with the US also caused considerable difficulties in its relations with the USSR. In these circumstances Japan's application for membership of the UN was vetoed by the Soviet Union in June 1952. A change was however noticeable in the Soviet attitude around the middle of 1954. Moscow began to imply that the Peace Treaty was not necessarily a roadblock to restoring normal ties with Japan. This point was clarified on 22 December 1954 in an article carried by *Izvestia*, a Soviet Government organ. The article categorically denied as false reports that the Soviet Union demanded as a preparatory step towards adjustment of relations with Japan rejection of the treaty and related pacts. The article also rejected as ridiculous the contention that the Soviet Union's condition for normalising relations was for Japan to sever its relations with the US.[36]

Soviet-Japanese peace negotiations began in London on 1 June 1955 and culminated after protracted and difficult negotiations in a Peace Declaration which was signed in Moscow on 19 October 1956. In May 1956 a treaty relating to fishery and an agreement relating to sea rescue had been signed. Without waiting for China the Soviet Union normalised its relations with Japan by the joint declaration of October 1956.[37] The state of war between the two countries was terminated and the exchange of diplomatic and consular representatives was agreed upon. The Soviet Union waived all reparations claims against Japan. It also agreed to support Japan's application for UN membership and to return Habomai and Shikotan Islands at the time of signing a formal peace treaty. No treaty has been signed so far because there is no agreement between the two countries regarding two other islands, Kunashiri and Etorofu. Japan became a member of the UN on 12 December 1956.

In January 1960 Khrushchev went back on the pledge to transfer Habomai and Shikotan unless Japan's security treaty with the US was abrogated. Soviet leaders after Khrushchev have not referred to the conditional reversion of the two islands but have taken the stand that the territorial question has already been settled on the basis of various international treaties. But in the wake of Nixon's visit to China and the ensuing Sino-US and Sino-Japanese rapprochement the rigid Soviet attitude in the matter appears to have changed. Foreign Minister Gromyko's visit to Tokyo in January 1972 reflected a new Soviet interest in Japan because ever since 1968 he had postponed the return engagement in connection with the annual ministerial talks. In his discussions with Japanese leaders Gromyko was reported to have stated that the question of the "northern territories" (the four islands in dispute) was very complicated and that it was necessary to consider it carefully. This remark signified flexibility in the Soviet approach to the question.

On Prime Minister Tanaka's visit to USSR in October 1973 the Soviet leaders refused however to go beyond agreeing to continue the talks on a peace treaty at an appropriate time in 1974.[38] Japanese Foreign Minister Kiichi Miyazawa continued the discussions in January 1975. The two sides were convinced of the desirability of such a treaty so as to develop their relations "on a firm and stable foundation," but in the absence of

agreement they decided to continue negotiating.[39]   Gromyko's
visit to Japan in January 1976 was likewise unproductive.

Eastern Europe

Restoration of Japanese-Soviet diplomatic relations on 12
December 1956 not only paved the way for Japan's admission
to the UN but also facilitated normalisation of ties between
Japan and the socialist countries of Eastern Europe. Poland
was the first of them to follow the Soviet example. Poland and
Czechoslovakia had participated in the San Francisco Peace
Conference but refused to sign the treaty which emerged from it.
The Polish Government formally requested resumption of relations through the Japanese Ambassador in Paris in December
1954. Several times after that, Poland proposed talks on this
issue, but the Japanese Government adhered to its policy of
normalising relations with the East European countries only
after ties had been re-established with the Soviet Union.[40]

As a result of negotiations between the Permanent Representatives of Poland and Japan to the UN an Agreement on the
Restoration of Normal Relations was signed in New York on
8 February 1957. It contained six articles, of which the first two
provided for ending the state of war between the two ations
nand re-establishment diplomatic relations and the exchange
of envoys of ambassadorial rank. Article III stated that Japan
and Poland would be guided by the principles of the UN
Charter particularly those mentioned in its second article. The
two countries also undertook not to intervene either directly or
indirectly in each other's internal affairs. By Article IV of the
agreement each state waived all claims against the other and its
organisations and nationals so far as they had arisen out of the
state of war between the two states.

By Article V they agreed to negotiate as soon as possible
treaties or agreements to place their trading, maritime and
other commercial relations on a stable and friendly basis.[41]   In
accordance with this article Japan and Poland concluded a
Treaty on Commerce and an Agreement on Trade and Payments on 26 April 1958. The Treaty on Commerce provided
broadly for non-discriminatory treatment in various matters
relating to commerce and navigation, including customs duties
and internal taxation and shipping. The Agreement on Trade

and Payments provided for the methods of granting permission for import and export of goods between the two countries as well as the method of payment for them.[42]

The Agreement on the Restoration of Normal Relations was considered "a new milestone in Japan's endeavour to normalise her relationship with the communist countries of East Europe."[43] Within five days of the re-establishing of relations with Poland Japan signed a protocol relating to the restoration of normal relations with Czechoslovakia which contained the identical text of the six articles of the Polish pact.[44] The Czechoslovak Government-in-Exile in London had declared war on Japan in December 1941, but no actual fighting had occurred between the two countries. Czechoslovakia had requested Japan to open talks on normalising relations from June 1956, but as in the case of Poland Japanese Government had stuck to its policy of considering this matter only after relations had been restored with the Soviet Union.[45]

As a result of negotiations carried on subsequently by the Japanese Ambassador stationed in Prague and Warsaw, agreements were reached on the re-establishment of diplomatic relations between Japan and Hungary on 29 August 1959,[46] between Japan and Romania on 1 September 1959,[47] and between Japan and Bulgaria on 12 September 1959.[48]

Yugoslavia was however the first socialist country of Europe to end the state of war with Japan and normalise its relations with Tokyo. Like India and Burma, Yugoslavia had declined the invitation to attend the San Francisco Conference. But when the San Francisco Peace Treaty came into force, Belgrade exchanged letters with Tokyo on ending the state of war.

Chapter 4

NATIONALIST CHINA

Since China had suffered most at the hands of the Japanese militarists even the Chiang Kai-shek Government adopted a stiff attitude on the terms of a peace settlement with Japan, before it was driven out of the mainland by the Communists. There was lurking suspicion in the Chinese nationalist mind that the United States was "building up Japan at the expense of China"[1] and General MacArthur found, in his discussions with the Chinese Foreign Minister Wang Shih-chieh on 28 October 1947, the Chinese "most desirous of obtaining a larger share of reparations out of current production." Disagreeing with Wang, MacArthur asked him how the Chinese could possibly expect Japan to produce sufficient goods and turn over a substantial amount thereof, out of current production, when Japan itself was just about keeping alive with American assistance. He also took serious note of the "current Chinese press campaign," which he said, was perpetrating "a huge fraud upon the Chinese people" who expected to receive an endless amount of goods, etc., from Japan, when in fact, "there is practically nothing to be given or taken."[2]

During April 1948, the Chinese National Assembly passed six resolutions which included proposals that the Ryukyu Islands be returned to China and that the Government oppose the new American plan for reducing Japan's reparations. These six resolutions, the US Ambassador in China pointed out, expressed serious apprehensions about US restoring Japan's military potential and, among other things, called for complete disarmament of Japan, maintenance of Japanese industry at a low level and control of Japan to be continued for fifty years.[3]

The Chinese Nationalist government also expressed its dis-agreement with the US proposal of 11 July 1947[4] that decisions at the proposed 11-Power Japanese peace should be approved by a simple two-thirds majority. In view of Chinese exclusion from the purely great power formulation of the peace terms in regard to Europe, which had been always resented by the Chinese public opinion, the Chinese Foreign Minister Wang found it very difficult for the Chinese Government to support before the people any procedures for the making of the Japanese peace which did not accord China some privileged position in view of the vital interest of China in the terms of the Japanese peace settlement.[5]

Another factor which undoubtedly influenced Nationalist Chinese thinking concerning the procedures for the Japanese peace settlement was its acute concern over the Soviet attitude and the consequences of Soviet refusal to go along with the American peace proposal.[6] The Chinese Government was apprehensive lest the Soviet Union would seize, from the fact that China had proceeded to negotiate and conclude a peace treaty with Japan without the participation of the Soviet Union, as grounds for abrogating the Sino-Soviet Treaty of Friendship of 1945,[7] which Chinese Foreign Minister Wang believed had operated as a restraining factor in the Soviet attitude towards the Chinese Communists. If a pretext was offered the Soviet Union through the conclusion by China of a separate peace with Japan, Wang observed, in his confidential discussions with US Department of State official Bohlen, the Russians might have grounds then for openly supporting the Chinese Communists even possibly to the extent of recognizing a Communist regime in Manchuria and North China. Offend-ing the Soviets had obvious bearing on the problem of Dairen too. These apprehensions, Wang added, might be groundless, but nevertheless his Government felt that they were a real possibility and in view of the geographic proximity of the Soviet Union his Government felt it would be unwise for them to take the risk.[8]

For the above-mentioned reasons, the Chinese Government believed that the most practicable and wisest method of handling the preparation for the Japanese peace treaty would be to adopt the membership and voting procedures of the Far Eastern Commission.[9] This idea was contained in the Chinese Aide-Memoire[10] on the calling of a Peace Conference regarding Japan to the US Secretary of State of 9 October 1947 and reiterated in the Chinese Note of 17 November 1947[11] to the Governments of the UK, the USA and the USSR, and the Chinese Note addressed to the Soviet Foreign Minister on 6 December 1947.[12] By its Far Eastern Commission and its voting procedure proposal, China sought to strike a via media between the Soviet viewpoint that the task of preparing a peace settlement for Japan must be confined to the four major Powers and the American suggestion of 11-Power peace Conference in which the Big Four concurrence or veto was to be dispensed with. At the same time, it enabled China to preserve for it a great power status keeping in view the Chinese national sensibility and to safeguard its vital national interests.

The US proposal was considered impractical in that it, in fact, prevented Russia from joining the peace conference. The American argument that the Soviet Union was not being kept out but rather that Russia was refusing to come in was described by the Chinese Foreign Minister Wang as "fallacious" for the following reason : a two-thirds majority could be obtained by the five British Commonwealths and the United States; Russia would have one vote, as would China; the other countries would not count. It would therefore be possible for Britain and the United States (plus the Philippines) to out vote Russia and China on all matters which these countries might consider of major importance and vital to their respective interests. For example, it might be possible to take away all territorial concessions which have been made to Soviet Russia; it would be possible to establish a post-treaty regime of control which might be entirely unacceptable to China; the question of war loot could easily be settled in such manner as to be detrimental to both China and Russia; the question of external assets might be resolved in favour of Japan; a reparations settlement might be made which would be unacceptable to China, though entirely acceptable to wealthier countries. In Dr. Wang's opinion, the realities of the situation made it impossible for Russia to join under the conference proposal advanced by the United States. On the other hand, Dr. Wang continued, his suggestion that the FEC set-up and procedure be adopted in drafting the treaty appeared to be "the only practical compromise" which might be acceptable both to Russia and to the United States.[13]

After its defeat on the mainland and its dependence on the United States for the maintenance of its position in Taiwan the Chiang Government was hardly in a position to oppose American views on the substance of a settlement. By December 1950 it was willing to waive reparations if other nations did so. It concurred in the proposed security arrangements, including US trusteeship of the Bonin and Ryukyu Islands. Most notable of all, it was prepared to see the future of Taiwan left undecided, provided Japan renounced all title to it. On these points it was acting as a good ally of the US, but the problem still remained of how other states could be induced to consent to the Chiang regime's representing China at the treaty talks.[14]

Taipeh struggled hard to get admittance to the San Francisco Conference. In a statement on 18 June 1951, Chiang made a strong case for Taipeh's participation in the following words :

> World War II was heralded by the aggression of Japan against the Republic of China. Of all the Allies, we fought the longest. Our losses in lives and property were the greatest. In the defeat of the aggressors China made a significant contribution. A treaty of peace with Japan without the participation of China is at once unrealistic and unjust.

The government based on Taiwan, Chiang stated, had exercised considerable restraint and demonstrated unstintedly its willingness to cooperate on such important questions as reparations and the security of Japan. Any denial of its right to participate in the conference would not only "dishearten the people now living in Free China but also dim the hopes of millions of mainlanders who await emancipation from Communist rule." The ultimate effect of such an unjust act would not be limited to the effectiveness of the peace treaty, "but may seriously damage the traditional friendship between the Chinese and American peoples." Chiang concluded his statement with these words :

Any instrument of peace concerning Japan concluded in violation of the position of the Government of the Republic of China would certainly be lacking in both moral force and legal justification and leave an indelible blot on the history of allied cooperation in resisting aggression. Such an unrealistic peace treaty will not only fail to terminate the state of belligerency of World War II, but also add confusion to the Far Eastern situation and sow the seeds for further world disaster.[15]

In a statement on 14 July 1951 George Yeh took strong exception to Article 23 of the draft treaty which failed to include China among its signatories. He considered the article "highly objectionable" and put forward the following eight reasons in support of the right of his government to participate on an equal footing with the other Allies in concluding treaty with Japan :

1. Our common war against Japan was begun with its armed invasion of China of September 18, 1931.
2. The Republic of China was the first country to take up arms against Japanese aggression.
3. The armed forces of the Republic of China suffered the heaviest casualties and the Chinese people were subjected to direct tribulations and sacrifices.
4. The Republic of China made important contributions to the defeat of Japan.
5. The government of the Republic of China was the government which declared war on, and did the actual fighting against, Japan.
6. The Government of the Republic of China had been, and still was, representing China in all the international setups for Japan such as the Allied Council.
7. The Government of the Republic of China was the legal Chinese Government, recognised by the UN and its specialized agencies.
8. The Government of the Republic of China was the legal Chinese Government recognised by the majority of the states at war, or in a state of war, with Japan.[16]

Which Chinese Government should be invited to the conference was the subject of disagreement between the two co-sponsors of the draft treaty, the US and Britain. London

recognised the Peking regime while Washington continued to
recognise the Taiwan-based one. Ultimately, a compromise
was reached by which it was agreed that neither Government
would be invited to the conference and that Japan would be
allowed to decide with which of them it might wish to negotiate
a bilateral treaty in the future along the lines of the San
Francisco pact. This was harmful to the Chinese interests in
that Japan was prevented from negotiating a bilateral settlement with China on terms more favourable than those incorporated in the multilateral treaty.

Japan's freedom of choice in this respect was much circum-
scribed, if not taken away altogether, by the remarks of US
Senators, subsequently endorsed by Dulles himself, that ratification of the treaty by the US Senate could not be guaranteed
unless Japan agreed not to recognise the Mao regime and
decided to conclude an early peace with the government in
Taiwan.

For a while Tokyo appeared reluctant to proceed with any
China treaty, but Yoshida was in no position to exploit the
Anglo-American differences on China. Compared with the
US, Britain was in no position to influence the Japanese decision. In the postwar world a weak Britain was in fact condemned to a role of always agreeing with its predominant ally,
the US. A defenceless Japan struggling to see the occupation
ended was scarcely in a better position. The Yoshida Government decided under US pressure to negotiate a treaty of normal
relations with Chiang. In a letter to Dulles on 24 December
1951 Yoshida made it clear that "the terms of such a bilateral
treaty shall, in respect of the Republic of China, be applicable
to all territories which are now, or which may hereafter be,
under the control of the National Government of the Republic
of China."[17] Yoshida at the same time asserted his government's desire *"ultimately* to have a full measure of political
peace and commercial intercourse with China, Japan's close
neighbour." Yoshida had no illusions about the reality of
Communist contral over the mainland. He clearly hinted that
Japan would seek to achieve peace with the Peking Government in future.

Meanwhile Yoshida sought to justify establishing relations
with Taipeh by stating that its government "has the seat, voice

and vote of China in the United Nations...exercised actual government authority over certain territory and...maintains diplomatic relations with most of the members of the United Nations." The Chinese Communist regime, on the other hand, Yoshida argued, stood condemned by the UN as an aggressor. He also accused Peking of seeking, through its support of the Japan Communist Party, to overthrow Japan's government and constitutional system by force. Moreover, he pointed out, the Mao regime had entered into a military alliance with the Soviet Union aimed at Japan.[18] These arguments, though plausible, could not obliterate the naked fact that the conservative government of Japan, in a period of national weakness, had "acquiesced definitely in America's China policy and had to live with the consequences of that policy."[19] This acquiescence was the price Japan paid for regaining its independence in 1952 after seven years of US occupation. Diplomatic recognition of the government in Taiwan, Richard Storry writes, hardly represented the true wishes of the Yoshida Cabinet. What Yoshida had in mind was a simultaneous de facto working arrangement with both Peking and Taipeh. But he was not allowed to make the experiment and US pressure compelled him to recognise Taipeh.[20]

Commenting on Yoshida's letter to Dulles, British Foreign Secretary Anthony Eden observed in the House of Commons on 5 February 1952 that it would have been better if the Japanese had remained free in the matter. He regretted Britain was in no position to prevent, this, adding that "only time will show whether the Japanese Government are acting wisely," in regard to Sino-Japanese relations.[21]

In fulfilment of his commitment to Dulles, Yoshida designated on 31 January 1952 Isao Kawada plenipotentiary of the Japanese Government to negotiate a bilateral treaty with Taipeh. That treaty would end the state of war and re-establish normal relations with the Chiang Government in conformity with the principles set out in the San Francisco Treaty. Although Chiang was in no position to make stringent demands on Japan he had the blessings of the US Government, and he was able to secure some modifications in his favour.

Taipeh succeeded in making Japan accede to its demand that the bilateral treaty to be concluded between them should be called a "treaty of peace." It is significant to recall here that Yoshida, both in his letter to Dulles and his communication to Ho Shai-lai, chief of the Chinese Mission in Japan, informing him of the appointment of Kawada as Japan's plenipotentiary for negotiating a bilateral treaty, had refrained from using this term for the treaty. He described it as "a bilateral treaty" to end the state of war and to re-establish normal relations.[22]

Although Japan pressed for a clause limiting the application of the treaty to those territories currently under the control of Chiang, or which might come under it in future, Taipeh was able to secure its omission from the text of the treaty. But Japan's standpoint was accepted in an exchange of notes. Taipeh further refused to forgo its claim for reparations, arguing that national sentiment would not allow China, chief victim of the war with Japan, to do so. The Chiang Government demanded reparations from Japan, but the Japanese Government maintained that war damages suffered on the Chinese continent was outside the scope of the treaty. In the end the clauses relating to reparations were deleted.

A comparison between the Taiwan draft Peace Treaty with Japan of 20 February 1952,[23] and the Treaty of Peace[24] finally signed on 28 April 1952 reveals that the Final Treaty did not contain any specific provision about reparations. There were also a number of other points on which Taipeh's wishes were not fulfilled. Its insistence that pending conclusion of relevant treaty or agreement to place their trading, maritime and other commercial relations on a stable and friendly basis, Japan would accord Taiwan, its nationals, products and vessels most-favoured-nation treatment with respect to customs duty and other dues, and national treatment with respect to shipping and navigation for four years after the treaty came into force found no mention in the flnal text. Likewise, the provision in the Taiwan draft that Japan would ensure that the external purchases and sales of Japanese state trading enterprises would be based solely on commercial considerations was not agreed to. After Japan established normal relations with the People's Republic of China under Prime Minister Tanaka the Japan-Taiwan Treaty was declared invalid and inoperative from 29 September 1972.

Chapter 5

PEOPLE'S REPUBLIC OF CHINA

Having suffered heavy losses at the hands of the Japanese militarists, the Chinese people felt intensely about the nature and content of a peace treaty, and demanded reparations, punishment of war criminals, and demilitarisation of Japan. As early as July 1947, when the US proposed preliminary discussions on a treaty in the 11-nation Far Eastern Commission, the Chinese Communists expressed apprehension about the Anglo-American group securing a two-thirds majority in that forum. Keeping in mind Chinese interests, Yu Shu-teh wrote an article in *Ta Kung Pao* insisting on the unity of the Big Four, which meant retention of a Chinese veto. He thereby sought to ensure that nothing contrary to Chinese wishes was decided at the peace conference. In this respect the Communist approach was in no way different from that of the Kuomintang.

Yu Shu-teh warned against the disastrous consequences of "an aimless and imprudent 'generosity' " shown towards Japan in a momentary impulse. To eliminate the danger of future invasion, he laid stress on a "thorough disbandment of Japanese troops" and of all instruments of Japanese economic invasion. Half the total reparations should go to China, which must also receive in view of its acute shortage of capital "part payment in gold."[1]

A commentary in another pro-Communist publication, *China Digest* (23 September 1947), referred to the US suggestion that the Powers concerned should instead of using the veto decide a peace settlement by a two-thirds majority and observed that China had been the victim of Japanese aggression and had fought Japan the longest. He therefore asserted that China should take "a decisive role in forming Japan's future." This was especially important since the US, represented by MacArthur in Japan, aimed at rebuilding a strong Japanese nation sufficiently powerful to menace China's security again. China should veto anything detrimental to its interests "no matter whether it comes from America or is agreed by majority."[2]

In a commentary on 24 February 1948, *China Digest* referred to the opposition which "America is now voicing against Japanese war reparations" and to the Chinese losses of approximately $30 billion, according to the UN Secretariat. The writer expressed serious concern at MacArthur's policy of building Japan into "a strong, American-controlled military, political and economic bulwark in the Far East to be the bastion of an anti-Bolshevism crusade and a secure base for American expansion." He denounced Nanking's "slavish dependence on America for action towards Japan" and declared : "Every war criminal must be punished . . . China's war losses *must* be reparated."[3]

Wen Hui-Pao and *World Culture* of 1 July 1949 criticised the US for trying to convert Japan into a military ally and an anti-Communist and anti-Soviet bastion. Drafting a peace treaty should be undertaken in accordance with the Potsdam Declaration by the Council of Foreign Ministers of China, the US, USSR and Britain. These organs opposed consideration of the Japanese peace treaty by the 11-nation Far Eastern Commission, where China would be deprived of its veto power and all resolutions adopted by a two-thirds majority under the manipulation of the "imperialist Powers."[4]

By the middle of 1949 the Chinese Communist views on Japan had crystalised in a policy framework which included : advocacy of an early peace treaty with Japan; emphasis on demilitarisation and democratisation of Japan; and an apprehension about the US policy in Japan, which favoured release of war criminals, cessation of payment of reparations, and preservation of the Zaibatsu. This was evident from a *New China News Agency* commentary[5] dated 21 June 1949 and from a joint statement of various parties and people's organisations of

China on the occasion of the 12th anniversary of the war of resistance against Japan.[6]

After the outbreak of the Korean War Japan was incorporated into the American strategic system against the strong opposition of China and USSR, and the US continued its preparations for a separate peace with Japan. China criticised the policy of the US occupation authorities in Japan which aimed at rebuilding the Japanese war machine, establishing military bases, cancelling reparations, and prevention of democratisation. Peking also opposed US attempts to conclude a separate peace without the participation of China and the Soviet Union. An article by Li Chung-ching in *World Culture* (March 1950) expressed concern about the conclusion of a United States-Japanese military alliance upon the conclusion of a peace treaty which "may possibly be developed into a 'Pacific Pact'."[7]

The official Chinese attitude on a peace treaty was spelt out in a statement of Premier Chou En-lai on 4 December 1950,[8] his letter to the Soviet Ambassador dated 22 May 1951,[9] his statement on the US-British draft dated 15 August 1951,[10] and his statements on the San Francisco treaty dated 18 September 1951,[11] and 5 May 1952.[12] These statements emphasised that an overall treaty should be concluded with the participation of Communist China and all the other countries which had fought Japan; that Taiwan and the Penghu Islands (Pescadores) should be restored to China in accordance with the Cairo Declaration; that the Kuriles, the southern part of Sakhalin and all islands adjacent to it should be returned to the Soviet Union; that the peace treaty should guarantee the genuine independence and sovereignty of Japan; that all foreign troops should be withdrawn from Japan; that there should be an assurance against the revival of Japanese militarism by limiting the size of the armed forces, which should not exceed the requirements of self-defence; that Japan must not join any alliance aimed at any of the Allied Powers; and that no restrictions should be imposed on the development of a peacetime Japanese economy and trade with other countries.

In putting forward these demands China expressed full support for the Soviet stand in the matter. Chou considered the joint US-British draft "in reality a treaty for preparing a new war not a genuine peace treaty." He reserved the right of

China, which had suffered great losses at the hands of Japan,
to claim reparations. Any treaty with Japan in the preparation, drafting and signing of which China did not participate
would be considered "illegal" and "null and void" by his
government, Chou said. Conclusion of a US-Japan Bilateral
Security Treaty soon after the San Francisco Treaty on 8
September 1951, he added, cleared the way for rearming Japan
and was "unmistakable evidence that the US Government was
preparing for another war of aggression in Asia and the Far
East on an even bigger scale."[13]

The American plan regarding the peace treaty with Japan,
Chou En-lai observed on 4 December 1950, flagrantly violated
the common war aims of the Allied Powers and all international agreements on policy towards Japan. It also utterly
disregarded the fundamental interests of the Chinese people
who fought a heroic war against Japan and also disregarded
the aspirations of the Japanese people for the future.[14] The
United States draft treaty with Japan, Chou En-lai stated on
22 May 1951, provided no guarantee at all for preventing the
revival of Japanese militarism, nor did it place any limitation
upon the size of the armed forces. The aim of the United States
Government, he stated, was clearly not to eliminate, but to revive, militarism in Japan and, with its territory as war base
and its people as cannon fodder, to make Japan a tool of the
United States in continuing and expanding aggression in Korea,
China and other Asian countries.[15]

The joint Anglo-American draft peace treaty with Japan,
Chou En-lai pointed out on 15 August 1951, provided that its
Article concerning the disposal of the property and rights or
interests in Japan of the Allied Powers and their nationals
during the war was applicable only to the period from 7 December 1941 to 2 September 1945, thus completely ignoring the
period before 7 December 1941 when the Chinese people were
carrying on the war against Japan single-handed. The provisions of the US-British draft treaty on territory, he said, were
designed entirely to suit the desire of the United States Government to expand its occupation and aggression. Chou En-lai
asserted, on behalf of the Chinese Government the inviolable
sovereignty of the People's Republic of China over Nansha and
Hsisha Islands in the South China Seas. Criticizing reparations

provisions in the joint draft treaty, he observed that those States which were occupied by Japan, suffered great losses and have difficulties in rehabilitating themselves, should reserve their right to claim reparations.[16]

In his statement of 18 September 1951, Chou En-lai criticized the American Government for dictatorially and stubbornly rejecting the suggestions of the Soviet Polish and Czechoslovak delegates at the San Francisco Conference to invite China to the Conference and for rejecting the various basic proposals of the Soviet Union concerning signing of the peace treaty with Japan. He also denounced the reactionary Japanese Government for selling out the national independence and sovereignty of the country by signing the San Francisco Peace Treaty and the US-Japan Bilateral Security Pact.[17]

Chou's statement when the "illegal" peace treaty with Japan became effective denounced it as a "forcible imposition on the Japanese people" which in no way restored sovereignty and independence to Japan and did not change its status as an occupied country. Chou also expressed his firm opposition to the Yoshida-Chiang treaty, which he described as "an open insult and act of hostility to the Chinese people."

Earlier on 22 January 1952, Chang Han-fu, Vice-Foreign Minister of China, issued a statement denouncing the US-Yoshida "plot" to conclude a treaty with the Chiang "clique". He referred to Yoshida's letter to Dulles dated 24 December 1951[18] in that regard and observed :

We consider this letter to be conclusive evidence of the collusion between the reactionary government of defeated Japan with American imperialism in preparing a new aggressive war against the people and the territory of China. This letter is another provocation of the imperialist government of the United States and the reactionary government of defeated Japan against the People's Republic of China— the most serious and most flagrant provocation since the conclusion of the San Francisco "peace treaty" with Japan in September 1951.[19]

Chang's statement also contained a bitter attack on the policies of the "reactionary" Yoshida Government, which he described as a betrayal of the national interests of Japan. He also accused it of turning itself into an instrument of American imperialist aggression in Asia.

Chapter 6

INDIA

While the Soviet Union accepted the invitation to attend the San Francisco Peace Conference even though China was not invited India, Burma and Yugoslavia declined to participate on principle. After the San Francisco Peace Treaty was concluded, India was the first country to end the state of war with Japan and to conclude a separate peace with it.[1] India took an independent stand in the matter and followed a policy of keeping aloof from the two Power blocs.

In the early stages, India, along with other nations represented on the Far Eastern Commission, demanded its share of reparations from Japan. Thus, a share of $12\frac{1}{2}$ per cent of the Japanese internal industrial facilities, amounting to Rs. 28,000 million had been claimed on behalf of India in pursuance to the Potsdam Declaration.[2] However, beginning 1949, India began to take a liberal and sympathetic approach towards the problem of reparations from Japan and the rehabilitation of the Japanese economy. Thus, in September 1949, the Indian Minister in Washington stated that his Government was in favour of halting reparations in view of the fact that the burden told heavily on the living standards of the Japanese people.[3] The liberal Indian attitude towards Japan was also reflected in the 240,000 word Dissenting Opinion of Justice R.B. Pal, which ran into 1235 pages. Pal expressed his disagreement with the judgement of the International Military Tribunal for the Far East. He dissented generally from the legal theories and disagreed with the facts upon which the judgement of the Tribunal was based. It was stated *inter alia* that the Allied Powers did not have the legal right under international law to treat Japanese leaders as war criminals; that an international tribunal however established was not bound by the will of the conqueror; that war had not been made a crime in international law; that aggressive war was not definable; that the Charter was *ex post facto* law. The separate opinion of Justice Pal concluded that each of the accused should have been found not guilty and acquitted. Commenting on the Dissenting Opinion of the Member from India, the Acting American Political Adviser in Japan, Sebald, remarked that Justice Pal's opinion appeared to adhere to "the positivist theory of international law, which holds that national sovereignty is the basis of the international community and that consent to qualification of national sovereignty must not be presumed."[4]

At the Canberra meeting of the Commonwealth countries (26 August-2 September 1947), which was held within a fortnight of India's attainment of independence, India seemed to have desisted from taking a strong line against the prevalent British-Australian view that in order to prevent Japanese resurgence it was necessary not only to limit its armaments but also restrict its industry and trade and bind its government to respect fundamental rights and develop and protect trade unions.[5] But, as an Indian researcher rightly points out, "a reasonable surmise is that India's arguments had a softening effect on those who wished to impose harsh conditions on Japan." While Britain was guided mainly by considerations of a possible Japanese competition in trade, India was anxious to see a speedy revival of Japanese industry and trade, so that Japan could play a useful role in the industrialization of Asia.[6] The difference of views among the Commonwealth nations persisted at the Colombo (Jan 1950) and London (Jan 1951) meetings. At both these meetings, India laid stress on associating Communist China and the Soviet Union with the peace treaty and opposed the idea of a Pacific Pact. While returning from the London meeting of the Commonwealth Prime Ministers, Prime Minister Jawaharlal Nehru, at the press conference in Paris, expressed his belief that it would be "conducive to the peace in the Far East if there were no rearmament of Japan." But he recognized that if the situation in the Far East continued to be tense, Japan would rearm itself whether there was permission from others or not.[7]

There was no possibility of Commonwealth nations formulating unanimity of views, but even if they had succeeded in hammering out a common stand, their views counted little in the changed US approach towards Japanese peace settlement. As *The Hindu* pointed out :

> The views of Britain, India, Australia and other such countries are in practice of less consequence to the future of Japan than the views of the various policy-making groups in Washington . . . Military considerations are the prime factor and the debate on the future of Japan centres on the role that she may play in a possible war between the United States and Russia.[8]

As time passed, Australia, Britain and New Zealand changed their positions considerably in return for certain promises or assurances from the USA. India, however, continued to stick to its independent position. New Delhi remained critical of the seven-point memorandum the US circulated to FEC members in October 1950. India was unwilling to see the Yalta decisions on Sakhalin and the Kuriles reopened. It desired that the Bonin and Ryukyu Islands should be left under the unqualified sovereignty of Japan and favoured restoration of Taiwan and the Pescadores to China. It was against any treaty provision to retain Allied troops on Japanese territory since that meant taking advantage of a temporary weakness that would be lastingly resented.

On the other hand India did not object to Japan's entering into security arrangements with the US or any other Power after the treaty came into force and was willing to waive reparations. India wanted the treaty to be drafted by a conference of all states belonging to FEC and with the Peking Government representing China. But it differed from USSR on voting and was willing to accept the American proposal that matters of substance be decided by a two-thirds majority. Thus while the Indian Government supported the Russians on Southern Sakhalin and the Kuriles, its stand on voting on the treaty would have given the deciding power to the Western Powers and would have been completely unacceptable to Moscow.[9]

Dulles made no serious effort to enlist Indian cooperation

in peacemaking. He visited Canberra and Manila in this connection, but not New Delhi. Indian objections to the joint Anglo-American draft, made available in July 1951, were communicated to the US Government on 30 July 1951. India stated that if the objective was to relieve tension in the Far East, it could not be achieved by excluding Communist China and the Soviet Union from the peace settlement with Japan. It suggested, therefore, that the terms of the treaty should be such that even if they did not participate in the settlement, they should not object to it, thereby leaving the door open for their adherence to the treaty at least in the future. India also demurred at the proposed continuance of US trusteeship of the Bonins and Ryukyus, which it considered should be returned to Japan. It declared furthermore that the treaty should contain a definite commitment to restore Formosa to China and asked for the deletion of the clause in Article 6(a) which envisaged the retention of foreign troops in Japan after the occupation ended.[10] In the US reply of 12 August 1951, none of the major suggestions put forward by India was accepted.

Since the final draft of the Anglo-American peace treaty, released on 15 August 1951, hardly afforded any satisfaction to India, New Delhi deemed it necessary to explain its attitude in detail in a note to the US Government on 23 August 1951. Throughout the negotiations, the note said, India had emphasised two fundamental objectives :

(1) The terms of the treaty should concede to Japan a position of honour, equality and contentment among the community of free nations;

(2) The terms should be so framed as to enable all countries specially interested in the maintenance of a stable peace in the Far East to subscribe to the treaty sooner or later.

In the opinion of the Indian Government the first condition was not satisfied because the Ryukyus and Bonins, which Japan had not acquired by aggression against any other country, and whose inhabitants had a historic affinity with the Japanese people, were placed under the legislative and administrative control of the US. India believed this was bound to be a source of dissatisfaction to large sections of the Japanese people and would carry the seeds of future conflict in the Far East. The *Times of*

India made this point emphatically when it said that both terri-
torially and historically these islands were Japanese and their
severance from Japan laid Washington open to the charge of
"expansionism," which, whether motivated by economic or
strategic reasons, was in Eastern eyes "equally imperialistic."[11]
It was not without reason that the representative of Egypt con-
considered it advisable in his statement before the San Francisco Conference to leave the question of the Ryukyus and
Bonins to the UN General Assembly.

India further believed that Japan should have entered into
a defence agreement with the US only after it had become
"truly sovereign." It pointed out that the provision in the
treaty which suggested that the occupation force might stay on
in Japan as part of such a defensive agreement was bound to
give rise to the impression that the agreement did not represent
"a decision taken by Japan in the full enjoyment of her freedom as a sovereign nation," and this would have unfortunate
effects both in Japan and the rest of Asia.

As regards the second condition India expressed the opinion
that the future status of Taiwan should not have been left
undetermined and that it should have been returned to China
although the time and manner of its return could be the subject
of separate negotiations. Similar considerations applied to the
Kuriles and southern Sakhalin. New Delhi also noted that the
conference convened in San Francisco to consider the draft
treaty was not open to negotiations. For all these reasons
India expressed its inability to participate in the conference
or to sign the treaty.[12]

Speaking in Parliament on 27 August 1951, Prime Minister
Nehru reaffirmed India's decision not to sign the peace treaty
or to participate in the San Francisco Conference. He added :

> It was further decided that immediately after Japan attained
> independent status, the Government of India would make a
> declaration terminating the state of war between India and
> Japan and, later, a simple, bilateral treaty with Japan should
> be negotiated.[13]

Acceptance of the controversial treaty, an Indian researcher
points out, would have meant a departure from the principle
on which its foreign policy rested. To reject it altogether
would have meant acting in concert with the Sino-Soviet bloc,

which was using the Japanese peace treaty to further its own ends. Either way there was the danger before it of its losing the goodwill of one group of nations and jeopardizing its independent position. To stay out of the San Francisco Peace Conference, therefore, seemed to be the only way out for India. The logic of non-alignment unavoidably led to abstention.[14]

In its reply to the Indian note of 23 August 1951, the US Government disputed the Indian points. In Washington's opinion the Anglo-American draft achieved the goal of restoring to Japan a position of honour and equaliy to "an unprecedented degree." The US accused India of applying "different tests" to the Kuriles and the Ryukyus. The Government of India, the US note observed, criticized the treaty provision with reference to the Kurile Islands because it did not explicitly transfer full sovereignty to the Soviet Union and criticized the provision with reference to the Ryukyus because, although it left sovereignty in Japan, it permitted UN trusteeship with the United States as administering authority. Moreover, the United States found a discrepancy in India's views on Taiwan. India, it was pointed out, was insisting on not leaving the future of Taiwan "undetermined." But if the return of Taiwan to China was provided in the Treaty with its future disposition depending upon future negotiations as to time and manner, as suggested by India, the island's future would remain "undetermined."

Washington also disagreed with India's view that Japan should have entered into a military agreement with the US only after the treaty came into force so as to prove it was a voluntary arrangement on Tokyo's part. The US Government considered the Indian suggestion to be full of grave hazards for Japan because of its "total defencelessness in close proximity to proved aggressors."[15]

Washington took great pride in forging military alliance systems all over the world and referred approvingly to the fact that not less than 32 of the Allied Powers, all members of the UN, had freely made or were making collective security arrangements to which the US was a party. The Japanese were also seen to be animated by the sentiment of forging military solidarity with the Western Powers.[16] In these circumstances it was not quite easy for the US to understand India's policy of avoiding involvement in the deepening struggle between the Communist and the non-communist world.

Replying to the US note of 25 August 1951, the Government of India sent a further communication to the US Government on 28 August 1951 in which it said that it would always gladly co-operate with the United States and other countries in maintaining peace and developing the nations of Asia, and expressed appreciation that the United States did not want to be a party to colonialism or imperialism. India denied any intention on its part to challenge the Potsdam terms of surrender and maintained that in suggesting the return of the Ryukyu and Bonin Islands to Japan, it understood that those terms left room for the addition of minor islands to the four main islands of Hokkaido, Honshu, Shikoku, and Kyushu, over which Japan was to be given sovereignty. Regarding the charge that it had applied one set of principles in regard to the Kuriles and another set in regard to the Ryukyu and Bonin Islands, the Indian communication of 28 August 1951 observed :

> If they excepted the Kurile Islands from the scope of their suggestion, it was because the Yalta Agreement provided, without any reservation, that 'the Kurile Islands shall be handed over to the Soviet Union'. The Government of India cannot be held responsible for an inconsistency, which is the result of the Yalta Agreement.

As regards Formosa, India suggested that in conformity with international obligations, the treaty should simply declare that Formosa would be returned to China. It was pointed out that such a declaration would settle the status of Formosa and would also create conditions helpful for a settlement in the Far East. The Indian note of 28 August 1951 suggested that the time and manner in which Formosa should be returned could be left for a future settlement. On the US comments regarding the defencelessness of Japan against proved aggressors, it said :

> The Government of India fail to find any warrant for such a conclusion from anything that they have said. The draft treaty recognizes that Japan as a sovereign nation possesses the inherent right of individual or collective self-defence and that Japan may voluntarily enter into collective security arrangements. Adequate provision is thus made for Japan independently to make whatever arrangement she considers

necessary for her self-defence as soon as she has signed the peace treaty and it is not clear to the Government of India why there should be any "period of total defencelessness" for Japan.

Countering the US contention that their view of the proposed treaty was shared by the people and Government of Japan, the Indian communication said : "The Government of India regret that their appreciation of the situation does not tally with that of the United States Government." Finally, it stated that in pointing out what appeared to it to be a major imperfection in the treaty, it was not coming in the way of any nation which was satisfied with the terms of the treaty and wanted to sign it. What it claimed for itself, the Indian note said, was its "inherent and unquestionable right" not to sign a treaty with the terms of which it was not fully satisfied.[17]

The correspondence between India and the United States reflected not only a basic difference in the thinking of the two countries, but also the increasing bitterness and irritation which had nothing to do with the Japanese peace treaty as such. While the US note betrayed irritation of a kind which was considered to be "unusual in its diplomatic exchanges with non-Stalinist countries," the Indian notes showed signs of distrust and fear and a love of technicalities. The exchange of notes between India and the USA also offered "exceptional insights into the mutual incomprehensions of the governments concerned." The sources of mutual incomprehension covered the whole gamut of Indo-US relations. There were the serious disagreement between the two nations on the question of recognizing the Peking regime, the American disappointment with India's refusal to join others in branding China an aggressor for intervening in the Korean War, and the Indian bitterness over the delaying attitude of the US Congress towards India's request for emergency food assistance in a critical situation. "These feelings were never completely forgotten, and they came to the surface again at the time of the Japanese peace treaty."[18]

Dunn writes that the reasons India adduced for not signing the peace settlement related to the timing of the security arrangement and the contents of some of the territorial clauses, questions largely about the prestige of Japan on which Prime

Minister Nehru "seemed to be more sensitive then most Japanese." Proceeding from the belief that Indian interests would have been better served by the Anglo-American bloc than by the Soviet Union and its allies, he expresses the opinion that if Dulles had visited New Delhi the case Nehru made "might not at that time have been strong enough to resist the analytical and persuasive powers of Mr. Dulles in person." In any event Dulles might have gained a better understanding than he seemed to have had of the real alternatives that he was facing in negotiating a settlement.[19]

Commenting on the announcement that India would not sign the treaty, the London *Times*, observed in an editorial on 27 August 1951 that a theoretically unassailable procedure for a general peace with Japan would probably not be possible to devise, and if it were possible it would not in practice produce a treaty. The American and British Governments had acted in the sensible belief that some kind of peace treaty was necessary and had done their best to see that it was as widely acceptable as it could be made in the prevailing circumstances. The Indian refusal to accept the results of these efforts had caused "disappointment in London and resentment in Washington."

The *Times* considered some of the Indian objections a little fine drawn and removed from the real world of international politics. It inquired : "Is it really supposed in India that the United States could now arrange to withdraw from the security arrangements of the West Pacific, or that such a withdrawal— unblemished though it would leave Japanese sovereignty—would be in the interest of Japan or of the world ?" The Indians probably did not propose this, but clearly they did not wish to associate themselves with arrangements which provided explicitly for American troops to remain.

The *Times* editorial said it understood the Indian stand on consulting China and inviting it to sign the peace treaty. It admitted there were great gaps in the settlement because with India's refusal only one of the three great land Powers of Asia—the Soviet Union—would be present at San Francisco, and that too not for signing but for recording its objections to the settlement. The result of all this would be not a general settlement but "a limited settlement with the Western Powers and those other governments that can conveniently follow their lead." The editorial considered this unfortunate, but because the events of the past six years had not created in East Asia or anywhere else a settled condition capable of being expressed in a general treaty of peace, it expressed the belief that for more limited purposes the treaty as drafted was "a reasonable, even elightened, instrument for regulating the relations of Japan with the West."[20]

Speaking on 1 October 1951, Dulles expressed disappointment at the Indian attitude. He said he had scarcely expected India to sign a peace treaty which Soviet Russia and Communist China had rejected as that might have involved a departure from a policy which the Indian Government had within its rights judged would best serve its national interests. But the reasons India had given for declining the US invitation to participate in the San Francisco Conference seemed at that time to give encouragement to the Chinese Communists, who had revived, "for their own imperialist purposes," the old battle cry of "Asia for the Asiatics," and who were demanding that all US influence should be eradicated from Japan. Dulles expressed satisfaction that India's example was not generally followed by the other Asian states. Their presence at San Francisco, he said, gave sufficient proof of their determination "to seek peace through world unity rather than to divide continents and races into hostile camps."[21] Dulles must have been disappointed to see that Asian states like Indonesia and the Philippines which had suffered much under Japanese occupation and were therefore seriously concerned with a peace settlement with Japan later refused to ratify the San Francisco treaty.

In an article in *Foreign Affairs* of January 1952, Dulles expressed his anger with India by saying that New Delhi did not believe that the Americans could have friendly cooperation with Japanese "as equals." According to Dulles this was the principal reason why the Indian Government wanted the peace treaty to stipulate that US forces should be wholly withdrawn from Japan and the Ryukyus. He believed that India seemed to align itself with those who employed fear and hatred to create disunity, which only benefitted "the new Communist imperialism." He reiterated his view that most of the Allied nations in Asia did not endorse the Indian position.[22]

Not all Americans were inclined to share the official US view. As early as 1950 Edwin O. Reischauer, later US Ambassador in Tokyo, said that the Japanese could probably welcome foreign military installations on their soil as a protection against external attack at least for a while and added : "But, however necessary, the stationing of foreign troops on Japanese soil after the conclusion of a peace treaty is not a desirable solution of the problem."[23] India's refusal to take part in the treaty negotiations, the *Christian Science Monitor* of 29 September 1951 remarked, "exposed a lack of statemanship on our part." This newspaper considered it "naive" to believe that because of "economic aid" India should have "swallowed American Far Eastern policy, hook, line and sinker." It was wrong to think that "dollars can buy international friendship and persuade sovereign nations to dance to whatever tune we choose to fiddle."[24]

India's abstention from the San Francisco Conference, *The Hindu* remarked, was "not simply a matter of ethics or idealism as some seem to imagine but also a matter of India's national interests" as it could not afford to antagonise neighbouring China, turn a blind eye to the limitation of Japanese sovereignty, and alter its chosen course of nonalignment in foreign affairs.[25] The US strategy in the Far East necessitated retention of Japan on the American side, and India's interests demanded keeping aloof from the Cold War rivalry of the two Power blocs.

On 8 September 1951 the head of the Indian Mission in Tokyo, K.K. Chettur, appraised the Japanese Foreign Office of India's intention to end the state of war with Japan as soon as the San Francisco treaty came into force and to conclude at the earliest practicable date a separate bilateral treaty with Japan.[26] The Government of India, accordingly, announced on 28 April 1952 the end of technical state of war between India and Japan and concluded on 9 June a treaty of peace with Japan.[27] Under its terms India waived all reparations claims against Japan and the two countries agreed to accord on a reciprocal basis for four years, certain privileges to each other's nationals in trade, shipping, navigation, air traffic and other interests until the conclusion of relevant agreements in the matter. As it was not possible for a variety of reasons to conclude the stipulated agreements by the end of this period the two countries decided on 6 October 1956 to continue the same privileges up to 31 March 1957.[28] With reference to Article 2 (b) of the Treaty of Peace, the Government of India, through exchange of letters between the Indian Ambassador in Japan and the Foreign Minister of Japan on 9 June 1952, reserved the right to give any preferences or advantages in future to Commonwealth countries and contiguous countries, it being understood that if, by the grant of such preferences or advantages in the future to Commonwealth countries and contiguous countries, the Government of India was required to give similar preferences or advantages to countries other than Commonwealth countries and contiguous countries, the Government of India would also extend the same preferences or advantages to Japan.[29]

The Government of India protested in 1954 against its exclusion from participation in framing decisions on persons sentenced for war crimes by the International Military Tribunal for the Far East (IMTFE). Explaining its stand in the matter, the US Government said in a press release dated 12 May 1954 that Pakistan was entitled under international law to seek and be accorded the rights and obligations which attached to British India as a participant in the war against Japan. Thus Pakistan's rights as regards the San Francisco treaty and its rights to be represented on IMTFE were considered justified. India's vote, it was clarified, was not transferred to Pakistan. Had India signed and ratified that treaty the US Government observed that both India and Pakistan would have been eligible to participate in the decisions on the sentenced persons.[30]

The Japanese Ambassador-designate to India, Tsutomu Nishiyama, said in an interview at Dum Dum on 15 September 1952 that while the San Francisco treaty was "the most liberal treaty ever concluded by victorious powers with a vanquished country" the Indo-Japanese treaty signed in June and ratified in August 1952 "goes much further." The Japanese greatly appreciated India's "unparalleled magnanimity." In waiving all claims to war reparations and agreeing to return or restore all Japanese property in India, India had set "a new pattern of international reconciliation after a war."[31]

Chapter 7

SOUTHEAST ASIA

The countries of Southeast Asia had suffered heavily both material and spiritual damage under the Japanese occupation. Therefore, besides demanding reparations payments, they desired to insure themselves against any resurgence of Japanese militarism. The Philippines demand of "positive safeguards against future Japanese aggression" was met by the conclusion, as a "collateral part" of the Japanese peace settlement, of a US-Philippines Mutual Defence Treaty which formalised US commitment to aid the Philippines against armed external attack, whatever the source, "whether from the resurgence of Japanese militarism or from an extension of communist imperialism." But Burma and Indonesia, which also had bitter experience of Japanese aggression and exploitation by Western Colonial Powers, refused to join in any security arrangement with the US. In pursuit of its policy of keeping aloof from the Cold War confrontation between the Western Colonial Powers and the communist states, Burma even declined to participate in the San Francisco Conference. Despite its serious reservations on the reparations clauses in the peace treaty Indonesia, in a "brief disgression" from its general nonaligned approach, signed the treaty, but it subsequently refused to ratify it and rejected compromising military aid from the US.[1]

Burma

Like India, Burma had also declined the US invitation to participate in the San Francisco Conference, though for different reasons. The Burmese Government informed Washington on

23 July 1951 that it could not approve the Anglo-American draft because this would enable Japan to evade reparations despite the enormous damage that the Japanese invasion had inflicted on Burma.[2] The Burmese Government further stated that it had received "no adequate contribution toward the rehabilitation of Burma . . . from any source at any time."[3] Rangoon was dissatisfied with the reparations clauses in Article 14 of the final text of the treaty and refused to be a party to it. The Burmese Prime Minister, U Nu, told newspaper correspondents in Rangoon on 23 October 1951 on his return from a visit to Delhi that he had discussed the treaty with Nehru. Burma wanted to conclude a separate treaty with Tokyo as soon as Japan regained full freedom—after the San Francisco treaty came into force—and that he hoped to get several million rupees worth of reparations. While reparations were no doubt an important factor in swaying the Burmese Government to abstain from signing the treaty, F.C. Jones remarks, it had also to bear in mind the attitude of its powerful neighbours, Communist China and India, though for the sake of prestige it could not put this forward as a cause of refusal.[4]

Burma was the first Southeast Asian country to conclude a bilateral Treaty of Peace and Reparations and an Economic Cooperation Agreement with Japan. An amicable settlement of the reparations problem was reached on 25 September 1954,[5] though the Agreement was signed on 5 November 1954. Against Burma's huge initial claims of reparations the Japanese offered less than $100 million. Under the compromise agreement they however agreed to pay the equivalent of $200 million in goods and technical services and to invest $50 million over 10 years in joint enterprises in Burma.[6]

The Treaty of Peace and the Agreement for Reparations and Economic Cooperation was also signed on 5 November 1954 and came into force on 16 April 1955. A joint communique issued on that date said the treaty established firm and perpetual relations of peace between the two countries and laid the foundation on which they could work hand in hand for their common welfare.[7] Speaking at the exchange of instruments of ratification of the treaty, Japanese Foreign Minister Shigemitsu observed that this act marked the beginning of a new era in the relations between the two countries.[8]

On 18 October 1955 the two Governments exchanged notes on implementing the agreement on reparations and economic cooperation.[9] In a joint communique of the Prime Ministers of the two countries issued at the end of Prime Ministers Kishi's visit to Burma on 23 May 1957, Kishi reaffirmed that his government would continue to implement the agreement in good faith. U Nu in turn acknowledged that its implementation had already contributed positively to the economy of Burma.[10]

Article V paragraph 1 (a) (iii) of the treaty between Japan and Burma provided for re-examination of Burma's reparations claims in the light of Japan's final settlement of such claims with other countries and its economic capacity to bear the overall burden of reparations. After Japan agreed to pay much larger reparations to other Southeast Asian countries Burma demanded that the procedure should be reopened for review, claiming that it wanted a sum proportionate to the payments to the Philippines and Indonesia. Japan rejected the Burmese demand until January 1961, but to settle the longstanding dispute it offered $40 million in economic aid. By July 1961 Tokyo was prepared to give $75 million, but Burma not only insisted on its original demand of $200 million but added a similar sum as "investments." All $400 million were to be invested in joint Japan-Burma enterprises.[11]

After prolonged negotiations the two governments signed a memorandum on 26 January 1963 for increased reparations. Japan agreed to assist Burma's economic and social development by supplying Japanese products and the services on a grant basis. The total value of this aid would be $140 million spread over 12 years beginning 16 April 1965. Japan also agreed to extend commercial loans of $30 million payable over six years at 6 per cent interest and redeemable in 15 years. Burma agreed not to present Japan with further claims based on Article V paragraph 1 (a) (iii) of their peace treaty.[12]

The Philippines

As early as May 1949 the Philippine Government objected to the decision of the US Government to halt shipment of reparations from Japan under the advance Transfers Programme, to withdraw its proposal on sharing out reparations, and to take no further action under its interim directive powers to facilitate reparations removals from Japan. In the opinion of the Philippines, this US stand, announced to FEC on 12 May 1949, conflicted with the Potsdam Declaration and was incompatible with FEC decisions on interim removals and reparations. The Philippine representative on the commission charged the US with impatience in proposing that the reparations accounts should be closed to enable Japan to have a self-sustaining economy as early as possible. Manila even believed that the US attitude conflicted with the effective and continuing disarmament and demilitarisation of Japan.[13]

The Philippine spokesman accused Washington of showing greater concern for the welfare of its late enemy than for the just reparations claims of its allies. He asserted that the Japanese, under the direction of the former Zaibatsu, were deliberately sabotaging economic recovery and that "the Japanese must first help themselves" before a solution was sought through Allied abstention from further reparations. The representative also contended that the US Government had implicitly undertaken in the Philippine Rehabilitation Act of 1946 to act as agent for the Philippines in collecting reparations from Japan at least to the extent of the balance of Manila's war-damage claims not met by the $520 million appropriation for the Philippines under the act. He further expressed his misgivings about the formation of a "Japanese national defence force" which was said to be under "vigorous study" in Washington. The US gave its answers to these charges on 10 June 1949.[14]

On 17 October 1949, Under-Secretary Felino Neri, Foreign Office spokesman of the Philippine Government, stated that the Philippines wanted an "early and material recognition of our just claims against Japan, and an unequivocal position against Japan's resurgence in the future as a dominant power capable once more of threatening the peace in this part of the world."[15] Manila, thus, laid emphasis on "just" reparations from Japan and adequate security guarantees against any possible revival of Japanese militarism. On the issue of Japanese fishing too, it was demanded on the Philippine side that the Japanese should not be permitted to fish within three hundred miles of Philippine territory.[16]

Washington's announcement on 14 September 1950 about

initiating discussions on a Japanese peace treaty with other
interested countries was welcomed by the Philippines Foreign
Minister on 18 September. As Manila was keen to see Japan's
relations with the victorious Allies regularised it desired that
the treaty should place on a permanent basis the programme of
FEC to demilitarise and democratise Japan so that it could
never again become a threat to the peace and freedom of its
neighbours.[17] The Filipinos apprised Dulles of their strong
views on reparations claims on his visit to Manila in February
1951.[18]

The US draft of March 1951, which provided for the complete waiver of reparations claims, came as a great disappointment to the Philippines. Foreign Secretary Carlos P. Romulo
reacted sharply to it and declared that his country would not
withdraw its claim for reparations which constituted an "inde-
feasible right." He maintained that the need to keep a self-
sustaining Japanese economy should not "supersede" the
Philippine claim for reparations and considered the reparations
question still remaining "open". On the question of security,
Romulo stated, in his letter to Dulles, dated 20 March 1951,
that the Philippines would not be "willing to risk the emergence
of a remilitarized Japan." He, therefore, wanted "adequate
and effective safeguards both on the restoration of Japanese
industry and rearmament of Japan." He observed that while
the Philippines would respect Japan "as an important bastion
of the proposed defensive wall against communism," it would
serve no purpose if the countries which were sought to be protected by that defensive wall were "permitted to fall into economic chaos to be subverted by communism from within." He
concluded that the Philippines would not withdraw its claim
for reparations as a "price of Japan's participation in a collective security arrangement for the Pacific."[19]

The Filipinos did not feel happy about the joint Anglo-
American draft of July 1951 either. The draft had filled them
"with profound disillusionment and dismay,"[20] Romulo said.
The speaker of the Philippine House of Representatives,
Eugenio Perez, felt so bitter about what he called "the suicidal
document" that he bluntly refused to sign the treaty and
threatened that the Filipinos "might conceivably turn to communism even if only for the sake of empty promises of better

treatment."[21]

President Quirino said the draft "practically sidetracks our claims for reparations." The whole nation was united in insisting that "our right to demand reparations from Japan be recognised." He observed : "They misread the temper of our people, those who refuse to respect that right."[22]

Responding to the strong Philippine reaction, the US Government deemed it necessary not only to remove what it called "a serious misunderstanding" on the part of its ally regarding the true meaning of the reparations clause in the draft treaty,[23] but also agreed to modify the relevant provisions in the final text of the treaty, which was released on 15 August 1951. The modified text, along with the text of the US-Philippines bilateral security pact released on 16 August 1951, seemed to go a long way in mollifying Filipino feelings. The final text was an improvement over the previous drafts in that it recognised Japan's obligations to pay reparations in more categorical terms. Moreover, the inclusion of the word "presently" in Article 14 (a) seemed to afford the Philippines much scope for negotiating a larger sum in reparations on the basis of increased Japanese ability to pay in the future.

In a statement before the San Francisco Conference Romulo generally supported the treaty but said it fell short in certain respects. But for the situation created by the "menace of Communist aggression" and the conclusion of the US-Philippines Mutual Defence Treaty, which protected the Philippines from armed attack "whether arising from a new source or from the renewal of Japanese aggression," the Philippines would have regarded as "completely intolerable the unrestricted right of Japan to organise its own military forces," Romulo observed. He expressed his profound dissatisfaction with the treaty provisions on reparations and demanded "an early and equitable reparation of the damage caused by Japan to the Philippines and other countries."[24]

He said Japan had been deprived of all its overseas territories under Article 2 and 3 and of its overseas assets under Article 14 (a) 2. The beneficiaries of these provisions were "almost exclusively the Great Powers." On the other hand payment of reparations, the only form in which smaller countries damaged and occupied by Japan might be indemnified for their losses, was severely restricted under the treaty. It was a treaty of forgiveness in respect of the claims of the smaller countries but plainly punitive in respect of the claims of the Great Powers.

Conceding the need for Japan to have a viable economy, Romulo was not prepared to foreclose the whole question of reparations in advance and to limit their payment to "services in production, salvaging and other work." He demanded a "freer hand" in negotiating with Japan in future for the payment of reparations "in forms other than those stipulated under Article 14 (a)1." He accordingly reserved the right of his government to negotiate "on the kinds and forms of reparations . . . and the manner of . . . payment or delivery."[25]

The Philippines signed the San Francisco treaty, but ratification was held up for want of agreement on the amount and form of reparations. The Nacionalista Party, which was bent on blocking ratification, had raised the slogan : "No ratification without adequate reparations." It considered the signing of the Peace Treaty by the Philippines "a great betrayal," "a new abdication of our rights," and "our Munich at San Francisco."[26] In an article entitled, "Dulles Final Draft Gives Philippines Nothing," Senator Recto stated that the Nacionalista Party wanted a categorical declaration that reparations would include "forms" other than mere Japanese services stipulated in the Treaty.[27] Another reason for the Nacionalista Party's dissatisfaction was that the Mutual Defence Treaty between the USA and the Philippines, signed on 30 August 1951,[28] did not contain automatic and obligatory action on the part of the United States in defence of the Philippines on the pattern of the North Atlantic Treaty Organization. Senator Recto believed that while the provision of meeting "the common dangers in accordance with its constitutional process" in Article IV of the bilateral security pact was sufficient to protect the Philippines against Communist aggression, it might not be satisfactory with regard to any possible Japanese attack through infiltration or subversion.[29]

On 4 April 1952 J.M. Elizalde, Secretary of Foreign Affairs, tried to impress upon the Philippine Senate the need for early ratification by dwelling on "the plans for the integration of Japan into the bloc of free nations," by emphasising that "what we may unfortunately have to forgo in reparations we are gaining in security," by pointing out that the treaty validated the seizure or disposition by the Allied Powers of Japanese properties within their jurisdiction, and by saying that the US had not only turned over to the government in Manila the proceeds from the sale of former Japanese properties within the Philippines and in several cases the properties themselves but had also contributed to "our rehabilitation in the form of war damages," extended substantial benefits to "our veterans," and provided financial, economic and military assistance under the ECA now the MSA.

The additional considerations Elizalde cited in support of early ratification of the treaty included the undesirability of allowing abnormal relations to continue indefinitely, participating effectively in coordinating the defence efforts of the "free world" countries, the possibilities of increased economic assistance from the US, trade benefits, and the need to give "fresh evidence of its alignment with the free world in the Cold War" against communism.

Elizalde said delay in ratification would hold in abeyance the benefits that would flow from it. He also pointed out there was no provision binding Japan to negotiate a bilateral treaty with a country which signed the treaty in San Francisco but refused to ratify it. He held out little prospect of the Philippines getting better and more advantageous terms in a bilateral treaty than those of the San Francisco treaty.

Despite the strenuous efforts of the Philippine leaders it was not possible to get ratification from the Senate in the absence of a satisfactory solution of the reparations problem. The Opposition Nacionalista Party demanded reparations worth $8 billion and that too in cash. Its spokesmen feared that payment in services might enable Japan to gain an economic foothold in the Philippines.

As a result of discussions in Manila and Tokyo, Japan and the Philippines signed on 12 March 1953 an interim agreement on the salvage of sunken vessels lying in Manila Bay and Cebu harbour. Japan agreed to lend the Philippines Government the services of Japanese and equipment and supplies for operatives and equipment and supplies for salvaging about 200,000 tons of vessels located in Philippine waters.[30] The salvage work was however delayed for two years because of the persistent disagreement on the expenses of the operation. Japan originally demanded $114 per ton, but the Philippines refused to accept this. It was only on 8 June 1955 that the revised Japanese offer of $92 per ton was accepted[31] and the operations finally got under way in August 1955.

After three months of reparations negotiations, which began in Manila in January 1954, Katsumi Ohno of Japan and Carlos P. Garcia, Vice-President and Foreign Secretary of Philippines, reached on 15 April a provisional agreement setting the total amount of reparations at $400 million payable over 20 years.[32] This was a considerable climbdown for the Nacionalista Party, which had assumed power, not only from its original claim of $8 billion but also the starting sum of $2 billion in the negotiations. Because of strong Senatorial opposition the agreement was scrapped and demands were made for fresh negotiations taking $1 billion as the irreducible minimum.[33]

The Philippines Government contention that the Ohno-Garcia memorandum was agreed upon "as no more than a starting point of negotiations" was apparently motivated by the desire to gain "further concessions," which Japanese Foreign Minister Katsuo Okazaki declared on 1 May 1954 meant "forcing the impossible on Japan." Japan would calmly watch developments.[34] In March 1955 Mitsuo Tanaka, Director of the Public Information and Cultural Affairs Bureau, Ministry of Foreign Affairs of Japan, deemed it necessary to categorically deny a report which had appeared in the *Asahi* of 10 March 1955 that the Philippines had demanded reparations amounting to $680 million, to be paid in 73 kinds of machinery and equipment.[35]

In May 1955, Manila presented new demands for $800 million to which the Japanese offered $600 million. In early June 1955 the Japanese were reported to be "earnestly studying payment of $800 million," but this was denied later in the month. The strain on Japan's economy would be too great, Tokyo maintained.[36] Agreed minutes[37] setting forth the various reparations requirements of the Philippines for its economic development and rehabilitation together with the Japanese findings and comments on them were signed on 14 June 1955.

Early in September Japanese Prime Minister Hatoyama

asked Yoshida for his support for the $800 million formula, but Yoshida refused. Hatoyama then offered the Philippines a compromise : $500 million over 20 years in reparations goods, $30 million in technical services including ship salvage, and $20 million in cash for Filipino war widows and orphans. In addition, he agreed to facilitate $250 million worth of private, long-term, low-interest "commercial" loans on terms to be negotiated later. The contradictory language in the agreement concerning these loans was to produce difficulties later.[38] It was not until after nine months of negotiations that a settlement was finally signed on 9 May 1956 in Manila to provide $800 million in 20 years, of which $550 million was payable in services and capital materials and $250 million in industrial loans. The agreement signed by Japan and the Philippines in 1953 concerning salvage of vessels sunk in Philippine waters was considered part of the settlement.[39]

The instruments of ratification in regard to the agreement were exchanged in Tokyo on 23 July 1956. The instrument of ratification of the treaty of Peace with Japan, signed at San Francisco on 8 September 1951, was also deposited by the Philippine Government in Washington the same day. Thus relations between the two countries were normalised and formal diplomatic relations established.

Indonesia

Like the Philippines, Indonesia had suffered heavily at the hands of the Japanese militarists and it was believed that in addition to requisitioning Indonesian natural resources, primarily petroleum products and railway rolling stock, they had taken millions of dollars worth of gold and diamonds back to their homeland.[40] In the words of the Indonesian delegate to the San Francisco Conference, Indonesia had to suffer the loss of approximately 4 million lives and material damages to the extent of billions of dollars under the Japanese occupation.[41] In these circumstances it was quite natural for Indonesia to hold strong views on reparations. In fact Indonesia claimed $17 billion, an amount larger than demanded by all the other Southeast Asian countries put together.[42]

Indonesia was not a member of the Far Eastern Commission but Dulles had brought it within the purview of the treaty talks after discussions with the Indonesian delegation at the UN. After the March 1951 US draft for a peace treaty was published a spokesman of the Indonesian Foreign Ministry declared that his country would prefer to sign a treaty along-with all the nations involved in the Pacific war. If this proved impossible Indonesia would join in a "partial peace settlement" without the Soviet Union.[42]

When the joint Anglo-American draft was made available to Indonesia, Jakarta, in its note to US dated 6 August 1951, made several suggestions. Among these were : the sovereignty of Japan over its territories and waters should be recognised; a plebiscite should be held in the territories detached from Japan to ascertain the wishes of their inhabitants; fair and just reparations should be made to Indonesia; an opportunity should be provided to the participants in the San Francisco Conference to discuss the final text; and attempts should be made to secure the participation of China and the Soviet Union "in the endeavours leading to a peace treaty with Japan."[44]

The final text of the treaty, circulated in August 1951, rejected all the Indonesian suggestions except that relating to the recognition of Japan's sovereignty over its territories and waters. This provision was included in the March draft, committed in the July draft, and later re-inserted in the final text.

Towards the end of August 1951 it was obvious that India and Burma would not participate in the peace conference. Their attitude, A. Brotherton remarks, was determined as much by the wish to maintain friendly relations with China as by understandable suspicion of US motives in maintaining a large measure of economic, political and military control—directly and indirectly—over a nominally independent Japan.[45] While the participation in the conference of the Philippines, the Bao Dai regime in Vietnam and the Songram Government in Thailand was never in doubt that there was a distinct possibility that Indonesia might follow India. Indonesia like India was reluctant to align itself irrevocably with one bloc or the other and had refused to allow refuelling of US vessels proceeding to Korea.

There was a violent press campaign in Indonesia against the proposed treaty, and Partai Nasional Indonesia, the second largest political grouping in the country, declared its unconditional rejection of the US invitation to attend the conference. The Indonesian Socialist Party also opposed participation and its influential leader Sultan Sjahrir pointed out the possible disadvantages that might result from signing the treaty. Only a small Catholic party believed that by signing it the Indonesian Government would be better able to press its claim to Western Irian.

Six of the 14 members of the coalition cabinet in Jakarta also opposed participation. That the dominant member of the coalition, the Masjumi (Muslim) Party, was deeply divided on the issue was evident from the fact that the decision to send a delegation to San Francisco was taken only after two days of intense debate at which only 33 of the 60 members of the party's central executive were present and the voting was 17 in favour, 14 against and two abstentions. It was believed that had there been a larger attendance the decision might have been in the negative, "more in keeping with the editorial policy of the Masjumi press."[46]

As if to placate public opinion government statements, issued prior to the departure of the Indonesian delegation to San Francisco emphasised that there was no commitment to sign the treaty as it stood. If Indonesia subsequently decided to sign the treaty in the face of "an all-embracing national unpopularity" it was because as Dr. Ahmed Subardjo claimed, Indonesia would have been forced into isolation.[47]

Presenting the views of the Indonesian Government at the conference, Dr. Subardjo expressed his government's dissatisfaction with the treaty provisions on reparations. He demanded more than mere good faith as a pledge and declared that Indonesia would have wished to move amendments, if permitted, to the articles on reparations and fisheries. He proposed that Japan should assist the Allied Powers who had suffered under Japanese occupation and desired compensations for damages not only by making available skills and services but also by paying all expenditure incurred by the consignment of raw materials for processing in Japan, by making available machinery and workshops required for reconstructing by the Allied Powers so desiring, by making available technicians and giving opportunities for trainees to work in Japan, and by making funds available to mitigate the sufferings of nationals of the Allied Powers in the war.[48]

The Indonesian suggestions would have made the stipulations under Article 14 of the treaty regarding the form of reparations more broad-based. But under the rules of procedure guiding the conference no opportunity was provided for considering the Indonesian amendments. The Indonesian delegate addressed three questions pertaining to reparations and regulation of fisheries to Yoshida, the chairman of the Japanese delegation. After receiving Yoshida's assurances about "a fair interpretation of Article 14 and 9 of the treaty" and about Japan's carrying out its obligation in "good faith."[49] Subardjo signed the treaty. This act did not however ensure its quick ratification by Indonesia. Although Indonesia was the first Southeast Asian nation with which Japan opened bilateral reparations negotiations it was not until January 1958 that a settlement on the amount of reparations was reached.

A provisional agreement was signed on 18 January 1952 by Japan and Indonesia under which Japan recognised the damage and suffering it had caused to Indonesia in World War II, and agreed to make reparations, as defined in Article 14 of the peace treaty, in the form of processing raw materials, ship salvage, technical assistance, and technical training of Indonesian workers.[50] The provisional agreement defined how Japan would pay rather than how much.[51]

After prolonged negotiations, Japan and Indonesia also signed on 16 December 1953 an interim agreement by which Japan agreed to bear expenses not exceeding $6.5 million for salvaging not less than 60 sunken vessels.[52] Speaking at the signing of the agreement, Japanese Foreign Minister Katsuo Okazaki observed that the first step had been taken towards the settlement of the long-pending question of reparations for Indonesia. He expressed the belief that it would contribute greatly to the establishment of normal relations and promoting friendship and goodwill between the two countries.[53] The salvage agreement was considered as constituting an integral part of the overall reparations agreement.

There was no difference of opinion on the form of reparations and the kinds or the way in which payments had to be made, but "the very great difference" on their amount persisted.

The Indonesian side insisted that talks should proceed on the basis of a huge estimate of damages—$17.3 billion.[54] On a visit to Indonesia in December 1952 a Japanese Government delegation headed by Majima Eiji reportedly offered only $125 million against an Indonesian claim of $8 billion.[55]

The conclusion of the Japan-Philippines Reparations Agreement of 9 May 1956 had a direct bearing on the reparations negotiations with Indonesia as both sides began to think of settling the problem on a realistic basis. Indonesian Prime Minister Djuanda asked in his note to Premier Nobusuke Kishi of Japan on 7 July 1957 for $400 million by way of pure reparations and another $400 million by way of economic cooperation loans. The problem of the trade deficit of $170 million could be settled separately over a fixed period.[56]

On Kishi's visit to Indonesia in November 1957 the reparation problem was discussed freely and thoroughly and an understanding reached in principle.[57] Ataru Kobayashi, personal representative of the Japanese Government, and Kishi were asked to remain in Indonesia to finalise details. Thus, a bilateral treaty of peace was signed on 20 January 1958. Japan agreed to supply Indonesia by way of reparations with Japanese products and services to the total value of $223.08 million over 12 years.[58] Under a protocol[59] signed separately on the same day Japan agreed to cancel the Indonesian trade deficit of $176,913,958.41, which virtually meant payment in cash. By an exchange of notes between the two governments Japan also agreed to provide the Government of Indonesia with $400 million in 20 years in commercial investments, long term loans or similar credit arrangements.[60]

South Vietnam

Like the Philippines and Indonesia, the Republic of Vietnam (South Vietnam) was also dissatisfied with the reparations clauses in the San Francisco treaty. Speaking at the conference on 7 September 1951, its delegate Tran Van Huu observed that the reparations, which were to be given mainly in the form of services, would not be of much use to Vietnam, which did not have any raw materials. Like Japan, he said, Vietnam needed great contributions of capital to re-establish its economy. To accept reparations principally in services therefore amounted to accepting currency which was not legal tender. He laid stress on "other more effective formulas for payment" under study and hoped that normal indemnification would come when the restored Japanese economy would make it possible for Japan to fulfil its obligations.[61]

Negotiations on reparations opened between Japan and South Vietnam in 1956 and continued on Kishi's visit to Saigon in November 1957.[62] An early settlement proved difficult because Vietnam claimed $2 billion. After protracted talks settlement was however reached and a Reparations and Loan Agreement signed in Saigon on 30 May 1959. Under the agreement Japan agreed to pay $39 million over a period of five years in the form of products and services. In the first three years it would pay $10 million annually, and $4.5 million yearly in the last two.[63]

In addition to these payments Japan also agreed to lend $7.5 million in 3 years and invest $9.1 million over a period of 5 years in economic cooperation projects. The agreement came into force in January 1960. Speaking at the exchange of ratification documents, Japanese Foreign Minister Fujiyama said the agreement not only meant that Japan desired to indemnify Vietnam for war damages but was also concrete evidence of the understanding between the two nations and "their friendship and solidarity in the community of Asian countries."[64]

North Vietnam

The Japanese efforts at normalising ties with South Vietnam invited protests from North Vietnam. As soon as Hanoi learnt of the contacts Saigon had established with Tokyo in regard to reparations for war damages it issued a statement on 25 August 1956 which said that the Japanese forces had inflicted considerable damages on the entire people of Vietnam in World War II. Reparations was therefore a question concerning the whole of Vietnam, and the Government of the Democratic Republic of Vietnam accordingly reserved its right to demand reparations from Japan.[65] The spokesman of the Japanese Foreign Ministry replied the following day that the Japanese Government would not consider this demand because Tokyo did not recognise the Hanoi regime as the legitimate government of Vietnam. Hanoi described the Japanese stand as "unjustified because it does not correspond with the actual situation in

Vietnam" and reiterated, in its statement of 29 August 1956, its "legitimate right" to demand reparations for war damages caused by Japanese troops on Vietnamese territory.[66]

The Foreign Minister of North Vietnam also issued a statement on 26 November 1957 criticising the separate negotiations between Japan and South Vietnam on the question of war indemnities. He said that according to the Geneva Agreements the South Vietnam administration was not qualified to represent all of the Vietnamese in demanding war compensations from Japan. The Government of North Vietnam did not recognise any agreement between Tokyo and Saigon on war compensations for the whole of Vietnam. He reserved the right of his government to demand war indemnities.[67]

Relations between North Vietnam and Japan remained abnormal for a long time. Because of its Mutual Security arrangements and deep political and economic involvement with US and also because Tokyo benefitted economically from the Vietnam war, Japan expressed understanding and approval of American policies in the Southeast Asian region and never openly questioned or criticised American policies or actions in Vietnam, including the bombing of the North. Even when Japan had doubts over the escalation of the Vietnam conflict and disagreed with the US approach, Tokyo was somewhat reticent about airing its differences with Washington publicly. Moves to normalise relations with North Vietnam were initiated on the visit of Wasuke Miyake, former chief of the Japanese Foreign Ministry's Southeast Asia Division, to Hanoi in February 1972. Subsequent visits to Hanoi in January 1973 and April 1973 and the signing of the Paris Agreements between the US and Vietnam in that year contributed to the beginning of formal negotiations on establishing diplomatic relations on 25 July 1973.

The two countries officially exchanged notes on the establishment of diplomatic relations in Paris on 21 September 1973. It was agreed that after the establishment of diplomatic relations Japan would provide $20 million in economic assistance to North Vietnam.[68] But it was not until October 1975 that Japan announced an outright grant of 8,500 million yen (nearly $30 million) and opened an embassy in Hanoi, thereby normalising relations. Even though Vietnam continues to be critical of Japan's security pact with the United States and supports the Japanese Communist Party's demand for a neutral Japan, Hanoi responded by opening its resident Mission in Tokyo under a charge d'Affaires in January 1976 and its attitude was not averse to Japanese economic overtures. For the fiscal year 1976, Tokyo announced a 5000 million yen non-reimbursable aid to Vietnam thereby embarking in right earnest to establish a solid economic relationship with the newly unified Vietnam—forgetting the past.

Laos and Cambodia

Unlike other Southeast Asian countries, Cambodia waived its claim for war indemnities against Japan in 1955 and Laos during 1957. Communicating his Government's renunciation to Japanese Vice-Foreign Minister Katsui Ohno on 27 March 1957, Laotian Ambassador Khammao hoped that Japan would aid the economic development of Laos by supplying goods and equipment, including small vessels for river transportation.

By way of returning the friendly gesture by Laos and Cambodia, as Japanese Minister of International Trade and Industries Hayato Ikeda put it, Tokyo, decided to offer economic and technical cooperation free of any obligation to them.[69] This matter was discussed on Kishi's visit to these two countries, in November-December 1957[70] and negotiations commenced in 1958. The agreements finally reached with Laos on 15 October 1958 and with Cambodia on 2 March 1959 provided for a grant of $2.777 or 1000 million yen for Laos in goods and services and $4.166 or 1500 million yen for Cambodia, a total of $6.944 million to both.[71]

The grant to Laos was to be used to construct water tanks and bridges in Vientiane while that for Cambodia was meant to establish an agricultural trading centre (with farming implements and a travelling clinic), a cattle breeding centre and similar facilities. The agreements provided the following procedures in the same way as reparations payments : the Japanese Government would sanction and issue export licences on contracts concluded with the Governments of Laos and Cambodia; and payment for such contracts would be made by the Japanese Government out of the Reparations Payment Special Account in the national budget to Japanese enterprises through banks designated by the Government of Laos or Cambodia.[72]

Chapter 8

KOREA

Korea was never at war with Japan, yet in a message signed by Dr. Kimm Kiusic as Chairman and all other members of the interim Legislative Assembly of South Korea, addressed to President Truman of the USA, Prime Minister Attlee of Britain and Generalissimo Chiang Kai-shek in August 1947, the direct participation of Korea in the coming peace conference with Japan was stated to be "justified by the fact that relationship between Korea and Japan had been very complicated for a long period." The American Political Adviser Jacobs in Seoul was inclined to feel that some representatives of the South Korea Government might well be permitted to attend the peace conference with Japan if only in the capacity of an observer. It was, however, realized that granting such permission to a representative of South Korea would probably move the USSR, if it attended the conference, to request that a representative from North Korea be present. To permit representatives from both North and South Korea to attend an international gathering such as the Japanese peace conference, Jacobs observed, might be objectionable from the viewpoint of emphasizing the division of Korea into two separate political entities.[1] That was in 1947. After the Korean War, many other complications arose and it was not possible to obtain a consensus in favour of inviting only South Korea to participate in the San Francisco Peace Conference among all the States whose participation in the Conference was deemed necessary.

Accordingly, it was decided to exclude both South and North Korea from the San Francisco Peace Conference. They did not sign the peace treaty which contained only brief references to Korea. Nevertheless, the treaty affected Korea, which had suffered heavy losses under Japanese occupation, in many ways. Japan recognised the independence of Korea under Article 2. Article 21 stipulated that Korea would enjoy the benefits of Articles 2, 4, 9 and 12. These provisions placed Korea on par with the Allied Powers with regard to postwar trading, fishing, commercial and maritime arrangements, and Japan was obligated to enter into negotiations for the transfer of large holdings of Japanese property to Korea.

South Korea

After protracted negotiations relations between Japan and the Republic of Korea (ROK) were normalised in 1965, but it has not yet been possible for Japan to normalise its relations with North Korea. In the Cold War context in which the San Francisco Peace Conference was convened the US could be said to have been favourably inclined towards South Korea. But guided by the maxim that caution was the better part of valour Washington decided not to invite either South or North Korea to participate in it. Under the Treaty Japan recognized the independence of Korea and renounced "all right, title and claim to Korea, including the islands of Quelpart, Port Hamilton and Dagalet."

Soon after the signing of the treaty the US tried to reconcile the differences between South Korea and Japan. Preliminary talks opened between the officials of the two countries through the good offices of SCAP on 20 October 1951 to settle some outstanding difficulties. The conference was attended by Sadao Iguchi of Japan, Ambassador You Chan Yang of South Korea and Ambassador William Sebald of the USA. Sebald points out that the situation was complicated by the effects of Japan's long domination of Korea and by South Korean President Syngman Rhee's intransigent attitude to the Japanese. Keeping this in view, Sebald tried in his opening statement to impress upon the parties directly concerned the need to solve their many outstanding problems in a reasonable manner. Iguchi made a conciliatory statement calling for give-and-take on both sides, but Yang delivered a scorching indictment of Japanese actions in Korea over the previous 40 years. The Korean diplomat demanded payment of such a huge indemnity that "it would have bankrupted Japan," Sebald remarks. Despite Sebald's attempts to restore harmony the conference slowly collapsed after futile attempts to agree on an agenda.[2]

Among the various problems in the way of normalising relations were the disputes over Takeshima Island, the fishery question, the status of Koreans in Japan (numbering about 600,000) and war claims. As early as 18 January 1952 Syngman Rhee established the "Rhee Line" over a wide area of the high seas adjacent to the territorial waters of Korea and declared that his government would exercise its sovereignty and jurisdiction in the area. Takeshima was included[3] and Japanese fishermen were prohibited entry across the line, which lies 60 to 179 miles off the Korean coast.

The Japanese Government, which held that Takeshima was Japanese territory historically (having been incorporated in Japan in 1905 prior to annexation of Korea in 1910) and under international law, protested. South Korean attempts to assert its control over the island were termed "unlawful invasion" and "illegal intrusions." The absence of Japanese renunciation of its claim, in the San Francisco Peace Treaty was cited by Tokyo in support of its rights.[4]

Seoul turned down the Japanese protests and in September 1953 launched what the spokesman of the Japanese Ministry of Foreign Affairs called "an indiscriminate and wholesale seizure" of some 41 Japanese fishing boats with their 484 crew members. By the middle of 1954, South Korea had succeeded in stationing its guards and erecting a lighthouse on the island.

The Japanese proposal of 25 September 1954 to refer the Takeshima issue to the International Court of Justice was rejected by South Korea as it maintained that the island was unquestionably Korean. Exchange of notes between the two governments, from Japan dated 13 July 1953, 20 September 1953 and 10 February 1954, and from Seoul dated 9 September 1953 and 25 September 1954, only added to the heat of the controversy.[5]

In the Japan-South Korea talks in March 1952, the South Korean delegate argued that his country should have demand-

ed reparations for Japan's occupation of Korea and enslavement of the Korean people for 35 years (1910-1945). To this
Tokyo replied that the Japanese administration of Korea was
not entirely an unmixed evil. Japan recognised that the Republic of Korea should take over in accordance with the San
Francisco treaty with Japanese Government property in Korea
before the end of the war, but at the same time it held that
Japanese citizens "have claims to their private assets owned in
Korea, estimated at 800-900 million US dollars." Japan considered it "an absurd exaggeration" to say that such assets
amount to 85 per cent of the total property value in ROK. The
Japanese denied that Tokyo had at any time made the "unreasonable demand" that even the assets destroyed on account
of the Korean War should be returned to Japan. The Korean
side contended that it had claims to assets in Japan estimated
at 600-800 million dollars.[6]

Japan made a compromise proposal by which it offered to
forfeit $100-300 million in favour of South Korea. This was
not acceptable to Koreans, who argued that the Japanese had
no claim to their private property in Korea but the Koreans
had claims to the Korean assets in Japan. In practice this
amounted to the demand that Japan should pay a sum exceeding $600 million to ROK. The talks broke down in April 1952,
with no agreement on war claims, fisheries or the status of
Koreans in Japan.[7]

Commenting on relations between the two countries on 30
January 1956, Japanese Foreign Minister Shigemitsu observed :

That our relations with the Republic of Korea remain un-
adjusted is deplorable for the sake of not only the two
nations but also East Asia as a whole. We are trying to
solve speedily the pending issues and establish diplomatic
relations between the two countries, but it seems we shall
have to rely on the equitable intercession of the United
States, the author of the San Francisco Peace Treaty. The
urgent problem of the fishermen detained in Korea has not
been solved. The government is exceedingly sorry for all
concerned. Since the Korean Government is demanding
the release of the Korean nationals being held in custody at
the Omura detention centre as a condition for the return of
the fishermen, we hope to arrive at an early solution of this
problem by proposing a practical scheme.[8]

As a result of talks in 1957 understanding was reached on measures to be taken about the Koreans detained in Japan and the Japanese fishermen detained in Korea as well as the resumption of negotiations on normalising relations and other pending issues. The Japanese withdrew the claim to property in Korea which Japan was not prepared to surrender in 1952.[9] On 16 April 1958, the Japanese Government transferred 106 pieces of Korean cultural property to South Korea. In December 1962 tentative agreement was reached on $300 million gratuitous and $200 million nongratuitous credits in preliminary negotiations on claims.[10]

On the Japanese Foreign Minister's visit to South Korea in February 1965 a Treaty on Basic Relations between the two countries was initialled.[11] On 6 March agreement was reached on a 150,000-ton annual catch of fish in joint restricted waters (10 per cent leeway both ways) at the fourth conference of Agriculture-Forestry Ministers. Subsequently agreed minutes on fisheries, claims and legal status of Koreans in Japan were initialled in Tokyo on 3 April 1965.[12] Finally, on 22 June 1965 Japan and South Korea signed a Treaty on Basic Relations and four agreements concerning fisheries, South Korean property claims and economic aid, legal status and treatment of South Korean residents in Japan, and return of South Korean cultural properties. More than 20 other related documents, including a protocol and the records of the agreed minutes, were attached to the agreements. The two countries also exchanged each other's views on jurisdiction over Takeshima and on how long the fishery agreement should be valid—two major bones of contention still unremoved.[13]

The Treaty on Basic Relations was ratified in Seoul on 18 December 1965. It provided for establishing diplomatic and consular relations, declared null and void all treaties and agreements concluded between the Empire of Japan and the Empire of Korea on or before 22 August 1910, and confirmed that the Government of the Republic of Korea was "the only lawful Government in Korea as specified in the Resolution 195(III) of the United Nations General Assembly."[14]

The 14-year-long negotiations were successfully concluded in 1965 only after Japan agreed to give South Korea $300 million in outright grants and $200 million in long-term, low-interest credits.[15]

North Korea

In a statement of its Foreign Minister in July 1951, the Democratic People's Republic of Korea (North Korea), fully shared the Soviet Government's stand concerning the conclusion of a peace treaty with Japan both as regards the procedure of preparing this treaty and its goal and contents. Separate drafting of a treaty by the US was considered as having been motivated by the "obviously self-seeking aims" of consolidating the American position in occupied Japan and converting it into "the main base of American aggression in Asia."[16]

Pyongyang referred to the tremendous losses suffered by the Chinese and Korean peoples as a result of the Japanese aggression and emphasised the right of China and Korea to participate in the preparation of a treaty. North Korean Foreign Minister demanded "sufficient guarantees against a revival of Japanese militarism," withdrawal of US occupation troops from Japan and a settlement of territorial and other questions in accordance with the provisions of the Cairo Declaration, the Yalta Agreement and the Potsdam Proclamation.[17]

North Korea, like South Korea, was excluded from the San Francisco Conference. Moreover, like Seoul, Pyongyang expressed concern over the return home of Korean citizens in Japan. In a statement of 30 December 1958 Nam Il Sung criticised the "unjust steps of the Kishi Government" in hindering the return home of the Korean citizens in Japan, not ensuring proper living conditions for them and subjecting them to "cruel suppression" in flagrant violation of humanitarian principles and publicly accepted international law.[18]

The statement of the Government of North Korea on "revision of the Japan-US Security Treaty" issued on 12 January 1959 accused Washington of converting Japan into a permanent military base and of using rejuvenated Japanese militarism as a tool for fresh aggression against the Asian peoples.[19]

The joint communique signed by President Kim Il Sung on behalf of the Korean Workers' Party and by Kenji Miyamoto on behalf of a visiting delegation of the Japanese Communist Party on 27 February 1959 demanded an end to the "semi-occupation of Japan," the abrogation of the security treaty, the return of Okinawa and Ogasawara to Japan, the return home of Korean citizens in Japan, and normalisation of relations between the two countries.[20]

As a result of the agreement reached between the Japanese and North Korean Red Cross in Calcutta on 13 August 1959, two Soviet ships left the port of Nigata in Northern Japan on 14 December 1959, carrying 975 repatriates to North Korea despite strong objections by the South Korean Government. In all, 5000 Koreans were registered for repatriation to North Korea under the Calcutta agreement.[21] There are about 600,000 Koreans in Japan. About one-third favour Republic of Korea, the other two-third are sympathetic to North Korea and the remaining are neutral. About half of them have got Republic of Korea passports and the others have been given identification cards simply as Koreans. There have been economic intercourse and political contacts between Japan and North Korea recently, but relations have not been normalised so far.

Chapter 9

JAPAN AND THE PEACE SETTLEMENTS

The Japanese surrender to the Allied Powers in August 1945 was a traumatic experience for the proud Japanese people who had never before been subjected to the humiliating experience of defeat in war. The unprecedented suffering caused by the atomic bombing of Hiroshima and Nagasaki added to their woes. The war-devastated nation, smarting under the indignity of occupation, was much concerned about rehabilitating its economy and an early termination of the state of war by the victorious countries, thereby regaining its independence and sovereignty.

As a result of the Pacific War, Prime Minister Shigeru Yoshida stated, Japan was stripped of 44 per cent of its huge overseas assets, some 80 per cent of its merchant marine, and large portions of its industrial equipment. It also lost 36 per cent of its national wealth, including civilian production.[1] According to Yoshiniko Morozumi, Chief, Research Section, Ministry of International Trade and Industry, the total war damage suffered by Japan drained away as much as 25 per cent of its national wealth; and the production in key industries in 1945, when compared with the prewar production volume (the average for 1934-36 taken as 100), was 66.5 per cent for rice, 4.2 per cent for cotton yarn, 12.8 per cent for raw silk, 58 per cent for coal, and 35.6 per cent for iron and steel. In addition to the loss of 44 per cent of its territory, its direct contact with the mainland of China was severed, and as a result it was deprived of important supply sources of rice, soy-bean, lumber, coal and iron ore, as well as of one of its most important overseas markets for manufactured goods. In contrast to such postwar industrial deterioration, the population of Japan, when repatriated ex-servicemen and civilians were added, increased by 6 million within two years after the end of the war. The acute shortage of food-stuffs, raw materials, fuel and electric power soon brought on a vicious inflation. The official commodity price level rose 60-fold during the four-year period of 1945-48.[2]

The economic instability of post-war Japan, Mitsuo Tanaka, Director, Public Information Bureau, Ministry of Foreign Affairs, pointed out in 1955, owed its origin to the following factors : (1) drastic shrinkage in territory, from 260,457 square miles in prewar years to 142,116 square miles under the San Francisco Peace Treaty, with Korea, Formosa, Kwantung Leased Territory, Mandated Islands of the Marianas truncated from Japan; (2) population increase from 72.2 million in 1945 to 88.8 million as of March 1955; (3) foreign debts, including reparations payments; and (4) loss of markets for exports, particularly that of China, which took as much as 34 per cent of Japanese total exports in 1939. The loss of possessions, Tanaka observed, meant that Japan had to face acute shortages in primary products and industrial materials for which it depended on them.[3]

If the rehabilitation of the war-torn Japanese economy was an uphill task, the conclusion of peace settlement with the victor nations was not an easy problem. The emergence of the two Power blocs, one headed by the United States and the other by the Soviet Union, in the postwar world and the atmosphere of the Cold War necessarily led to delay in the signing of treaty of peace with Japan. In the process, however, Japan benefitted. Because of the differences among the victorious Powers and the delay caused thereby, Japan was able to obtain non-punitive and lenient peace terms which otherwise would not have been possible. Guided by considerations of power politics and the realities of the changing world situation, including success of communists in China, the United States, as the principal occupying Power, modified its stance in favour of a liberal treaty of "reconciliation."

Taking advantage of the persisting stalemate among the victorious "allies" about the procedure to be followed in the drafting of a peace treaty, Washington adopted a so-called policy of "de facto peace," by which the United States allowed Japanese Government increasing degree of freedom in managing its own economic and political affairs. Japan was, thus, permitted to send representatives to international conferences, not only as observers, but also as formal participants.[4] The US Government's interim decision of May 1949 to suspend the removal of industrial facilities as reparation had the wholesome effect on the Japanese industries, which started to become active again. However, the Japanese could not but be concerned about the ad hoc nature of such decisions and the uncertainty in regard to reparations persisting so long as the peace treaty was not signed. Arguing the case for an early peace settlement, Shigeru Yoshida observed :

In order that Japan may become a real workshop of East Asia and contribute abundantly to its progress and prosperity she must have a peace treaty. It is essential that we be guaranteed an equitable and equal treatment in international commerce, the rights of travel and residence, and full freedom of trade and shipping in this and other quarters of the globe. Such conditions of commerce and navigation can be realized only after the conclusion of peace and Japan's restoration as a free and independent member to the society of nations. There are inevitable and severe limitations to any *de facto* peace arrangement.

A protracted occupation, no matter how efficient, wise and benevolent, Yoshida stated, tended to destroy the people's self-respect and their spirit of self-reliance; it militated against the growth of true democracy in the country. The presence of the Allied forces in Japan, he said, had been the prime factor for ensuring the country's tranquility and internal security. Nevertheless, he pointed out, it could not be denied that a military occupation, was prejudicial to the fostering of initiative and enterprise, the sense of responsibility, the spirit of self-reliance and independence, pride and patriotism. These qualities of the spirit, he added, could not be fully developed until the Japanese nation was restored to complete sovereignty and reinstated in the community of nations as a free and independent member.[5]

In the prevailing international conditions, particularly after the Korean War, it did not at all seem possible for the victor nations to come to an agreement on the terms of peace treaty with Japan or the kind of a Japan they would like to see. Fully cognisant of this fact, the Japanese Government, in a statement issued on 1 June 1950, declared that it could not be so nonchalant as to assert that it would be advisable to hope for overall peace and have the present system of control continue indefinitely. Our nation, it stated, should embark on a program of steadily achieving normal international status by concluding peace treaties with nations willing to accord it independence and equality.[6] From this statement, it was quite evident that the ruling Liberal Democratic Party under the leadership of Yoshida was prepared to accept a separate peace treaty with the United States.

In opting for a separate peace settlement, which omitted the Communist Powers, the conservative Government of Japan was ignoring the widespread demand in Japan for an overall peace. The Social Democratic Party advocated the "three Principles of Peace," namely : an overall peace treaty with all nations, including USSR and China; opposition to political or military agreements permitting establishment of foreign bases in Japan; and preservation of the country's neutrality and disarmament.[7]

The Japanese Socialist leaders, Inejiro Asanuma and Masaburo Suzuki among others, put forward the idea of "positive neutrality" with a view to avoiding involvement in the Cold War. They also laid considerable stress on the withdrawal of US forces and bases and keeping Japan totally unarmed.[8] The leaders of the Japanese Socialist Party and certain other parties were of the opinion that Japan could not afford to take sides in the Cold War and that a separate peace and grant of military bases to the US would set USSR against Japan, with the result that not only the prospects of reviving Japan's vital trade with China and USSR and recovery of the northern fisheries would be impaired but there was also the risk that the two Communist Powers, still enjoying belligerent rights, might seize Japanese shipping, demand large reparations payments or even occupy a portion of Japan.[9]

The Communist Party of Japan took through and through a pro-Soviet line. Thus, speaking in the Lower House of the Japanese Diet on 1 February 1951, Communist Deputy Kawakami demanded withdrawal of all occupation troops from Japan "as speedily as possible." The Japanese people, he said, were not supporting the preparations for war against the USSR, China, and Korea. He denounced the aggressive policy of Yoshida's government to conclude a separate peace in the interests of the imperialists, to convert the country into a military base of international imperialism, and to utilize the Japanese as cannon fodder in the war against Japan's neighbours. Japan, he stated, had been turned altogether into an operational base and arsenal of the American interventionists in Korea. Kawakami characterized the rearmament of Japan as a plot to make the Japanese people the slaves of the imperialists and branded former Prime Minister Ashida, who recently advocated the rearmament of Japan, as a warmonger. He also accused the Japanese government of destroying the Japanese economy, through the complete consent of the Japanese government to the imperialist policy of war, and demanded that the ban against trading with China be annulled immediately. People who insisted that the Kurile Islands and south Sakhalin be returned to Japan, he remarked, were instigating war against the Soviet Union.[10]

The ruling Liberal Democratic Party of Japan responded to Opposition parties' criticism of separate peace by saying that the importance of Japan's China trade was being exaggrated, that in the face of Sino-Soviet alliance which was directed against Japan, it was dangerous for defenceless Japan, which was marked as "a special prize" by the Communists, to remain exposed to the Communist "war threat."[11] The Korean War, Shigeru Yoshida pointed out, was proof of how real and close the Communist danger to Japan was.[12]

In the opinion of the Japanese Foreign Office, there was no room for "non-involvement" or "neutrality" in the face of the world-wide struggle between the two incompatible forces-communism and democracy. Tokyo realized that it was not possible for Japan to please both the sides. It, therefore, saw no other alternative but to co-operate with the democracies and assist in strengthening their unity, which was considered as nothing less than a measure for Japan's own self-defence.[13] Shigeru Yoshida openly declared : "We cannot afford to sit on the fence....We are definitely and irrevocably on the side of the free world." He preferred a peace treaty with as many as nations as possible to no peace at all.[14]

After the outbreak of the Korean War Prime Minister Yoshida emphatically asserted that the proposals of overall peace and neutrality not only ignored reality but also played into the hands of Communist propagandists. Japan could preserve its security only by showing its resolve to contribute to world peace in concert with all free nations and by being welcomed into the ranks of those free nations dedicated to peace and international justice.[15]

Yoshida believed that a separate treaty with the US was less likely to contain punitive measures directed against Japan. But in the face of strong opposition from a formidable array of political, religious and social groups in Japan to both rearmament and a closer alliance with the US, Yoshida seemed somewhat reluctant to take a public stand about committing his government to granting military bases to the US even after concluding the peace treaty.

The Korean War seemed to settle that question for Yoshida, who it is stated was now persuaded that South Korea must not be permitted to fall into the hands of a hostile Power and that "retention of American forces in Japan would be necessary in order to protect Japan's security interests in Korea." To what extent Yoshida was moved by this consideration of Japan's national security is difficult to say, but the fact remained that the treaty allowing US forces to be stationed in Japan became "the unavoidable quid pro quo for the non-punitive peace settlement—a concession to irresistible American pressure."[16]

Moreover, under Article 2 of the Security Treaty US forces in Japan could be used not only for the maintenance of international peace and security in the Far East and for the security of Japan against armed attack from without but also to assist the Japanese Government, at its express request, to put down large-scale internal riots and disturbances caused through instigation or intervention by an outside Power or Powers.[17] The novel provision about internal riots, Dulles explained, was included in view of "a known and proclaimed Communist threat" and because Japan, disarmed physically, legally and psychologically, was not able to defend itself.[18] The provision was designed to deter a Communist-led revolt supported by USSR or China. But, as Roger Dingman rightly points out, there is also evidence to suggest that those who wrote the Security Treaty felt that Japan mattered a great deal but could not yet be fully trusted. Leaving American forces in Japan, giving them rights of intervention, and entrusting them with supervision of Japanese rearmament constituted insurance against Tokyo's defection to the Soviet side in the Cold War.[19]

At the time Secretary of State Acheson gave evidence on the treaty before the Senate MacArthur Inquiry Committee on 2 June 1951, Senator B. Hickenlooper emphatically declared that the US had the power to force any terms they wanted on the Japanese. He expressed his doubts about including the question of military alliances or bases in Japan in such a treaty. That would mean negotiation of a security treaty by Japan not as a sovereign nation but "under its restrictions as a conquered nation not yet re-admitted to sovereignty or full sovereignty of an independent nation."

Acheson had no convincing answer to Hickenlooper. He said this was a matter "which is not thought of in any way as being imposed upon the Japanese, but in which they will have a perfectly free choice." He claimed to believe that the Japanese and their government looked with favour on the security arrangements they and the US would work out together "as equal partners" and which would be "mutually beneficial to the security interests of both countries and to the entire Pacific area."[20] Many Japanese tended not to agree with Acheson's views.

In his statement before the San Francisco Peace Conference, Prime Minister Shigeru Yoshida, while appreciating the non-punitive nature of the treaty, spoke of certain points which caused Japan pain and anxiety. Among others, he mentioned the arrangement about Ryukyu and the Kurile Islands and pronounced himself in favour of their restoration to Japan. He also expressed his dissatisfaction with the Treaty provisions depriving Japan of its vast overseas assets and empowering Allied nations which had suffered no damage from the war to seize Japanese private property in their country. In the end, Yoshida regretted the absence of India and Burma, sought to allay the fears of Japanese neighbours about resurgence of Japanese militarism, and justified conclusion of the security pact with the United States in view of Japan's exposure to the "menace of communist imperialism from the North."[21]

Speaking before the Diet on 12 October 1951, Yoshida referred to the various difficult problems involved in peacemaking, e.g. the manifest concern of several countries of Asia over Japan's execution of its reparation commitments, the desire of Canada, Australia and others about an early conclusion of a convention for the conservation of fishery resources, because of the unwarranted overharvesting by Japanese fishing vessels in the past, and certain apprehensions voiced by other countries regarding the resurgence of Japan's militarism and aggression or unfair trade competition. The reparation burden, he said, would be "undeniably heavy" but Japan would not refuse to shoulder the treaty obligation in that regard or in regard to fishery question. He, however, could not understand the fear expressed by some delegates of Japanese competition after the restoration of peace. It was unthinkable, he stated, that Japan defeated in war and handicapped on all hands owing to loss of territory, scarcity of resources, war devastations of land, loss of shipping, deterioration of industrial plants and equipment, and the reparations obligations it had undertaken, could ever be an economic menace to any country. Moreover, Yoshida pointed out, Japan had enacted labour legislation of the highest order in the world, setting up unprecedented working conditions that would seem too idealistic for the country's actual state of affairs. Again, in the peace treaty Japan was pledged to observe all internationally accepted fair trade practices. Such being the case, Yoshida remarked, it was puzzling indeed why Japan's entry into world markets should occasion any apprehension or why any restrictions should be proposed on her economic activities in the international field. He criticised Soviet policy aimed at rendering Japan defenceless, internally and externally, and denying it any benefits of a collective security arrangement. The talk of the Japanese militarism by the Soviet delegate, he observed, could not but be dismissed as a piece of absurd and groundless propaganda. Yoshida justified Japan's security pact with the United States on the ground that neutrality was not suitable for Japan in the current international situation.[22]

A large number of Japanese, both of the Left and the Right, did not feel happy at the retention of American troops in the main islands of their country as garrison forces, at their great dependence on the US for raw materials and markets, at the restrictions on Japan's trade with China, the extra-territorial rights enjoyed by the US armed forces, and the semi-independent status accorded to Japan by the San Francisco settlement. In the opinion of a Japanese scholar Japan had neither the appearance nor the standing of an independent country but was "in a position of subservience to the United States."[23] The Anglo-American draft, Krishna Menon remarked towards the end of August 1951, had the effect of a third party holding together Japan's relations with the rest of Asia.[24]

A number of Japanese clamoured for revision of the security pact. Commenting on the Administrative Agreement signed between the US and Japan on 28 February 1952 in pursuance of the security treaty, the conservative newspaper *Nihon Keizai* observed : "Frankly speaking, we get the impression that the will of the US has been forcibly imposed upon Japan. This is a fact we cannot overlook in criticising the results of the US-Japanese negotiations on the agreement."[25] Under the Administrative Agreement Japan had agreed to cede to the US the use of facilities and areas necessary for "the maintenance of international peace and security in the Far East." *Asahi* remarked : "Friendship between Japan and the United States will become everlasting only when the two peoples stand in equal autonomy."[26]

When the peace treaty and the security pact came before the Japanese Diet for ratification, Socialist members described them as onesided, unequal and slavish. They maintained that these treaties reduced Japan to a colony.[27] Quite a few members of the ruling Liberal Democratic Party also expressed dissatisfaction with the security pact. Some members were of the opinion that the security arrangements should have been made after signing the peace treaty.[28] One member demanded abrogation of the unequal security treaty and conclusion of a new one based on equality and fairness.[29] Others declared that the Administrative Agreement was inconsistent with the independence of Japan.[30]

In view of these unfavourable reactions it is not at all

surprising that a former US Ambassador to Japan, Douglas MacArthur II, remarked : "Japan's restoration of sovereignty and independence was not complete."[31] It was hard to believe, an Indian researcher observes, that Japan, still under occupation at the time the treaty was being drafted, took an independent decision without being influenced by the US Government. Moreover, stationing foreign troops in Japan ran counter to the provisions on sovereignty. The fact of the matter was that the Japanese Conservative leaders had to consent knowing there would not be an early peace settlement with the Western Powers unless US armed forces were allowed to stay in Japan after the conclusion of the treaty.[32] Dunn points out :

> In place of requiring Japan, as a condition of peace, to allow American troops to remain indefinitely in Japanese territory, the proposed treaty provision was put in the form of a request by Japan for American military aid and an acceptance by the United States. This appeared to give Japan the initiative in the arrangement and did not formally impair the grant of full sovereignty to Japan.[33]

US troops, one American diplomat asserts, were kept in Japan after the treaty "not as a result of a dictated peace settlement" but under the security treaty concluded with an independent, equal and sovereign Japan.[34] This statement could have had greater credibility if the security pact had been concluded after Japan had regained its independence and the Treaty of Peace had come into effect and restored Japanese sovereignty. Only then could Japan have rightfully claimed that it had entered into security arrangements with the US of its own free will. In the words of Hugh Borton, the occupation forces were transformed into security forces, but outwardly there seemed to be no difference before and after the treaty. The return of independence seemed illusory to many Japanese. US military personnel and their families were not subject to Japanese police control as before. "Naturally, they continued to assume a condescending if not haughty attitude toward their hosts." So long as foreign troops remained on Japanese soil, Borton remarks, "the change from occupation to autonomy under the peace treaty seemed to be only a technical matter." No wonder the Prime Minister of Japan was accused of being more pro-American than pro-Japanese.[35]

Dulles, whom President Truman had assigned the task of negotiating the peace and security treaties in 1950, also sought to put pressure on Yoshida to accept the rearmament of Japan and to participate in regional collective defence arrangements with US with a pledge to contribute positively to defend the entire Pacific region.[36] Dulles forcefully argued that the US Senate would not ratify the mutual security treaty unless it met the requirements of the Vandenberg resolution of June 1948 that regional and other collective arrangements in which the US would be associated, must be based on "continuous and effective self-help and mutual aid," meaning military self-help and action.[37]

The Japanese Government could not at that stage commit itself to "continuous and effective self-help and mutual aid" in the form of military force partly because of economic considerations, partly because Japan's first task was to create internal security through an adequate police force and coastal patrol, and partly because of the provisions of the Japanese Constitution which, in renouncing war, stated that "land, sea and air forces, as well as other war potentials, will never be maintained." In view of this the US was not disposed to assume obligations Japan could not reciprocate. It assumed no treaty obligation to maintain land, air and sea forces in and about Japan or to guarantee that country's security and independence although, as Dulles pointed out, "this will be a practical result of the exercise by the United States of the right to station its forces in Japan."[38]

So long as US troops were stationed in Japan an attack on Japan would involve an attack on the US. The bilateral Security Treaty providing provisionally for stationing of US troops in Japan gave de facto protection to Japan. Dulles stated that the US was not prepared to guarantee Japan's security permanently until it was clear what Japan's own contribution would be. Protection "would be de facto, not a legal guarantee." The US was not willing to give a legal undertaking except under the terms of the Vandenberg resolution.[39]

In the circumstances Yoshida chose to remain contented with an implicit, de facto guarantee of defence, but avoided in the process a commitment in regard to large-scale rearmament or military responsibility for regional defence. This lacuna was sought to be filled to a certain extent by the Mutual Defence Assistance Agreement of March 1954, by which both Japan and the US pledged themselves to mutual defence against the communist world.[40] Thus the final step was taken to bind Japan militarily to the Western democracies.[41]

The two governments subsequently signed the Treaty of Mutual Cooperation and Security on 19 January 1960. Article 3 of the Treaty committed Japan to maintain and develop its "capacity to resist armed attack" and provided for cooperation and mutual aid. Article 5 recognised that an armed attack against either party would be dangerous to its own peace and safety and contained a pledge to "act to meet the common danger." It thereby provided the formal commitment for the defence of Japan Yoshida sought.[42]

The territorial clauses of the San Francisco Peace Treaty have been the subject of much controversy in the period of peacemaking and afterwards. Under Article 2 Japan renounced all claims to most of its former territories outside the home islands. These included Formosa, the Pescadores, the Spratly and Paracel Islands, South Sakhalin and the Kurile Islands. The status of Formosa and the Pescadores continued to be a subject of dispute among the Powers.[43] The Spratly and the Paracel Islands are claimed by China, Vietnam, Taiwan and the Philippines. The controversy over the Kurile Islands has blocked for over three decades a peace treaty between Japan and USSR.

After the conclusion of the peace treaty, the US continued to maintain close relations with Japan, though the occupation of Okinawa, the presence of US military bases and the testing of US nuclear weapons in the South Pacific often created problems in the relations between the two countries. Article 3 of the Treaty provided that Japan "will concur in any proposal of the United States to the United Nations to place under its trusteeship system" the Bonin and Ryukyu Islands or Okinawa as the islands were commonly called after the largest of them, where nearly a million people live. Washington later abandoned the trusteeship scheme and publicly recognised that Japan had "residual sovereignty" over the islands.

The US agreed in December 1953 to return to Japan the Amami Oshima Group in the Ryukyus. The *Mainichi* of

Tokyo summed up the reasons for this decision as follows

1. Strategically these islands are not so valuable as other islands under US trusteeship.

2. Anti-American sentiment among the islanders had grown to such an explosive point that it had become difficult for the US to control it.

3. Amid the intensified Communist peace offensive directed against Japan by such means as repatriation of Japanese detainees in China, the US found it necessary to forestall these moves.[44]

Agreement on the return of the Bonin Islands was reached in April 1968, but Okinawa's return to Japan was delayed as the island was considered not only the "keystone of the Pacific" but also of the American war effort in Vietnam. An agreement about its return to Japan was however reached in November 1969. Prime Minister Sato said this agreement had brought about the "end of the postwar period." The actual transfer of the island was accomplished in 1972.

On 12 June 1952, the Japanese Government and a number of Governments of the Allied Powers signed an Agreement for the Settlement of Disputes concerning the interpretation and execution of Article 15 (a) of the San Francisco Peace Treaty. The agreement established procedures for the settlement of disputes under that article[45] and entered into force for various signatories at different dates. Thus, with Canada, Ceylon, Dominican Republic, New Zealand and the USA it entered into force in June 1952; with France, Pakistan, Turkey and UK in July 1952; with Australia, Belgium, Cambodia, Cuba and Mexico in August 1952; with Norway on 9 September 1952; with Argentina on 3 October 1952; with Liberia on 29 December 1952; with South Africa on 7 January 1953; with Haiti and Greece in May 1953; with the Netherlands on 10 September 1953; with Labanon on 7 January 1954; with Venezuela on 3 February 1954; and with Chile on 28 April 1954.[46]

The potential value of Japan as "an ally against expanding Soviet communism"[47] spared that nation many of the deprivations, as well as humiliations, which commonly follow abject defeat in a big, prolonged war. Thus the reparations provisions of the San Francisco Peace Treaty formulated by the US were strikingly moderate. Desirous of giving liberal non-punitive treatment to this former enemy, the US favoured waiver of all reparations claims beyond the war-time seizures by the Allied Powers of certain properties, rights and interests of Japan and its nationals, sanctioned under Article 14 (a) 2 of the treaty.

It was very reluctantly, owing chiefly to the insistence of the Philippines and Indonesia, that the US finally agreed to make Japan pay token reparations in the form of manufacturing and technical services. Article 14 of the treaty obligated Japan to negotiate reparations agreements, with "Allied Powers so desiring," whose territories had been occupied and damaged in the war. The treaty stipulated that reparations were to take the form of Japanese services in production, salvaging and other work. The treaty specifically stated that where reparations took the form of manufacturing raw materials these materials "shall be supplied by the Allied Powers in question, so as not to throw any foreign exchange burden upon Japan."[48]

Negotiations on reparations settlements between the concerned countries of Southeast Asia and Japan proved a long-drawn-out and difficult affair. There was a wide discrepancy between the reparations demands of the countries which had suffered heavily under the Japanese occupation and the amount Japan was willing to pay. Satisfactory agreements were however ultimately reached and led to normalisation of political and trade relations between Japan and these countries. Such agreements would not have been possible if Japan had not been able to pay and had it not realised the importance of Southeast Asia as potentially its most important market and source of raw materials such as tin, rubber, oil and iron ore.

Tokyo therefore felt the need for early restoration of normal trade relations with the Southeast Asian countries and expressed its eagerness to settle the pending reparations problem. Describing economic cooperation with Southeast Asia as an important factor in Japan's foreign policy, one Japanese commentator, Arata Sugihara, observed : "Whatever the future developments may be, it will be definitely advantageous for Japan to import the raw materials for her heavy industries, such as iron ore, from the Southeast Asian countries."[49] The reparations payments to these countries even at the peak averaged only 2 per cent or less of Japan's annual budget. They were thus not a serious burden to Japan at any time and the fear that they would seriously injure Japan's ordinary exports also proved unfounded.

It took almost 30 years from the date of the Japanese surrender to the Allied Powers in 1945 and about 24 years from the date of the signing of the San Francisco Peace Treaty for Japan to settle the reparations claims of Southeast Asian countries. The reparations initially claimed by four countries amounted to about $30 billion ($8 billion by the Philippines, $17 billion by Indonesia, $2.5 billion by Burma and $2 billion by Vietnam). Even if this huge amount had been made payable in 20 years Japan's annual quota of payments would have been around $1.5 billion whereas its payment capacity at that time was estimated at between $50 million and $100 million. The variance between the claims and Japan's capacity for payment was very great, and this was the main cause of the delay in settling the reparations problem.[50]

The final reparations settlements obligated Japan to pay in pure reparations to the above-mentioned four Southeast Asian countries a total of $1012.08 million or 364,348.8 million yen. The average annual payment of $75 million or 27,000 million yen corresponded to 0.3 per cent of Japan's total national income (for 1958), 2.1 per cent of the total budget expenditure (for the 1958-59 fiscal year), and 2.6 per cent of the total figure for exports (in 1958). These figures, Itagaki Yoichi points out, suggested that the yearly reparations payments were not too heavy a burden on Japan's economy and that the reparations programme would be carried out smoothly. However, as compared to West Germany's reparations of $830 million and Italy's $360 million, Japan's total of $1012.08 millions, Itagaki Yoichi adds, was not necessarily small.[51]

Japan completed all World War II indemnity payments demanded by the above mentioned four Southeast Asian states on 22 July 1976 by paying the final payment of $17.5 million to the Philippines. The details of the reparations payments are as follows :

Reparations

	Total Amount	Period of payment	Annual payment
Burma	72,000 million yen ($200 million)	10 years 16 Apr 1955- 12 Apr 1965	7,200 million yen ($20 million)
Philippines	198,000 million yen ($550 million)	20 years 23 Jul 1956- 22 Jul 1976	First ten years 9000 million yen ($25 million) Last ten years 10,800 million yen ($30 million)
Indonesia	80,308.8 million yen ($223.08 million)	12 years 15 Apr 1958- 14 Apr 1970	First 11 years 7200 million yen ($20 million) Last year 1,108.8 million yen ($3.08 million)
South Vietnam	14,040 million yen ($39 million)	5 years 12 Jan 1960- 11 Jan 1965	First 3 years 3,600 million yen ($10 million) Last 2 years 1,620 million yen ($4.5 million)
TOTAL	364,348.8 million yen ($1012.08 million)		

It might be recalled here that under the interim reparations settlement, directed by the Far Eastern Commission, Japan in 1949 surrendered industrial machinery, generating plants, etc., amounting in value of 160,000,000 yen to the Allied Powers. Appropriations made from this were 5,600 tons for Nationalist China, 23,000 tons for Philippines, 8,000 tons for the Netherlands, and 22,000 tons for the United Kingdom.[52]

Apart from pure reparations, Japan was obligated to cancel credits worth $117 million in case of Indonesia and to provide $716.7 million in long-term loans or similar credit arrangements to the above-mentioned four nations as follows :

Country	Amount (in million dollars)	Terms (years)	Remarks
Burma	50	10	Investments in kind in joint enterprises
Philippines	250	20	Commercial loans
Indonesia	400	20	Commercial loans and investments
South Vietnam	7.5	3	Government loans
	8.1	5	Commercial loans
TOTAL	716.6		

In addition to payments made, either in pure reparations, cancellations of credits or in long-term loans, etc. to the four Southeast Asian countries, Japan has also undertaken to pay in the form of grant aids a sum of 11,000 million yen (approximately $37 million) to Laos, Cambodia and North Vietnam and $348.86 million to other countries (see below), who had relinquished their rights to demand reparations from Japan, in order to compensate them for "the sufferings caused by Japan during the War." The details of these Grants-in-Aid, which excludes $200 million in long-term, low interest credits given by Japan to South Korea and 13.5 billion yen aid extended by Japan to Vietnam in 1976, are given below :

Grants-in-Aid

Country	Amount	Period (years)
Laos	1,000 million yen ($2.777 million)	1959-61
Cambodia	1.500 million yen ($4.166 million)	1959-62
North Veitnam	8,500 million yen (about $30 million)	1975
TOTAL	11,000 million yen	

(in million US dollars)

Country	Amount	Period (years)
Thailand	26.7	1962-70
Singapore	8.16	1968-72
Malaysia	8.16	1968-72
South Korea	300.00	1965-75
Micronesia	5.84	1972-76
TOTAL	$348.86	

Unlike the reparation payments Germany made in cash after World War I the Japanese reparations were paid wholly in capital goods and services for the economic development of the recipients. The settlement of reparations was carried out in accordance with annual schedules agreed by the Japanese Government and the governments concerned and in which various construction projects were included. This opened opportunities for the Japanese construction industry to extend its activities abroad. Before the implementation of the reparations agreements started in 1955 the industry's activities had been strictly confined to Japan.

Through reparations the industry began to take an active part in the economic development of the countries to which

Japan paid reparations. By the summer of 1961 the value of projects initiated or scheduled to be implemented under reparations or economic aid agreements were as follows: Burma, 12,200 million yen; the Philippines (including loans secured on reparations), 13,100 million yen; Indonesia (including loans secured on the reparations) 4,400 million yen; South Vietnam, 13,300 million yen; Laos, 64 million yen; and Cambodia, 1,200 million yen.[53]

Principal overseas construction projects related to the Reparations and Grant aid programmes, which were in the process of construction by middle of 1961, were as follows :

Burma
Balu Chaung Hydro-electric Project : The first stage of the project was completed in March 1960 (84,000 kilowatts) at a cost of 19,000 million yen of which 60 per cent was covered by reparations.

Philippines
Markikina Multi-purpose Dam Project : Of the total of $54 million, a credit of $35.5 million was secured on the reparations payment.

Indonesia
Nejama Diversion Tunnel Project (cost 1,138 million yen); Kali Brantas Multipurpose Dam Project (cost 212 million yen); Construction of Graving Dock (cost 1440 million yen); Construction of the Hotal Indonesia (cost 4000 million yen).

Laos
Nam Ngum River Development Project (cost $16 million); Vientiane Water Supply System Project (cost 1000 million yen).

South Vietnam
Da Nhim Development Project (cost 17,000 million yen).[54]

The problem concerning Japan's "liabilities" have been multitudinous and complicated. The payment of reparations to Asian countries under Article 14 of the San Francisco Peace Treaty was only one of them. The return of property, all rights and interests, owned by the Allied Powers and their nationals, which existed in Japan, and compensation for the loss and damage thereof (Article 15 of the San Francisco Peace Treaty and also Article 5 of the Peace Treaty between India and Japan) involved payments amounting in total to 30,000,000,000 yen ($81,000,000). The countries concerned were the United States, the United Kingdom, France, Australia, Canada, Belgium, Turkey, New Zealand, Greece, the Union of South Africa, Pakistan, Norway, Syria, Mexico, Argentina, the Netherlands, and India. The individual cases of claims numbered as many as 1,300. The indemnities paid to the members of the Allied forces who suffered undue hardships while being held as prisoners of war in Japan (Article 16 of the San Francisco Treaty) amounted in total of 4,500,000,000 yen ($12,500,000). These payments were effected through the transfer of Japanese assets in the neutral and Axis countries to the International Committee of the Red Cross, who liquidated such assets for the benefit of the claimants. During 1955, Japan reached an agreement with Switzerland and Denmark respectively, with regard to their indemnity claims : she paid 1,800,000,000 yen (12,250,000 Swiss fr.) to Switzerland, and 300,000,000 yen to the Great Northern Telegraph Company of Denmark. By the end of 1956, no agreement had been reached as regards the claim of 9,900 million yen ($27.5 million) presented by the Netherlands on behalf of its 110,000 nationals, and the claims of the nationals of Spain, Portugal and Ireland.[55]

Besides, Japan was obligated, under Article 18 of the San Francisco Treaty, to pay pecuniary debts arising from obligations and contracts (including those in respect of bonds which existed before the war). Under the agreement reached in 1952, Japan's liability for the prewar external debts of the Japanese State and its corporate bodies was fixed at 47,000 million yen and 133,100 million yen, which Japan had to pay in ten years to the USA and the UK respectively. The settlement of external debts in French francs, which consisted mainly of the unsettled account of bonds issued by the Japanese government in 1910 (450,000,000 fr.) and by the Tokyo Municipal Government in 1912 (180,000,000 fr.), cost Japan around 3,700 million yen, approximately 14 times over the original value of the debt.[56]

Last to be mentioned but none the less important has been

the settlement of the special yen account, set up by Japan during the war. In order to cover deficits, the special yen, which had no currency value, were issued and used in trade transactions. The major countries concerned were Thailand, Italy and French Indo-China. The special yen account problem with Thailand arose because, during the war, a yen counterpart fund had been set up in Japan to match the financing in bahts of the expense for the stationing of Japanese forces in Thailand. Under the agreement signed in 1955, Japan agreed to pay 15,000 million yen to Thailand. During 1955-60, Japan paid 5,400 million yen in pound sterling, but differences arose about the remaining amount of 9,600 million yen. Japan wanted to pay this amount in the form of credits or loans while Thailand demanded outright payments. Ultimately, the problem was settled by Japan making payment of $26.7 million to Thailand between 1962 and 1970.

As many as 49 states had declared belligerence against Japan at different dates beginning from 7 December 1941 to 10 August 1945. All these states, except China, Italy and Mongolia, plus Burma, Cambodia, Ceylon, Colombia, Indonesia, Laos, Pakistan and Republic of Vietnam (South Vietnam) were invited to participate in the San Francisco Peace Conference in September 1951. Of these 54 invitee states, 48 signed the multilateral Treaty of Peace with Japan at San Francisco on 8 September 1951 (it came into force on 28 April 1952), three (Burma, India and Yugoslavia) declined to participate in the conference, while the Soviet Union, Poland and Czechoslovakia refused to sign the treaty documents. Quite a few states which had signed the Treaty of Peace with Japan at San Francisco delayed ratification of the San Francisco Treaty documents. For instance, Gautemala deposited instruments of ratification with the Government of the United States on 23 September 1954, Iraq on 18 August 1955 and Ecuador did that on 27 December 1955 with reservations. The Philippines ratified the San Francisco Treaty of Peace with Japan only after a mutually acceptable settlement of its reparations claims had been reached. Indonesia not only declined to ratify the treaty till the reparations problem had been solved but also deemed it necessary to conclude a separate bilateral treaty of peace with Japan.

Those states which did not attend the San Francisco Conference or declined to append their signatures to the San Francisco Peace Treaty obviously chose to enter into separate arrangements with Japan for terminating state of war, normalising relations and/or concluding bilateral peace treaties. In some cases, for instance India and Yugoslavia, this was done immediately; in the case of Burma that became possible only after the settlement of the reparations problem; while in the case of three Communist States of Europe—the Soviet Union, Poland and Czechoslovakia—the termination of the state of war and normalisation of relations was agreed to in 1956-57, but the formal peace treaties have not yet been concluded.

As regards the countries which were excluded from participation in the San Francisco Peace Conference, the most significant case was that of China. Japan entered into a bilateral Peace Treaty with Nationalist China (Taiwan) in April 1952 under circumstances discussed in Chapter Four. Relations with the People's Republic of China were, normalised only on 29 September 1972 when the state of war between the two countries was terminated, the war reparations claims waived, and the Treaty of Peace between Japan and the Republic of China declared to have lost its *raison d'etre*. The problem of normalisation of relations between China and Japan has been examined in depth in the study *China and Japan, 1949-1976* already published. Japan succeeded in normalising relations with South Korea in 1965 by agreeing to pay $300 million as grant-in-aid and $200 million in long-term low-interest credits, and with North Vietnam in 1975 by extending 8500 million yen as grant-in-aid, but relations with North Korea have yet to be normalised.

NOTES

Chapter 1 : United States of America

1. USA, Department of State Publication 2671, Far Eastern Series 17, 53.
2. See Edwin O. Reischauer, *The United States and Japan* (Cambridge, 1950) Appendix II, 321-8.
3. See Richard Storry, "The New Tensions in Japan : The American Connection and the Future," *Conflict Studies* (Aug. 1974) 14. Over five million acres of land was purchased from the old absentee landlords and sold to working farmers, with the result that tenant cultivated land decreased from 46% of cultivated land in 1944 to 12% in 1949. By the middle of 1951, about 90% of all cultivated land belonged to those who worked on it.
4. See *Keesings Contemporary Archives 1946-1948*, 8561.
5. US. Department of State, *Foreign Relations of the United States*, (hereafter cited as *Foreign Relations*) *1947, vol. VI, The Far East* (Washington, D.C., 1972) 377.
6. Policy Decision on Basic Surrender Policy, adopted by the Far Eastern Commission on 19 June 1947. Far Eastern Commission Press Release 34, 11 July 1947; *Department of State Bulletin*, Vol. 17, 216.
7. In 1947, the American economic aid to Japan amounted to $400 million.
8. *Department of State Bulletin* (18 May 1947) 991.
9. *Foreign Relations, 1947*, n. 5, 485-6.
10. *New York Times*, 22 Jan 1948.
11. Frederick S. Dunn, *Peace-Making and the Settlement with Japan* (Princeton, N.J., 1963) 76-7.
12. Storry, n. 3, 14.
13. *Ibid*.
14. See Department of Army *Press Release*, 19 May 1948 and USA, Department of State, *A Decade of American Foreign Policy 1941-1949* (Washington, D.C., 1950) 1017-20. Since the issuance of the stabilization directive on 14 December 1948, the removal of any further materials from Japan for the reparations account was considered as

placing a significant added burden on Japan's strained economy,
materially handicapping the stabilization and recovery of Japan. See
MacArthur's comment on the tentative State-Army reparations proposals. *Foreign Relations, 1948, Vol. VI; The Far East and Australasia* (Washington, D.C., 1974) 1064-5.

15. National Percentage Shares to be applicable to Japanese industrial
facilities available for reparations to the members of the Far Eastern
Commission (FEC):

Country	As claimed by members of FEC in May 1947	As presented by R.W. Barnett, US delegate to the FEC in May 1947	Department of State proposal, 25 Sep 1947	Revised US plan suggested by Secretary of State, 26 Aug 1948
Australia	28	9	8	8
Canada	1½	2	1	1
China	40	25	30	30
France	12	2	2	2½
India	18	5	5	5
Netherlands	15	5	4	5
New Zealand	2	2	1	1
Philippines	15	9	8	8
Soviet Union	14	3	4	4
United Kingdom	25	9	10	12½
United States	34	29	28	23
TOTAL	176½	100	100	100

In the revised US plan of 26 August 1948 for apportionment of re-
paration-shares, it was stated that the United States for its own part
will hold 18 of its 23% share of industrial facilities for redistribution
among those Far Eastern countries which approved the schedule of
percentage shares and which desired increments to industrial facilities
which they were entitled to receive by their share. The United States
Government would allow a period not to exceed one month for
negotiation among countries wishing to participate in the redistribution of this 18% in which these countries could seek a mutually
acceptable redistribution of that share. If no agreement was reached
within this period the said 18% for redistribution would be divided
among interested countries in proportion to their accepted percentage
shares of the total reparations. See *Foreign Relations*, 1947, n. 5,395,
397 and 430 and *Ibid.*, 1948, n. 14,1001.

16. Department of State *Press Release*, 350, 12 May 1949.

17. For text of the US statement sent to the ten missions by telegram on
11 July 1947, see *Foreign Relations*, n. 5, 468-9. For a summary of
the replies of the Governments represented on the Far Eastern Commission to the US suggestion of 11 July 1947, see *Ibid.*, 489-90.

18 For the text of US Aide Memoire to the Soviet Union dated 12 August 1947, see *Ibid.*, 488-9; see also *Department of State Bulletin* (24 Aug. 1947) 395-6.

19 *Foreign Relations*, n. 5, 1942, vol. 1, 25.

20 *Ibid.*, 1943, Vol. I, 755.

21 *Ibid.*, *The Conferences at Cairo and Tehran*, 1943, 640.

22 *Ibid.*, *The Conferences at Malta and Yalta*, 1945, 968 and 975.

23 *Ibid.*, *1947*, n. 5, 483-5.

24 See Hugh Borton, *Japan's Modern Century* (New York, 1955) 426, footnote 29.

25 *Foreign Relations*, 1948. n. 14, 862 and 713.

26 William Sebald and Russel Brines, *With MacArthur in Japan* (New York, 1965) 243.

27 *Foreign Relations*, 1948, n. 14, 656-60.

28 *Ibid.*, 1947, n. 5, 454.

29 Dunn, n. 11, 58-60.

30 For Kennan's views, see *Foreign Relations*, 1947, n. 5, 537-43 and *Ibid.*, 1948, n. 14, 691-6 and 712-9. In his memorandum of 11 August 1947, John P. Davies of the Policy Planning Staff stated that the central American objective in peace settlement for Japan should be "a stable Japan, integrated into the Pacific economy, friendly to the U.S. and, in case of need, a ready and dependenable Ally of the U.S." He found fault with the Draft Treaty of Peace for its pre-occupation with drastic disarmament and democratization under continuing international supervision, including the U.S.S.R. The presence of the Soviet Union, on an international supervisory body, he observed, would be "a disruptive influence in Japan, placing the onus for continued supervision on the U.S. and conspiring to bring about sovietized totalitarianism." *Foreign Relations*, 1947, n. 5, 485-6.

31 *Ibid.*, n. 14, 708-9. The United States was committed to policy of complete and continuing Japanese disarmament expressed in the Potsdam Declaration, Far Eastern Commission Basic Post-Surrender Policy for Japan and Far Eastern Commission decision of February 1948 on Prohibition of Military Activity in Japan, *Ibid.*, 863.

32 As early as August 1947, the Navy Department had desired base rights at Yokosuka and necessary air fields to provide protection for the base. See memorandum by Rear Admiral E.T. Wooldrige, 18 August 1947. *Foreign Relations*, 1947, n. 5, 495. On 1 September 1947, General MacArthur considered US control of Ryukyu group of Islands as "absolutely essential to the defense of our Western Pacific Frontier." Failure to secure it for control by the United States, he said, "might prove militarily disastrous." *Ibid.*, 512-5.

33 *Foreign Relations*, 1948, n. 14, 858-62 and 877.

34 Roger Dingman, "Reconsiderations: The United States—Japan Security Treaty," *Pacific Community* (Jul 1976) 473.

35 *Foreign Relations*, n. 14, 806.

36 Sebald, n. 26, 245.

37 *New York Times*, 27 May 1950.

38   *Foreign Relations*, 1948, n. 14, 858-62, 877, and 691-719.

39   The invitation to the Far Eastern Commission nations, Dunn re-
     marks, could be cited as evidence to the US Congress and public
     that steps were being taken to negotiate peace with Japan while the
     non-cooperation of China, the Commonwealth nations (the date of
     19 August 1947 proposed by the US for convening a Peace Conference
     was not suitable to the Commonwealth countries as it conflicted with
     their own meeting scheduled for 26 August in Canberra) and USSR
     could be cited as reasons for not attaining this objective. Dunn has
     described this as "nothing more than minor Machiavellianism" with
     the avowed purpose of gaining time. Dunn, n. 11, 66.

40   *Ibid* , 90.

41   Sebald, n. 26, 261-2.

42   See Borton, n. 24, 423 and 427.

43   Dunn, n. 11, 88.

44   *Department of State Bulletin* (23 Jan 1950) 115-6.

45   Soon after the San Francisco Peace Treaty came into effect, the
     National Police Reserve Force was reorganized into a 100,000 men
     National Safety Force and an 8900 men Maritime Safety Force. In
     1954, the name was again changed to National Defence Force, which
     by 1960 had emerged as a fully military organization, having land, sea
     and air arms of substantial size, all equipped with the most modern
     weapons. By 1972, the ground forces contained 155,000 men, whose
     equipment included 500 tanks and 360 aircraft; the air force had
     42,000 men and 930 aircraft; the naval arm with 37,000 men was
     operating 200 combat vessels and 266 aircraft. The defence budget
     expanded to 677,000 million in 1971. See W.G. Beasley, *The Modern
     History of Japan* (London, 1973) 290-1.

46   President Truman stated on 14 September 1950 that he had authoriz-
     ed the Department of State to initiate informal discussions on the
     Peace Treaty with Japan. *Department of State Bulletin* (25 Sep 1950)
     513.

47   In 1961, the Japanese Prime Minister Ikeda settled, despite consider-
     able leftist opposition, this debt of Occupation days to the United
     States by agreeing to pay back $490 million, or about one-third of
     the original sum, on much the same terms as an earlier German
     settlement of a similar debt. Edwin O. Reischauer, *Japan : Past
     and Present* (New York, 3rd edn., 1964) 286.

48   See Dunn, n. 11, 83-6.

49   *Ibid.*, 99-102.

50   It was made public on 24 November 1950, only after the Soviet Union
     had published its reply.

51   *Department of State Bulletin* (4 Dec. 1950) 881. See also Dunn, n. 11,
     107-8.

52   USA, Department of Press Release 1267, 28 December 1950.

53   See Dunn, n. 11, 108.

54   Japan, Ministry of Foreign Affairs, *Collection of Official Foreign
     Statements on Japanese Peace Treaty*, vol. II (Tokyo, 1951) 12.

55 *Ibid.*, 14-25.

56 *Contemporary Japan* (Jan-Mar 1951) 126-7.

57 Dulles' Speech in Manila, 12 February 1951. *Collection of Official Foreign Statements on Japanese Peace Treaty*, n. 54, 26-8.

58 Borton, n. 24, 443.

59 Address by Dulles over the Columbia Broadcasting System, 1 March 1951. *Department of State Bulletin* (12 Mar 1951) 403-7.

60 *Ibid.*

61 *Collection of Official Foreign Statements on Japanese Peace Treaty*, n. 54, 73-80.

62 *Department of State Bulletin* (12 Mar. 1951) 403-4.

63 Address by Dulles, 31 March 1951. *Ibid.* (9 Apr 1951) 576-80.

64 *Ibid.*

65 *Ibid.* (16 Apr 1951) 618.

66 See American Draft of the Japanese Peace Treaty, 29 March 1951 published on 5 April 1951. *Collection of Official Foreign Statements on Japanese Peace Treaty*, n. 54, 55-62. See also Dulles Press Conference, 19 April 1951. *Ibid.*, 73-80.

67 *Department of State Bulletin* (7 May 1951) 726-31.

68 Dulles Press Conference in Tokyo, 19 April 1951. *Collection of Official Foreign Statements on Japanese Peace Treaty*, n. 54, 73-80.

69 US memorandum to the USSR, 19 May 1951. *Department of State Bulletin* (28 May 1951) 852-6.

70 *Ibid* , (23 Jul 1951) 143-4.

71 *Ibid.* (17 Sep 1951) 461-3.

72 *Collection of Official Foreign Statements on Japanese Peace Treaty*, Vol. 3, n. 54, 35.

73 *Ibid.*, 13.

74 Dunn, n. 11, 142.

75 *Department of State Bulletin* (23 Jul 1951) 132.

76 Dulles Statement of 15 August 1951. See *Ibid.*, (27 Aug 1951) 346-8.

77 *Collection of Official Foreign Statements on Japanese Peace Treaty*, Vol. 3, n. 72, 23. See also US note of 16 August 1951. *Department of State Bulletin* (27 Aug 1951) 348.

78 Acheson's Statement at the San Francisco Conference, 5 September 1951 *Ibid.* (17 Sep 1951) 450.

79 Dunn, n. 11, 175.

80 Dulles Statement, 15 August 1951. *Department of State Bulletin* (27 Aug 1951) 346-8.

81 Dunn, n. 11, 169.

82 *Department of State Bulletin* (17 Sep 1951) 452-9.

83 Dunn, n. 11, 184.

84 Japan, Ministry of Foreign Affairs, *Japanese Peace Conference*, San Francisco, Provisional Verbatim Minutes (Tokyo, undated) 353-4.

85 USA, Department of State, *Conference for the Conclusion of the Treaty of Peace with Japan*, San Francisco, California, September 4-8, 1951, Record of Proceedings (Washington, 1951) 189-98, 219-24 and 144-5.

86 United States, Department of State, *United States Treaties and Other*

International Agreements Vol. 3, Part 3, 1952 (Washington, 1955) 3326-8.

87 See F.C. Jones, "Japan", in Royal Institute of International Affairs, *Survey of International Affairs 1951* (London, 1954) 415.

88 *United States Treaties and Other International Agreements*, n. 86, 3341-62.

89 UK, Command Papers, *Cmd.*, No. 8601.

90 Sebald, n. 26, 242.

91 John Foster Dulles, "Security in the Pacific," *Foreign Affairs* (Jan 1952).

92 Dulles Statement, 2 December 1951. *Department of State Bulletin* (17 Dec 1951) 973-5.

93 US, Department of State, *American Foreign Policy, 1950-55, Basic Documents* Vol. 1 (Washington, 1957) 463-83.

94 *Ibid.*

95 *Ibid.*

96 *Information Bulletin* (Embassy of Japan, New Delhi), 1 Oct 1956.

Chapter 2 : United Kingdom

1 UK, Parliamentary Debates, *House of Commons* (hereinafter cited as *H.C. Deb.*) 437 (1947) 1969-70.

2 US, Department of State, *Foreign Relations, 1947 Volume VI : The Far East* (Washington, D.C., 1972) 410-1.

3 See *Keesings Contemporary Archives*, 8875. For an account of the Canberra meeting of representatives of the British dominions, given by the British Embassy to the US Department of State on 9 October 1947, see *Foreign Relations*, n. 2, 532-4.

4 *H.C. Deb.*, 437(1947) 1933, 1069-70 and 1762.

5 *Ibid.*, 457 (4 Nov 1948) 1030 and 1034.

6 Statement by Secretary of State for Overseas Trade, Bottomley, 19 May 1949. *Ibid*, 465 (1949) 589.

7 *H.C. Deb.*, 470 (25 Nov 1949) 58

8 *Ibid.*, 473 (28 Mar 1950) 210-1.

9 *The Economist* (26 May 1951) 1218-9.

10 *H.C. Deb.*, 475 (24 May 1950) 2102-3.

11 *Ibid.*, 476 (26 Jun 1950) 2066-8.

12 British Information Service, *The Peace Treaty with Japan*, R. 2217 (New Delhi, 1951) 2.

13 *H.C. Deb.*, 446 (22 Jan 1948) 408-9.

14 *Ibid.*, 461 (21 Feb 1949) 238-9.

15 *Ibid.*, 468 (19 Oct 1949) 25.

16 *Ibid.*, 535-6.

17 *Ibid.*, 476 (26 Jun 1950) 2066-8.

18 Statement by Minister of State, Younger, 15 March 1951. *Ibid.*, 485 (15 Mar 1951) 1976-8.

19 See *Ibid.* Written Answers 242-3.

20 Japan, Ministry of Foreign Affairs, *Collection of Official Foreign Statements on Japanese Peace Treaty* vol. III (Tokyo, 1951) 109.

21 Frederick S.Dunn, *Peace-Making and the Settlement with Japan* (Princeton, N.J., 1963) 138-9.

22 *Ibid.*, 137-8.

23 *Collection of Official Foreign Statement on Japanese Peace Treaty*, n. 20, 35.

24 Dunn, n. 21, 160.

25 *Ibid.*, 163.

26 *Ibid.*, 160 and 164-5.

27 *H.C. Deb.*, 490 (12 Jul 1951) 49-51.

28 Dunn, n. 21, 164. As early as November 1948, the US officials found Britain "most reluctant" to consider the extension of most favoured nation treatment to Japan unless it received definite assurances from the United States to the effect that Japan would not become a serious competitor in the field of international trade. See Memorandum by D.M. Bane on the discussion between the officials of the British Commonwealth and the United States. US, Department of State, *Foreign Relations, 1948, Vol. VI, The Far East and Australasia*, (Washington, D. C. 1974) 1050-4.

29 US, Department of State, *American Foreign Policy 1950-55, Basic Documents* Vol. I (Washington, 1957) 463-83.

30 *H.C. Deb.*, 494 (26 Nov 1951) 1000-4.

31 *Ibid.*, 491 (25 Jul 1951) 478-84.

32 *Ibid.*, 494 (26 Nov 1951) 883-7.

33 *Ibid.*, 491 (25 Jul 1951) 574-81.

34 *Ibid.*, 490 (12 Jul 1951) 632-7.

35 See Statement by the President of the Board of Trade. *Ibid.*, 49-51.

36 *Ibid.*, 491 (25 Jul 1951) 574-81.

37 See J.P. Jain, *China in World Politics : A Study of Sino-British Relations, 1949-1975* (New Delhi, 1976) 94-5.

38 Japan, Ministry of Foreign Affairs, *Japanese Peace Conference*, San Francisco : Provisional Verbatim Minutes (Tokyo, undated) 87-98.

39 See *Keesings Contemporary Archives 1950-1952*, 11949.

40 *H.C. Deb.*, 494 (1951-2) Written Answers 328.

Chapter 3 : Soviet Union and Eastern Europe

1 United States, Department of State, *Foreign Relations of the United States : the Conferences at Malta and Yalta, 1945* (Washington, 1955) 984.

2 Government of the USSR, Ministry of Foreign Affairs, *Correspondence between the Chairman of the Council of Ministers of the USSR and the President of the USA and the Prime Minister of Great Britain during the Great Patriotic War of 1941-45* (London, 1958) Vol. II, 266. See also Harry S. Truman *Memoirs*, Vol. I. : *Year of Decisions* (Garden City, 1955) 440.

3 See Reply of the Soviet Government, 22 July 1947. *Soviet News*, 25 July 1947.

4 See Chapter 1 : The United States.

5 The Far Eastern Commission consisted initially of eleven members : Australia, Canada, China, France, India, the Netherlands, New Zealand, the Philippines, the UK, the USA and the USSR. In November 1949 Pakistan and Burma also became members of the Commission. Decisions of the Commission were by a majority vote but were to include the concurring votes of China, the UK, the USA and the USSR.

6 See Soviet notes of 22 July 1947 and 29 August 1947 and the US note dated 12 August 1947. For the Soviet notes, see *Soviet News*, 25 Jul 1947 and 2 Sep 1947. For the US note, see *Department of State Bulletin* (24 Aug 1947) 395-6.

7 *New York Times*, 16 Aug 1947.

8 See Chinese note of 17 November 1947. *China Newsweek*, 27 Nov 1947 and US, Department of State, *Foreign Relations, 1947, Vol. VI, The Far East*, (Washington, 1972) 568-9.

9 See the Soviet note of 27 November 1947, *Soviet News*, 29 Nov 1947.

10 See Chinese note of 5 December 1947 and Soviet note of 30 December 1947. *Soviet News*, 5 Jan 1948.

11 *Foreign Relations*, n. 8. 1948, *Volume VI, The Far East and Australasia* (Washington, 1974) 879 and 887.

12 USA. Army Department, Civil Affairs Division, *183rd Weekly Report on Japan*, Appendix A, 7-8. Cited in Raymond Dennet and Robert T. Turner, ed., *Documents on American Foreign Relations*, Vol. XI (Princeton, 1950) 182-4.

13 *Department of State Bulletin* (25 Jul 1949) 107-8.

14 Soviet note of 11 May 1950. *Department of State Bulletin* (10 Jul 1950) 60-1.

15 United States note of 8 June 1950. *Ibid.*, 60.

16 *Keesings Contemporary Archives*, 1950-52, 10920.

17 *News and Views of the Soviet Union* (19 Feb 1951) 6-10.

18 See *Soviet Press Translations* (15 Mar 1951) 57-8.

19 Department of State Press Release 1180, 24 Nov 1950.

20 Japan, Ministry of Foreign Affairs, *Collection of Official Foreign Statements on Japanese Peace Treaty*, Vol. II (Tokyo, 1951) 121.

21 *Department of State Bulletin* (19 Mar 1951) 453.

22 *Ibid.* (23 Jul 1951) 138-43.

23 *Ibid.* (28 May 1951) 856-8.

24 *Ibid.* (23 Jul 1951) 138-43.

25 *Ibid.*

26 Japan, Ministry of Foreign Affairs, *Japanese Peace Conference, San Francisco, Provisional Verbatim Minutes* (Tokyo, undated) 105-28.

27 *Ibid.*

28 *Ibid.*

29 *Ibid.*, 338-40 and 346-9.

30 *Keesings Contemporary Archives, 1950-52*, 11724.

31 *Soviet Press Translations* (5 Oct 1951) 554-5.
32 *Times* (London), 27 May 1952.
33 *Soviet News*, 10 May 1952.
34 See *Nippon Times*, 13 Jun 1952.
35 *Ibid.*
36 *Information Bulletin* (Embassy of Japan, New Delhi) (1 Jul 1955) 2-4.
37 *Ibid.*, (15 Nov 1956) 1-4.
38 *Soviet Review* (18 Oct 1973) 52-5.
39 Joint Communique of 17 January 1975. *Pravda*, 19 Jan 1975, as translated in *Daily Review*, 20 Jan 1975.

Other Socialist Countries of East Europe

40 *Information Bulletin* (Embassy of Japan, New Delhi) 1 Mar 1957.
41 *Ibid.*
42 *Ibid.*, 15 May 1958.
43 *Ibid.*, 1 Mar 1957.
44 *Contemporary Japan* (Apr 1957) 731.
45 *Information Bulletin*, n. 1.
46 *Contemporary Japan* (Dec 1959) 369.
47 Japan, Ministry of Foreign Affairs, *Press Releases and Other Materials* p. 153.
48 *Ibid.*

Chapter 4 : Nationalist China

1 US, Department of State, *Foreign Relations of the United States, 1947, Vol. VI, The Far East* (Washington, D.C., 1972) 548.
2 *Ibid.*, 554-5.
3 *Ibid., 1948, Volume VI. The Far East and Australasia* (Washington, D.C., 1974) 799-800.
4 *Ibid.*, 1947, n. 1., 468-9.
5 *Ibid.*, 520. In his discussions with the US Ambassador in China, the Chinese Vice Minister of Foreign Affairs drew attention to the pressure of public opinion in China, as exemplified by the influential *Ta Kung Pao*, which feared a resurgence of Japanese power under American protection and agitated against abridgement of Chinese veto powers and also the unremitting pressure of the Soviets. *Ibid.*, 585.
6 *Ibid.*, 496.
7 Article 11 of the Sino-Soviet Treaty of 14 August 1945 provided : "The High Contracting Parties undertake not to enter into separate negotiation with Japan and not to conclude, without mutual consent, any armistice or peace treaty either with the present Japanese Government or with any other government or authority set up in Japan which do not renounce all aggressive intentions". *Ibid.*, 529.
8 *Ibid.*, 520.
9 *Ibid.*

10 For text, see *Ibid.*, 528-9.

11 For text, see *Ibid.*, 568-9.

12 For text, see *Ibid.*, 588, also see *Soviet News*, 5 Jan 1948.

13 *Foreign Relations of the United States*, 1947, n. 1, 548.

14 See Frederick S. Dunn, *Peace-Making and the Settlement with Japan* (Princeton, N.I., 1963) 114.

15 *China Handbook, 1952-53* (Taipeh, 1952) 160-1.

16 *Ibid.*, 161.

17 *Department of State Bulletin* (28 Jan 1952) 120.

18 *Ibid.*

19 Lawrence Olson, *Japan in Post-War Asia* (London, 1970) 75.

20 Richard Storry, "Options for Japan in the 1970s." *The World Today* (Aug 1970).

21 UK Parliamentary Debates, *House of Commons Debates*, 495 (5 Feb 1952) 828.

22 *China Handbook, 1952-53* (Taipeh, 1952) 163-4.

23 For the text of the Nationalist Chinese Draft of the Treaty of Peace with Japan handed to the Japanese Chief Delegate Isao Kawada by the Chinese Foreign Minister George Yeh in the first formal session on 20 February 1952, see *The Mainichi*, 9 and 10 March 1952.

24 *China Handbook*, n. 22, 154-60.

Chapter 5 : People's Republic of China

1   *China Digest* (4 Nov 1947) 8-11.

2   *Ibid.* (23 Sep 1947) 3.

3   *Ibid.* (24 Feb 1948) 10-1.

4   *China Weekly Review* (2 Jul 1949) 109 and (9 Jul 1949) 127.

5   *China Digest* (28 Jun 1949) 14-5.

6   *China Weekly Review* (16 Jul 1949) 151.

7   *Ibid.* (25 Mar 1950) 68.

8   *People's China* (16 Dec 1950) Supplement, 17-9.

9   *Ibid.* (1 Jun 1951) Supplement, 3-5.

10 *Ibid.* (1 Sep 1951) Supplement, 3-6.

11 *Ibid* (1 Oct 1951) 38-9.

12 *Ibid* (16 May 1952) 4-6.

13 *Ibid.* (1 Oct 1951) 38-9.

14 *Ibid.* (16 Dec 1950) Supplement 17-9.

15 *Ibid.* (1 Jun 1951) Supplement 3-5.

16 *Ibid.* (1 Sep 1951) Supplement 3-6.

17 *Ibid.* (1 Oct 1951) 38-9.

18 *Department of State Bulletin* (28 Jan 1952) 120.

19 *People's China* (1 Feb 1952) 11-2.

Chapter 6 : India

1 Lok Sabha Secretariat, *Foreign Policy of India* : *Texts of Documents* (New Delhi, 1959) 71-5.

2 See India, *Constituent Assembly Debates*, Vol. 3, pt. 1, 19 Mar 1949, Col. 1680 and *Ibid.*, vol. 4 pt. 1, 1 December 1949, col. 137.

3 *The Hindu*, 2 Oct 1949.

4 US, Department of State, *Foreign Relations of the United States 1948, Volume VI, The Far East and Australasia* (Washington, D.C., 1974), 907.

5 See New Zealand, Department of External Affairs, *Japanese Peace Settlement* 38 (Wellington, 1947) 5.

6 P.A.N. Murthy, "India and the Peace Settlement with Japan," in M.S. Rajan, ed., *Studies in Politics* (Delhi, 1971) 468.

7 *The Hindu*, 19 Jan 1951.

8 *Ibid.*, 26 Jun 1950.

9 Frederick S. Dunn, *Peace-Making and the Settlement with Japan* (Princeton, N.J., 1963) 113-4.

10 *The Hindu*, 1 Aug 1951, see also *New York Times*, 30 Jul 1951 and *Survey of International Affairs 1951* (London, 1954) 402.

11 *Times of India* (Bombay) 28 Aug 1951.

12 Indian Note to US Government, 23 August 1951. *Department of State Bulletin* (3 Sep 1951) 385-6.

13 India, House of the People, *Parliamentary Debates*, Vol. 14, pt. 2, 27 August 1951, col. 1358-61.

14 Murthy, n. 6, 484.

15 US Note to India, 25 Aug 1951. *Ibid.*, 387-8.

16 *Ibid.*

17 India, Ministry of External Affairs, *Japanese Peace Treaty* (U.S.–U.K. Draft) : *Selected Documents, 1951* (New Delhi, 1951).

18 See Council of Foreign Relations, *The United States in World Affairs, 1951* (New York, 1952) 192 and Murthy, n. 6, 489.

19 Dunn, n. 9, 132-3.

20 *The Times* (London), 27 Aug 1951.

21 *Department of State Bulletin*, Vol. 25, (15 Oct 1951) 616-20.

22 John Foster, Dulles, "Security in the Pacific", *Foreign Affairs* (Jan 1952) 175-86.

23 Edwin O. Reischauer, *The United States and Japan* (Cambridge, Mass., 1950) 315.

24 *Christian Science Monitor*, 29 Sep 1951.

25 *The Hindu*, 4 Sep 1951.

26 Government of India, Press Information Bureau, *Press Release*, 10 Sep 1951.

27 *Foreign Policy of India*, n. 1, 71-5.

28 *Information Bulletin* (Embassy of Japan, New Delhi), 15 Oct. 1956.

29 Indo-Japanese Association, *Treaty and Agreements between Japan and India* (Tokyo, undated) 10-2.

30 *Department of State Bulletin*. vol. 30 (1954) 802.

31   *The Statesman*, 15 Sep 1952.

Chapter 7 : Southeast Asia
   1   Frederick S. Dunn, *Peace-Making and the Settlement with Japan*
       (Princeton, N.J., 1963) 196.

Burma
   2   *Manchester Guardian*, 24 Jul 1951.
   3   *Nippon Times*, 25 Jul 1951.
   4   F.C. Jones. "China and Japan" in Peter Calvocoressi, *Survey of Inter-*
       national Affairs 1951 (London, 1954) 403-4.
   5   *Gaimusho Bulletin* (Tokyo), 25 Sep 1954.
   6   *Contemporary Japan*, Vol. 23 (Nos. 4-6, 1955) 424-9.
   7   *Gaimusho Bulletin*, 16 Apr 1955.
   8   *Ibid*.
   9   *United Nations Treaty Series*, Vol. 251, No. 3543. pp. 226-42.
  10   *Information Bulletin*, 15 Jun 1957.
  11   *Japan Times Weekly*, 25 Nov 1961.
  12   *Contemporary Japan* (Oct 1963) 795.

Philippines
  13   *Department of State Bulletin* (22 May 1949) 831-3.
  14   *Ibid*.
  15   Republic of Philippines, *Official Gazette*, Oct 1949, 4358.
  16   George H. Blakeslee, *The Far Eastern Commission : A Study in*
       International Cooperation, 1945 to 1952 (Washington, D.C., 1953)
       121.
  17   Japan Ministry of Foreign Affairs, *Collection of Official Foreign*
       Statements on Japanese Peace Treaty, Vol. II, (Tokyo, 1951) 115-6.
  18   See Chapter 1.
  19   *Manila Chronicle*, 27 Mar 1951.
  20   *New York Times*, 21 Jul 1951.
  21   *The Hindu*, 26 Jul 1951.
  22   *Collection of Official Foreign Statements on Japanese Peace Treaty*,
       n. 17, Vol. III, 55.
  23   *Ibid.*, 22.
  24   Japan, Ministry of Foreign Affairs, *Japanese Peace Conference*, San
       Francisco, California, Sep 1951, Provisional Verbatim Minutes.
       (Tokyo, undated) 258-65.
  25   *Ibid*.
  26   Senator Recto's speech in *Manila Chronicle*, 9 Sep 1951.
  27   See Senator Recto's article, "Dulles' Final Draft Gives Philippines
       Nothing," in *Ibid.*, 17 Aug 1951.
  28   For text, see, United States Department of State, *United States*
       Treaties and Other International Agreements, Vol. 3, Part 3, 1952

(Washington, D.C., 1955) 3947-51.

29 *Manila Chronicle*, 2 Sep 1951.

30 *Gaimusho Bulletin*, 12 Mar 1953.

31 *Official Gazette* (Manila), Jun 1955. Cited in K.V. Kesavan, *Japan's Relations with Southeast Asia, 1952-60* (Bombay 1972), 81, footnotes.

32 See *Contemporary Japan* (Mar 1959) 551-3.

33 *Manila Times Bulletin*, 19 and 21 Apr 1954.

34 *Gaimusho Bulletin*, 1 May 1954.

35 *Ibid.*, 10 Mar 1955.

36 Lawrence Olson, *Japan in Postwar Asia* (New York, 1970) 25.

37 Japan, Embassy in India, *Press Release*, 14 Jun 1955.

38 Olson, n. 36, 25.

39 *Contemporary Japan*, Vol. 24 (1956) 362-9.

Indonesia

40 Claude A. Buss, "Making Peace with Japan, U.S. Policy on the Japan Treaty," *Far Eastern Survey* (15 Jun 1951) 115. See also US, Department of State, *Conference for the Conclusion and Signature of the Treaty of Peace with Japan*, San Francisco 4-8 September 1951 (Washington, 1951) 220-1.

41 Japan, Ministry of Foreign Affairs, *Japanese Peace Conference*, San Francisco, Provisional Verbatim Minutes (Tokyo, undated) 250-5.

42 Tsunezo Ichikawa, "Japan's Liabilities—Reparations and External Debts," *Contemporary Japan*, Vol. 24 (Nos. 4-6. 1956) 337-41.

43 See Dharmasathiawan's statement, *Report on Indonesia* (Information Office of the Republic of Indonesia, New York) 16 Apr 1951.

44 Japan, Ministry of Foreign Affairs, *Collection of Official Foreign Statements on Japanese Peace Treaty*, Vol. 3 (Tokyo, August 1951) 79.

45 A. Brotherton, "Indonesia and the Japanese Peace Treaty," *Eastern World* (Feb 1952) 15-6.

46 *Ibid.*

47 *Ibid.*

48 *Japanese Peace Conference*, n. 41, 250-5.

49 *Ibid.*, 327–32. See also *Indonesia Review* (Oct–Dec 1951) 424-5.

50 *Report on Indonesia*, 13 Feb 1952.

51 *Ibid.*, 31 Jan 1952.

52 *Gaimusho Bulletin*, 16 Dec 1953.

53 *Ibid.*

54 Statement of the Government of Japan, 1 November 1956. *Information Bulletin* (Embassy of Japan, New Delhi), 1 Nov 1956.

55 Address by Indonesian Foreign Minister Sunario before the opening session of the Asian conference for the Ministry of Foreign Affairs of Indonesia, 9 March 1954. Indonesia, Ministry of Foreign Affairs, *Indonesia and its Foreign Policy* (Jakarta, 1955) 18-9. See also K.V. Kesavan, n. 31, 1972) 99. footnote.

56 *Ibid.*, 101.

57 *News from Indonesia* Press Note, No. 7, 30 Nov 1957.
58 Indonesia, Ministry of Information, *Special Release*, 7-13.
59 *Ibid.*, 34-5.
60 *Ibid.*, 40-3.

South Vietnam

61 Japan, Ministry of Foreign Affairs, *Japanese Peace Conference*, San Francisco, Provisional Verbatim Minutes (Tokyo, undated) 304-5.
62 *Information Bulletin* (Embassy of Japan in India) 1 Jan 1958.
63 *Contemporary Japan*, Vol. 26 (1959-60) 185.
64 *Times of Vietnam* (Saigon), 16 Jan 1960.

North Vietnam

65 *Vietnam Information* (Rangoon), 3 Sep 1956.
66 *Ibid.*, 8 Sep 1956.
67 *Ibid.*, 20 Dec 1957.
68 *Japan Review* (Oct 1973) 16-7.

Laos and Cambodia

69 Hayato Ikeda, "Japan's Share in Economic Cooperation," *Contemporary Japan* (Aug 1959) 22.
70 *Information Bulletin*, 1 Jan 1958, 1-3.
71 Ikeda, n. 69, 22.
72 *Contemporary Japan*, Vol. 25 (1957-9) 718.

Chapter 8 : Korea

1 US Department of State, *Foreign Relations of the United States 1947, Volume VI, The Far East*, (Washington, D.C., 1972) 511-2.

South Korea

2 William Sebald and B. Russel, *With MacArthur in Japan* (New York, 1965) 287-8.
3 *Information Bulletin* (Embassy of Japan, New Delhi), 1 Jan 1957.
4 *Ibid.*
5 *Ibid.*
6 *Ibid.*, 22 Oct 1953.
7 *Gaimusho Bulletin*, 22 Oct 1953.
8 *Information Bulletin*, Vol. 3 (No. 4, 1956) 4-7.
9 *Ibid.*, 1 Feb 1958.
10 *Japan Times*, 23 Jun 1965.
11 See Joint Communique dated 20 February 1965 *Contemporary Japan* (Jun 1965) 471.
12 *Japan Times*, 23 Jun 1965.
13 *Ibid.*, 22 and 23 Jun 1965.

14 See *Ibid.*, 23 Jun 1965. See also Contemporary Japan (May 1966) 677-8.
15 *Japan Times*, 23 Jun 1965.

North Korea

16 *News and Views from the Soviet Union* (30 Jul 1951) 1-6.
17 *Ibid.*
18 See *Korea Today* (No. 33, 1959) Supplement, Documents II, 6-7.
19 *Ibid.*, 4-5.
20 *Ibid.*, Documents III, 6-7.
21 *Hindustan Times*, 16 Dec 1959. About 3000 of the 5000 registered for repatriations under the Calcutta agreement were expected to be returned to North Korea by the end of 1959.

Chapter 9 : Japan and the Peace Settlements

1 Shigeru Yoshida, "Japan and the Crisis in Asia," *Foreign Affairs* (Jan 1951) 177.
2 *Contemporary Japan*, Vol. 24 (Nos. 1-3, 1956).
3 *Ibid.*, Vol. 23 (Nos. 10-12, 1955) 669-74.
4 See State by Japanese Foreign Ministry on Peace Treaty, 1 June 1950. *New York Times*, 2 Jun 1950.
5 Yoshida, n. 1, 171 and 180-1.
6 *New York Times*, 2 Jun 1950.
7 *Contemporary Japan* (Jan-Mar 1951) 39.
8 William Sebald and Russel Brines, *With MacArthur in Japan* (New York, 1965) 261-2.
9 Robert A. Fearey, *The Occupation of Japan : Second Phase 1948-50* (New York, 1950) 189.
10 *Soviet Press Translations* (15 Mar 1951) 157-8.
11 Statement issued by the Japanese Foreign Office for the purpose of clarifying Japan's position in the Korean conflict, 19 August 1950. *Contemporary Japan* (Jul-Sep 1950) 463-9.
12 Yoshida, n. 1, 174.
13 Statement by Japanese Foreign Office, n. 11.
14 Yoshida, n. 1, 173.
15 Speech before the Diet, 14 ful 1950. *Ibid.*, (Jul-Sep 1950) 459-60.
16 Martin E. Weinstein, *Japan's Post-War Defence Policy, 1947-1968* (New York, 1971) 50, 55 and 63. Japanese appeared willing to tolerate US troops in their midst, but only for a very short time and as a matter of necessity. Roger Dingman, "Reconsiderations : The United States-Japan Security Treaty," *Pacific Community* (Jul 1976) 478.
17 United States, Department of State, *United States Treaties and Other International Agreements*, Vol. 3, Part 3, 1952 (Washington, D.C., 1955) 3331-2.
18 J.F. Dulles, "Security in the Pacific," *Foreign Affairs*, (Jan 1952).

19 Dingman, n. 16, 480-1.

20 Japan, Ministry of Foreign Affairs, *Collection of Official Foreign Statements on Japanese Peace Treaty*, Vol. 3 (Tokyo, Aug 1951) 4-6.

21 Japan, Ministry of Foreign Affairs, *Japanese Peace Conference*, San Francisco, Provisional Verbatim Minutes (Tokyo undated) 327-32.

22 *Contemporary Japan* (Jul-Sep 1951) 423-8.

23 Royama Masamichi, "The US-Japanese Security Treaty—A Japanese View," *Japan Quarterly* (Jan-Mar 1957) 288 and 294.

24 *The Hindu*, 28 Aug 1951.

25 See *New York Times*, 3 Mar 1952.

26 *Ibid.*

27 Japan, House of Councillors, *The Official Gazette Extra*, 12th Session (18 Oct 1951) 3. The Peace Treaty and the Security Treaty were approved in the House of Representatives by 307 votes to 47 and 289 votes to 71 respectively and in the House of Councillors by 174 to 45 and 147 to 76 respectively.

28 Japan, House of Representatives, *The Official Gazette Extra*, 12th Session (27 Oct 1951) 30.

29 Japan, House of Councillors, *The Official Gazette Extra*, 12th Session (17 Oct 1951) 3.

30 See Mallappa Amravati, *Relations Between Japan and the United States Since 1945 with special reference to the Peace Treaty and the Security Pact*, Ph. D. Dissertation of Jawaharlal Nehru University, New Delhi, 1969, 340.

31 Address before the America-Japan Society of Tokyo, 7 March 1961. Embassy of the United States in Japan, *Press Release* No. 65, 2-3. Quoted in Mallappa, n. 30, 313.

32 Mallappa, n. 30, 301-2.

33 Frederick S. Dunn, *Peace-Making and the Settlement with Japan* (Princeton, N.J., 1963) 106.

34 Sebald and Russel, n. 8, 256.

35 See Hugh Borton, *Japan's Modern Century* (New York, 1955) 443 and 445.

36 It might be recalled here that when the British Under Secretary for Foreign Affairs, in his conversation with US Department of State Officials on 2 June 1948, broached the idea of the USA securing its strategic interests in the Western Pacific meeting the Soviet threat without postponing a peace treaty with Japan through the conclusion of a US-Japanese bilateral pact, the US officials questioned the feasibility of such a bilateral pact. They pointed out that there would undoubtedly be attempts to introduce clauses in the treaty stipulating that any defense of Japan should be on a multilateral basis. Such clauses, if accepted, the US official remarked, would obstruct the possibility of a bilateral pact and the US would find itself in the indivious position of prematurely being required to withdraw its forces and to destroy its airfields. US Department of State, *Foreign Relations 1948, Vol. VI, The Far East and Australasia* (Washington, D. C., 1974) 797.

37 Dulles Broadcast, 1 March 1951, *Department of State Bulletin* (12 Mar 1951) 404-5.

38 Dulles, *Ibid.*

39 See Dulles Press Conference in Tokyo, 19 April 1951. Japan, Ministry of Foreign Affairs, *Collection of Official Foreign Statements on Japanese Peace Treaty*, Vol. II (Tokyo, 1951) 73-80.

40 Weinstein, n. 16, 61-3 and 74-5.

41 Borton, n, 35, 449.

42 For the text of the Treaty and Related Documents, see *Department of State Bulletin* (8 Feb 1960) 185-6. For further details and comments on the provisions of the 1960 Security Treaty, see Weinstein, n. 16, 87-90.

43 See J.P. Jain, *China in World Politics* (New Delhi, 1976) 82-111 and J.P. Jain, "The Legal Status of Formosa : A Study of British, Chinese and Indian Views," *American Journal of International Law* (Jan 1963) 25-45.

44 *Mainichi*, 15 Dec 1953.

45 *United Nations Treaty Series No. 1869*, vol. 138, 184-8.

46 *Ibid.*, Vols. 150, 396, Vol. 184, 359 and vol. 199, 346.

47 Dunn, n. 33, 171.

48 See Text of the San Francisco Peace Treaty, 8 September 1951, *Department of State Bulletin* (27 Aug 1951) 349-55.

49 *The Shinron*, Jan 1956.

50 Tsunezo Ichikawa, "Japan's Liabilities—Reparations and External Debts," *Contemporary Japan*, Vol. 24 (Nos. 4-6, 1956) 337-41.

51 Itagaki Yoichi, "Reparations and Southeast Asia," *Japan Quarterly*, Vol. VI (1959) 411.

52 Ichikawa, n. 50.

53 *Information Bulletin*, 1 May 1961, 1-2.

54 *Ibid.*, 4-6.

55 Ichikawa, n. 50.

56 *Ibid.*

DOCUMENTS

1. Cairo Declaration by US President F.D. Roosevelt, British Premier Winston Churchill and Generalissimo Chiang Kai-shek of China, 27 November 1943 (Extract).

The three great Allies are fighting this war to restrain and punish the aggression of Japan. They covet no gain for themselves and have no thought of territorial expansion. It is their purpose that Japan shall be stripped of all islands in the Pacific which she has seized and occupied since the beginning of the first World War in 1914, and that all the territories Japan has stolen from the Chinese, such as Manchuria, Formosa, and the Pescadores, shall be restored to the Rupublic of China. Japan will also be expelled from all other territories which she has taken by violence and greed.

2. Agreement regarding entry of the Soviet Union into the war against Japan: Yalta Agreement, 11 February 1945 (Extracts).

The leaders of three Great Powers—the Soviet Union, United States of America and Great Britain—have agreed that in two or three months after Germany has surrendered and the war in Europe has terminated the Soviet Union shall enter into the war against Japan on the side of the Allies on condition that :

2. The former rights of Russia violated by the treacherous attack of Japan in 1904 shall be restored, viz :

    (a) The southern part of Sakhalin as well as all islands adjacent to it shall be returned to the Soviet Union. . .

3. The Kurile Islands shall be handed over to the Soviet Union.

The Heads of the three Great Powers have agreed that these claims of the Soviet Union shall be unequestionably fulfilled after Japan has been defeated.

3. Potsdam Proclamation by China, the USA, and the UK defining terms for the Japanese surrender, 26 July 1945 (Extracts).

(1) We—the President of the United States, the President of the National Government of the Republic of China, and the

Prime Minister of Great Britain, representing the hundreds of millions of our countrymen, have conferred and agree that Japan shall be given an opportunity to end this war. . . .

(6) There must be eliminated for all time the authority and influence of those who have deceived and misled the people of Japan into embarking on world conquest, for we insist that a new order of peace, security and justice will be impossible until irresponsible militarism is driven from the world.

(7) Until such a new order is established *and* until there is convincing proof that Japan's war-making power is destroyed, points in Japanese territory to be designated by the Allies shall be occupied to secure the achievement of the basic objectives we are here setting forth.

(8) The terms of the Cairo Declaration shall be carried out and Japanese sovereignty shall be limited to the islands of Honshu, Hokkaido, Kyushu, Shikoku and such minor islands as we determine.

(9) The Japanese military forces, after being completely disarmed, shall be permitted to return to their homes with the opportunity to lead peaceful and productive lives.

(10) We do not intend that the Japanese shall be enslaved as a race or destroyed as a nation, but stern justice shall be meted out to all war criminals, including those who have visited cruelties upon our prisoners. The Japanese Government shall remove all obstacles to the revival and strengthening of democratic tendencies among the Japanese people. Freedom of speech, of religion, and of thought, as well as respect for the fundamental human rights shall be established.

(11) Japan shall be permitted to maintain such industries as will sustain her economy and permit the exaction of just reparations in kind, but not those which would enable her to re-arm for war. To this end, access to, as distinguished from control of, raw materials shall be permitted. Eventual Japanese participation in world trade relations shall be permitted.

(12) The occupying forces of the Allies shall be withdrawn from Japan as soon as these objectives have been accomplished and there has been established in accordance with the freely expressed will of the Japanese people a peacefully inclined and responsible government.

(13) We call upon the government of Japan to proclaim

now that unconditional surrender of all Japanese armed forces, and to provide proper and adequate assurances of their good faith in such action. The alternative for Japan is prompt and utter destruction.

UNITED STATES OF AMERICA

4. **Replies of the Governments represented on the Far Eastern Commission to the US suggestion of 11 July 1947 about holding a Japanese Peace Conference as reproduced in US Acting Secretary of State Telegram, 13 August 1947.**

The status of Japanese peace treaty discussions is currently as follows :

1. A. Replies to our July 11 suggestion of a conference of deputies and experts on August 19 have been received from the 10 Govts. approached, which offered the following views on leading questions involved :

(a) *Composition :* All states consulted except Soviets indicated willingness attend an all-power peace conference. Soviets took position Far Eastern Big Four possessed special interests postwar treatment of Japan, Council of Foreign Ministers had been organized particularly for preparatory work of drawing up peace treaties, and question of convening a conference to draw up Japanese treaty should therefore be provisionally examined by CFM.

(b) *Date :* France, Netherlands, and Philippines considered August 19 satisfactory date. Britain, Australia, New Zealand, Canada and India supported suggestion for an early conference but stated it would be difficult or impossible to attend on August 19. Soviets emphasized desirability of haste in convening CFM.

(c) *Level of Representation :* US proposal that conference initially be composed of deputies and experts accepted by France, Netherlands and Philippines. Canada reserved position. Chinese, Indian and New Zealand positions not clarified. Britain expressed view questions of policy and principle would have to be determined first at ministerial level before deputies and experts could usefully begin to operate. Australia also took this position and stated Australian Minister of External Affairs must represent Australia at any peace conference on Japan. Soviets proposed whole question of Japanese treaty be first considered by CFM.

(d) *Place* : No Govt. expressed clear preference regarding site of suggested conference but several representatives have expressed preference for Washington because of presence here of Far Eastern experts attached to FEC. Chinese Ambassador urged preliminary or formal conference be held in China.

(e) *Voting* : Australia, Canada and Philippines expressly accepted American proposal voting at conference be by simple two thirds majority. France accepted for initial conference with understanding voting procedures at a subsequent meeting of 11 Foreign Ministers to pass on draft would be determined at the time. New Zealand and India approved suggested abandonment EFC veto rights. Britain and Netherlands did not question US proposal for two-thirds voting system. China proposed decision by two-thirds majority including majority Far Eastern Big Four. Soviets gave no indication voting preferences beside proposal treaty be considered by CFM.

5. Memorandum by the Director of the Policy Planning Staff (Kennan) on results of Planning Staff study of questions involved in the Japanese Peace Settlement, 14 October 1947 (Extracts).

1. *Timing of Settlement*

The staff sees great risks in an early relinquishment of Allied control over Japan. It has no satisfactory evidence that Japanese society would be politically or economically stable if turned loose and left to its own devices at this stage. If Japan is not politically and economically stable when the peace treaty is signed, it will be difficult to prevent communist penetration.

Nevertheless, we recognize that the occupation is in many ways entering on a period of diminishing returns. Furthermore, we are already committed to proceed with peace discussions by the invitations we have issued to other governments.

The Staff considers, therefore, that we cannot very well

refuse to proceed with the negotiations at this time. On the other hand, we should not force the pace in any way but should keep the talks exploratory and non-binding and hold open some possibility of further postponement of final decisions, until we can arrive at a firm judgement on certain of the basic issues involved. Accordingly, discussions of substance should not be begun until after January first at the earliest, and we should not plan on completing them before about next June.

2. *Voting Procedure*

If possible, the U.S.S.R. should be included in the negotiations. If it is to exclude itself, it would be better that this occur on a substantive issue damaging to the U.S.S.R. in Japanese eyes rather than on a procedural question such as voting arrangements.

If the other drafting powers will agree to a veto, on the FEC rules or otherwise, the U.S. should concur reluctantly. Otherwise, assuming that there is no agreement on a two-thirds rule, we should permit the whole question to carry over to next spring before proceeding with the talks at all. . . .

4. *Territory*

A. The southern-most islands of the Kurile archipelago would be retained by Japan.

B. The Bonins, Volcano Islands and Marcus would be detached from Japan, with a view to their being placed under U.S. strategic trusteeship.

C. A decision on the disposition of the Ryukyu islands south of 29° would be held in abeyance pending the receipt from SWNCC of information regarding the relative desirability of

    a. a U.S. strategic trusteeship over those islands and

    b. a long-term lease of base areas, nominal sovereignty over the islands being retained by Japan.

5. *United States Security*

As stated above, we would insist on U.S. strategic trusteeship of the Bonins, Volcano and Marcus Islands.

In addition to this, we should proceed in the negotiations

on the assumption that we will require military facilities in Okinawa. . . .

6. *Military Defence of Japan*

The staff considers that the idea of a four-power agreement on Japanese demilitarization should be abandoned but that the Treaty should provide for complete Japanese disarmament, with the reservation that Japan should be permitted to maintain a civil police force, including a constabulary and coast guard, at a strength to be defined initially by SCAP. A Council of Ambassadors should be charged with the continued supervision of demilitarization and disarmament.

Admittedly, this leaves the Japanese without means of self-defense against foreign aggression. The Staff sees no means of avoiding this. It feels that in the coming period Japanese military security must rest primarily on the proximity (or in extreme event, the presence in Japan) of adequate U.S. forces, and that it should be accepted as a principle of American defence policy to retain in the Pacific areas sufficient armed strength to make plain our will and determination to prevent any other military power from establishing itself in the Japanese home islands.

7. *Political and Economic Defence of Japan*

The Staff does not consider that there should be any formal allied control or supervision of Japan's political life following entrance into force of a peace treaty. One of the greatest values of a peace treaty, from our standpoint, is its psychological effect on the Japanese. This would be lost if formal political controls were to be retained. If we must retain controls, it would be better to have no treaty. . . .

8. *Reparations*

The reparations program should be wound up at the earliest possible date. Minimum reparations, consistent with existing commitments, should be exacted, and none out of current production. The Council of Ambassadors should be charged with the administrative supervision of reparations in the post-war period.

9. *Industrial Disarmament*

Japan's industrial disarmament should be limited to the prohibition of the manufacture of weapons of war and aircraft and the minimum of restrictions on industrial production which can be advocated in the light of commitments already made by the U.S. regarding the reduction of industrial war potential. Japan's economic war potential should be controlled by restrictions on allowable stockpiling of designated strategic raw materials within Japan. Japan should be permitted to operate at least domestic civil air transport and a merchant marine, although she should not be permitted to manufacture aircraft. In defining our position on the limitations on merchant shipping, primary consideration should be given to the views of the Navy.

10. *Provision in Treaty for Future Revision*

It is absolutely essential that a peace treaty contain adequate provision for revision. A peace treaty imposing servitudes of indefinite duration rests on the inexcusable assumption of a static world and constitutes an infallible invitation to eventual unilateral violation.

6. Analysis of the Japanese Peace Treaty Draft of 8 January 1948, submitted by US Department of State official Hugh Borton to John P. Davies of the Policy Planning Staff, 30 January 1948 (Extracts).

Territorial Clauses

The territorial clauses (Articles 1—9) are based largely on international agreements made at Cairo, Yalta and Potsdam. The disposition of the Bonin and Volcano Islands and Marcus Island (Article 5) is based on a decision of SWNCC of September 17, 1946 to the effect that these islands be placed under a strategic trusteeship under the administration of the United States. Although the trusteeship agreement for the Trust Territory of the Pacific, the former Japanese Mandated Islands, was approved by the President on July 18, 1947, title to this territory is to be renounced by Japan (Article 6) in order to nullify any possible residual claims that Japan may have to it. The main outstanding problems in the territorial clauses concern the southern Kurile Islands and the Ryukyus. In reference to the Kuriles, they are not defined in the Yalta Agreement, which simply states that "The Kurile Islands shall be handed over to the Soviet Union." If the United States proposes a narrow interpretation of the "Kurile Islands", the southern-most islands of Kunashri and Etorofu, the Habomai group and Shikotan would be retained by Japan. In reference to the Ryukyu Islands, the Joint Chief of Staff have recommended a U.S. strategic trusteeship for all of the islands south of 29 degrees north latitude but the State Department has not yet concurred with this proposal.

Extent of Allied Authority

The sovereign independence and territorial integrity of Japan is recognized by the Allied and Associated Powers in Article 10 and SCAP, the FEC and the Allied Council for Japan are abolished by Article 11. Such control as the Allies are to exercise over Japan in post-treaty-period is to be through the Council of Ambassadors (Chapter 6). While most of this authority is limited to problems of disarmament and demili-tarization, Article 32(h) gives the Council authority for a period of 5 years to determine whether Japan has vitiated the pro-visions concerning limitations on holding public offices (Annex A) and those on economic reform. . . .

4. Disarmament and Demilitarization

The provisions for disarmament and demilitarization, con-tained in Chapter 5, follow the revision of November 1947 of the draft treaty for disarmament and demilitarization of Germany insofar as these provisions are applicable to Japan. On April 29, 1946 the United States circulated to the Govern-ment of China, the Soviet Union and the United Kingdom a draft four-power treaty on the disarmament and demilitariza-tion of Japan. It was originally intended that this four-power treaty would be separate from the peace treaty and would be binding upon the four contracting powers. The January 8 draft of the Japanese peace treaty does not envisage a separate disarmament and demilitarization treaty. By incorporating the disarmament provisions in the peace treaty, the obligation to carry out these provisions is placed directly on Japan rather than on the four powers. Allied control over these provisions is limited to 25 years and is to be exerted through the Council of Ambassadors for Japan. Revisions of the disarmament and demilitarization provisions of the treaty are possible through the operation of Article 32(c) 4, whereby the governments represented on the Commission of Inspection may agree to the discontinuance of the functions of the Commission prior to the expiration of the 25-year period. These articles may further be revised through the operation of Article 58 which provides that the Allied and Associated Powers may hold a conference for the purpose of considering revision of the treaty "in the light of the progress of Japan toward the fulfilment of the provisions of the present treaty after its entry into force," whenever such a recommendation is made by the Council of Ambassadors for Japan or by a majority of the states represented on the Council. The articles on disarmament and demilitarization are also in conformity, in most respects, with the corresponding section in the Far Eastern Commission policy decision on Basic Post-Surrender Policy for Japan, approved on June 19, 1947.

No provision is made in the draft treaty for a permanent level of industry in Japan. Such controls as are to be exercised over Japanese industry are limited to the prohibition of the stockpiling of strategic raw materials in excess of normal requirements for current consumption and the prohibition of any attempt to subsidize war shipping industries directly or indirectly for the purposes of expanding their capacity to produce (Article 26). The levels of industrial capacity specified in Annex D are not intended as establishing a level of industry but are for the purposes of determining availability of facilities for claims reparations.

5. General Reform Program

As stated above, the Council of Ambassadors is given limited authority to supervise the carrying out by Japan of the provision in Annexes A and D (Limitations on Office Holding and Economic Reform). The Council of Ambassadors has no direct authority, however, in reference to the carrying out by Japan of other reform proposals such as those concerning commercial policy (Article 49 and Annex L) and restrictive trade practices (Article 50 and Annex L). The provisions for limitation upon holding of certain public offices allow for the continuation, in exceptional cases, of the purge. . . .

6. *Reparations and Restitution*

The present draft of the treaty provides that Japan shall make equitable reparation for the damage caused by it to the Allied and Associated Powers (Article 33). This general provision is based on the Potsdam Declaration and on the pertinent section in the FEC Basic Post-Surrender Policy on Japan of June 19, 1947. More detailed provisions concerning reparations are contained in Annex D and are based on FEC policy decisions on interim removals and on agreed U.S. policy decision determination of the peaceful needs of Japan (SWNCC 236/43)...The United States reparations proposal does not advocate reparation from current production but it is understood that the Chinese Government will press for adoption of such a policy by the Far Eastern Commission. The Chinese position is based on the fact that our insistence on a prior claim on Japanese assets for payment of the costs of occupation, a principle already approved by the FEC, would result in less reparations to the other Allied [powers ?]. The Chinese will formally recommend, therefore, that this discrepancy be met by reparations from current production.

The draft treaty further provides that the supervision of the implementation of the reparation and restitution articles of the treaty shall be by the Council of Ambassadors (Article 33 and Annex F, paragraph 11).

7. *Technical Problems connected with the Liquidation of the War*

The remainder of the draft of the treaty of the Annexes, with the exception of the general political clauses (Articles 13, 14 and 15), is devoted to the settlement of technical questions connected with the liquidation of the war with Japan. Such questions as adherence by Japan to international conventions and treaties, war criminals, claims, United Nations property rights and interests, special economic clauses, concerning contracts, decisions of price courts, industrial and artistic property rights and settlement of disputes are treated in general terms in the body of the treaty and are elaborated in Annexes B, C, G,

H, I, J, K and N. In general, these provisions and annexes follow the pattern already established in the Italian Treaty and do not raise any basic issues.

It should be pointed out, however, that there is a provision for revision of the treaty (Article 58). Such a provision is not contained in the Italian or satellite treaties.

8. *Summary of Unsettled Issues in Draft Treaty*

From the foregoing, it is clear that if a complete draft treaty of peace for Japan is to be prepared, the United States Government must reach a definitive decision on the following points : (a) disposition of the southern Kurile Islands; (b) disposition of the Ryukyu Islands; (c) extent of authority of Council of Ambassadors over economic reform provisions; (d) economic reform program, particularly in reference to the purge, agrarian, reform, and excessive concentration of economic power; (e) determination of the peaceful needs of Japan as a basis for availability of reparations; (f) reparations from current production.

7. **Report by Director of the Policy Planning Staff George F. Kennan together with Explainatory Notes on his Conversations with General MacArthur, 25 March 1948 (Extracts).**

Reparations

We should announce that our Government is not prepared to permit the removal of reparations items from Japan in excess of the existing 30% project; that removals under this project will be restricted to such as do not materially prejudice the economic recovery of Japan; and that these removals will have to be completed by July 1, 1949; that no plants not earmarked for removal under this project will be retained on the reparations list; and that the United States will oppose the exaction of reparations from Japan under any future peace treaty unless a form can be found for such reparations payments which is practical, economical, favourable to the general economic development of the Far Eastern area and not burdensome to any single one of the Allied nations, directly or indirectly...

I agree strongly with General MacArthur that Japan must not be left defenceless in the period before the conclusion of a treaty of peace. It is with respect to the period subsequent to the entry into effect of the treaty that my views diverge from his.

World conditions are now in a state of extreme flux. Plainly, we are not going to have a treaty, or even proceed to the negotiation of a treaty, for some time. We do not know today what the situation of Russia will be when the time comes to negotiate the treaty. Yet this will be the decisive point. If Russia still presents the same sort of threat to world security that she presents today, then I see only two alternatives : either we must not have the treaty at all and retain allied troops in Japan or we must permit Japan to re-arm to the extent that it would no longer constitute an open invitation to military aggression. If, on the other hand—as I consider possible—the course of events should have served to weaken Russia's military-political potential and to take off the aggressive edge of Russian policy, and if there were to be a good prospect that this situation would endure for some time, then we might proceed to the negotiation of a treaty of demilitarization and place our reliance upon that treaty to assure Japanese military security. We would still have to make sure that Japanese society was not too vulnerable politically, however, before we could take this step.

It is clear from the above that we cannot make a decision on this point at the present time. This decision will have to be taken later, in the light of prevailing circumstances. However, we should have it prominently in mind throughout the coming period, and we should observe developments closely from this standpoint. . . .

The deleterious effect of the unresolved reparations program on Japanese industry cannot be over-emphasized. In every category of plant subject to reparations removal—aircraft, arsenals, munitions, laboratories, chemicals, shipbuilding, iron and steel, oil synthetic rubber, machine tools, etc.—there are some plants now engaged in turning out products which are either vital to the recovery of Japan, or at least completely unrelated to war manufacturing. . . .

Altogether about a thousand Japanese plants, both integrated and non-integrated facilities, have been earmarked for removals, but only about 20 of these plants have so far been subjected to actual removal of some of their equipment. . . .

General Harrison, Chief of SCAP's Reparations Section, informed me that there is totally inadequate shipping available for the purpose of transporting even the 1.6 million tons of equipment scheduled for removal under the interim program. In the case of China he estimates that it will require about 20 years, with the shipping now available, to transfer her requested share from Japan. In the meantime this equipment will either be maintained by the Japanese at a huge cost or left to deteriorate beyond the point of repair. If and when transferred to claimant countries (such as China and the Philippines) which lack technicians, skilled labour and power sources, the reparations equipment will in many instances be consigned to scrap or remain unused.

Reparations have been justified on the grounds that they will neutralize Japan as a future military threat and that they will provide Far Eastern countries with equipment which will contribute to their recovery. With her army, navy and air force abolished, her fighting equipment scuttled, her overseas empire liquidated, and 30% of her home industries destroyed, others damaged, and the remainder largely obsolete, Japan cannot be regarded as a potential military threat in the predictable future. The control of her sources of critical raw materials, if carefully conducted, would be a far more effective measure against military resurgence than an extensive system of reparations removals.

It is absurd to suppose that many of the facilities tentatively scheduled for removal from Japan could ever be effectively utilized in other Far Eastern countries or could contribute in this way to the basic recovery of the Far East.

8. Note from the US Secretary of State to the Ambassador of the Soviet Union in reply to latter's note of 3 January 1948, 1 April 1948 (Extracts).

On October 28, 1947, in a memorandum for the Soviet Member of the Allied Council for Japan, the Supreme Commander for the Allied Powers referred to the fact that one hundred and thirty-five vessels had already been divided (among the four powers) and stated that: "It is not contemplated that

further deliveries of these vessels can be made for a considerable period or months in view of the present employment of the
remaining vessels in occupation duties and other tasks required
in implementation of the Japanese surrender. The Soviet
Member, Allied Council for Japan, will be advised sufficiently
in advance of any future division to allow for designation of
representatives to participate in the inspection and drawing."
A similar communication was addressed to the Chiefs of the
United Kingdom and Chinese Missions in Japan.

It is the view of the United States Government that the
action of the Supreme Commander for the Allied Powers in
deferring the final disposition of these vessels neither contradicts nor violates the agreement of the four powers in October
1945 regarding the disposition of combatant vessels of the former Japanese Navy.

**9. Memorandum by the US Assistant Secretary of State for
Economic Affairs (Thorp) to Director of the Office of Far
Eastern Affairs (Butterworth) on Japanese reparations, 6
April 1948 (Extracts).**

Whether or not to have reparations is essentially a political
problem, the form which they are to take is an economic one.
A decision to reduce reparations will have major political re-
percussions. All Far Eastern countries feel deeply that simple
justice requires that Japan make reparation in some form. They
have also associated intimately in their minds the reparations
and security problems. The objections which General Mac-
Arthur raises to remilitarization of Japan are objections which
they would level against Mr. Kennan's views on reparations.
The ERP countries with colonies in Asia, notably the U.K. and
France, have found it necessary to consider the prestige as well
as the economic implications of demands upon them for
Japanese industrial reparations which have arisen in their
colonies. As a country which built up its plant during the
War, it is difficult for us to understand the pressures from
other countries for reparations but it is a strong political
fact.

These political considerations which would justify standing
on present policy may not outweigh others which justify its

abandonment. We should be aware, however, of what is involved in adopting Mr. Kennan's recommendation. The FEC would not agree to a reparations program going no further than—and perhaps not as far as—the existing 30% project. The U.S. Government could not take unilateral action without exciting the deepest resentment and inviting the antagonism of the FEC countries. They would certainly regard such a move as violating both existing international reparations commitments and the terms of reference of the Commission; they might regard it as requiring break-up of the Commission itself. . . .

If one assumes that reparations are politically necessary, the present 30% plan cannot be regarded as a solution since it relates to only four countries. There may be room for some adjustment, but the present program is probably, from an economic point of view, as good as any. I am not convinced either that it imposes a heavy burden on the Japanese economy or that it will seriously hamper recovery. No reparation formula can meet the tests suggested by Mr. Kennan—it necessarily constitutes a loss and cost to the paying country. However, it seems to me that the form of reparations is a less crucial problem than the more fundamental one of the attitude of the other countries on this matter, and our commitments to them. It is obvious that the U.S. interest and approach differs from that of other countries, just as it did in the negotiations of the Paris peace treaties.

Most important of all, it is urgent that some definite and final settlement of the reparations problem be reached promptly. Further delay, review, or restudy of details would reflect a type of vacillation which is more damaging to Japan than almost any kind of concrete program, not to mention the damage it does to the standing and purposes of the U.S. in the rest of the world.

10. Note from the US Secretary of State to the French Ambassador (Bonnet) in reply to French Note of 21 May 1948, 26 July 1948.

The United States Government named China, the Netherlands, the Philippines and the United Kingdom as beneficiaries

of the so-called Advance Transfer Program, which the United
States Government initiated in April 1947, because these four
countries had been at war with Japan at least for as long as the
period from December 7, 1941 to September 2, 1945, because
their territories were occupied by Japanese armed forces and
because, within their powers, these countries fought continuo-
usly against the Japanese during periods of occupation. The
United States Government regarded these qualifications as
justifying the giving of special consideration to the reparations
claims of these four countries, and hoped that issuance of an
interim directive on this urgent matter would stimulate the Far
Eastern Commission to agree upon a comprehensive and final
reparations program in Japan. Since the reparations percentage
shares assigned to the four designated countries were clearly
beyond challenge by any other Far Eastern Commission members and the assigned shares applied to no more than a total of
30 per cent of the industrial facilities declared available
for removal in the Far Eastern Commission policy decisions embodied in the Interim Removals Program, it was believed that the interests of all reparations claimants were in the
meanwhile safeguarded. The interests of other reparations
claimants were also protected by the requirement that the four
designated countries could lodge claims for particular facilities
only if they could provide evidence that such facilities were
capable to immediate useful employment.

The United States Government is aware of the dissatisfaction of the Far Eastern countries including, as a matter of
fact, China, the Netherlands, the Philippines and the United
Kingdom, which results from the fact that the Far Eastern
Commission has not reached those decisions on reparations
shares and on availability of Japanese assets for removal as reparations which could be the basis for a comprehensive,
practical and final reparations program. This Government
hopes that at an early time the problem of Japanese reparations may be discussed with the French Government and other
governments concerned as a integral program, action upon
which will contribute both to the attainment of occupation
objectives in Japan and to the satisfaction of the just desires
of the Far Eastern countries which were at war with Japan.

This Government does not consider it appropriate at this

time to approach reparations problems on anything less than the comprehensive basis outlined above. It therefore seems unwise that additional governments, even though their territories may also have suffered directly from Japanese aggression and occupation, should be given individually the benefit to an emergency allotment as a result of any further action by the United States Government alone.

11. Report by the National Security Council on recommendations with respect to United States policy toward Japan, 7 October 1948 (approved by President on 5 November 1948) (Extracts).

1. *Timing and Procedure.* In view of the differences which have developed among the interested countries regarding the procedure and substance of a Japanese peace treaty and in view of the serious international situation created by the Soviet Union's policy of aggressive Communist expansion, this Government should not press for a treaty of peace at this time. It should remain prepared to proceed with the negotiations, under some generally acceptable voting procedure, if the Allied Powers can agree among themselves on such a procedure. We should, before actually entering into a peace conference, seek through the diplomatic channel the concurrence of a majority of the participating countries in the principal points of content we desire to have in such a treaty. Meanwhile, we should concentrate our attention on the preparation of the Japanese for the eventual removal of the regime of control.

2. *The Nature of the Treaty.* It should be our aim to have the treaty, when finally negotiated, as brief, as general, and as nonpunitive as possible. . . .

3. *The Pre-Treaty Arrangements.* Every effort, consistent with the proper performance of the occupational mission as envisaged in this policy paper and with military security and morale, should be made to reduce to a minimum the psychological impact of the presence of occupational forces on the Japanese population. The numbers of tactical, and especially non-tactical, forces should be minimized. In determining the location of occupation forces, their employment, and support from the Japanese economy in the pre-treaty period, full weight should be given to the foregoing.

4. *The Post-Treaty Arrangements*. United States tactical forces should be retained in Japan until the entrance into effect of a peace treaty. A final U.S. position concerning the post-treaty arrangements for Japanese military security should not be formulated until the peace negotiations are upon us. It should then be formulated in the light of the prevailing international situation and of the degree of internal stability achieved in Japan.

5. *The Ryukyu, Nanpo and Marcus Islands*. The United States should make up its mind at this point that it intends to retain on a long-term basis the facilities of Okinawa *and such other facilities as are deemed by the Joint Chiefs of Staff to be necessary in the Ryukyu Islands south of 29 degree N., Marcus Island and the Nanpo Shoto south of Sofu Gan. The base on Okinawa should be developed accordingly*. The United States agencies responsible for administering the *above-mentioned* islands should promptly formulate and carry out a program on a long-term basis for the economic and social well-being and, to the extent practicable, for the eventual self-support of the natives. At the proper time, international sanction should be obtained by the means then most feasible for United States longterm strategic control of the Ryukyu Island south of latitude 29 degrees N., *Marcus Islands and the Nanpo Shoto south of Sofa Gan*.

6. *Naval Bases*. The United States Navy should shape its policy in the development of the Yokosuka base in such a way as to favour the retention on a commercial basis in the post-treaty period of as many as possible of the facilities it now enjoys there. Meanwhile, it should proceed to develop the possibilities of Okinawa as a naval base, on the assumption that we will remain in control there on a long-term basis. This policy does not preclude the retention of a naval base as such at Yokosuka if, at the time of finalizing the U.S. position concerning the post-treaty arrangements for Japanese military security, the prevailing international situation makes such action desirable and if it is consistent with U.S. political objectives.

7. *The Japanese Police Establishment*. The Japanese Police establishment, including the coastal patrol, should be strengthened by the re-enforcing and re-equipping of the present forces, and by expanding the present centrally directed police organisation.

8. *Supreme Commander for the Allied Powers.* This Government should not at this time propose or consent to any major change in the regime of control. SCAP should accordingly be formally maintained in all its existing rights and powers. However, responsibility should be placed to a steadily increasing degree in the hands of the Japanese Government. To this end the view of the United States Government should be communicated to SCAP that the scope of its operations should be reduced as rapidly as possible, with a corresponding reduction in personnel, to a point where its mission will consist largely of general supervisory observation of the activities of the Japanese Government and of contact with the latter at high levels on questions of broad governmental policy. . . .

13. *The Purge.* Since the purpose of the purge has been largely accomplished, the U.S. now should advise SCAP to inform the Japanese Government informally that no further extension of the purge is contemplated and that the purge should be modified along the following lines : (1) Categories of persons who have been purged or who are subject to the purge by virtue of their having held relatively harmless positions should be made re-eligible for governmental, business and public media positions; (2) certain others who have been barred or who are subject to being barred from public life on the basis of positions occupied should be allowed to have their cases re-examined solely on the basis of personal actions; and (3) a minimum age limit should be fixed, under which no screening for public office would be required.

14. *Occupation Costs.* The occupational costs borne by the Japanese Government should continue to be reduced to the maximum extent consonant with the policy objectives of the pre-treaty period as envisaged in this paper.

15. *Economic Recovery.* Second only to U.S. Security interests, economic recovery should be made the primary objective of United States policy in Japan for the coming period. . .

18. *War Crime Trials.* The trial of Class A suspects is completed and decision of the court is awaited. We should continue and push to an early conclusion and screening of all "B" and "C" suspects with a view to releasing those whose cases we do not intend to prosecute. Trials of the others should be instituted and concluded at the earliest possible date.

19. *Control of Japanese Economic War Potential.* Production in, importation into, and use within Japan of goods and economic services for bonafide peaceful purposes should be permitted without limitation, except;

a. Japan's economic war potential should be controlled by restrictions on allowable stockpiling of designated strategic raw materials in Japan.

b. Japan's industrial disarmament should be limited to the prohibition of the manufacture of weapons of war and civil aircraft and the minimum of temporary restrictions on industrial production which can be advocated in the light of commitments already made by the United States regarding the reduction of the industrial war potential

12. Memorandum of the US Assistant Secretary of State for Occupied Areas (Saltzman), 10 November 1948 (Extract).

In addressing itself to the problem of how much industrial capacity should be removed from Japan as reparations, the Departments of State and Army have adhered to the principle that this Government should not agree to the removal of an amount of industrial capacity which would obstruct the recovery of Japanese economy as soon as practicable to a point where a reasonable degree of self-support will be achieved. I pointed out that there are two very important reasons why such a degree of self-support must be realized as soon as possible : (1) Without such self-support Japan cannot survive as an independent democratic nation and will fall prey to communism or some form of totalitarian government with resultant trouble for the United States and other nations of the world; and (2) self-support must be gained as soon as possible in order that the present huge expense of the United States, now in order of a total of approximately one billion dollars a year may be reduced and eliminated. These principles apply to our policy in regard to the removal for reparations of Japanese shipbuilding capacity and it is our view that not more than approximately 300,000 tons of annual shipbuilding capacity out of the present total of approximately 800,000 tons should be permitted to be removed from Japan, lest the effect of further removals impede the necessary Japanese economic recovery as described above.

13. United States Memorandum to the Governments on the Far Eastern Commission, 26 October 1950 (Released to the Press on 24 November 1950).

There is given below a brief general statement of the type of Treaty envisioned by the United States Government as proper to end the state of war with Japan. It is stressed that this statement is only suggestive and tentative and does not commit the United States Government to the detailed content or wording of any future draft. It is expected that after there has been an opportunity to study this outline there will be a series of informal discussions designed to elaborate on it and make clear any points which may be obscure at first glance.

The United States proposes a treaty with Japan which would end the state of war, restore Japanese sovereignty and bring back Japan as an equal in the society of free peoples. As regards specific matters, the treaty would reflect the principles indicated below :

1. *Parties.* Any or all nations at war with Japan which are willing to make peace on the basis proposed and as may be agreed.

2. *United Nations.* Membership by Japan would be contemplated.

3. *Territory.* Japan would (a) recognize the independence of Korea; (b) agree to U.N. trusteeship with the U.S. as administering authority, of the Ryukyu and Bonin Islands and (c) accept the future decision of the U.K., U.S.S.R., China and U.S. with reference to the status of Formosa, Pescadores, South Sakhalin and the Kuriles. In the event of no decision within a year after the Treaty came into effect, the U.N. General Assembly would decide. Special rights and interests in China would be renounced.

4. *Security.* The Treaty would contemplate that, pending satisfactory alternative security arrangements such as U.N. assumption of effective responsibility, there would be continuing cooperative responsibility between Japanese facilities and U.S. and perhaps other forces for the maintenance of international peace and security in the Japan area.

5. *Political and Commercial Arrangements.* Japan would agree to adhere to multilateral treaties dealing with narcotics

and fishing. Pre-war bilateral treaties could be revived by
mutual agreement. Pending the conclusion of new commercial
treaties, Japan would extend most-favoured-nation treatment,
subject to normal exceptions.

6. *Claims.* All parties would waive claims arising out of
war acts prior to September 2, 1945, except that (a) the Allied
Powers would, in general, hold Japanese property within their
territory and (b) Japan would restore allied property or, if not
restorable intact, provide yen to compensate for an agreed percentage of lost value.

7. *Disputes.* Claims disputes would be settled by a special
neutral tribunal to be set up by the President of the International Court of Justice. Other disputes would be referred
either to diplomatic settlement, or to the International Court of
Justice.

14. US Reply to Soviet Notes of 20 November 1950, 28 December 1950 (Extracts).

1. The United States Government hopes that all nations
at war with Japan will participate in the conclusion of peace.
The United States does not, however, concede that any one
nation has a perpetual power to veto the conclusion by others
of peace with Japan.

2. The Cairo Declaration of 1943 stated the purpose to
restore 'Manchuria, Formosa and the Pescadores to the Republic of China.' That Declaration, like other wartime declarations such as those of Yalta and Potsdam, was in the opinion
of the United States Government subject to any final peace
settlement where all relevant factors should be considered. The
United States cannot accept the view, apparently put forward
by the Soviet Government, that the views of other Allies not
represented at Cairo must be wholly ignored. Also the United
States believes that declarations such as that issued at Cairo
must necessarily be considered in the light of the United Nations
Charter, the obligations of which prevail over any other international agreement.

3. The United States Government does not understand the
reference by the Soviet Union to "territorial expansion" in
connection with the suggestion that the Ryukyu and Bonin

Islands might be placed under the United Nations trusteeship system, with the United States as administering authority. Article 77 of the United Nations Charter expressly contemplated the extension of the trusteeship system to "territories which may be detached from enemy state as a result of the Second World War" and certainly the trusteeship system is not to be equated with "territorial expansion."

The Government of the United States also does not understand the suggestion of the Soviet Union that because the Ryukyu and Bonin Islands are not mentioned in either the Cairo Declaration or the Potsdam Agreement, their consideration in the peace settlement is automatically excluded. The Government of the Soviet Union seems to have ignored the fact that the Potsdam Declaration provided that Japanese sovereignty should be limited to the four main islands, which were named, and "such minor islands as we determine." It is, therefore, strictly in accordance with the Potsdam Agreement that the peace settlement should determine the future status of these other islands.

4. It is the view of the United States Government that, upon conclusion of a peace settlement, the military occupation of Japan would cease. The fact that a "new order of peace, security, and justice," as envisaged in the Potsdam Declaration, has not been established, and that irresponsible militarism has not been driven from the world, would at the same time make it reasonable for Japan to participate with the United States and other nations in arrangements for individual and collective self-defence, such as are envisaged by the United Nations Charter and particularly Article 51 thereof. These arrangements could include provisions for the stationing in Japan of troops of the United States and other nation. . . .

6. The United States considers that the Japanese peace treaty should not limit the Japanese peacetime economy nor deny Japan access to sources of raw material or participation in world trade.

15. Address by Dulles on his trip to the Far East made over the Columbia Broadcasting System, 1 March 1951 (Extracts).

In the still free area, that communism has not conquered,

Japan occupies a key position. Japan's industrial potential is great and unique in that part of the world. That fact, of course, increases the danger, for Japan's industrial capacity is something that Russia covets. If Japan should succumb to communist aggression, there would be a combination of Russian, Japanese and Chinese power in the East which would be dangerously formidable. Therefore, the free nations face the task of turning what was an enemy into a dependable friend and uniting separate and discordant elements into a harmonious whole. That is not easy. But our mission now feels confident that it can be done. . . .

In the Philippines we found much concern with the problem of reparations. The Philippines had gravely suffered from its cruel invasion and occupation by Japan. Although much has been rebuilt, there are signs of devastation on every hand, and almost every family has had one or more members killed by the Japanese. It is only natural that there should be bitterness and a demand for at least material reparation. The amount sought reached $8,000,000,000. The mood is like that of the French at the end of World War I.

We sympathized totally with the Philippines sentiment. We had no argument to make against the justice of reparation claims. We had to point out, however, that reparation is not merely a matter of justice, it is a matter of economics.

The fact is that a nation situated as is Japan can barely pay for its essential imports in food and raw materials. To require reparation payments means either that the United States must pay the reparation bill or there will be default preceded by widespread starvation and unemployment. This would assure the conquest of Japan by communism and not be in the real interest of the Philippines.

The peoples of Australia and New Zealand did not like to contemplate a future where they might stand alone against a Japan which might be rearmed in collusion with Russia and communist China. Public opinion favoured a peace treaty which would prescribe severe limits on any future Japanese rearmament.

This attitude, like the Philippines demand for reparations, was quite understandable. Again, it corresponded with the mood of the French after World War I. We pointed out, however, that the Versailles Treaty experience indicates the surest way to induce rearmament is to forbid it. Treaty restrictions of that kind are inherently unenforceable except by war, and they are discriminatory because they do not reflect a general program of disarmament. Therefore, they seem to be a challenge to a nation's dignity and stature.

16. American Draft of Japanese Peace Treaty, 29 March 1951.

WASHINGTON ? Apr. 5—(UP). The Japanese peace treaty prepared by Special Presidential Representative John Foster Dulles "will come into force" when the United States and six other members of the 13-nation Far Eastern Commission have signed it.

This was revealed Thursday in an official copy of the treaty text secured by the United Press which also disclosed the United States will insist that any post-treaty reductions of the sentences of convicted Japanese war criminals must have the approval of the majority of the Allied Powers.

Here is the text of the proposed treaty which Dulles has given to the 15 other countries most actively engaged in the Pacific war.

Preamble—The Allied Powers and Japan are resolved that hence-forth their relations shall be those of nations; which as sovereign equals shall cooperate in a friendly association to promote their common welfare and maintain international peace and security.

Japan declares its intention to apply for membership in the United Nations and under all circumstances to conform to the principles of the Charter of the United Nations, to strive to realize the objectives of the United Nations' Universal Declaration of Human rights, to create internationally conditions of stability and well being as envisaged by Articles 55 and 56 of the Charter of the United Nations and already initiated by postwar Japanese legislation, and in public and private trade and commerce to conform to internationally accepted fair practices.

The Allied Powers welcome the intentions of Japan in these respects and will seek to facilitate their realization.

In order to put their future relations on a stable and peaceful basis, the Allied Powers make this treaty with Japan :

Chapter I. Peace. The state of war between the Allied

Powers and Japan is ended.

Chapter II. Sovereignty. The Allied Powers recognize the full sovereignty of the Japanese people over Japan and its territorial waters.

Chapter III. Territory. Japan renounces all rights, titles and claims to Korea, Formosa, and the Pescadores and also all rights, titles and claims in connection with the mandate system or deriving from the activities of Japanese nationals in the Antarctic area. Japan accepts the action of the United Nations Security Council of April 2, 1947, in relation to extending the trusteeship system to the Pacific islands formerly under mandate to Japan. The United States may propose to the United Nations to place under its trusteeship system with the United States as the administering authority the Ryukyu Islands south of 29 degrees north latitude, the Bonin Islands including Rossario Island, the Volcano Islands, Parce Vela and Marcus Island.

Japan will concur in any such proposal. Pending the making of such a proposal and affirmative action thereunder, the United States will have the right to exercise all and any powers of administration, legislation and jurisdiction over the territory and inhabitants of these islands, including their territorial waters.

Japan will return to the U.S.S.R. the southern part of Sakhalin Island as well as all islands adjacent to it and will hand over to the Soviet Union the Kurile Islands.

Chapter IV. Security. Japan accepts the obligations set forth in Article two of the Charter of the United Nations and, in particular, obligations......to settle its international disputes by peaceful means in such a manner that international peace, security and justice are not endangered; to refrain in its international relations from threat or the use of force against the territorial integrity or political independence of any state or in any manner inconsistent with the purposes of the United Nations; to give the United Nations every assistance in any action it takes in accordance with the Charter and to refrain from giving assistance to any state against which the United Nations make a preventive or enforcement action.

The Allied Powers undertake reciprocally to be guided by the principles of Article II of the Charter of the United Nations in their relations with Japan.

The Allied Powers recognize that Japan as a sovereign nation possesses what the Charter of the United Nations refers to as inherent right of individual or collective self-defence and Japan may voluntarily enter into collective security arrangement or arrangements participated in by one or more of the Allied Powers. Such arrangements shall be designed solely for security against armed attack.

(The foregoing suggestions are recognized as being not in themselves complete in respect to security and are to be supplemented in the light of the outcome of current exchange of views designed to maintain security in the Pacific and enable Japan hereafter to contribute to its security without developing the arrangement which could be an offensive threat or serve other than to promote peace and security in accordance with the purposes and principles of the United Nations.)

Chapter V. Political and Economic Clauses. Japan will continue to be a party or if not now a party will seek adherence to existing multilateral treaties and agreements designed to promote fair trade practices, prevent misuse of narcotics and conserve fish and wild life.

Japan agrees to enter promptly into negotiations with parties so desiring for formulation of new bilateral or multilateral agreements for regulation, conservation and development of high seas fisheries

Each of the Allied Powers within a year after the present treaty has come into force between it and Japan will notify Japan which of its pre-war bilateral treaties with Japan it wishes to keep in force or revise and such treaties shall continue in force or be revised except for any provisions thereof not in conformity with the present treaty, which provision shall be deleted. All such treaties not so notified shall be regarded as abrogated.

Japan renounces all special rights and interests in China.

Power to grant clemency, reduce sentences, parole and pardon with respect to war crimes sentences imposed by military tribunals of the Allied Powers on persons who are incarcerated in Japan, may not be exercised except jointly by Japan and the government or governments which imposed the sentence in each instance.

In the case of those persons sentenced by the International Military Tribunal for the Far East, such power may not be exercised except jointly by Japan and the majority of governments represented in the tribunal.

Japan declares its readiness promptly to conclude with each of the Allied Powers treaties or agreements to put on a stable and friendly basis commercial and trading relations between them.

In the meantime, the Government of Japan will, during the period of three years from the first coming into force of the present treaty, accord the most-favoured nation treatment to each of the Allied Powers with respect to customs, duties, charges and all other regulations imposed on or in connection with importation or exportation of foods and will accord national treatment or the most-favoured nation treatment, whichever is most favourable, with respect to vessels, nationals and companies of the Allied Powers and their property, interests and business within Japan. National treatment shall not be deemed to include Japanese coastal and inland navigation.

In respect of any of the above matters, the Government of Japan may withhold from any power application of more favourable treatment than such power, subject to exceptions customarily included in commercial agreements, is prepared to accord Japan in that respect.

Notwithstanding the provisions of the first paragraph of this article, the Government of Japan will be entitled to apply measures to safeguard its external financial position and balance of payments or its essential security interests and to reserve exceptions customarily contained in commercial agreements.

Pending conclusion of civil air agreements, Japan during a period of three years, shall extend to each of the Allied Powers not less favourable civil air traffic rights and privileges than those they exercise at the time of coming into force of the present treaty.

Japanese submarine cables connecting Japan with territory removed from Japanese control pursuant to the present treaty shall equally be divided. . . . Japan retaining the Japanese terminal and adjoining half of the cable and the detached territory the remainder of the cable and connecting terminal facilities.

Chapter VI. Claims and Property. The Allied Powers recognize Japan lacks the capacity to make payments in bullion money, property or services which would enable Japan to maintain a viable economy to meet its obligations for relief and economic assistance furnished since September 2, 1945 in furtherance of the objectives of the occupation and also make adequate reparations to the Allied Powers for war damages.

However, Japan grants to each of the Allied Powers the rights to vest, retain and dispose of all property rights and interests of Japan and Japanese nationals which between December 7, 1941 and September 2, 1945 were within territories renounced by Japan or within territories administered by any of them under trusteeship except,

1. Property of Japanese nationals permitted to reside in territory of one of the Allied Powers and not subjected to special measures before September 2, 1945.

2. Tangible diplomatic or consular property, net of any expenses incidental to its preservation.

3. Property of non-political, religious, charitable; cultural or educational institutions.

4. Property located in Japan despite the presence elsewhere of paper or similar evidence of the right to title or interest in such property or any debt claimed with respect thereto.

5. Trademarks identifying products originating in Japan.

In the case of any Allied Power which has taken property rights or interest of any industrial character of Japan or Japanese nationals from the territory of another Allied Power, it will account to the other.

Reparations claims of Allied Powers and their claims for direct military costs of the occupation shall be deemed satisfied out of Japanese assets, subject to their respective jurisdictions in accord with the foregoing and out of assets received from the Japanese home islands during the occupation.

(Note : The foregoing suggestions regarding reparations are made subject to current exchanges of views).

Japan will return upon demand within six months from the first coming into force of treaty, property, tangible and intangible, and all rights and interests of any kind in Japan of each Allied Power and its nationals unless the owner has freely disposed thereof without duress or fraud.

In the case of war loss or damage to property of nationals of Allied Powers in Japan, compensation will be made in accordance with Japanese domestic legislation in yen, subject to Japanese foreign exchange regulations.

Japan waives all claims of Japan and its nationals against the Allied Powers for action taken during the state of war, hereby ended, and waives all claims arising from the presence, operations or actions of forces of authorities of any of the Allied Powers in Japanese territory prior to coming into force of the present treaty.

Chapter VII. Settlement of Disputes. Any dispute between an Allied Power and Japan concerning interpretation of execution of the present treaty, which is not settled through diplomatic channels, shall, at the request of the party to the dispute, be referred for decision to the International Court of Justice.

Japan and those Allied Powers which are not already parties to the Statute of the International Court, will deposit with the registrar of the court, at the time of their respective ratification of the present treaty and in conformity with the resolution of the Security Council dated October 15, 1946, a general declaration accepting jurisdiction without special agreement of the court generally in respect of all disputes of character referred to in this article.

Chapter VIII. Final Clauses. The Allied Powers for purposes of the present treaty shall be deemed to be those states at war or in a state of belligerency with Japan and which becomes parties to the present treaty.

Except for provisions of Article XI (note : fourth paragraph of Chapter V referring to China), the present treaty shall not confer any rights, title or benefits to or upon any state unless and until it signs, ratifies or adheres to this treaty nor with that exception shall any right, title or interest of Japan be deemed to be diminished or prejudiced hereof in favour of the state which does not sign and ratify or adhere to this treaty.

Japan will not make a peace settlement or war claims settlement with any state which would grant that state greater advantage than contemplated by the present treaty to be granted to parties thereto.

The present treaty shall be ratified by the Allied Powers and by Japan and will come into force as between Japan and other ratifying states when the instruments of ratification by Japan and by the majority, including the United States of America as the principal occupying power, of the states which are members of the Far Eastern Commission, have been deposited with the Government of the United States of America.

If such coming into force has not occurred within nine months after ratification by Japan, then any Allied Power may at its election bring the treaty into force as between itself and Japan by notification to Japan and to the Government of the United States of America.

The Government of the United States of America shall notify all signatory and adhering states of all ratifications deposited and of all notifications received pursuant to this article.

Any state not a signatory to the present treaty which is at war or in a state of belligerency with Japan may adhere to the present treaty at any time within three years after the treaty has come into force as between Japan and any ratifying state.

Adherence shall be effective by deposit of instrument of adherence with the Government of the United States of America which shall notify all signatory and adhering states of each deposit.

17. Address by John Foster Dulles at the Whittier College, Whittier, California, 31 March 1951 (Extracts).

Two principal postwar goals of the Soviet Communists are Japan and Germany. If Russians rulers could exploit the industrial and human potential of either Japan or Germany, it would be a sad day for peace. That would involve such a shift in the balance of world power that these new imperialists might calculate that they could start a general war with good prospect of success. They know that Japan, even alone, was able seriously to menace the free world in the Pacific and they imagine vast possibilities out of a combination, under their direction, of the Asiatic Power of Russia, China and Japan. . . .

The South Sakhalin and Kurile Islands were allotted to Russia at Yalta and are actually in Russian possession. Any peace-treaty validation of Russia's title should, we suggest, be dependent upon Russia's becoming a party to that treaty. . . .

If the Japanese wanted it, the United States would sympathetically consider the retention of United States armed forces in and about Japan, so that the coming into force of a treaty of peace would not leave Japan a vacuum of power and, as such, an easy prey to such aggression as has already shown itself in nearby Korea. . . .

As regards reparations, the United States does not question the inherent justice of the proposition that Japan should make good the damage to others by its aggression. Reparation is, however, not merely a matter of what is just but of what is economically practicable, without disastrous consequences. We have closely examined this problem. Considerable industrial machinery has already been removed from Japan and given to countries having reparation claims. Also there is substantial Japanese property within allied countries which, as indicated, should be applicable to the satisfaction of claims. It is, however, not easy to see the possibility of Japan's providing future reparation out of her remaining capital assets or as a surplus from her current economic activity over coming years.

One of the gravest problems which confront Japan, and it equally concerns the reparation creditors, is whether Japan, deprived of its formerly owned sources of raw materials and with a population of 85 million on four relatively small and barren islands, can maintain the standard of living and employment necessary to prevent widespread social unrest. This, if it occurred, would inevitably give rise to dangerous expansionist and explosive tendencies, which Japan's Communist neighbours would joyously exploit.

The United States, to prevent social and economic unrest within Japan since the occupation began, has advanced about 2 billion dollars for relief and economic assistance. That is a realistic measure of how seriously the United States views this problem and its responsibility as principal occupying power. However, the United States is not prepared after the occupation ends to continue indefinitely such economic relief. Neither is it willing in effect to pay Japanese reparations by putting into Japan what reparation creditors would take out. The United States considers indeed that its postwar advances have a certain priority status.

We doubt that it is practicable to get the essential over-all and long-range results which are sought, if the treaty also seeks to extract reparation payments other than in terms of the Japanese assets already received from Japan or within the territory of the Allied Powers. However, the United States has not closed its mind on this subject, and it is, with an open mind, actively exchanging views with countries which were most grievously damaged by Japanese aggression.

18. US Memorandum in answer to Remarks of the Soviet Government dated 7 May 1951, 19 May 1951 (Extracts).

The Potsdam Agreement (2 August 1945) between the Government of the Soviet Union, the United Kingdom and the United States did not mention the Japanese Peace Treaty. This was natural, for the war with Japan was then in full vigour and the Soviet Union was then neutral in that war.

The Council of Foreign Ministers can, of course, deal with "other matters" than the European matters specified, but only "by agreement between the Member Governments."

The United States has not agreed and does not agree to the reference to the Council of Foreign Ministers of the matter of making a Japanese peace treaty. The reason, among others, is that the systematic misuse in the Council of veto power militates against the speedy achievement, through the Council, of an early peace treaty. Furthermore, the procedures of the Council would give a secondary role to Allied Powers which bore a greater burden of the Pacific war than did the Soviet Union.

The Government of the Soviet Union urges that the Peace-making procedure should fully take account of the interests of China in a Japanese peace treaty. The procedure being presently followed does that. It is true that the United States does not seek guidance from a convicted aggressor, but the real interests of China are fully reflected in the present draft treaty. . . .

The Government of the United States notes that the remarks of the Soviet Government fail to quote accurately the Cairo Declaration. The word "Manchuria" is deleted and "China" is substituted for "the Republic of China." . . . .

The Government of the Soviet Union criticizes the provision that the Ryukyu, Bonin, and certain other islands may be placed under United Nations trusteeship with the United States as administering authority. . . .

Since, however, the Surrender Terms provided, ... that Japanese sovereignty should be limited to the four main islands and such minor islands as may be determined, it is consonant with the Surrender Terms for the Allied Powers by treaty of peace with Japan to deal with Japanese islands other than the four main islands, mentioned. . . .

(b) As to demilitarization . . . . the United States Government is satisfied that "Japan's war-making power is destroyed." Apparently the Soviet Government shares that conviction, since it says that the occupation of Japan has "impermissibly dragged on." Furthermore, the United States, so far as it is concerned, has in fact completely disarmed the Japanese military forces under its control and has assured that they now lead peaceful and productive lives. . . .

The United States Government is not disposed to rely upon the dependability of treaty limitations on armament such as were imposed upon Rumania, Bulgaria and Hungary by the Treaties of Peace and which limitations already are being grossly exceeded. . . .

As to ending the Occupation, the Soviet Government alleges that the present draft does not establish any period for the withdrawal of occupation troops from Japan. On the contrary, under the draft treaty, the occupation would cease upon the coming into force of the treaty. If, after the treaty comes into force, any allied troops are in Japan they will not be there as occupation troops but pursuant to such collective security arrangement as Japan may make voluntarily. Such arrangement would carry no offensive threat. . . .

The assistance which the Japanese in fact are rendering to the United Nations action in Korea is within the demilitarization limits established by Far Eastern Commission decisions, is non-belligerent in character, and is in accord with the Charter and recommendation of the United Nations. . . .

As to Japan's peacetime economy, the Soviet Government alleges that the draft treaty "ignores the necessity of removing limitations with respect to the free development of the peaceful economy of Japan." In reality, the draft treaty, by restoring to Japan complete sovereignty without any limitation upon the development of its peaceful economy and without imposing burdensome current reparation liabilities, would accomplish completely the result which the Government of the Soviet Union professes to desire. . . .

To define "the size of Japanese armed forces" needed for "requirements of self-defense" as the Government of the Soviet Union now proposes, would not only be difficult, but might be dangerous. Japanese land, sea, and air forces adequate for self-defense under present troubled circumstances might also, under other circumstances, be adequate for offense.

It is the hope and expectation of the United States Government that application of the policy of collective security envisaged by Article 7 of the draft treaty will provide Japan with effective security with much less Japanese armament than would be required if the Treaty reflected the policy of "let each country defend itself." . . .

It is the view of the Government of the United States that Japan should not enter into any coalition directed against *any* state, whether or not it was a belligerent in the war against Japan. This is provided for by Article 6 of the draft Treaty whereby Japan would agree, in accordance with Article 2 of the Charter of the United Nations, to refrain from the threat or use of force against the territorial integrity or political independence of any state. . . . .

19. US Memorandum in Reply to Soviet Memorandum of 10 June 1951, 9 July 1951 (Extracts).

The Government of the Soviet Union would have the peace treaty deny to Japan the right hereafter to enter into collective security arrangements with other countries of its choosing. This is a viewpoint which the Government of the United States cannot accept.

Section 2 of the Soviet memorandum dealt with procedure. It again "insists on observance of the Potsdam Agreement" which, according to the Government of the Soviet Union, means that "preparation of a peace treaty with Japan is placed upon four countries—the United States of America, U.S.S.R., Great Britain, and China" constituting the Council of Foreign Ministers.

This would commit the preparation of the treaty to the veto-bound processes of that Council and would exclude from the preparatory work France and many Pacific and Asiatic countries which bore a far heavier burden in the Japanese war than did the Soviet Union. . . .

In the concluding Section 3 of its memorandum of June 10, 1951, the Soviet Government says that the "peace treaty with Japan should be multilateral and not separate" both as to preparation and as to signing.

The July 3, 1951, draft reflects the operation of those very principles. Many interested nations have participated in its preparation. The fact that they have done so through diplomatic channels makes their participation no less real than if they had participated in some other manner. The terms of the treaty would recognize and protect equally the legitimate interests of each and every state which took part in the Japanese war. At the same time the terms embody not merely the formality of peace, but the spirit of peace. The Government of the Soviet Union will further observe that, as it desire, the text is prepared as a multilateral instrument.

20. Anglo-American Draft of Japanese Peace Treaty, 3 July 1951 (Released to the Press on 12 July 1951) (Extracts)*.

Article 1

The state of war between Japan and each of the Allied Powers is hereby terminated as from the date on which the present Treaty comes into force between Japan and the Allied Powers concerned, as provided for in Article 23. . . .

Article 6

(a) All occupation forces of the Allied Powers shall be withdrawn from Japan as soon as possible after the coming into force of the present Treaty, and in any case not later than 90 days thereafter. Nothing in this provision shall however prevent the stationing or retention of foreign armed forces in

* Only those Articles, which were substantially modified in the Final Text (Document 24 below) approved at the San Francisco Conference, are given here.

Japanese territory under or in consequence of any bilateral or multilateral agreements which have been or may be made between one or more of the Allied Powers, on the one hand, and Japan on the other.

(b) All Japanese property for which compensation has not already been paid, which was supplied for the use of the occupation forces and which remains in the possession of those forces at the time of the coming into force of the present Treaty, shall be returned to the Japanese Government within the same 90 days unless other arrangements are made by mutual agreement.

CHAPTER V : CLAIMS AND PROPERTY

Article 14

(a) It is recognized that, although Japan should in principle pay reparation for the damage and suffering caused by it during the war, nevertheless Japan lacks the capacity, if it is to maintain a viable economy, to make adequate reparation to the Allied Powers and at the same time meet its other obligations.

However,

1. Japan will promptly enter into negotiations with Allied Powers so desiring, whose present territories were occupied by Japanese forces and damaged by Japan, with a view to assisting to compensate those countries for the cost of repairing the damage done, by making available the skills and industry of the Japanese people in manufacturing, salvaging and other services to be rendered to the Allied Powers in question. Such arrangements shall avoid the imposition of additional liabilities on other Allied Powers, and, where the manufacturing of raw materials is called for, they shall be supplied by the Allied Powers in question, so as not to throw any foreign exchange burden upon Japan.

2. (I) Each of the Allied Powers shall have the right to seize, retain, liquidate or otherwise dispose of all property, rights and interests of

(a) Japan and of Japanese nationals

(b) persons acting for or on behalf of Japan or Japanese nationals, and

(c) entities owned or controlled by Japan or Japanese nationals

which on the coming into force of the present Treaty were subject to its jurisdiction, except :

 (i) property of Japanese nationals who during the war resided with the permission of the Government concerned in the territory of one of the Allied Powers, other than territory occupied by Japan, except property subjected during that period to measures not generally applied by the Government of the territory where the property was situated to the property of other Japanese nationals resident in such territory;

 (ii) all real property, furniture and fixtures owned by the Government of Japan and used for diplomatic or consular purposes, and all personal furniture and furnishings and other private property not of an investment nature which was normally necessary for the carrying out of diplomatic and consular functions, owned by Japanese diplomatic and consular personnel;

 (iii) property belonging to religious bodies or private charitable institutions and used exclusively for religious or charitable purposes;

 (iv) property rights arising after the resumption of trade and financial relations between the country concerned and Japan before the coming into force of the present Treaty, except in the case of any rights resulting from transactions contrary to the laws of the Allied Power concerned;

 (v) obligations of Japan or Japanese nationals, any right, title or interest in tangible property located in Japan, interests in enterprises organized under the laws of Japan, or any paper evidence thereof; provided that this exception shall only apply to obligations of Japan and its nationals expressed in Japanese currency.

(II) Property referred to in exceptions (i) to (v) above shall be returned subject to reasonable expenses for its preservation and administration. If any such property has been liquidated the proceeds shall be returned instead.

(III) The right to seize, retain, liquidate or otherwise dispose of Japanese property referred to above shall be exercised in accordance with the laws of the Allied Power concerned, and the Japanese owner shall have only such rights as may be given him by those laws.

(IV)   The Allied Powers agree to deal with Japanese trademarks and literary and artistic property rights on a basis as favorable to Japan as circumstances ruling in each country will permit.

(V)   Except as otherwise provided in the present Treaty, the Allied Powers waive all reparations claims of the Allied Powers, other claims of the Allied Powers and their nationals arising out of any actions taken by Japan and its nationals in the course of the prosecution of the war, and claims of the Allied Powers for direct military costs of occupation.

21.   Opening Address by President Truman at the San Francisco Conference, 4 September 1951 (Extracts).

The treaty we are gathered here to sign has not been drawn in a spirit of revenge.   The treaty reflects the spirit in which we carried on the war.

There were, of course, differences of opinion among the nations concerned as to many of the matters covered by this treaty.   The text of the treaty now before us is the product of long and patient negotiations, among many nations, which were undertaken to reconcile these differences.   I think it is fair to say that it is a good treaty.   It takes account of the principal desires and ultimate interests of all the participants. It is fair to both victor and vanquished.   But more than that, it is a treaty that will work.   It does not contain the seeds of another war.   It is a treaty of reconciliation, which look to the future, not the past.

The treaty re-establishes Japan as a sovereign, independent nation.   It provides for the restoration of Japanese trade with other nations, and it imposes no restrictions upon Japan's access to raw materials.   The treaty recognizes the principle that Japan should make reparations to the countries which suffered from its aggression.   But it does not saddle the Japanese people with a hopeless burden of reparations which would crush their economy in the years to come.

**22. Statement by John Foster Dulles made on behalf of US
delegation at the San Francisco Conference, 5 September
1951 (Extracts).**

The treaty before us is a step toward breaking the vicious
cycle of war—victory—peace—war. The nations will here
make a peace of justice, not a peace of vengeance. . . .

Every nation which has constructively interested itself in the
treaty can claim authorship of important parts of the present
text.   Also each of these nations can claim the equally honor-
able distinction of voluntarily subordinating some special
interest so that a broad base of unity might be found. The
Allied Powers have been conducting what in effect, is an 11
month's peace conference participated in by so many nations
as to make this treaty the most broadly based peace treaty in
all history. . . .

The treaty remains, as first agreed, a nonpunitive, nondis-
criminatory treaty, which will restore Japan to dignity, equality
and opportunity in the family of nations. But it has been
found increasingly possible to do justice to particular situations
without violating these basic concepts.

I now turn to a consideration of the principal provisions of
the text. . . .

Some question has been raised as to whether the geographical name "Kurile Islands" mentioned in article 2(c) includes
the Habomai Islands. It is the view of the United States that
it does not. If, however, there were a dispute about this, it
could be referred to the International Court of Justice under
article 22.

Some Allied Powers suggested that article 2 should not
merely delimit Japanese sovereignty according to Potsdam, but
specify precisely the ultimate disposition of each of the ex-
Japanese territories. This, admittedly, would have been neater.
But it would have raised questions as to which there are now
no agreed answers. We had either to give Japan peace on the
Potsdam Surrender Terms or deny peace to Japan while the
Allies quarrel about what shall be done with what Japan is
prepared, and required, to give up. Clearly, the wise course
was to proceed now, so far as Japan is concerned, leaving the
future to resolve doubts by invoking international solvents

other than this treaty.

Article 3 deals with the Ryukyus and other islands to the south and southeast of Japan. These, since the surrender, have been under the sole administration of the United States.

Several of the Allied Powers urged that the treaty should require Japan to renounce its sovereignty over these islands in favour of United States sovereignty. Others suggested that these islands should be restored completely to Japan.

In the face of this division of Allied opinion, the United States felt that the best formula would be to permit Japan to retain residual sovereignty, while making it possible for these islands to be brought into the U.N. trusteeship system, with the United States as administering authority. . . .

There can be nothing more sweeping than the renunciation of offensive force expressed in article 5(a) (ii) of the treaty. . . .

Article 6 of the treaty calls for ending the Occupation not later than 90 days after the treaty comes into force. However, Japan, as contemplated by article 51 of the U.N. Charter, may enter into collective security arrangements, and these might, in part, be implemented by Allied elements which were in Japan when the treaty came into force. Accordingly, it seemed useful to make it clear that, under such circumstances, these elements would not have to be physically removed from Japan before they could serve as collective security forces. This would be a burdensome requirement, and a risky one for it would for a time leave Japan wholly defenseless, in close proximity to proved aggressors possessed of great military strength. To avoid that danger, article 6 provides that Occupation elements now in Japanese territory may stay on for Japan's defense, if this is wanted by Japan.

These remaining military elements would, of course, have characteristics and powers very different from what they had as occupation forces. They would have only such status in Japan as Japan would voluntarily have given them.

The security provisions which we have reviewed are necessary if the treaty of peace is honestly to restore sovereignty to Japan. It has been suggested that the treaty ought to deny to Japan "the inherent right of collective self-defense" and permit only a token right of "individual self-defense."

That kind of a peace, in this present kind of a world,

would be a fraud. To give a sovereignty which cannot be defended, is to give an empty husk. Indefensible sovereignty is not sovereignty at all. An undefended and indefensible Japan would be so subject to the menace of surrounding power that Japan would not in fact be able to lead an independent existence.

It has been suggested that a collective security arrangement with the United States, such as Japan is considering, would not be a free act or what the Japanese people really want.

That is not a suggestion which will command credence here. Nearly two-thirds of the delegations here are from countries which either have, or are about to have, voluntary association in collective security arrangements which include the United States. These delegations will assume, and rightfully assume, that the Japanese people are like their own people, and like most free peoples, in wanting the collective security which may deter aggression. . . .

No person in this room, and I mean that literally, honestly believes that Japan seeks collective security with the United States because it is coerced. That is palpably absurd. . . .

If today we are compelled to think in terms of a treaty which will enable Japan to protect its sovereignty and independence it is not because we seek a re-militarized Japan—that we have done everything in our power to prevent—but because social and economic progress cannot be achieved in the cold climate of fear. . . .

Chapter IV deals with trade and commerce. The text is somewhat technical but the words add up to this; Japan is not subjected to any permanent discriminations and disabilities, her economy is unrestricted and no limitations whatever are placed upon her right to trade with each and every country. . . .

Reparations is usually the most controversial aspect of peace making. The present peace is no exception. . . .

On the one hand, there are claims both vast and just. Japan's aggression caused tremendous cost, losses, and suffering. Governments represented here have claims which total many billions of dollars and China could plausibly claim as much again. One hundred thousand million dollars would be a modest estimate of the whole.

On the other hand, to meet these claims, there stands a

Japan presently reduced to four home islands which are unable to produce the food its people need to live, or the raw materials they need to work. Since the surrender, Japan has been 2 billion dollars short of the money required to pay for the food and raw materials she had to import for survival on a minimum basis. The United States had made good that 2 billion dollar deficit. We accepted that as one of our occupation responsibilities. But the United States is entitled to look forward to Japan's becoming economically self-sustaining, so as to end dependence on us; and it is not disposed, directly or indirectly, to pay Japan's future reparations.

Under these circumstances, if the treaty validated, or kept contingently alive, monetary reparation claims against Japan, her ordinary commercial credit would vanish, the incentive of her people would be destroyed and they would sink into a misery of body and spirit which would make them an easy prey to exploitation. Totalitarian demagogues would surely rise up to promise relief through renewed aggression with the help of those nearby who, as we have seen in Korea, are already disposed to be the aggressors. The old menace would appear in aggravated form.

Such a treaty, while promoting unity among aggressors would promote disunity among many Allied Powers. There would be bitter competition for the largest possible percentage of an illusory pot of gold. Already, several countries have approached the United States with suggestions that their particular claims for reparation should be favored at the expense of others.

A treaty which, on the one hand, encouraged division among the nonaggression states and, on the other hand, brought recruits to the side of the aggressive states, would be a treaty which would recklessly squander the opportunity of victory. The parties to such a treaty would expose themselves to new perils greater than those which they have barely survived.

These conflicting considerations were fully discussed, until there emerged a solution which gives moral satisfaction to the claims of justice and which gives material satisfaction to the maximum extent compatible with political and economic health in the Pacific area.

The treaty recognizes, clearly and unambiguously, that

Japan *should* pay reparation to the Allied Powers for the damage and suffering caused by it during the war.

It then goes on to dedicate to the implementation of that principle, certain assets which Japan does have in surplus and which could be put to work to help to compensate those nations which suffered the most from Japan's wartime acts.

Japan has a population not now fully employed, and it has industrial capacity not now fully employed. Both of these aspects of unemployment are caused by lack of raw materials. These, however, are possessed in goodly measure by the countries which were overrun by Japan's armed aggression. If these war-devastated countries send to Japan the raw materials which many of them have in abundance, the Japanese could process them for the creditor countries and by these services, freely given, provide appreciable reparations. The arrangements could cover not merely consumers goods but machinery and capital goods which would enable underdeveloped countries to speed up developing their own industry, so as thereafter to lessen their dependence on outside industrial power.

This is, in essence, the formula expressed in article 14(a) 1. It results from prolonged exchanges of views, particularly with such countries as the Philippines and Indonesia, which were occupied by Japanese forces and injured in a way which places on the Allied Powers as a whole, and on Japan, a very clear duty to seek all means of reparation which are realistic.

I am frank to say that the treaty is a better, fairer treaty than first drafted. That results from the proper insistence of some governments that all possibilities of reparation should be exhaustively explored, That has been done, and the result is a fresh demonstration of the worth of the free processes of free and equal people. Those processes have here produced a treaty formula which serves the ideal of justice within an economic framework which can benefit all concerned.

In addition to this source of future reparation, the treaty validates the taking, by Allied Powers, of Japanese property within their jurisdictions.

By article 16, Japanese property in neutral and ex-enemy countries is to be transferred to the International Red Cross for the benefit of former prisoners of war and their families, on the basis of equity, to make some compensation for undue hardship suffered, often in violation of the Geneva conventions. The United States, in response to some Allied inquiries, has indicated that, since its own prisoners of war have received some indemnification out of proceeds of Japanese property we seized, we would assume that equity would require first distribution to those who have had no comparable indemnification.

Allied property within Japan is to be returned. Where this cannot be done, because of war damage, there will be compensation in blocked yen in accordance with pending Japanese domestic legislation. . . .

China. The absence of China from this conference is a matter of deep regret. Hostilities between Japan and China first began in 1931 and open warfare began in 1937. China suffered the longest and the deepest from Japanese aggression. It is greatly to be deplored that the Sino-Japanese War cannot be formally terminated at this occasion. Unhappily, civil war within China and the attitudes of the Allied Governments have created a situation such that there is not general international agreement upon a single Chinese voice with both the right and the power to bind the Chinese nation to terms of peace. Some think that one government meets these tests. Some think another meets them. Some doubt that either meets them. No majority can be found for any present action regarding China. Thus, the Allies were faced with hard choices.

They could defer any peace with Japan until they could agree that there was in China a government possessed of both legitimacy and authority. It would, however, be wrong, cruel and stupid to penalize Japan because there is civil war in China and international disagreement regarding China.

As another approach, each Allied Power could refuse to sign a treaty of peace with Japan unless a Chinese government of its choice was cosigner with it. That, we ascertained, would leave Japan at war with so many Allied Powers that Japan would get only a small measure of the peace she has earned. Indeed, there is no reason to believe that Japan, an essential party, would willingly cooperate in a program leading to that end. To exert compulsion, in this matter, would create resentment in Japan, and it would activate and aggravate Allied division in the face of a grave world-wide menace which requires maximum unity.

The remaining choice was for the Allied Powers generally to proceed to conclude peace without any present Chinese cosignature, leaving China and Japan to make their own peace, on terms, however, which would guarantee full protection of the rights and interests of China.

That is the choice reflected by the present treaty. By article 26, China is given the right to a treaty of peace with Japan, on the same terms as the present treaty. The victorious Allies, which sign the treaty, take nothing for themselves that they do not assure equally to China. Also, by article 21, China, without need of signature, gets the sweeping renunciation by Japan (article 10) of all Japan's special rights and interests in China, in accordance with a formula suggested by the Republic of China. Also, China receives automatically, and without need of signature, the benefit of article 14(a) 2 which validates the seizure of Japanese property subject to its jurisdiction. The treaty preserves, in full, the rights of China as one of the Allied victors in this war.

Final Clauses. Chapter VII contains clauses which are largely matters of protocol. Of these articles, 32 dealing with ratification, gives those signatories to the treaty which have been actively concerned with the Occupation, a special position, for 9 months, regarding the bringing of the treaty into force. But after 9 months all of the Allied Powers stand on an equal footing as regards bringing the treaty into force as between themselves and Japan.

Such, in broad outline, are the main aspects of the treaty that awaits our signature.

It contains, no doubt, imperfections. No one is completely satisfied. But it is a good treaty. It does not contain the seeds of another war. It is truly a treaty of peace. . . .

23. Statement by John Foster Dulles at the San Francisco Conference, 7 September 1951 (Extract).

The sum total of these (Soviet) proposals is to create a situation where Japan would be so defenseless from an internal standpoint and from an external standpoint that she would readily fall a victim to any strong, dynamic power in her vicinity, and we all know that there is such a strong, dynamic power in close proximity to Japan.

For example, proposal No. 6, says that Japan shall be bound to put no obstacles in the way of what is referred to as organizations which are supposed to develop "democratic" tendencies in Japan. Well, in Soviet vocabulary the only vehicle for "democratic" tendencies is the Communist Party and that clause, if adopted, would in this instance mean that the Japanese Government is not allowed to take any measures whatever against the activities in Japan of the Communist Party. So much for its defenselessness as regards internal situation.

As regards the external situation, what are the proposals? First, the proposal is that Japan itself shall be allowed only a token defense force and on top of that she shall not be allowed to enjoy any benefits of collective security. She is denied the right given to every other sovereign state, exercised by the Soviet Union itself, to make collective arrangements with other states; that is to be denied to Japan. So Japan, without any opportunity for help from abroad, without any opportunity to make collective security arrangements which the Charter of the United Nations says are the inherent rights of every sovereign nation; denied that, denied the right to have more than a token force of her own, would stand exposed to external aggression.

And I was interested this afternoon in looking up something that may have not caught the attention of most of you, which is a provision contained in their proposal No. 13, which says that the straits about Japan, (indicating, on a map, the straits of Le Perouse, Memoru, Tsugaru, and Tsushima) may be used only by battleships and the navy of such countries as are based upon the Sea of Japan. What does that mean? Under this proposal the only naval force there, would be the great force based upon Vladivostok, which will patrol the waters in and about Japan, which will cut Japan in two and divide Japan from Korea, so that not even a United Nations force could operate in the straits between Korea and Japan. That is the kind of thing, the "jokers" that are contained in the series of proposals that are put before us, and that is the kind of thing we have had to face for 11 months, and that is why it is not possible for us to come to any agreement with the

Soviet Union despite our sincere desire to do so.

24. San Francisco Peace Treaty, 8 September 1951 (Text of the Treaty was released to the Press on 15 August 1951).

Whereas the Allied Powers and Japan are resolved that henceforth their relations shall be those of nations which, as sovereign equals, cooperate in friendly association to promote their common welfare and to maintain international peace and security, and are therefore desirous of concluding a Treaty of Peace which will settle questions still .outstanding as a result of the existence of a state of war between them;

Whereas Japan for its part declares its intention to apply for membership in the United Nations and in all circumstances to conform to the principles of the Charter of the United Nations; to strive to realize the objectives of the Universal Declaration of Human Rights; to seek to create within Japan conditions of stability and well-being as defined in Articles 55 and 56 of the Charter of the United Nations and already initiated by post-surrender Japanese legislation; and in public and private trade and commerce to conform to internationally accepted fair practices;

Whereas the Allied Powers welcome the intentions of Japan set out in the foregoing paragraph;

The Allied Powers and Japan have therefore determined to conclude the present Treaty of Peace, and have accordingly appointed the undersigned Plenipotentiaries, who, after presentation of their full powers, found in good and due form, have agreed on the following provisions :

CHAPTER I

PEACE

Article 1

(a) The state of war between Japan and each of the Allied Powers is terminated as from the date on which the present treaty comes into force between Japan and the Allied Power concerned as provided for in Article 23.

(b) The Allied Powers recognize the full sovereignty of the Japanese people over Japan and its territorial waters.

CHAPTER II

TERRITORY

Article 2

(a) Japan, recognizing the independence of Korea renounces all right, title and claim to Korea, including the islands of Quelpart, Port Hamilton and Dagelet.

(b) Japan renounces all right, title and claim to Formosa and the Pescadores.

(c) Japan renounces all right, title and claim to the Kurile Islands, and to that portion of Sakhalin and the islands adjacent to it over which Japan acquired sovereignty as a consequence of the Treaty of Portsmouth of September 5, 1905.

(d) Japan renounces all right, title and claim in connection with the League of Nations Mandate System, and accepts the action of the United Nations Security Council of April 2, 1947, extending the trusteeship system to the Pacific Islands formerly under mandate to Japan.

(e) Japan renounces all claim to any right or title to or interest in connection with any part of the Antarctic area, whether deriving from the activities of Japanese nationals or otherwise.

(f) Japan renounces all right, title and claim to the Spratly Islands and to the Paracel Islands.

Article 3

Japan will concur in any proposal of the United States to the United Nations to place under its trusteeship system, with the United States as the sole administering authority, Nansei Shoto south of 29° north latitude (including the Ryukyu Islands and the Daito Islands), Nanpo Shoto south of Sofu Gan (including the Bonin Islands, Rosario Islands and the Volcano Islands) and Parece Vela and Marcus Islands. Pending the making of such a proposal and affirmative action thereon, the United States will have the right to exercise all and any powers

of administration, legislation and jurisdiction over the territory
and inhabitants of these islands, including their territorial
waters.

Article 4

(a) Subject to the provisions of paragraph (b) of this
Article, the disposition of property of Japan and of its nationals
in the areas referred to in Article 2, and their claims, including
debts, against the authorities, presently administering such
areas and the residents (including juridical persons) thereof,
and the disposition in Japan of property of such authorites and
residents, and of claims, including debts, of such authorities
and residents against Japan and its nationals, shall be the
subject of special arrangements between Japan and such authorities. The property of any of the Allied Powers or its nationals
in the areas referred to in Article 2 shall, in so far as this has
not already been done, be returned by the administering
authority in the condition in which it now exists. (The term
nationals whenever used in the present Treaty includes juridical
persons).

(b) Japan recognizes the validity of dispositions of property of Japan and Japanese nationals made by or pursuant to
directives of the United States Military Government in any of
the areas referred to in Articles 2 and 3.

(c) Japanese owned submarine cables connecting Japan
with territory removed from Japanese control pursuant to the
present Treaty shall be equally divided, Japan retaining the
Japanese terminal and adjoining half of the cable, and the
detached territory the remainder of the cable and connecting
terminal facilities.

CHAPTER III

SECURITY

Article 5

(a) Japan accepts the obligations set forth in Article 2 of the
Charter of the United Nations, and in particular the obligations

(i) to settle its international disputes by peaceful means in such a manner that international peace and security, and justice, are not endangered;

(ii) to refrain in its international relations from the threat or use of force against the territorial integrity or political independence of any State or in any other manner inconsistent with the Purposes of the United Nations;

(iii) to give the United Nations every assistance in any action it takes in accordance with the Charter and to refrain from giving assistance to any State against which the United Nations may take preventive or enforcement action.

(b) The Allied Powers confirm that they will be guided by the principles of Article 2 of the Charter of the United Nations in their relations with Japan.

(c) The Allied Powers for their part recognize that Japan as a sovereign nation possesses the inherent right of individual or collective self-defense referred to in Article 51 of the Charter of the United Nations and that Japan may voluntarily enter into collective security arrangements.

Article 6

(a) All occupation forces of the Allied Powers shall be withdrawn from Japan as soon as possible after the coming into force of the present Treaty, and in any case not later than 90 days thereafter. Nothing in this provision shall, however, prevent the stationing or retention of foreign armed forces in Japanese territory under or in consequence of any bilateral or multilateral agreements which have been or may be made between one or more of the Allied Powers, on the one hand, and Japan on the other.

(b) The provisions of Article 9 of the Potsdam Proclamation of July 26, 1945, dealing with the return of Japanese military forces to their homes, to the extent not already completed, will be carried out.

(c) All Japanese property for which compensation has not already been paid, which was supplied for the use of the occupation forces and which remains in the possession of those forces at the time of the coming into force of the present Treaty, shall be returned to the Japanese Government within the same 90 days unless other arrangements are made by mutual agreement.

CHAPTER IV

POLITICAL AND ECONOMIC CLAUSES

Article 7

(a)   Each of the Allied Powers, within one year after the present Treaty has come into force between it and Japan, will notify Japan which of its prewar bilateral treaties or conventions with Japan it wishes to   continue in force or revive, and any treaties or conventions so notified shall continue in force or be revived subject only to such amendments as may be necessary to ensure conformity with the present Treaty. The treaties and conventions so notified shall be considered as having been continued in force or revived three months after the date of notification and shall be registered with the Secretariat of the United Nations. All such   treaties and conventions as to which Japan is not so notified shall be regarded as abrogated.

(b)   Any notification made under paragraph (a) of this Article may except from the operation or revival of a treaty or convention any territory for the international relations of which the notifying Power is responsible, until three months after the date on which notice is given to Japan that such exception shall cease to apply.

Article 8

(a)   Japan will recognize the full force of all treaties now or hereafter concluded by the Allied Powers for terminating the state of war initiated on September 1, 1939, as well as any other arrangements by the Allied Powers for or in connection with the restoration of peace.   Japan also accepts the arrangements made for terminating the former League of Nations and Permanent Court of International Justice.

(b)   Japan renounces all such rights and interests as it may derive from being a signatory power of the Conventions of St. Germain-en-Laye of September 10, 1919, and the Straits Agreement of Montreux of July 20, 1936, and from Article 16 of the Treaty of Peace with Turkey signed at Lausanne on July 24, 1923.

(c)   Japan renounces all rights, title and interests acquired under, and is discharged from all obligations resulting from, the Agreement between Germany and the Creditor Powers of January 20, 1930, and its annexes, including the trust agreement, dated May 17, 1930; the Convention of January 20, 1930, respecting the Bank of International Settlements; and the Statutes of the Bank for International Settlements. Japan will notify to the Ministry of Foreign Affairs in Paris within six months of the first coming into force of the present Treaty its renunciation of the rights, title and interests referred to in this paragraph.

Article 9

Japan will enter promptly into negotiations with the Allied Powers so desiring for the conclusion of bilateral and multilateral agreements providing for the regulation or limitation of fishing and the conservation and development of fisheries on the high seas.

Article 10

Japan renounces all special rights and interests in China, including all benefits and privileges resulting from the provisions of the final Protocol signed at Peking on September 7, 1901, and all annexes, notes and documents supplementary thereto, and agrees to the abrogation in respect to Japan of the said protocol, annexes, notes and documents.

Article 11

Japan accepts the judgments of the International Military Tribunal for the Far East and of other Allied War Crimes Courts both within and outside Japan, and will carry out the sentences imposed thereby upon Japanese nationals imprisoned in Japan. The power to grant clemency, to reduce sentences and to parole with respect to such prisoners may not be exercised except on the decision of the Government or Governments represented on the tribunal, and on the recommendation of Japan, which imposed the sentence in each instance, and on the recommendation of Japan. In the case of persons sentenced by the International Military Tribunal for the Far East, such power may not be exercised except on the decision of a majority of the Governments represented on the Tribunal, and on the recommendation of Japan.

Article 12

(a) Japan declares its readiness promptly to enter into negotiations for the conclusion with each of the Allied Powers of treaties or agreements to place their trading, maritime and other commercial relations on a stable and friendly basis.

(b) Pending the conclusion of the relevant treaty or agreement, Japan will, during a period of four years from the first coming into force of the present Treaty

(1) accord to each of the Allied Powers, its nationals, products and vessels

(i) most-favored-nation treatment with respect to customs duties, charges, restrictions and other regulations on or in connection with the importation and exportation of goods;

(ii) national treatment with respect to shipping, navigation and imported goods, and with respect to natural and juridical persons and their interests—such treatment to include all matters pertaining to the levying and collection of taxes, access to the courts, the making and performance of contracts, rights to property (tangible and intangible), participation in juridical entities constituted under Japanese law, and generally the conduct of all kinds of business and professional activities;

(2) ensure that external purchases and sales of Japanese state trading enterprises shall be based solely on commercial considerations.

(c) In respect to any matter, however, Japan shall be obliged to accord to an Allied Power national treatment, or most-favored-nation treatment, only to the extent that the Allied Power concerned accords Japan national treatment or most-favored-nation treatment, as the case may be, in respect of the same matter. The reciprocity envisaged in the foregoing sentence shall be determined, in the case of products, vessels and juridical entities of, and persons domiciled in, any non-metropolitan territory of an Allied Power, and in the case of juridical entities of, and persons domiciled in, any state or province of an Allied Power having a federal government, by reference to the treatment accorded to Japan in such territory, state or province.

(d) In the application of this Article, a discriminatory measure shall not be considered to derogate from the grant of national or most-favored-nation treatment, as the case may be, if such measure is based on an exception customarily provided for in the commercial treaties of the party applying it, or on the need to safeguard that party's external financial position or balance of payments (except in respect to shipping and navigation), or on the need to maintain its essential security interests, and provided such measure is proportionate to the circumstances and not applied in an arbitrary or unreasonable manner.

(e) Japan's obligations under this Article shall not be affected by the exercise of any Allied rights under Article 14 of the present Treaty; nor shall the provisions of this Article be understood as limiting the undertakings assumed by Japan by virtue of Article 15 of the Treaty.

Article 13

(a) Japan will enter into negotiations with any of the Allied Powers, promptly upon the request of such Power or Powers, for the conclusion of bilateral or multilateral agreements relating to international civil air transport.

(b) Pending the conclusion of such agreement or agreements, Japan will, during a period of four years from the first coming into force of the present Treaty, extend to such Power treatment not less favorable with respect to air traffic rights and privileges than those exercised by any such Powers at the date of such coming into force, and will accord complete equality of opportunity in respect to the operation and development of air services.

(c) Pending its becoming a party to the Convention on International Civil Aviation in accordance with Article 93 thereof, Japan will give effect to the provisions of that Convention applicable to the international navigation of aircraft, and will give effect to the standards, practices and procedures adopted as annexes to the Convention in accordance with the terms of the Convention.

CHAPTER V

CLAIMS AND PROPERTY

Article 14

(a) It is recognized that Japan should pay reparations to the Allied Powers for the damage and suffering caused by it during the war. Nevertheless it is also recognized that the resources of Japan are not presently sufficient, if it is to maintain a viable economy, to make complete reparation for all such damage and suffering and at the same time meet its other obligations.

Therefore,

1. Japan will promptly enter into negotiations with Allied Powers so desiring, whose present territories were occupied by Japanese forces and damaged by Japan, with a view to assisting to compensate those countries for the cost of repairing the damage done, by making available the services of the Japanese people in production, salvaging and other work for the Allied Powers in question. Such arrangements shall avoid the imposition of additional liabilities on other Allied Powers, and, where the manufacturing of raw materials is called for, they shall be supplied by the Allied Powers in question, so as not to throw any foreign exchange burden upon Japan.

2. (I) Subject to the provisions of sub-paragraph (II) below, each of the Allied Powers shall have the right to seize, retain, liquidate or otherwise dispose of all property, rights, and interest of

(a) Japan and Japanese nationals,
(b) persons acting for or on behalf of Japan or Japanese nationals, and
(c) entities owned or controlled by Japan or Japanese nationals,

which on the first coming into force of the present Treaty were subject to its jurisdiction. The property, rights and interests specified in this sub-paragraph shall include those now blocked, vested or in the possession or under the control of enemy property authorities of Allied Powers, which belonged to, or were held or managed on behalf of, any of the persons or entities mentioned in (a), (b) or (c) above at the time such assets came under the controls of such authorities.

(II)   The following shall be excepted from the right specified in sub-paragraph (I) above :

(i)   property of Japanese natural persons who during the war resided with the permission of the Government concerned in the territory of one of the Allied Powers, other than territory occupied by Japan, except property subjected to restrictions during the war and not released from such restrictions as of the date of the first coming into force of the present Treaty;

(ii)   all real property, furniture and fixtures owned by the Government of Japan and used for diplomatic or consular purposes, and all personal furniture and furnishings and other private property not of an investment nature which was normally necessary for the carrying out of diplomatic and consular functions, owned by Japanese diplomatic and consular personnel;

(iii) property belonging to religious bodies or private charitable institutions and used exclusively for religious or charitable purposes;

(iv)   property, rights and interests which have come within its jurisdiction in consequence of the resumption of trade and financial relations subsequent to September 2, 1945, between the country concerned and Japan, except such as have resulted from transactions contrary to the laws of the Allied Power concerned;

(v)   obligations of Japan or Japanese nationals, any right, title or interest in tangible property located in Japan, interests in enterprises organized under the laws of Japan, or any paper evidence thereof; provided that this exception shall only apply to obligations of Japan and its nationals expressed in Japanese currency.

(III) Property referred to in exceptions (i) through (v) above shall be returned subject to reasonable expenses for its preservation and administration. If any such property has been liquidated the proceeds shall be returned instead.

(IV) The right to seize, retain, liquidate or otherwise dispose of property as provided in sub-paragraph (I) above shall be exercised in accordance with the laws of the Allied Power concerned, and the owner shall have only such rights as may be given him by those laws.

(V)   The Allied Powers agree to deal with Japanese trade marks and literary and artistic property rights on a basis as favourable to Japan as circumstances ruling in each country will permit.

(b) Except as otherwise provided in the present Treaty, the Allied Powers waive all reparations claims of the Allied Powers, other claims of the Allied Powers and their nationals arising out of any actions taken by Japan and its nationals in the course of the prosecution of the war, and claims of the Allied Powers for direct military costs of occupation.

Article 15

(a) Upon application made within nine months of the coming into force of the present Treaty between Japan and the Allied Power concerned, Japan will, within six months of the date of such application, return the property, tangible and intangible, and all rights or interests of any kind in Japan of each Allied Power and its nationals which was within Japan at any time between December 7, 1941, and September 2, 1945, unless the owner has freely disposed thereof without duress or fraud. Such property shall be returned free of all encumbrances and charges to which it may have become subject because of war, and without any charges for its return. Property whose return is not applied for by or on behalf of the owner or by his Government within the prescribed period may be disposed of by the Japanese Government as it may determine. In cases where such property was within Japan on December 7, 1941, and cannot be returned or has suffered injury or damage as a result of the war, compensation will be made on terms not less favorable than the terms provided in the draft Allied Powers Property Compensation Law approved by the Japanese Cabinet on July 13, 1951.

(b) With respect to industrial property rights impaired during the war, Japan will continue to accord to the Allied Powers and their nationals benefits no less than those heretofore accorded by Cabinet Orders No. 309 effective September 1, 1949, No. 12 effective January 28, 1950, and No. 9 effective February 1, 1950, all as now amended, provided such nationals have applied for such benefits within the time limits prescribed therein.

(c) (i) Japan acknowledges that the literary and artistic

property rights which existed in Japan on December 6, 1941, in respect to the published and unpublished works of the Allied Powers and their nationals have continued in force since that date, and recognizes those rights which have arisen, or but for the war would have arisen, in Japan since that date, by the operation of any conventions and agreements to which Japan was a party on that date, irrespective of whether or not such conventions or agreements were abrogated or suspended upon or since the outbreak of war by the domestic law of Japan or of the Allied Power concerned.

(ii) Without the need for application by the proprietor of the right and without the payment of any fee or compliance with any other formality, the period from December 7, 1941, until the coming into force of the present Treaty between Japan and the Allied Power concerned shall be excluded from the running of the normal term of such rights; and such period, within an additional period of six months, shall be excluded from the time within which a literary work must be translated into Japanese in order to obtain translating rights in Japan.

Article 16

As an expression of its desire to indemnify those members of the armed forces of the Allied Powers who suffered undue hardships while prisoners of war of Japan, Japan will transfer its assets and those of its nationals in countries which were neutral during the war, or which were at war with any of the Allied Powers, or, at its option, the equivalent of such assets, to the International Committee of the Red Cross which shall liquidate such assets and distribute the resultant fund to appropriate national agencies, for the benefit of former prisoners of war and their families on such basis as it may determine to be equitable. The categories of assets described in Article 14(a) 2(II) (ii) through (v) of the present Treaty shall be excepted from transfer, as well as assets of Japanese natural persons not residents of Japan on the first coming into force of the Treaty. It is equally understood that the transfer provision of this Article has no application to the 19,770 shares in the Bank for International Settlements presently owned by Japanese financial institutions.

Article 17

(a) Upon the request of any of the Allied Powers, the Japanese Government shall review and revise in conformity with international law any decision or order of the Japanese Prize Courts in cases involving ownership rights of nationals of that Allied Power and shall supply copies of all documents comprising the records of these cases, including the decisions taken and orders issued. In any case in which such review or revision shows that restoration is due, the provisions of Article 15 shall apply to the property concerned.

(b) The Japanese Government shall take the necessary measures to enable nationals of any of the Allied Powers at any time within one year from the coming into force of the present Treaty between Japan and the Allied Power concerned to submit to the appropriate Japanese authorities for review any judgment given by a Japanese court between December 7, 1941, and such coming into force, in any proceedings in which any such national was unable to make adequate presentation of his case either as plaintiff or defendant. The Japanese Government shall provide that, where the national has suffered injury by reason of any such judgment, he shall be restored in the position in which he was before the judgment was given or shall be afforded such relief as may be just and equitable in the circumstances.

Article 18

(a) It is recognized that the intervention of the state of war has not affected the obligation to pay pecuniary debts arising out of obligations and contracts (including those in respect of bonds) which existed and rights which were acquired before the existence of a state of war, and which are due by the Government or nationals of Japan to the Government or nationals of one of the Allied Powers, or are due by the Government or nationals of one of the Allied Powers to the Government or nationals of Japan. The intervention of a state of war shall equally not be regarded as affecting the obligation to consider on their merits claims for loss or damage to property or for personal injury or death which arose before the existence of a state of war, and which may be presented or represented by the Government of one of the Allied Powers to the Government of Japan, or by the Government of Japan to any of the Governments of the Allied Powers. The provisions of this paragraph are without prejudice to the rights conferred by Article 14.

(b) Japan affirms its liability for the prewar external debts of the Japanese State and for debts of corporate bodies subsequently declared to be liabilities of the Japanese State, and expresses its intention to enter into negotiations at an early date with its creditors with respect to the resumption of payments on those debts; to encourage negotiations in respect to other prewar claims and obligations; and to facilitate the transfer of sums accordingly.

Article 19

(a) Japan waives all claims of Japan and its nationals against the Allied Powers and their nationals arising out of the war or out of actions taken because of the existence of a state of war, and waives all claims arising from the presence, operations or actions of forces or authorities of any of the Allied Powers in Japanese territory prior to the coming into force of the present Treaty.

(b) The foregoing waiver includes any claims arising out of actions taken by any of the Allied Powers with respect to Japanese ships between September 1, 1939 and the coming into force of the present Treaty, as well as any claims and debts arising in respect to Japanese prisoners of war and civilian internees in the hands of the Allied Powers, but does not include Japanese claims specifically recognized in the laws of any Allied Power enacted since September 2, 1945.

(c) Subject to reciprocal renunciation, the Japanese Government also renounces all claims (including debts) against Germany and German nationals on behalf of the Japanese Government and Japanese nationals including inter-governmental claims and claims for loss or damage sustained during the war; but excepting (a) claims in respect of contracts entered into and rights acquired before September 1, 1939, and (b) claims arising out of trade and financial relations between Japan and Germany after September 2, 1945. Such renunciation shall not prejudice actions taken in accordance with

Articles 16 and 20 of the present Treaty.

(d) Japan recognizes the validity of all acts and omissions done during the period of occupation under or in consequence of directives of the occupation authorities or authorized by Japanese law at that time, and will take no action subjecting Allied nationals to civil or criminal liability arising out of such acts or omissions.

Article 20

Japan will take all necessary measures to ensure such disposition of German assets in Japan as has been or may be determined by those powers entitled under the Protocol of the proceedings of the Berlin Conference of 1945 to dispose of those assets, and pending the final disposition of such assets will be responsible for the conservation and administration thereof.

Article 21

Notwithstanding the provisions of Article 25 of the present Treaty, China shall be entitled to the benefits of Articles 10 and 14 (a) 2; and Korea to the benefits of Articles 2, 4, 9 and 12 of the present Treaty.

CHAPTER VI

SETTLEMENT OF DISPUTES

Article 22

If in the opinion of any Party to the present Treaty there has arisen a dispute concerning the interpretation or execution of the Treaty, which is not settled by reference to a special claims tribunal or by other agreed means, the dispute shall, at the request of any party thereto, be referred for decision to the International Court of Justice. Japan and those Allied Powers which are not already parties to the Statute of the International Court of Justice will deposit with Registrar of the Court, at the time of their respective ratifications of the present Treaty, and in conformity with the resolution of the United Nations

Security Council, dated October 15, 1946, a general declaration accepting the jurisdiction, without special agreement, of the Court generally in respect to all disputes of the character referred to in this Article.

CHAPTER VII

FINAL CLAUSES

Article 23

(a) The present Treaty shall be ratified by the States which sign it, including Japan, and will come into force for all the States which have then ratified it, when instruments of ratification have been deposited by Japan and by a majority, including the United States of America as the principal occupying Power, of the following States, [here would appear the names of such of the following States as are signatories to the present Treaty] namely Australia, Burma, Canada, Ceylon, France, India, Indonesia, the Netherlands, New Zealand, Pakistan, the Philippines, the United Kingdom of Great Britain and Northern Ireland, the Union of Soviet Socialist Republics and the United States of America. The present Treaty shall come into force for each State which subsequently ratifies it, on the date of the deposit of its instrument of ratification.

(b) If the Treaty has not come into force within nine months after the date of the deposits of Japan's ratification, any State which has ratified it may bring the Treaty into force between itself and Japan by a notification to that effect given to the Governments of Japan and of the United States of America not later than three years after the date of deposit of Japan's ratification.

Article 24

All instruments of ratification shall be deposited with the Government of the United States of America which will notify all the signatory States of each such deposit, of the date of the coming into force of the Treaty under paragraph (a) of Article 23, and of any notifications made under paragraph (b) of

Article 23.

Article 25

For the purposes of the present Treaty the Allied Powers shall be the States at war with Japan, or any State which previously formed a part of the territory of a State named in Article 23, provided that in each case the State concerned has signed and ratified the Treaty. Subject to the provisions of Article 21, the present Treaty shall not confer any rights, titles or benefits on any State which is not an Allied Power as herein defined; nor shall any right, title or interest of Japan be deemed to be diminished or prejudiced by any provision of the Treaty in favor of a State which is not an Allied Power as so defined.

Article 26

Japan will be prepared to conclude with any State which signed or adhered to the United Nations Declaration of January 1, 1942, and which is at war with Japan, or with any State which previously formed a part of the territory of a State named in Article 23, which is not a signatory of the present Treaty, a bilateral Treaty of Peace on the same or substantially the same terms as are provided for in the present Treaty, but this obligation on the part of Japan will expire three years after the first coming into force of the present Treaty. Should Japan make a peace settlement or war claims settlement with any State granting that State greater advantages than those provided by the present Treaty, those same advantages shall be extended to the parties to the present Treaty.

Article 27

The present Treaty shall be deposited in the archives of the Government of the United States of America which shall furnish each signatory State with a certified copy thereof.

25. Declarations by the Government of Japan, 8 September 1951.

Declaration

With respect to the Treaty of Peace signed this day, the Government of Japan makes the following declaration :

1. Except as otherwise provided in the said Treaty of Peace, Japan recognizes the full force of all presently effective multilateral international instruments to which Japan was a party on September 1, 1939, and declares that it will, on the first coming into force of the said Treaty, resume all its rights and obligations under those instruments. Where, however, participation in any instruments involves membership in an international organization of which Japan ceased to be a member on or after September 1, 1939, the provisions of the present paragraph shall be dependent on Japan's re-admission to membership in the organization concerned.

2. It is the intention of the Japanese Government formally to accede to the following international instruments within the shortest practicable time, not to exceed one year from the first coming into force of the Treaty of Peace :

(1) Protocol opened for signature at Lake Success on December 11, 1946, amending the agreements, conventions and protocols on narcotic drugs of January 23, 1912, February 11, 1925, February 19, 1925, July 13, 1931, November 27, 1931, and June 26, 1936;

(2) Protocol opened for signature at Paris on November 19, 1948, bringing under international control drugs outside the scope of the convention of July 13, 1931, for limiting the manufacture and regulating the distribution of narcotic drugs, as amended by the protocol signed at Lake Success on December 11, 1946;

(3) International Convention on the Execution of Foreign Arbitral Awards signed at Geneva on September 26, 1927;

(4) International Convention relating to Economic Statistics with protocol signed at Geneva on December 14, 1928, and Protocol amending the International Convention of 1928 relating to Economic Statistics signed at Paris on December 9, 1948;

(5) International Convention relating to simplification of Customs Formalities, with protocol of signature, signed at Geneva on November 3, 1923;

(6) Agreement of Madrid of April 14, 1891, for the Prevention of False Indication of Origin of Goods, as

revised at Washington on June 2, 1911, at The Hague
on November 6, 1925, and at London on June 2,
1934;

(7) Convention for the unification of certain rules relating
to international transportation by air, and additional
protocol, signed at Warsaw on October 12, 1929;

(8) Convention on safety of life at sea opened for signature
at London on June 19, 1948;

(9) Geneva conventions of August 12, 1949, for the protection of war victims.

3. It is equally the intention of the Japanese Government,
within six months of the first coming into force of the Treaty of
Peace, to apply for Japan's admission to participation in (a)
the Convention on International Civil Aviation opened for
signature at Chicago on December 7, 1944, and, as soon as
Japan is itself a party to that Convention, to accept the International Air Services Transit Agreement also opened for
signature at Chicago on December 7, 1944; and (b) the Convention of the World Meteorological Organization opened for
signature at Washington on October 11, 1947.

Another Declaration

With respect to the Treaty of Peace signed this day, the
Government of Japan makes the following declaration:

Japan will recognise any Commission, Delegation or other
Organization authorized by any of the Allied Powers to identify,
list, maintain or regulate its war graves, cemeteries and memorials in Japanese territory; will facilitate the work of such
Organizations; and will, in respect of the above mentioned war
graves, cemeteries and memorials, enter into negotiations for
the conclusion of such agreements as may prove necessary with
the Allied Power concerned, or with any Commission, Delegation or other Organization authorized by it.

Japan trusts that the Allied Powers will enter into discussions with the Japanese Government with a view to arrangements being made for the maintenance of any Japanese war
graves or cemeteries which may exist in the territories of the
Allied Powers and which it is desired to preserve.

26. Protocol, 8 September 1951.

The undersigned, duly authorized to that effect, have agreed on the following provisions for regulating the question of Contracts, Periods of Prescription and Negotiable Instruments, and the question of Contracts of Insurance, upon the restoration of peace with Japan :

CONTRACTS, PRESCRIPTION AND NEGOTIABLE INSTRUMENTS

A. Contracts

1. Any contract which required for its execution intercourse between any of the parties thereto having become enemies as defined in part F shall, subject to the exceptions set out in paragraphs 2 and 3, below, be deemed to have been dissolved as from the time when any of the parties thereto become enemies. Such dissolution, however, is without prejudice to the provisions of Article 18 of the Treaty of Peace signed this day, nor shall it relieve any party to the contract from the obligation to repay amount received as advances or as payments on account and in respect of which such party has not rendered performance in return.

2. Notwithstanding the provisions of paragraph 1 above, there shall be excepted from dissolution and, without prejudice to the rights contained in Article 14 of the Treaty of Peace signed this day, there shall remain in force such parts of any contract as are severable and did not require for the execution intercourse between any of the parties thereto, having become enemies as defined in part F. Where the provisions of any contract are not so severable, the contract shall be deemed to have been dissolved in its entirety. The foregoing shall be subject to the application of domestic laws, orders or regulations made by a signatory hereto which is an Allied Power under the said Treaty of Peace and having jurisdiction over the contract or over any of the parties thereto and shall be subject to the terms of the contract.

3. Nothing in part A shall be deemed to invalidate transactions lawfully carried out in accordance with a contract between enemies if they have been carried out with the authorization of

the Government concerned being the Government of a signatory hereto which is an Allied Power under the said Treaty of Peace.

4. Notwithstanding the foregoing provisions, contracts of insurance and reinsurance shall be dealt with in accordance with the provisions of part D and E of the present Protocol.

B. Periods of Prescription

1. All periods of prescription or limitation of right of action or of the right to take conservatory measures in respect of relations affecting persons or property, involving nationals of the signatories hereto who, by reason of the state of war, were unable to take judicial action or to comply with the formalities necessary to safeguard their rights, irrespective of whether these periods commenced before or after the outbreak of war, shall be regarded as having been suspended, for the duration of the war in Japanese territory on the one hand, and on the other hand in the territory of those signatories which grant to Japan, on a reciprocal basis, the benefit of the provisions of this paragraph. These periods shall begin to run again on the coming into force of the Treaty of Peace signed this day. The provisions of this paragraph shall be applicable in regard to the periods fixed for the presentation of interest of dividend coupons or for the presentation for payment of securities drawn for repayment or repayable on any other ground, provided that in respect of such coupons or securities the period shall begin to run again on the date when money becomes available for payments to the holder of the coupon or security.

2. Where, on account of failure to perform any act or to comply with any formality during the war, measures of execution have been taken in Japanese territory to the prejudice of a national of one of the signatories being an Allied Power under the said Treaty of Peace, the Japanese Government shall restore the rights which have been detrimentally affected. If such restoration is impossible or would be inequitable the Japanese Government shall provide that the national of the signatory concerned shall be afforded such relief as may be just and equitable in the circumstances.

C. Negotiable Instruments

1. As between enemies, no negotiable instrument made before the war shall be deemed to have become invalid by reason only of failure within the required time to present the instrument for acceptance or payment, or to give notice of non-acceptance or non-payment to drawers or endorsers, or to protest the instrument, nor by reason of failure to complete any formality during the war.

2. Where the period within which a negotiable instrument should have been presented for acceptance or for payment, or within which notice of non-acceptance or non-payment should have been given to the drawer or endorser, or within which the instrument should have been protested, has elapsed during the war, and the party who should have presented or protested the instrument or have given notice of non-acceptance or non-payment has failed to do so during the war, a period of not less than three months from the coming into force of the Treaty of Peace signed this day shall be allowed within which presentation, notice of non-acceptance or non-payment, or protest may be made.

3. If a person has, either before or during the war, incurred obligations under a negotiable instrument in consequence of an undertaking given to him by a person who has subsequently become an enemy, the latter shall remain liable to indemnify the former in respect of these obligations, notwithstanding the outbreak of war.

D. Insurance and Reinsurance Contracts (other than Life) which had not terminated before the date at which the Parties became Enemies

1. Contracts of Insurance shall be deemed not to have been dissolved by the fact of the parties becoming enemies, provided that the risk had attached before the date at which the parties became enemies, and the insured had paid, before that date, all moneys owed by way of premium or consideration for effecting or keeping effective the Insurance in accordance with the Contract.

2. Contracts of Insurance other than those remaining in force under the preceding clause shall be deemed not to have

come into existence, and any moneys paid thereunder shall be returnable.

3. Treaties and other Contracts of Reinsurance, save as hereinafter expressly provided, shall be deemed to have been determined as at the date the parties became enemies, and all cession thereunder shall be cancelled with effect from that date. Provided that cessions in respect of voyage policies which had attached under a Treaty of Marine Reinsurance shall be deemed to have remained in full effect until their natural expiry in accordance with the terms and conditions on which the risk had been ceded.

4. Contracts of Facultative Reinsurance, where the risk had attached and all moneys owed by way of premium or consideration for effecting or keeping effective the Reinsurance had been paid or set off in the customary manner, shall, unless the Reinsurance Contract otherwise provides, be deemed to have remained in full effect until the date at which the parties became enemies and to have been determined on that date.

Provided that such Facultative Reinsurances in respect of voyage policies shall be deemed to have remained in full effect until their natural expiry in accordance with the terms and conditions on which the risk had been ceded.

Provided further that Facultative Reinsurances in respect of a Contract of Insurance remaining in force under clause I above shall be deemed to have remained in full effect until the expiry of the original Insurance.

5. Contracts of Facultative Reinsurance other than those dealt with in the preceding clause, and all Contracts of Excess of Loss Reinsurance on an "Excess of Loss Ratio" basis and of Hail Reinsurance (whether facultative or not), shall be deemed not to have come into existence, and any moneys paid thereunder shall be returnable.

6. Unless the Treaty or other Contract of Reinsurance otherwise provides, premiums shall be adjusted on a *pro rata temporis* basis.

7. Contracts of Insurance or Reinsurance (including cessions under Treaties of Reinsurance) shall be deemed not to cover losses or claims caused by belligerent action by either Power of which any of the parties was a national or by the Allies or Associates of such Power.

8. Where an insurance has been transferred during the war from the original to another Insurer, or has been wholly reinsured, the transfer or reinsurance shall, whether effected voluntarily or by administrative or legislative action, be recognised and the liability of the original Insurer shall be deemed to have ceased as from the date of the transfer or reinsurance.

9. Where there was more than one Treaty or other Contract of Reinsurance between the same two parties, there shall be an adjustment of accounts between them, and in order to establish a resulting balance there shall be brought into the accounts all balances (which shall include an agreed reserve for losses still outstanding) and all moneys which may be due from one party to the other under all such contracts or which may be returnable by virtue of any of the foregoing provisions.

10. No interest shall be payable by any of the parties for any delay which, owing to the parties having become enemies, has occurred or may occur in the settlement of Premiums or claims or balances of account.

11. Nothing in this part of the present Protocol shall in any way prejudice or affect the rights given by Article 14 of the Treaty of Peace signed this day.

E. Life Insurance Contracts

Where an insurance has been transferred during the war from the original to another insurer or has been wholly reinsured, the transfer of reinsurance shall, if effected at the instance of the Japanese administrative or legislative authorities, be recognized, and the liability of the original insurer shall be deemed to have ceased as from the date of the transfer of reinsurance.

F. Special Provision

For the purposes of the present Protocol, natural or juridical persons shall be regarded as enemies from the date when trading between them shall have become unlawful under laws, orders, or regulations to which such persons or the contracts were subject.

Final Article

The present Protocol is open for signature by Japan and any State signatory to the Treaty of Peace with Japan signed this day, and shall, in respect of the matters with which it deals, govern the relations between Japan and each of the other States signatory to the present Protocol as from the date when Japan and that State are both bound by the said Treaty of Peace.

The present Protocol shall be deposited in the archives of the Government of the United States of America which shall furnish each signatory State with a certified copy thereof.

In faith where of the undersigned plenipotentiaries have signed the present Protocol.

Done at the city of San Francisco this eighth day of September, 1951, in the English, French, and Spanish languages, all being equally authentic, and in the Japanese language.

Signatories to the Protocol

Australia	Laos
Belgium	Lebanon
Cambodia	Liberia
Canada	Luxembourg
Ceylon	Netherlands
Dominican Republic	Pakistan
Egypt	Saudi Arabia
Ethiopia	Syria
France	Turkey
Greece	United Kingdom
Haiti	Uruguay
Indonesia	Vietnam
Iran	Japan
Iraq	

27. Security Treaty between the United States and Japan, 8 September 1951.

Japan has this day signed a Treaty of Peace with the Allied Powers. On the coming into force of that Treaty, Japan will not have the effective means to exercise its inherent right of self-defense because it has been disarmed.

There is danger to Japan in this situation because irresponsible militarism has not yet been driven from the world. Therefore Japan desires a Security Treaty with the United States of America to come into force simultaneously with the Treaty of Peace between the United States of America and Japan.

The Treaty of Peace recognizes that Japan as a sovereign nation has the right to enter into collective security arrangements, and further, the Charter of the United Nations recognizes that all nations possess an inherent right of individual and collective self-defense.

In exercise of these rights, Japan desires, as a provisional arrangements for its defense, that the United States of America should maintain armed forces of its own in and about Japan so as to deter armed attack upon Japan.

The United States of America, in the interests of peace and security, is presently willing to maintain certain of its armed forces in and about Japan, in the expectation, however, that Japan will itself increasingly assume responsibility for its own defense against direct and indirect aggression, always avoiding any armament which could be an offensive threat or serve other than to promote peace and security in accordance with the purposes and principles of the United Nations Charter.

Accordingly, the two countries have agreed as follows:

Article I

Japan grants, and the United States of America accepts, the right, upon the coming into force of the Treaty of Peace and of this Treaty, to dispose United States land, air and sea, forces in and about Japan. Such forces may be utilized to contribute to the maintenance of international peace and security in the Far East and to the security of Japan against armed attack from without, including assistance given at the express request of the Japanese Government to put down large scale internal riots and disturbances in Japan, caused through instigation or intervention by an outside power or powers.

Article II

During the exercise of the right referred to in Article I, Japan will not grant, without the prior consent of the United States of America, any bases or any rights, powers or authority whatsoever, in or relating to bases or the right of garrison or of maneuver, or transit of ground, air, or naval forces to any third power.

Article III

The conditions which shall govern the disposition of armed forces of the United States of America in and about Japan shall be determined by administrative agreements between the two Governments.

Article IV

This Treaty shall expire whenever in the opinion of the Governments of the United States of America and Japan there shall have come into force such United Nations arrangements or such alternative individual or collective security dispositions as will satisfactorily provide for the maintenance by the United Nations or otherwise of international peace and security in the Japan Area.

Article V

This Treaty shall be ratified by the United States of America and Japan and will come into force when instruments of ratification thereof have been exchanged by them at Washington.

IN WITNESS THEREOF the undersigned Plenipotentiaries have signed this Treaty.

DONE in duplicate at the city of San Francisco, in the English and Japanese languages, this eighth day of September 1951.

28. Declaration of the United States Senate, 20 March 1952.

As part of such advice and consent [is regards the ratification of the Treaty of Peace with Japan by the United States] the Senate states that nothing the treaty contains is deemed to diminish or prejudice, in favor of the Soviet Union, the right, title, and interest of Japan, or the Allied Powers as defined in said treaty, in and to South Sakhalin and its adjacent islands, the Kurile Islands, the Habomai Islands, the island of Shikotan, or any other territory, rights, or interests possessed by Japan on December 7, 1941, or to confer any right, title, or benefit therein or thereto on the Soviet Union; and also that nothing in the said treaty, or the advice and consent of the Senate to the ratification thereof, implies recognition on the part of the United States of the provisions in favor of the Soviet Union contained in the so-called "Yalta agreement" regarding Japan of February 11, 1945.

29. United States Aide-Memoire on Japan-Soviet Talks, 7 September 1956.

Pursuant to the request made by the Japanese Foreign Minister, Mr. Shigemitsu, in the course of recent conversations in London with the Secretary of State, Mr. Dulles, the Department of State has reviewed the problems presented in the course of the current negotiations for a Treaty of Peace between the Union of Soviet Socialist Republics and Japan, with particular reference to the interest of the United States as a signatory of the San Francisco Peace Treaty, and on the basis of such review makes the following observations.

The Government of the United States believes that the state of war between Japan and the Soviet Union should be formally terminated. Such action has been overdue since 1951, when the Soviet Union declined to sign the San Francisco Peace Treaty. Japan should also long since have been admitted to the United Nations, for which it is fully qualified; and Japanese prisoners of war in Soviet hands should long since have been returned in accordance with surrender terms.

With respect to the territorial question, as the Japanese Government has been previously informed, the United States regards the so-called Yalta Agreement as simply a statement of common purpose by the then heads of the participating powers, and not as a final determination by those powers or of any legal effect in transferring territories. The San Francisco Peace

Treaty (which conferred no rights upon the Soviet Union because it refused to sign) did not determine the sovereignty of the territories renounced by Japan, leaving that question, as was stated by the Delegate of the United States at San Francisco, to "international solvents other than this Treaty."

It is the considered opinion of the United States that by virtue of the San Francisco Peace Treaty/Japan does not have the right to transfer sovereignty over the territories renounced by it therein. In the opinion of the United States, the signatories of the San Francisco Treaty would not be bound to accept any action of this character and they would presumably reserve all their rights thereunder.

The United States has reached the conclusion after careful examinations of the historical facts that the islands of Etorofu and Kunashiri (along with the Habomai islands and Shikotan which are a part of Hokkaido) have always been part of Japan proper and should in justice be acknowledged as under Japanese sovereignty. The United States would regard Soviet agreement to this effect as a positive contribution to the reduction of tension in the Far East.

UNITED KINGDOM

30. Communication from the British Embassy to the US Department of State on the Canberra meeting of representatives of British Dominions, 9 October 1947 (Extract).

The Conference was an exchange of views on the broad issues, and detailed discussion of technical matters, for which in any case there would have been insufficient time, was never contemplated so that no statements of agreed policy were formulated and the Conference entailed no kind of commitment on any government represented at it.

2. The consensus of opinion was that all countries represented on the Far Eastern Commission should be entitled to representation in the framing of the peace settlement and that in addition Pakistan's claims for operate representation were incontestable. Decisions at the conference should be by two-

thirds majority on matters of substance but by a simple majority on drafting and procedural matters; the use of the veto should be avoided. Washington was generally favoured as the venue of the conference. It was generally hoped that the conference would begin with a short initial meeting at a Governmental level as soon as possible.

3. There was general agreement that the treaty could hardly do other than endorse the territorial agreements made at Cairo, Yalta, and Potsdam. In view of the uncertain future of Korea it was suggested for consideration that it might be advisable to leave Quelpart Island under Japanese sovereignty in spite of the fact that its population is Korean. The question was raised (but left unanswered) as to how the advantages of civil aviation bases in the Southern Kuriles could be obtained. It was generally contemplated that the Ryukyus and the Bonins should continue under United States administration presumably under some form of strategic trusteeship.

4. The conference agreed that Japan should remain completely disarmed and demilitarised, that armament manufacture and naval shipbuilding should be prohibited and that there should be careful supervision to ensure the observance of these sections of the treaty.

5. The majority of Delegations favoured the prohibition of the manufacture of aircraft in Japan; internal operation by Japan should be confined to a limited number of imported civil aircraft for specified purposes and under strict control.

6. The consensus of opinion was that the democratic principles broadly outlined in the Potsdam declaration and already included in the Japanese constitution should be written into the treaty but that the constitution itself should not be so written.

7. There was general support for the view that provision should be made in the treaty for the protection of civil rights of alien residents in Japan who should be accorded treatment at least no worse than that enjoyed by Japanese nationals in their own countries and in accordance with generally approved international standards.

8. On economic matters the majority of the Delegation were agreed that

(a) The manufacture of synthetic oil and rubber should be completely prohibited;

(b) Although it would be impracticable to include detailed provisions in the treaty referring to the freedom of trade unions, the general principle of freedom of association should be included leaving the Japanese to work out the details for themselves;

(c) It would be a mistake to incorporate any scheme of land reform in the treaty;

(d) The process of dissolving the Zaibatsu should be completed by the Japanese Government as soon as possible;

(e) The treaty should not attempt to lay down details regarding such subjects as economic equality, maintenance of full employment, fiscal policy;

(f) Japanese external assets should be taken into account in assessing total reparations and their percentages distribution (Delegates did not discuss the division of shares of reparations in general);

(g) Japanese shipping should be limited to vessels not exceeding 5000 gross registered tons. The construction of vessels should be limited to those not exceeding a stipulated speed. Japan's total merchant shipping tonnage should be limited to a maximum sufficient for the conduct of such trade as the Allies deem necessary.

9. With regard to post-treaty control the general feeling of the conference was that all the countries who share in the initial drafting of the treaty (i.e. the eleven Far Eastern Commission Powers plus any agreed additions) should be represented on whatever supervisory body may be set up. It was not thought that any military occupation force in Japan would be necessary after the treaty but it was considered that forces outside Japan should be available for enforcing the treaty if necessary. It was recognised that special regard should be paid to the views of the United States Government on this subject in view of the special responsibilities already undertaken by the United States. Voting in the supervisory body should be by simple majority. The conference gave consideration to the United Kingdom view that it might be desirable to conclude an agreement between the controlling powers separate from the treaty of peace. In order to minimise possible delays the treaty should come into force upon ratification by two-thirds of the treaty-making powers.

10. The conference recognised that provisions should be made for the acceptance of the treaty by belligerents who did not participate in the drafting.

11. The conference agreed that Japan should be compelled to observe the international whaling conventions if it were agreed that Japan should be allowed to participate in whaling at all.

12. Amongst other aspects of the settlement discussed in general terms by the conference were atomic research, education, emigration, Japanese membership of international bodies.

31. Note from the British Embassy to the US Department of State on Japanese Reparations, 30 June 1947 (Extracts).

In the course of discussions in the Reparations Committee of the Far Eastern Commission of the shares of reparations from Japan in the form of industrial equipment, the United States member of the Committee has put forward two lists of percentages. The first of these, which was presented on 12th May 1947, represented the personal views of the United States member and proposed that the United Kingdom should receive 9%. The second, which was presented on 29th May, represented the official views of the United States Government and proposed an even smaller percentage for the United Kingdom, viz. 8%.

His Majesty's Government in the United Kingdom are very much disappointed at the ungenerous treatment which the United States representative has proposed for the United Kingdom. . . .

The United Kingdom has a major claim on any of the three main grounds on which claims to internal assets in Japan can be based, viz. (a) extent of devastation, (b) war effort, and (c) paucity of holding of Japanese external assets.

With regard to the first of these, the extent of the devastation of British territories in the Far East appears to have been insufficiently recognised. Burma, for example, twice suffered serious devastation in the war against Japan, first from a scorched earth policy and then from bombing and a military campaign which traversed the whole country. Similar considerations apply to Malaya, Hong Kong and Borneo, where an immense task of reconstruction and rehabilitation has been left for His Majesty's Government to deal with.

With regard to war effort, His Majesty's Government wish to mention that British forces fought a major land campaign, with the result that the whole Japanese military and administrative machine in Southeast Asia was destroyed. On the sea, His Majesty's Navies drove the Japanese naval forces from the Indian Ocean and neighbouring waters, contained capital forces in the South-east Asia zone, took part in the naval advance to the shores of Japan and mounted a full scale operation for the recapture of Singapore.

It is difficult to believe that, in proposing the figure of 8% for the United Kingdom, the United States Government have given full weight to all the relevant factors. For instance, the United States Government propose to give China more than three and a half times the share of the United Kingdom, which cannot be consistent with any just appraisal of relative deserts in relation to war effort and holding of Japanese external assets. Nor does it appear that the United States Government have properly appreciated that the share of the United Kingdom is intended to cover Burma and the Colonies as well. It would be difficult to maintain that, taking Burma as a single unit, she should be less generously treated than the Philippines, to which the United States Government propose to give as great a share as to the United Kingdom, Burma and the Colonies taken together.

32. Statement by the Foreign Secretary, Herbert Morrison, on Draft Peace Treaty with Japan, 12 July 1951 (Extracts).

A peace treaty with Japan is now of great importance. We do not consider that we should continue to postpone a peace treaty which would materially aid a settlement in the Far East, simply because a small minority are not prepared to negotiate a treaty unless the veto is retained. . . .

If a treaty is not to be indefinitely delayed the only alternative has seemed to us to be that China should not be invited to sign the present treaty. The interests of the Chinese people are, however, safeguarded by the provisions in the draft which is being published today. Once the treaty has been signed and Japan becomes responsible for her own foreign relations, it will be for Japan herself to decide her future relations with China.

As to the security aspects of the treaty, Japan accepts the obligation of Article 2 of the Charter of the United Nations. At the same time she retains the right of self-defence implicit in Article 51 of the Charter. The defence of Japan against aggression is expected to be assured by an arrangement consistent with the purposes and principles of the United Nations between Japan and the United States. In relation to general security in the Pacific . . . special arrangements are contemplated in a pact to be concluded between Australia, New Zealand and the United States. . . .

33. Statement by H. Shawcross, President of the Board of Trade, on the Economic Aspects of the Draft Japanese Peace Treaty, 12 July 1951.

In the first place, it should be realised that we have been guided by the same considerations as those which determined our attitude on security provisions. We attach importance to the early resumption of full sovereignty by Japan; and we place little reliance in the effectiveness of punitive restrictions embodied in a peace treaty.

In one particular, in relation to the Congo-Basin Treaties, we have considered it appropriate to re-define Japan's position. Japan was a signatory to the Conventions concluded at St. Germain-en-Laye in 1919 in connection with the trade of the Congo-Basin territories. She will be required to renounce such rights as she possesses as a signatory Power to these Conventions. It should be noted, however, that certain benefits in this area were accorded by the Berlin Act of 1885 to all countries of the world.

We recognise that Japan's economic circumstances are very similar to those of the United Kingdom; she must export to live. Japan must succeed in paying her way without United States support which has sustained her economy during the occupation. This will be a difficult task, with her rapidly increasing population and lack of raw materials, and we therefore attach special importance to the intention expressed by

Japan in the Preamble to the draft Treaty of conforming in public and private trade and commerce to internationally accepted fair practices.

In token of this, Japan will, in a separate declaration to accompany the Treaty, record her full recognition of her obligations under various international instruments to which she is already a party, and her intention to accede to certain others. Under the guidance of the occupation authorities, Japan has introduced legislation for the regulation of working conditions and a trade union movement has been established. Japan has also recently sought and secured her re-admission to the International Labour Organisation. This should be a potent influence in promoting the maintenance and improvement of labour and living standards.

Pending the conclusion of bilateral trade agreements, Japan is required by the draft Treaty to accord for a period of four years to each of the Allied Powers and their nationals, subject to reciprocity, most-favoured-nation treatment in connection with the importation and exportation of goods and national treatment in respect of shipping, navigation and the activities of persons and companies.

On 19th March my right hon. Friend, who was then President of the Board of Trade, told the House that His Majesty's Government at present extends most-favoured-nation treatment to Japanese trade in goods but is not prepared to enter into any formal undertaking to continue to do so. The full resumption of Japanese sovereignty with the coming into force of this Treaty will test Japanese intentions; she will be answerable to world opinion for the manner in which she carries them out. She must expect other nations, sympathetic as they may be with the difficulties which she is bound to encounter in regaining her important place in world trade, to take appropriate action if their own economic well-being is gravely imperilled.

For our own part, bearing in mind the pre-war record of Japanese competition, especially in the textile trades, we have decided not to accord most-favoured-nation rights to Japan because we feel that we must for the present retain our freedom to protect our economy if necessary against abnormal and injurious competition. In an expanding world economy the establishment of new markets should afford Japan opportunity to achieve a reasonable standard of living for her people without menacing that of other countries and at the same time to help to satisfy the growing needs of consumers in the underdeveloped countries of the world.

We have observed the co-operative attitude shown in the post-war years by the leaders of Japanese industry, but the circumstances of international trade have not so far put these matters to the test. The conception of friendly contacts and joint consultation between industrial interests in the United Kingdom and in Japan, instanced by the Anglo-American Cotton Textile Mission to Japan in 1950, is of considerable importance in this connection.

We earnestly hope that by consultation between the industries principally concerned, policies and practices may develop which will make it possible for Japan and all other countries participating in world trade in commodities of importance to the various national economies, to develop their economic activities on a basis of live-and-let-live

34. Statement by Herbert Morrison in the House of Commons, 25 July 1951 (Extracts).

The principal Powers are not agreed as to the Government which could properly represent China in the signature of a multilateral Peace Treaty with Japan. Indeed, the 14 Powers who are regarded as those principally concerned in the war with Japan are almost equally divided between those who recognise the Central People's Government of China—and that number includes the United Kingdom—and those who recognise the Nationalist Government of Chiang Kai-shek. . . .

It therefore seemed that the only course to adopt would be to set aside this question of China's participation and, while safeguarding Chinese rights and interests, not to invite any Chinese to participate in the signature of the multilateral treaty now contemplated. This is a course much to be regretted but, after exhaustive consideration of the subject, there seemed to be no other way. . . .

The text of the Treaty provides that Japan will, for a period of three years after the present Treaty comes into force, be prepared to make a substantially similar Treaty of Peace with any State at war with her which signed the United Nations' Declaration of 1st January, 1942, but which does not sign the present draft Peace Treaty. China's rights and interests are thus safeguarded, as she was one of the States which signed the United Nations' Declaration referred to. In addition, the Treaty gives China, although not a signatory, the benefit of certain articles. It can fairly be said, therefore, that we have not been unmindful of China's position or of her rights and interests in the matter. . . .

We might have adopted a Versailles policy over the Japanese Peace Treaty, but after careful thought we felt that the contrary policy of a liberal treaty would give us the best chance of seeing Japan develop along liberal Parliamentary lines and play her part in the free world. . . .

In the present draft Treaty there are no actual restrictions upon Japanese re-armament. Such restrictions have been written into treaties in the past, and with the passage of time they have not been observed. Experience shows that such restrictions in a treaty not only do not ensure the desired result, but tend to provide a focus for the worst evils of nationalism. In point of fact, Japan, having been deprived by her loss of territory of important sources of raw materials will not be able in the fore-seeable future to re-arm to the extent of becoming a potential aggressor.

This question, however, is closely bound up with that of the defence of Japan itself. . . .

As at present contemplated, the security of Japan will be ensured by the voluntary conclusion by Japan of a defence pact with the United States of America, whereby balanced forces will be maintained for the defence of Japanese territory. It will, no doubt, be argued by those who are opposed to the security of Japan from aggression that such a pact represents an attempt by the United States to build up Japan in order that she may commit aggression against China or Russia, or both. We are satisfied that no such intention exists and that all that is contemplated is that the necessary forces will be stationed in and around Japan by arrangement between Japan and the United States which will ensure that Japan herself cannot become a victim of aggression.

One of the main security factors from the point of view of the United Kingdom has been the effect which the contemplated defence agreement between Japan and the United States and the consequent partial re-armament of Japan might be expected to have upon the defence of other members of the Commonwealth particularly that of Australia and of New Zealand. This question is one of the major problems connected with the Japanese Peace Treaty to which most careful thought has been given for a long time.

It has now been found possible to achieve a significant contribution to the security of Australia and of New Zealand in the Pacific area by the negotiation of a Tripartite Defence Agreement between these two members of the Commonwealth and the United States. His Majesty's Government, as is well known, have been in close consultation with the Governments of Australia and New Zealand throughout the negotiation of this Defence Agreement. . . .

I fully realise the anxieties of Lancashire and the fears held there of a revival of Japanese competition. . . .

I think, it is impossible to write into the Treaty effective restrictions. In the long run the future prosperity of Lancashire, like the rest of Britain, will depend upon the sustained pursuit of the right economic policies at home and on international co-operation in economic affairs.

There has been considerable discussion, especially among holders of Japanese sterling bonds, about the possibility of Japan resuming payments on her external debt. The draft Treaty emphasises that pre-war obligations have not been affected by the war, and it includes a Japanese affirmation of liability for the pre-war external debt, as well as undertakings about early negotiations between debtors and creditors for the resumption of service of the debts. . . .

35. Statement by Minister of State, Kenneth Younger, at the San Francisco Conference, 5 September 1951 (Extracts).

The principal document we have to consider is the text to the proposed Treaty of Peace with Japan, to which are attached three other documents—a Declaration on War Graves, a Declaration on International Agreements and Conventions, and a

Protocol on Contracts. The first three are jointly sponsored by the two Governments. For constitutional reasons it is not possible for the United States Government to sponsor the Protocol, which is therefore presented to you by the British Government alone. . . .

We could not accept the view that the Treaty should be prepared by the Council of Foreign Ministers of the United Kingdom, United States, Soviet Union and China. The argument that it should be so prepared rested on a misinterpretation of the Potsdam agreement. But apart from this we did not want to be held up indefinitely by a veto, and finally we felt most strongly that this procedure would not have been fair to many countries which had had long, close and bitter experience of the war against Japan. . . .

The Treaty safeguards the interests of the Chinese people by provisions designed to ensure that major benefits will accrue to China notwithstanding the absence of any signature or ratification of the Treaty on China's behalf. The Treaty thus provides that, when it comes into force, all Japan's special rights and interests in China will automatically be renounced, and that China will have the right to deal on its own account with Japanese property in China. . . .

The Treaty also provides for Japan to renounce its sovereignty over Formosa and the Pescadores islands. The treaty itself does not determine the future of these islands. The future of Formosa was referred to in the Cairo Declaration but that Declaration also contained provisions in respect to Korea, together with the basic principles of non-aggression and no territorial ambitions. Until China shows by her action that she accepts these provisions and principles, it will be difficult to reach a final settlement of the problem of Formosa. In due course a solution must be found, in accord with the purposes and principles of the Charter of the United Nations. . . .

As regards the Ryukyu and Bonin Islands, the treaty does not remove these from Japanese sovereignty; it provides for a continuance of United States administration over the Ryukyu islands south of 29° North latitude; that is to say that those islands nearest to Japan itself are to remain not only under Japanese sovereignty, but under Japanese administration as well. This is in marked contrast with the provision for the complete renunciation of Japanese sovereignty over the Kurile islands. . . .

Much concern has been expressed in Britain about the risk to our own economy from a revival of Japanese competition. This anxiety has been widespread and sincerely felt, but we recognized that the imposition of economic restrictions in the Treaty would have been inappropriate. . . .

We have,. . . . agreed that Japan should make such reparation as, on a realistic estimate, we believe she can afford. In the first place Japan will, if required, render to any of the Allied Powers, whose territory she overran, assistance in repairing the damage done by Japanese occupation. The draft treaty provides for the resumption by Allied nationals of their property and all their property rights in Japan. If these have been destroyed or cannot be returned, the Japanese Government has undertaken to pay compensation. Finally the draft treaty gives each of the Allies the right to seize all Japanese assets within its territory (subject to certain customary exceptions) and expresses Japan's desire to make recompense, out of the proceeds of Japanese assets in neutral and ex-enemy countries, for the suffering endured by prisoners of war who fell into her hands. . . .

A war completely disrupts international trade and commerce, and it is in our view right that a peace settlement should attempt to lay down general rules to govern their resumption. It was for this reason that the United Kingdom has sponsored the Protocol which has been circulated as one of the Peace Treaty documents. Its first three Sections follow the precedent of Annex 16 to the peace treaty with Italy and provide on similar lines rules to govern contracts, periods of prescription and negotiable instruments as between Japan and those states at war with her which may decide to sign it. Parts D and E of the protocol provide procedure for the settlement by Japanese and Allied insurance companies of all matters outstanding in connexion with insurance contracts affected by war. We hope that the protocol, by obviating the necessity for lengthy and expensive litigation, will materially help to restore that basis of confidence and willingness to meet obligations which is so important to the smooth conduct of international trade. . . .

SOVIET UNION

36. Soviet Note to USA seeking explanation on points raised in the US Memorandum of 26 October 1950, 20 November 1950 (Extracts).

Signatories of the Declaration by United Nations in Washington on January 1, 1942, obligated themselves not to conclude a separate peace with the enemy states.

In as much as the above obligation exists, an explanation is desired as to whether a peace treaty with Japan is contemplated in which are meant to participate the U.S.A., Great Britain, China and the U.S.S.R., in whose name the surrender terms for Japan were signed, as well as any other country which took an active part in the war against Japan, or whether the possibility exists of concluding a separate peace with Japan with only a few of the above-mentioned powers participating. . . .

In as much as the... [Cairo, Potsdam and Yalta] agreements exist, how should the proposal contained in the memorandum be interpreted which would make the status of Formosa, the Pescadores, Southern Sakhalin and the Kurile Islands subject to a new decision by the U.S.A., Great Britain, China and the U.S.S.R., and in case the states mentioned fail to reach an agreement in the course of a year, to a decision of the General Assembly of the United Nations.

Neither the Cairo Declaration nor the Potsdam Agreement mention that the Ryukyu and Bonin Islands should be taken out from under Japanese sovereignty; moreover, in signing those agreements the states announced that they "had no thoughts of territorial expansion."

In this connection the question arises as to what is the basis for the proposal contained in the memorandum to the effect that the Ryukyu and Bonin Islands should be placed under the trusteeship of the United Nations with the United States as the administrative power. . . .

The Soviet Government desires to know whether it contemplated that in the peace treaty with Japan a definite period of time must be provided for the withdrawal of the occupation forces from Japan's territory as provided in peace treaties already concluded with other states. . . .

In as much as in the memorandum is mentioned . . . "joint responsibility" for the maintenance of international peace and security in the region of Japan, the Soviet Government desires to receive explanations on the following two questions :

Firstly, whether it is proposed in connection with the above-mentioned "joint responsibility," to create Japanese armed forces, that is, a Japanese army, a Japanese navy and a Japanese air force, as well as the corresponding Japanese staffs.

Secondly, whether the above-mentioned "joint responsibility" means that even after the conclusion of a peace treaty with Japan American military, naval and air force bases will be maintained on the territory of Japan.

Nothing is said in the memorandum concerning the necessity of ensuring for the Japanese people on opportunity to develop freely its peacetime economy.

The Soviet Government desires to receive an explanation whether it is intended to include in the peace treaty provisions for the annulment of all limitations on the development of Japanese peacetime economy and for granting Japan access to the sources of raw materials, and also for Japan's participation in world trade with equal rights.

In as much as it is perfectly evident that in the matter of the peace treaty with Japan, China has a special interest, because China in particular was subjected for many years to aggression on the part of Japanese militarists, the Soviet Government desires to know what is being done to determine the point of view of the Government of the Chinese People's Republic on this matter. . . .

37. Soviet Government Remarks on 29 March 1951 US draft of Japanese Peace Treaty handed over by Acting Foreign Minister Begomolov to the US Ambassador Kirk, 7 May 1951 (Extracts).

That the drafting of a peace treaty with Japan has been laid upon the U.S.A., the U.S.S.R., China and Great Britain, who, as is known, signed the Japanese surrender document, also flows from the Potsdam Agreement referred to. . . .

The Soviet Government considers it necessary to mention

particularly the impermissibility of excluding China from the
preparation of a peace treaty with Japan. . . .

Without the participation of the Chinese People's Republic
in the work of preparing a peace treaty with Japan a real
peaceful settlement in the Far East is not possible. . . .

The American draft of a peace treaty with Japan contains,
from the point of view of the substance of the matter, several
incorrect contentions incompatible with existing agreements
between the powers. . . .

The draft leaves the present situation with Taiwan and the
Pescadores Islands, which have actually been torn away from
China, without change, in violation of the Cairo Agreement
concerning the return of these islands to China.

The American draft provides further, for taking the Ryukyu,
Bonin, Rosario, Volcano, Parece Vela, and Marcus Islands out
from under the sovereignty of Japan and transferring them
under the administration of the U.S.A. under the pretext of
establishing a trusteeship over them allegedly on the part of
the United Nations Organization. Inasmuch, however, as the
wresting of the islands named away from Japan is envisaged
neither by agreement between the powers nor by decision of
United Nations in the person of the Security Council, such
wresting away does not have any justification. . . .

The American draft not only does not contain a guarantee
against the restoration of Japanese militarism but in general
does not set forth any limitations with relation to the size of
the armed forces in Japan. . . .

The American draft does not establish any period for the
withdrawal of occupation troops from Japan and is directly
designed to leave American occupation troops and military
bases in Japan even after the conclusion of a peace treaty.
Consequently, even after that "peaceful settlement" which the
United States is preparing for Japan, the military occupation of
Japan will not be discontinued and the United States of
America will remain the real master in Japan. . . .

Finally, the American draft ignores the necessity of removing limitations with respect to the free development of the
peaceful economy of Japan. . . .

38. Soviet Memorandum in reply to US Memorandum of 19 May 1951, 10 June 1951 (Extracts).

For the Soviet Union as well as for other countries interested in a guarantee of lasting peace in the Far East question that Japan not become an aggressive state again and that *revival of Japanese militarism be prevented* possesses most important significance. . . .

Is there in the American draft peace treaty with Japan a guarantee against the rebirth of Japan as an aggressive state ? Acquaintance with the draft shows that it does not possess any guarantee in this respect. . . .

Inasmuch as no limitations on the armed forces of Japan are contained in the American draft, there are no guarantees there against the restoration of Japanese militarism and the possibility of repetition of Japanese aggression. It is clear that no state that experienced the aggressive attack of Japan and is interested in the guarantee of lasting peace in the Far East can agree with such a position.

Together with this, the Government of the United States of America, with the help of its occupation authorities, is in reality already carrying out of a policy of restoring Japanese militarism. . . .

The task of not permitting the rebirth of Japanese militarism and guaranteeing in the future the security of countries that suffered from Japanese aggression is being replaced by the Government of the United States of America by the conclusion of a military agreement with Japan which would push Japan even more toward the restoration of militarism. Inasmuch as it is perfectly obvious that such countries as the Chinese People's Republic and the Soviet Union are excluded from participation in this military agreement of the United States of America with Japan, there can be no doubt that this military agreement of the United States of America with Japan is directed primarily against these very states and possesses an obvious aggressive character. . . .

In refusing to set a time limit for the withdrawal of the occupation troops from Japanese territory, the Government of the United States of America breaks one of its important obligations under international agreements. Leaving foreign

troops in Japan after conclusion of a peace treaty, under whatever pretext it is done, contradicts the Potsdam declaration of
July 26, 1945, which provides for the withdrawal of foreign
troops from Japan and signifies camouflaged prolongation of
the occupation of Japan for an indefinite protracted period.

In intending to prolong the occupation even after the con-
clusion of the peace treaty, the Government of the United
States of America is thus aspiring to remain the real master in
Japan for a long time. . . .

It is necessary that in the peace treaty with Japan the time
limit for withdrawal of occupation troops from Japanese
territory be precisely fixed and that in this treaty it should be
established that no foreign state should have troops or military
bases in Japan. . . .

The proposal of the Soviet Government concerning the non-
participation of Japan in a coalition acquires important and
immediate significance on the strength of possible military agreement of the United States of America with Japan. . . .

The memorandum of the United States of America of May
19 bypasses the question of the peacetime economy of Japan
being placed in servile dependence on the United States of
America as the result of all kinds of limitations with respect to
the Japanese peacetime economy and the establishment of privileges for American firms sponsored by American occupation
authorities. Japan is deprived of the opportunity of engaging
in normal trade with neighboring states, which still further
harms prospects for the upsurge of Japanese national economy.

The Soviet Government considers that without the
effective removal of these restrictions imposed from outside, it
would be impossible to create conditions for the upsurge of a
peaceful economy and for improving the life of the Japanese
people. . . .

Judging from the memorandum of the United States of
America of March 19 everything essential has already been
achieved with respect to the democratization of Japan. But
this is wholly untrue. In fact, in Japan, police suppression of
organs of the democratic press, repressions against trade unions
and other democratic organizations and persecutions for political convictions are being fully revived, with the cooperation of
the occupation authorities, and a return to the pre-war fascist

order in Japan when the shameful law on the struggle against "dangerous thoughts" existed, is taking place.

All this confirms the necessity for adopting these proposals concerning the democratization of Japan which were put forward in the comments of the Soviet Government. . . .

It cannot be considered accidental that the Government of the United States of America does not want an over-all peace treaty with Japan, but aspires to a separate treaty. Only with conclusion of a separate treaty can the United States of America secure the dependence of Japan for several years hence, and inasmuch as the conclusion of a military agreement between the United States of America and Japan is also envisaged by the draft treaty it becomes clear the goal of the separate treaty is the transformation of Japan into a shameful weapon for carrying out the aggressive plans of the United States of America in the Far East. . . .

39. Statement by Soviet Deputy Foreign Minister, Andrei Gromyko at the San Francisco Conference, 5 September 1951 (Extracts).

The American-British draft of a peace treaty with Japan submitted to the Conference goes to show that the authors of this draft are more anxious to clear the path for the rebirth of Japanese militarism and to push Japan again along the path of aggression and military adventure. . . .

The prevention of the rebirth of Japanese militarism is closely interlinked with the task of the democratisation of the political and social life of the country, with the task of establishing in Japan a democratic order under which the fate of the country will not depend on the arbitrariness of a group of reactionary militarists. . . .

The peace treaty with Japan should have clauses providing for both restrictions of armed forces of Japan and the prevention of militarisation of its economy. At the same time, the peace treaty must not place obstacles in the path of the development of peaceful Japanese economy. . . .

The American-British draft peace treaty imposes on Japan an obligation to join a military grouping directed against the countries near Japan and first and foremost against the Soviet

Union and the Chinese People's Republic. . . .

The American-British draft provides for the exclusion of the Islands of Ryukyu, Bonin, Rosario, Volcano, Parece Vela, Marcus and Daito from the sovereignty of Japan and their transfer under the administration of the United States of America under the pretext of including them in the trusteeship system of the United Nations. However, it is well known that such a severance of the said islands from Japan is not provided for by the above-mentioned agreements of the powers, or by the decision of the Security Council which alone has the rights to take decisions regarding trusteeship over territory of strategic importance. This means that the requirement contained in the American-British draft is arbitrary and illegal. . . .

The American-British draft peace treaty does not and cannot satisfy any State that in deed and not in word stands for the establishment of a durable peace and the elimination of a threat of a new war. Such a draft cannot satisfy especially the countries of Asia and the Far East whose peoples have suffered most from the consequences of Japanese aggression and cannot permit a revival of Japanese militarism that is bearing a permanent threat to the peaceful existence of its neighbour countries in the Far East. It is for this reason that the American-British draft Peace Treaty met with opposition on the part of a number of countries: the Chinese People's Republic, India, Burma and others. . . .

To sum up, the following conclusions regarding the American-British draft peace treaty can be drawn :

1. The draft does not contain any guarantees against the re-establishment of Japanese militarism, the transformation of Japan into an aggressive state. The draft does not contain any guarantees ensuring the security of countries which have suffered from aggression on the part of militarist Japan. The draft creates conditions for the re-establishment of Japanese militarism, creates a danger of a new Japanese aggression.

2. The draft treaty actually does not provide for the withdrawal of foreign occupation forces. On the contrary, it ensures the presence of foreign armed forces on the territory of Japan and the maintenance of foreign military bases in Japan even after the signing of a Peace treaty. Under the pretext of self-defence of Japan the draft provides for the participation of

Japan in an aggressive military alliance with the United States.

3. The draft treaty not only fails to provide for obligations that Japan should not join any coalitions directed against any of the states which participated in the war against Japan but on the contrary is clearing the path for Japan's participation in aggressive blocs in the Far East created under the aegis of the United States.

4. The draft treaty does not contain any provisions on the democratization of Japan, on the ensurance of democratic rights to the Japanese people, which creates a direct threat to a rebirth in Japan of the pre-war fascist order.

5. The draft Treaty is flagrantly violating the legitimate rights of the Chinese people to the integral part of China—Taiwan (Formosa), the Pescadores and Paracel Islands and other territories severed from China as a result of Japanese aggression.

6. The draft Treaty is in contradiction to the obligations undertaken by the United States and Great Britain under the Yalta Agreement regarding the return of Sakhalin and the transfer of the Kurile Islands to the Soviet Union.

7. The numerous economic clauses are designed to ensure for foreign, in the first place American, monopolies the privileges which they have obtained during the period of occupation, Japanese economy is being placed in a slavery-like dependence from these foreign monopolies.

8. The draft actually ignores the legitimate claims of states that have suffered from Japanese occupation regarding the redemption by Japan for the damage that they have suffered. At the same time, providing for the redemption of losses direct by the labour of the Japanese population it imposes on Japan a slavery-like form of reparations.

9. The American-British draft is not a Treaty of Peace but a treaty for the preparation of a new war in the Far East. . . .

The Soviet Union has not refused to take part in the San Francisco Conference. The reason for this is that it is necessary to voice publicly the truth about the American-British draft and to oppose it with demands for such a peace treaty with Japan that shall in fact meet the interests of a peace settlement in the Far East and serve to strengthen a universal peace. . . .

The Soviet Delegation proposes the following amendments to be made in the draft of a peace treaty submitted by the Governments of the U.S.A. and Great Britain to the Conference for its consideration. . . .

1. *To Article 2.*

(a) To include, instead of paragraphs "B" and "F", a paragraph reading as follows: "Japan recognises full sovereignty of the Chinese People's Republic over Manchuria, the Islands of Taiwan (Formosa) with all the islands adjacent to it, the Penhuletao Islands (the Pescadores), the Tunshatsuntao Islands (the Bratas Islands), as well as over the Islands of Sishatauatao and Chunshatsuntao (the Paracel Islands, the group of Amphitrites, the choal of Maxifild) and Nanshatsuntao Islands including the Spratly, and renounces all right, title and claim to the territories named herein."

(b) Paragraph "c" is to be amended to read as follows: "Japan recognises full sovereignty of the Union of Soviet Socialist Republics over southern part of the Sakhalin Island, with all the islands adjacent to that part, and over Kurile Islands and renounces all right, title and claim to these territories."

2. *To Article 3.*

Article 3 to be amended to read as follows: "The sovereignty of Japan will extend to the territory consisting of the Islands of Honshu, Kushu, Sikoku, Hokkaido, as well as the Islands of Ryulayu, Bonin, Rosario, Volcano, Parece Vela, Marcus Tsushima and other islands which formed part of Japan prior to December 7, 1941, except those territories and islands which are named in Article 2."

3. *To Article 6.*

Paragraph "a" to be amended to read as follows: "All armed forces of the Allied and Associated Powers shall be withdrawn from Japan, as soon as possible and, in any case, not later than 90 days since the date of the coming into force of the present Treaty, and after that no Allied or Associated Power or any other foreign power shall have its troops or military bases on the territory of Japan."

4. *To Article 14.*

Paragraph "a" and sub-paragraph I of the same paragraph to be replaced by the following text: "Japan undertakes to compensate the damage caused by military operations against the Allied or Associated Powers, as well as by the occupation of the territories of certain Allied and Associated Powers. The amount and the sources of payment of the reparations to be paid by Japan shall be considered at a conference of the States concerned with the express participation of the nations which were subjected to Japanese occupation, namely, the Chinese People's Republic, Indonesia, the Philippines, Burma, with Japan being invited to that conference."

5. *To Article 23.*

To insert, instead of paragraph "a" and "b", a paragraph reading as follows: "The present Treaty shall be ratified by the States which sign it, including Japan, and will come into force for all the States, which will then ratify it, when the instruments of ratification have been deposited by Japan and by a majority of the following States, including the United States of America, the Soviet Union, the Chinese People's Republic and the United Kingdom of Great Britain and Northern Ireland, namely, Australia, Burma, Canada, Ceylon, France, India, Indonesia, the Netherlands, the Mongolian People's Republic, New Zealand, Pakistan, the Philippines, the United Kingdom of Great Britain and Northern Ireland, the Union of Soviet Socialist Republics, the Chinese People's Republic and the United States of America. It shall come into force for each State which subsequently ratifies it, on the date of the deposit of the instrument of ratification."

6. *A New Article* (*in Chapter IV*).

"Japan undertakes to remove all obstacles to the revival and strengthening of democratic tendencies among the Japanese people, to take all measures necessary to secure to all persons under Japanese jurisdiction, without distinction as to race, sex, language or religion, the enjoyment of human right and of the fundamental freedoms, including freedom of expression, of press and publication, of religious worship, of political opinion and of public meetings."

7. *A new article* (*in Chapter IV*).

"Japan undertakes not to permit the resurgence on Japanese territory of Fascist and militarist organisations, whether political, military or semi-military, whose purpose it is to deprive the people of their democratic rights."

8. *A new article* (*in Chapter VIII*).

"Japan undertakes not to enter into any coalitions or military alliances directed against any Power which participated with its armed forces in the war against Japan."

9. *A new article* (*in Chapter III*).

"Japanese land, air and naval armaments shall be closely restricted to meeting exclusively the tasks of self-defence. In accordance with the foregoing, Japan is authorized to have armed forces, including the frontier guards and gendarmerie, of not more than:

(a) A Land army, including anti-aircraft artillery, with a total strength of 150,000 personnel;

(b) A navy with a personnel strength of 25,000 and a total tonnage of 75,000 tons;

(c) An air force, including naval air arm, of 200 fighter and reconnaissance aircraft and of 150 transport, air-sea rescue, training and liason aircraft including reserves aircraft, with a total personnel strength of 20,000. Japan shall not possess or acquire any aircraft designed primarily as bombers with internal bomb-carrying facilities.

(d) The total number of medium and heavy tanks in the Japanese armed forces shall not exceed 200.

(e) The strength of the armed forces shall in each case include combat, service and overhead personnel."

10. *A new article* (*in Chapter III*).

"Japan is prohibited to conduct in any form military training of the population on the scale exceeding the requirements of the armed forces which Japan is permitted to maintain under Article . . . of the present Treaty Laying down the size of the armed forces of Japan."

11. *A new article* (*in Chapter III*).

"Japan shall not possess, construct or experiment with: (I) any atomic weapon and other means of mass destruction of human life, including bacteriological and chemical weapons; (II) any self-propelled or guided missiles or apparatus connected with their discharge (other than torpedoes and torpedo launching gear comprising the normal armament of naval vessels permitted by the present Treaty); (III) any guns with a range of over 30 kilometres; (IV) sea mines or torpedoes of noncontact types actuated by influence mechanisms; (V) any torpedoes capable of being manned."

12. *A new article* (*in Chapter IV*).

"No restrictions shall be imposed on Japan in developing her peaceful industries or in developing her trade with other States or in obtaining access to raw materials in accordance with the requirements of the peaceful economy of Japan. Similarly, no restrictions shall be imposed on Japan in developing her commercial shipping or in the construction of merchant vessels."

13. *A new article* (*in Chapter III*).

"1. The Straits of La Perouse (Soya) and Nemuro, along the entire Japanese coast, as well as the straits of Tsugaruand Tsushima shall be demilitarized. These straits shall always be open for the passage of merchant ships of all countries.

2. The straits named in paragraph 1 of this Article shall be open for the passage of only such warships as belong to the Powers adjacent to the Sea of Japan."

40. Joint Declaration by Japan and the Soviet Union, 19 October 1956 (Extracts).

1. The state of war between Japan and the Union of Soviet Socialist Republics is terminated as from the date on which the present Declaration enters into force, and relations of peace, amity and good neighbourhood shall be restored between them.

2. Diplomatic and consular relations shall be re-established between Japan and the Union of Soviet Socialist Republics. . . .

3. Japan and the Union of Soviet Socialist Republics confirm that they will be guided in their mutual relations by the principles of the Charter of the United Nations and in particular the principles set forth in Article 2 thereof.

(a) to settle their international disputes by peaceful means in such a manner that international peace and security, and justice are not endangered;

(b) to refrain in their international relations from the threat or use of force against the territorial integrity or political independence of any State or in any other manner inconsistent with the Purposes of the United Nations.

Japan and the Union of Soviet Socialist Republics confirm that each other country possesses the inherent right of individual or collective self-defence referred to in Article 51 of the Charter of the United Nations.

Japan and the Union of Soviet Socialist Republics mutually undertake that they will not intervene, either directly or indirectly, in the internal affairs of each other, regardless of whether for economic, political or ideological reasons.

4. The Union of Soviet Socialist Republics shall support the application by Japan for membership in the United Nations.

5. All the Japanese nationals convicted in the Union of Soviet Socialist Republics shall be released upon the entry into force of the present Joint Declaration and be repatriated to Japan.

The Union of Soviet Socialist Republics shall, in compliance with the request of Japan, continue investigations on missing Japanese nationals.

6. The Union of Soviet Socialist Republics waives all reparations claims against Japan.

Japan and the Union of Soviet Socialist Republics mutually waive all claims of the respective State and its organizations and nationals against the other State and its organizations and nationals arising out of the war since August 9, 1945.

7. Japan and the Union of Soviet Socialist Republics agree to enter into negotiations as soon as possible for the conclusion of treaties or agreements to place their trading, maritime and

other commercial relations on a stable and friendly basis. . . .

9. Japan and the Union of Soviet Socialist Republics agree to continue their negotiations for the conclusion of a peace treaty after normal diplomatic relations have been re-established between the two countries.

The Union of Soviet Socialist Republics, in response to the desire of Japan and in consideration of her interests, agrees to transfer the Habomai Islands and the island of Shikotan to Japan, provided, however, that the actual transfer of these islands shall be effected after the peace treaty between Japan and the Union of Soviet Socialist Republics is concluded.

10. The present Joint Declaration shall be ratified. It shall enter into force on the date of exchange of instruments of ratification. The instruments of ratification shall be exchanged in Tokyo as soon as possible.

POLAND

41. Agreement on the Restoration of Normal Relations between Japan and Poland, 8 February 1957.

Preamble. The Government of Japan and the Government of Poland,

Desiring to put an end to the state of war which has existed between the two countries, and to restore relations of peace and amity between them in conformity with the principles of the Charter of the United Nations,

Have agreed as follows :

Article I

The state of war between Japan and the People's Republic of Poland is terminated as from the date on which the present Agreement enters into force.

Article II

Diplomatic relations shall be re-established between Japan and Poland, and the two countries shall exchange diplomatic envoys with the Ambassadorial rank without delay.

Article III

(1) Japan and Poland confirm that they will be guided by the principles of the Charter of the United Nations, and in particular the following principles set forth in Article II thereof:

(a) to settle their international disputes by peaceful means in such a manner that international peace and security, and justice, are not endangered;

(b) to refrain in their international relations from the threat or use of force against the territorial integrity or political independence of any State or in any other manner inconsistent with the Purposes of the United Nations.

(2) Japan and Poland mutually undertake that they will not intervene, either directly or indirectly, in the internal affairs of each other, regardless of whether for economic, political or ideological reasons.

Article IV

Japan and Poland mutually waive all claims, of the respective State and its organizations and nationals against the other State and its organizations and nationals in so far as they have arisen out of the state of war between the two countries.

Article V

Japan and Poland agree to enter into negotiations as soon as possible for the conclusion of treaties or agreements to place their trading, maritime and other commercial relations on a stable and friendly basis.

Article VI

The present agreement shall be ratified. The instruments of ratification shall be exchanged in Warsaw as soon as possible. This agreement enters into effect on the day of exchange of instruments of ratification.

IN WITNESS WHEREOF, the undersigned, duly authorized by their respective Governments, have signed the present

Agreement.

DONE in duplicate, in the French language, at New York this 8th day of Feburary, 1957.

CZECHOSLOVAKIA

42. Protocol Relating to the Restoration of Normal Relations, between Japan and Czechoslovakia, 13 February 1957.

The Government of Japan and the Government of the Czechoslovak Republic, between the two countries, and to restore relations of peace and amity between them in conformity with the principles of the Charter of the United Nations.

Have agreed as follows :

Article 1

The state of war between Japan and the Czechoslovak Republic is terminated as from the date on which the present Protocol enters into force.

Article 2

Diplomatic relations shall be re-established between Japan and the Czechoslovak Republic, and the two countries shall exchange diplomatic envoys with the Ambassadorial rank without delay.

Article 3

1. Japan and the Czechoslovak Republic, confirm that they will be guided by the principles of the Charter of the United Nations and in particular the following principles set forth in Article 2 thereof :

(a) to settle their international disputes by peaceful means in such a manner that international peace and security, and justice, are not endangered;

(b) to refrain in their international relations from the threat or use of force against the territorial integrity or political independence of any State or in any other manner inconsistent with the Purposes of the United Nations.

2. Japan and the Czechoslovak Republic mutually undertake that they will not intervene, either directly or indirectly, in the internal affairs of each other, regardless of whether for economic, political or ideological reasons.

Article 4

Japan and the Czechoslovak Republic mutually waive all claims of the respective State and its organizations and nationals against the other State and its organizations and nationals in so far as they have arisen out of the state of war between the two countries.

Article 5

Japan and the Czechoslovak Republic agree to enter into negotiations as soon as possible for the conclusion of treaties or agreements to place their trading, maritime and other commercial relations on a stable and friendly basis.

Article 6

The present Protocol shall be ratified, and shall enter into force on the date of exchange of instruments of ratification. The instruments of ratification shall be exchanged at London as soon as possible.

IN WITNESS THEREOF, the undersigned, being duly authorized by their respective Governments, have signed the present Protocol.

DONE in duplicate, in the English language, at London, this thirteenth day of February, one thousand nine hundred fifty-seven.

For Japan : Haruhiko Nishi
For the Czechoslovak Republic : Jiri Hajek

NATIONALIST CHINA

43. Letter from the US Ambassador in China (Stuart) to the US Secretary of State transmitting Chinese National Assembly Resolutions, 2 June 1948.

The Ambassador has the honor to refer to the Department's telegram No. 678, dated May 5, and to transmit translations of six resolutions passed by the National Assembly during April 1948 on the subject of the Japanese Peace Conference. The subjects of the resolutions are as follows :

Resolution 108 : Principles to be advocated by the Chinese Government in connection with the Japanese Peace Treaty.

Resolution 141 : Proposal that a Japanese Peace Conference based on the Potsdam Declaration be called at once.

Resolution 196 : Proposal that the Ryukyu Islands be returned to China.

Resolution 199 : Proposal that Taiwanese representatives be sent with the Chinese delegation to the Peace Conference.

Resolution 294 : Proposal that the maximum level of production of the rehabilitated Japanese textile industry be stipulated in the peace treaty.

Resolution 769 : Proposal that the Government oppose the new American plan for reducing Japan's reparations.

These six resolutions embody ideas which frequently appear in the Chinese press. They express the lively apprehension among many Chinese that the United States may be engaged in restoring Japan's military potential and the fear that the Chinese Government is not sufficiently active in opposing this trend. Among other things the resolutions call for complete disarmament of Japan, abolition of the mikado system, maintenance of Japanese industry and standard of living at a low level and control of Japan to be continued for fifty years.

44. Letter from the Japanese Prime Minister Shigeru Yoshida to John Foster Dulles regarding Japan's policy towards China, 24 December 1951.

While the Japanese Peace Treaty and the U.S.-Japan Security Treaty were being debated in the House of Representatives and the House of Councillors of the Diet, a number of questions were put and statements made relative to Japan's future policy towards China. Some of the statements, separated from their context and background, gave rise to misapprehensions which I should like to clear up.

The Japanese Government desires ultimately to have a full measure of political peace and commercial intercourse with China which is Japan's close neighbour.

At the present time it is, we hope, possible to develop that kind of relationship with the National Government of the Republic of China, which has the seat, voice and vote of China in the United Nations, which exercises actual government authority over certain territory, and which maintains diplomatic relations with most of the members of the United Nations. To that end my Government on November 17, 1951, established a Japanese Government Overseas Agency in Formosa, with the consent of the National Government of China. This is the highest form of relationship with other countries which is now permitted to Japan, pending the coming into force of the multilateral Treaty of Peace. The Japanese Government Overseas Agency in Formosa is important in its personnel, reflecting the importance which my government attaches to relations with the National Government of the Republic of China. My government is prepared as soon as legally possible to conclude with the National Government of China, if that government so desires, a Treaty which will re-establish normal relations between the two Governments in conformity with the principles set out in the multilateral Treaty of Peace. The terms of such bilateral treaty shall, in respect of the Republic of China, be applicable to all territories which are now, or which may hereafter be, under the control of the National Government of the Republic of China. We will promptly explore this subject with the National Government of China.

As regards the Chinese Communist regime, that regime stands actually condemned by the United Nations of being an aggressor and in consequence, the United Nations has recommended certain measures against that regime, in which Japan is now concurring and expects to continue to concur when the multilateral Treaty of Peace comes into force pursuant to the provisions of Article 5 (a) (iii), whereby Japan has undertaken 'to give the United Nations every assistance in any action it takes in accordance with the Charter and to refrain from giving assistance to any State against which the United Nations may take preventive or enforcement action.' Furthermore, the Sino-Soviet Treaty of Friendship, Alliance, and Mutual Assistance concluded in Moscow in 1950 is virtually a military alliance aimed against Japan. In fact there are many reasons to believe that the Communist regime in China is backing the Japan Communist Party in its program of seeking violently to overthrow the constitutional system and the present Government of Japan. In view of these considerations, I can assure you that the Japanese Government has no intention to conclude a bilateral Treaty with the Communist regime of China.

45. Dulles' reply to Shigeru Yoshida, 16 January 1952.

I acknowledge the receipt by pouch of your letter of December 24, 1951, in which you express the intentions of your Government with reference to China.

This clear statement should dispel any misapprehensions which, as you suggest, may have arisen from statements, separated from their context and background, made during the course of debate in Japan on the ratification of the Japanese Peace Treaty and the U.S.-Japan Security Treaty.

I am grateful to you for your letter and I respect the courageous and forthright manner in which you face up to this difficult and controversial matter.

46. Treaty of Peace between the Republic of China and Japan, 28 April 1952.

The Republic of China and Japan,

Considering their mutual desire for good neighborliness in view of their historical and cultural ties and geographical prioximity; Realizing the importance of their close cooperation to the promotion of their common welfare and to the maintenance of international peace and security;

Recognizing the need of a settlement of problems that have arisen as a result of the existence of a state of war between them; Have resolved to conclude a Treaty of Peace and have accordingly appointed as their Plenipotentiaries,

His Excellency the President of the Republic of China:

Mr. Yeh Kung Chao;

The Government of Japan: Mr. Isao Kawada;

Who, having communicated to each other their full powers found to be in good and due form, have agreed upon the following articles :

Article I

The state of war between the Republic of China and Japan is terminated as from the date on which the present Treaty enters into force.

Article II

It is recognized that under Article 2 of the Treaty of Peace which Japan signed at the city of San Francisco in the United States of America on September 8, 1951 (hereinafter referred to as the San Francisco Treaty), Japan has renounced all right, title and claim to Taiwan (Formosa) and Penghu (the Pescadores) as well as the Spratly Islands and the Paracel Islands.

Article III

The disposition of property of Japan and of its nationals in Taiwan (Formosa) and Penghu (the Pescadores), and their claims, including debts, against the authorities of the Republic of China in Taiwan (Formosa) and Penghu (the Pescadores) and the residents thereof, and the disposition in Japan of property of such authorities and residents and their claims, including debts, against Japan and its nationals, shall be the subject of special arrangements between the Government of the Republic of China and the Government of Japan. The terms nationals and residents whenever used in the present Treaty include juridical persons.

Article IV

It is recognized that all treaties, conventions and agreements concluded before December 9, 1941, between China and Japan have become null and void as a consequence of the war.

Article V

It is recognized that under the provisions of Article 10 of the San Francisco Treaty, Japan has renounced all special rights and its interests in China, including all benefits and privileges resulting from the provisions of the final Protocol signed at Peking on September 7, 1901, and all annexes, notes and documents supplementary thereto, and has agreed to the abrogation in respect to Japan of the said protocol, annexes, notes and documents.

Article VI

(a) The Republic of China and Japan will be guided by the principles of Article 2 of the Charter of the United Nations in their mutual relations.

(b) The Republic of China and Japan will cooperate in accordance with the principles of the Charter of the United Nations and, in particular, will promote their common welfare through friendly cooperation in the economic field.

Article VII

The Republic of China and Japan will endeavor to conclude, as soon as possible, a treaty or agreement to place their trading, maritime and other commercial relations, on a stable and friendly basis.

Article VIII

The Republic of China and Japan will endeavor to conclude, as soon as possible, an agreement relating to civil air transport.

Article IX

The Republic of China and Japan will endeavor to conclude, as soon as possible, an agreement providing for the regulation or limitation of fishing and the conservation and development of fisheries on the high seas.

Article X

For the purposes of the present Treaty, nationals of the

Republic of China shall be deemed to include all the inhabitants and former inhabitants of Taiwan (Formosa) and Penghu (the Pescadores) and their descendants who are of the Chinese nationality in accordance with the laws and regulations which have been or may hereafter be enforced by the Republic of China in Taiwan (Formosa) and Penghu (the Pescadores); and juridical persons of the Republic of China shall be deemed to include all those registered under the laws and regulations which have been or may hereafter be enforced by the Republic of China in Taiwan (Formosa) and Penghu (the Pescadores).

Article XI

Unless otherwise provided for in the present Treaty and the documents supplementary thereto, any problem arising between the Republic of China and Japan as a result of the existence of a state of war shall be settled in accordance with the relevant provisions of the San Francisco Treaty.

Article XII

Any dispute that may arise out of the interpretation or application of the present Treaty shall be settled by negotiation or by other Pacific means.

Article XIII

The present Treaty shall be ratified and the instruments of ratification shall be exchanged at Taipei as soon as possible. The present Treaty shall enter into force as from the date on which such instruments of ratification are exchanged.

Article XIV

The present Treaty shall be in the Chinese, Japanese and English languages. In case of any divergence of interpretation, the English text shall prevail.

IN WITNESS WHEREOF, the respective Plenipotentiaries have signed the present Treaty and have affixed thereto their seals.

DONE in duplicate at Taipei, this Twenty Eighth day of the Fourth month of the Forty First year of the Republic of

China corresponding to the Twenty Eighth day of the Fourth month of the Twenty Seventh year of Showa of Japan and to the Twenty Eighth day of April in the year One Thousand Nine Hundered and Fifty Two.

47. Protocol, 28 April 1952.

At the moment of signing this day the Treaty of Peace between the Republic of China and Japan (hereinafter referred to as the present Treaty), the undersigned Plenipotentiaries have agreed upon the following terms which shall constitute an integral part of the present Treaty :

1. The application of Article XI of the present Treaty shall be subject to the following understandings :

(a) Wherever a period is stipulated in the San Francisco Treaty during which Japan assumes an obligation or undertaking, such period shall, in respect of any part of the territories of the Republic of China, commence immediately when the present Treaty becomes applicable to such part of the territories.

(b) As a sign of magnanimity and goodwill towards the Japanese people, the Republic of China voluntarily waives the benefit of the services to be made available by Japan pursuant to Article 14 (a) 1 of the San Francisco Treaty.

(c) Articles 11 and 18 of the San Francisco Treaty shall be excluded from the operation of Article XI of the present Treaty.

2. The commerce and navigation between the Republic of China and Japan shall be governed by the following Arrangements :

(a) Each Party will mutually accord to nationals, products and vessels of the other Party :

(i) Most-favored-nation treatment with respect to customs duties, charges, restrictions and other regulations on or in connection with the importation and exportation of goods; and

(ii) Most-favored-nation treatment with respect to shipping, navigation and imported goods, and with respect to natural and juridical persons and their interests—, such treatment to include all matters pertaining to the levying and collection of taxes, access to the courts, the making and performance of contracts, rights to property (including those relating to intangible property and excluding those with respect to mining), participation in juridical entities, and generally the conduct of all kinds of business and professional activities with the exception of financial (including insurance) activities and those reserved by either Party exclusively to its nationals.

(b) Whenever the grant of most-favored-nation treatment by either Party to the other Party, concerning rights to property, participation in juridical entities and conduct of business and professional activities, as specified in sub-paragraph (a) (ii) of this paragraph, amounts in effect to the grant of national treatment, such Party shall not be obliged to grant more favorable treatment than that granted by the other Party under most-favored-nation treatment.

(c) External purchases and sales of government trading enterprises shall be based solely on commercial considerations.

(d) In the application of the present Arrangements, it is understood

(i) that vessels of the Republic of China shall be deemed to include all those registered under the laws and regulations which have been or may hereafter be enforced by the Republic of China in Taiwan (Formosa) and Penghu (the Pescadores); and products of the Republic of China shall be deemed to include all those originating in Taiwan (Formosa) and Penghu (the Pescadores); and

(ii) that a discriminatory measure shall not be considered to derogate from the grant of treatments prescribed above, if such measure is based on an exception customarily provided for in the commercial treaties of the Party applying it, or on the need to safeguard that Party's external financial position or balance of payments (except in respect to shipping and navigation), or on the need to maintain its essential security interests, and provided such measure is proportionate to the circumstances and not applied in an arbitrary or unreasonable manner.

The Arrangements set forth in this paragraph shall remain in force for a period of one year as from the date on which the present Treaty enters into force.

DONE in duplicate at Taipei, this Twenty Eighth day of the

Fourth month of the Forty First year of the Republic of China
corresponding to the Twenty Eighth day of the Fourth month
of the Twenty Seventh year of Showa of Japan and to the
Twenty Eighth day of April in the year One Thousand Nine
Hundred and Fifty Two.

48. Exchange of Notes between Japanese and Chinese Plenipotentiaries, 28 April 1952.

(I) Note from the Japanese Plenipotentiary Isao Kawada to the Chinese Plenipotentiary, Yeh Kung Chao, 28 April 1952.

In regard to the Treaty of Peace between Japan and the
Republic of China signed this day, I have the honor to refer,
on behalf of my Government, to the understanding reached
between us that the terms of the present Treaty shall, in respect
of the Republic of China, be applicable to all the territories
which are now, or which may hereafter be under the control of
its Government.

I shall be appreciative, if you will confirm the understanding
set forth above.

Reply from Yeh Kung Chao, 28 April 1952.

In connection with the Treaty of Peace between the Republic
of China and Japan signed this day, I have the honor to
acknowledge receipt of your Excellency's Note of to-day's date
reading as follows : . . .

I have the honour to confirm, on behalf of my Government,
the understanding set forth in Your Excellency's Note under
reply.

(II) Note from Yeh Kung Chao to Isao Kawada, 28 April 1952.

I have the honor to state that it is the understanding of my
Government that pending the conclusion of the agreement
envisaged in Article VIII of the Treaty of Peace between the
Republic of China and Japan signed this day, the relevant provisions of the San Francisco Treaty shall apply.

I have the honor to request that Your Excellency will be so
good as to confirm that this is also the understanding of the
Government of Japan.

Reply from Isao Kawada, 28 April 1952.

In connection with the Treaty of Peace between Japan and the Republic of China signed this day, I have the honor to acknowledge receipt of Your Excellency's Note of to-day's date reading as follows : . . .

I have the honor to confirm that this is also the understanding of the Government of Japan.

49. Agreed Minutes between Japanese and Chinese Plenipotentiaries, 28 April 1952.

I

Chinese Delegate:

It is my understanding that the expression "or which may hereafter be" in the Notes No. I exchanged to-day can be taken to mean "and which may hereafter be". Is it so ?

Japanese Delegate:

Yes, it is so. I assure you that the Treaty is applicable to all the territories under the control of the Government of the Republic of China.

II

Chinese Delegate:

It is my understanding that the property, rights or interests in Japan of the collaborationist regimes created in China, as a result of the so-called "Mukden incident" of September 18, 1931, such as "Manchukuo" and the "Wang Ching Wei regime," shall be transferrable to the Republic of China upon agreement between the two Parties in accordance with the relevant provisions of the present Treaty and of the San Francisco Treaty. Is it so ?

Japanese Delegate:

It is so.

III

Chinese Delegate:

I understand that nothing in the provisions under Article 14 (a) 2 (II) (ii) of the San Francisco Treaty shall be construed to extend any exceptions to the real property, furniture and fixtures used by such set-ups as were established since September 18, 1931, without the concurrence of the Republic of China and were once claimed to be diplomatic or consular set-ups of the Japanese Government in China and the personal furniture and furnishings and other private property used by the personnel of such set-ups. Is it so ?

Japanese Delegate:

It is so.

IV

Japanese Delegate:

It is my understanding that since the Republic of China has voluntarily waived the service compensation as stated in paragraph I (b) of the Protocol of the present Treaty, the only benefit that remains to be extended to her under Article 14 (a) of the San Francisco Treaty is Japan's external assets as stipulated in Article 14 (a) 2 of the same Treaty. Is it so ?

Chinese Delegate:

Yes, it is so.

(Signed) Yeh Kung Chao
(Signed) Isao Kawada

PEOPLE'S REPUBLIC OF CHINA

50. Article by Yu Shu-teh in *Ta Kung Pao* on Peace Treaty with Japan, 10 October 1947 (Extracts).

The drawing up of the Japanese Peace Treaty is a matter of life and death to the future of our country, so it must be carefully studied. It must skilfully provide for the establishment of permanent peace and security, so as to eliminate the danger of future invasion. It would be disastrous to show an aimless and imprudent "generosity" in a momentary impulse, or to pander to any friendly nation, to the detriment of our own interests and security. . . . Most of the countries attending the conference belong to the Anglo-American group, so the

United States can secure the two-third majority. But our country is weak and stands alone, and our interests, which are far greater than Russia's, are at stake. Therefore, before the participants of this conference decide upon anything running contrary to our interests, we must never agree to such a proposal. In order to support the UN Charter and protect our interests, we need not evade the accusation of siding with Russia. We must insist on the unity of the Four Powers, and the retention of the veto. . . .

As to the limitation of Japanese armaments, we should persistently claim a thorough disbandment of Japanese troops, refuse to allow any part of the armed forces to be retained under any pretext, disallow reconstruction of the navy, army and air force; in fact annihilate the potential fighting power of Japan, and so eliminate the possibility of renewed aggression. . . .

Regarding restriction of the level of Japanese industry, we should adamantly claim disbandment of all instruments for Japanese economic invasion, and so nullify this possibility. . . .

As to Japanese reparations we should insist that the minimum standard acceptable according to the plan of Japanese indemnity should be as suggested by Porley, and that our country should obtain half the total of reparations. . . . Out of reparations to our country, apart from equipment taken from Japanese factories including steel, machinery and textiles, and electrical apparatus, we should further demand part payment in gold. Our country lacks capital. If we only demand equipment taken from factories, we will be in the difficult economic situation of a shortage of capital and unable to take possession of such reparations, or to transport them from Japan to China.

As to how to supervise the execution of the Japanese Peace Treaty, this is still problematic.

51. Observer's Commentary in *China Digest*, 24 February 1947 (Extract).

America is now voicing opposition against Japanese war reparations. China's losses during the war according to UNO's Secretariat, approximate to US $30,000,000,000. As victor she is more crippled and stricken than the conquered Japan. Her people will never agree with America's designs against Japan's war preparations. MacArthur's policy is clearly that of building Japan into a strong, American controlled military, political and economic bulwark in the Far East—to be the bastion of anti-Bolshevism crusade and a secure base for American exapansion.

The Chinese who have fought the war cannot endorse Nanking's slavish dependence on America for action towards Japan. China must have a clear-cut policy: to uproot all latent fascist forces in Japan which may prepare her for another aggression. In doing this, MacArthur's dictatorship must be eliminated. Every war criminal must be punished; none shall escape. True representatives of the masses of the Japanese people should be given a fair chance to carry out a thorough social revolution to clean up the mechanism through which the former ruling class: militarists and the Zaibatsu, operated. China's war losses must be reparated.

52. *Hsinhua* Commentary on Peace Treaty with Japan, 21 June 1949 (Extracts).

At a time when the American Government is continually adopting a separatist policy on the German question and at a time when the American Government is adopting a policy of protecting Japan's aggressive forces, the Chinese people cannot but be more seriously on the vigilant to the schemes of the United States to put off preparations for the peace treaty with Japan and for long term occupation of Japan. . . .

American imperialism has long ago unilaterally taken the steps of releasing war criminals, preserving the Zaibatsu and fostering reactionary forces. Recently it has more frenziedly carried out a series of illegal acts.

These illegal acts were mainly :

1. On May 12, the United States Government unilaterally announced its decision to cancel the provisional plan for Japanese reparation and put an end to all reparations payment by Japan. On June 10, the United States State Department again made a statement, re-affirming the stand to cancel Japanese reparations.

2. On May 16, the Japanese House of Representatives passed, under MacArthur's direction, an act to expand the police force. As everyone knows, the American occupying

force is secretly training and equipping Japanese troops under
the cloak of strengthening the police force.

3. Under the so-called 9 point plan for stablising Japanese
economy promulgated last December, American monopoly
capital is pouring into Japan and dominating all Japan's important industries and the export trade. . . .

4. Recently MacArthur's Headquarters is more frenziedly sup-
pressing the democratic movement of the Japanese people. . . .

This imperialist policy of the United States Government
towards Japan and its various acts directly threaten the peace
and security in the Far East, directly violate the Potsdam
Declaration and the rights of countries who fought against
Japan and directly destroy Japan's independence and democracy
and her peaceful economic development. Is this not obvious?

The Chinese people have firmly opposed this criminal policy
of the United States towards Japan and will continue to oppose
it to the end. The Chinese people have suffered the most and
sacrificed the most at the hands of the Japanese invaders. She
has every right to demand the prompt fixing of a date to hold
a preliminary conference which should be participated by delegates with full powers of the People's Democratic New China,
to prepare the peace treaty with Japan, in accordance with
principles of the Potsdam Agreement and other international
agreements and to work out a peace treaty with Japan which
will eliminate Japanese militarism and realise a democratic
Japan. At the same time, the Chinese people have every right
to declare as illegal the unilateral decisions carried out by the
United States which has time and again violated international
agreements during the past four years, such as releasing war
criminals, ceasing the payment of reparations and preserving
the Zaibatsu. . . .

53. *Wen Hui Pao* Blames the United States for Delay in Conclu-
ding Peace with Japan, 1 July 1949 (Extract).

It has been four years since Japan surrendered, and yet the
Peace Treaty with Japan is still an outstanding issue. The
basic reason for this is American imperialism's attempt to
occupy Japan permanently and all by itself, to convert Japan
into its military ally, and to make that country the springboard

for the invasion of Continental Asia. In accordance with the principle laid down in the Potsdam Agreement, the Japan Peace Treaty should be prepared for by the Council of Foreign Ministers. But . . . as for back as July 11, 1947, American imperialism unilaterally announced the preliminary discussion on the Japan Peace Treaty on August 19 of the same year by the 11 nations which participated in the Far Eastern Commission . . . Most of the 11 nations in the Commission are satellites of the US-British bloc. American imperialism obviously intended thus to realize her aims through the overpowering of the minority by the majority. . . .

54. *World Culture* Protests against American action in Delaying Peace with Japan, 1 July 1949 (Extracts).

On June 20, Soviet Foreign Minister Vishinsky proposed at the meeting of the Council of Foreign Ministers in Paris that the Foreign Ministers of the Big Four, including China, meet to prepare a peace treaty for Japan in accordance with the provisions of the Potsdam Agreement. He pointed out that the question of writing a Japanese peace treaty could not be delayed any longer. Vishinsky's proposal is both justified and necessary.

It is almost four years since the Japanese surrender and yet no Japanese peace treaty is in sight. Taking advantage of this indefinite delay, American imperialism intends to occupy Japan as long as possible, with General Douglas MacArthur holding the whip, for the purpose of preparing a war venture by building up the reactionary forces in Japan and by consolidating Japan's position as an anti-Communist and anti-Soviet bastion. . . .

In addition, American imperialism is doing everything in its power to tighten its control over South Korea and to seize Formosa. It is quite clear that this plan of American imperialism is aimed at bottling up the Soviet Union in the East and at throwing obstacles in the path of the growth of the new democratic China. . . .

55. Article by Li Chung-ching in *World Culture* on Peace Treaty with Japan, March 1950 (Extract).

The importance of the Japan problem is growing with the passage of each single day. . . .

Today Japan is the major military base in the campaign against the Soviet Union, against the democratic movements of Asia.

American monopolistic capital, backed by US militarism now controls Japan's economic and political life—in contravention of the terms of the Potsdam Declaration. This dangerous situation can only be rectified by an early Peace Conference and the framing of a Peace Treaty designed to lay the foundations for an independent, peaceful and democratic Japan. In the meantime American imperialism is using every tactic in its power to delay the calling of such a Conference, while lining up a "unilateral peace," which will provide for :

1. The continued garrisoning of American forces in Japan after the conclusion of the Peace Treaty, ostensibly to supervise the implementation of the peace terms. (But to the Japanese people the act will be explained as a measure to protect Japan from 'aggression', since Japan has already declared her disarmament in the Constitution.)

2. The conclusion of a United States-Japanese Military Alliance upon the conclusion of the Peace Treaty. This alliance may possibly be developed into a "Pacific Pact."

3. The demand by the United States to establish military bases in Japan, so as to legalize and perpetuate its encroachment on Japan's sovereign rights.

4. The cancellation of reparations, and the raising of Japan's industrial level. The United States will further ensure continuous economic aid to Japan, and invest in Japan so as to place its economy under complete control.

5. With reference to the question of Japan's territorial definitions, the United States will encourage Japanese expansion among the islands to the north of the four principal islands.

These plans will not only preserve the present status of Japan, but will turn Japan into a military base and colonial possession of American imperialism. . . .

These plans would not lack support from Japan's former

ruling classes. . . .

56. Chou En-lai's Statement on the Peace Treaty with Japan, 4 December 1950 (Extracts).

The Central People's Government consider all activities for the preparation and drafting of a peace treaty with Japan, no matter what their contents and results, are illegal and invalid unless the People's Republic of China takes part in them. . . .

The United States Government adopted a policy of procrastination with regard to the peace treaty with Japan in order to carry out its longterm military occupation of Japan. The United States Government has, since 1947, repeatedly attempted to upset the procedure for the conclusion of the peace treaty with Japan, has undermined the principle under which the peace treaty with Japan should first be jointly discussed and prepared by the foreign ministers conference of the four countries, China, the Soviet Union, the United States and Great Britain, and has also undermined the principle of unanimity of the great Powers. Now the United States Government is not only attempting to undermine the procedure for the peace treaty with Japan, but is further attempting to wreck the basis of a joint peace treaty with Japan. . . .

4. With regard to Taiwan and Penghu Islands, it has been decided that they be restored to China in accordance with the Cairo Declaration. With regard to the southern part of Sakhalin and Kurile Islands, it has been decided that they be restored and handed over to the U.S.S.R. in accordance with the Yalta Agreement. There is absolutely no reason for renewed discussion of these questions of territories which have already been decided. The demand of the United States Government for a renewed decision of these territorial questions is a flagrant violation of established international agreements, a deliberate violation of the legal rights and interests of the People's Republic of China and the U.S.S.R. and an attempt to attain its aggressive aims in the process. This is clearly proved by the fact that the United States Government has already engaged in armed aggression against China's Taiwan. As to the Ryukyu Archipelago and the Bonin Islands, there is no decision regarding trusteeship over these in the Cairo Declaration or the Pots-

dam Declaration, much less mention of such a thing as the appointment of "the United States as the administering authority." Such ambitions of the United States Government constitute nothing but a false borrowing of the name of the United Nations to carry out the long-term occupation of the Ryukyu Archipelago and the Bonin Islands and to establish military bases for aggression in the Far East.

5. Occupation troops should be withdrawn from Japan, according to the Potsdam Declaration. But the United States Government has not shown the slightest indication from beginning to end that the American occupation forces have any intention of withdrawing from Japan at an early date, but, instead, have been using Japan as a war base to invade Korea and China. The United States Government, in its memorandum to the Government of the Union of Soviet Socialist Republics, demands the inclusion in the Japanese peace treaty of permission to continue co-operative responsibility between Japanese facilities and United States forces for the maintenance of international peace and security in the Japan area. This is identical with coercing the Japanese people into accepting the stationing of United States troops for a long period in Japan to carry on aggression against the peoples of Asia.

6. In the Far Eastern Commission's basic policy regarding Japan after her surrender, it was originally set out that Japan would not have any army, navy or air force, secret police or gendarmerie, that is to say, Japan must not be re-armed. Nevertheless, just as the United States Government has today openly re-armed Western Germany, it is now openly re-arming Japan. As is generally known, the United States occupation troops are rebuilding the Japanese army under the pseudonym of the Japanese police; rebuilding the Japanese navy by means of the Maritime Security Bureau; preserving and reconstructing Japanese naval ports; rebuilding the Japanese air force by the training of Japanese aviators and preserving and reconstructing Japanese air bases. American occupation authorities are rebuilding the aggressive forces of Japan by releasing a large number of top war criminals, lifting the purge, and restoring a large number of fascist elements to their activities.

The United States Government, through its military control,

attempts to make Japan a United States colony, and drive Japan forward as the United States' tool in aggression against the Asian peoples.

7. In order to improve the livelihood of the Japanese people, the Central People's Government of the People's Republic of China strongly desires that Japan's peaceful industry develop on the basis of serving the Japanese people. At the same time, in accordance with the basic policies stipulated in regard to Japan after her surrender by the Far Eastern Commission, the economic basis of Japan's military strength must be destroyed and not allowed to revive. But actually, working in the interests of American monopoly capital, the American occupation authorities are reviving Japan's war industry and developing and utilising it in order to carry out aggression against Korea and China's Taiwan. At the same time, Japan's peaceful industry is deteriorating. This policy of the United States Government of stifling Japan's peaceful industry and encouraging her war industry, only results in undermining the peaceful life of the Japanese people and in intensifying the exploitation of the economy of the Japanese nation.

8. The plan envisaged in the memorandum of the United States Government regarding the peace treaty with Japan flagrantly violates the common war aims of the allied nations which opposed Japan, and, furthermore, violates all international agreements on policy towards Japan, utterly disregards the fundamental interests of the Chinese people who fought a heroic war against Japan and also disregards the aspirations of the Japanese people for the future. The United States Government has only the utterly selfish aim of forcibly occupying Japan, enslaving the Japanese people and transforming Japan into an American colony and a military base for aggression against the peoples of Asia. Therefore, the proposals set forth in the memorandum of the United States Government on the question of peace treaty with Japan do not conform to the interests of the Chinese and Japanese peoples. The Chinese people strongly desire the early conclusion of a joint peace treaty with Japan together with the other allied nations of the Second World War period. But the basis of the peace treaty must entirely conform to the Cairo Declaration, the Yalta Agreement, the Potsdam Declaration and the basic policies

therein prescribed towards Japan after her surrender. Only a peace treaty with Japan based on such international agreements can bring about the democratisation of Japan, can eliminate the aggressive forces of Japan. Only a democratic Japan, free from the control of foreign influence, can contribute to the peace and security of Asia.

57. *People's Daily* **Editorial, "Smash America's Plot to Re-arm Japan and Fight for a General and Just Peace with Japan," 28 January 1951 (Extracts).**

The American plan to conclude a separate peace and to re-arm Japan will, of course, arouse most stubborn and severe opposition from China, the Soviet Union, and the peoples of the Asian countries, and will produce most serious consequences. For about fifty years before Japan's surrender on August 15, 1945, imperialist Japan was the most prominent and vicious enemy of the Chinese people. The Chinese people won their victory only after a long and hard struggle; and consequently, they cannot tolerate America's re-armament of Japan and Japan as an enemy. For similar reasons of security, the peoples of the Soviet Union, too, can never agree to the emergence of an aggressor on their eastern borders. It is known to everyone that one of the chief purposes of the Sino-Russian Treaty of Alliance and Friendship is jointly to prevent the emergence of Japanese armed aggression. . . .

A separate peace with America would mean that Japan, politically speaking, will not only still be at war with the People's Republic of China and the Soviet Union, on, but also that Japan has sided with American imperialism, which is antagonistic to the two great powers of China and Soviet Russia. . . .

58. **Chou En-lai's Note to Soviet Ambassador in China supporting Soviet Remarks on US Draft Peace Treaty with Japan, 22 May 1951 (Extracts).**

China fully supports the Soviet Government's views on the United States Draft Peace Treaty with Japan and its concrete proposals concerning the preparation of a peace treaty with

Japan. . . .

The United States Government has tried hard to exclude the People's Republic of China, the Soviet Union and other Allied Powers from the work of preparing the peace treaty with Japan, and to monopolise the preparation and drafting of the Japanese peace treaty, so that it may utilise the dependence of the Japanese Government on the United States occupation authorities to dictate to Japan and force her to accept peace treaty terms favourable to the United States Government. It is very obvious that the Japanese Government, which is now utilised by the United States occupation authorities, cannot represent the free will of the Japanese people and that the peace terms which the United States Government imposes upon Japan can only bring calamity to the Japanese people.

2. The Government of the Soviet Union very properly points out that the contents of the United States Draft Peace Treaty with Japan flagrantly violate the important international agreements, the Cairo Declaration of 1943, the Potsdam Declaration of 1945 and the Yalta Agreement of 1945. . . .

In accordance with above-mentioned international agreements, the United States armed forces were authorised by the Allies to occupy Japan, with the sole purpose of eliminating Japanese militarism and carrying out the democratisation of Japan. But the policy carried out by the United States occupation authorities in Japan has been to do their utmost in preserving Japanese militarism and preventing the democratisation of Japan, and is therefore incompatible with the above-mentioned international agreements and illegal. . . .

The United States Draft Peace Treaty with Japan provides no guarantee at all for preventing the revival of Japanese militarism, nor does it place any limitation upon the size of the Japanese armed forces. The aim of the United States Government is clearly not to eliminate, but to revive, militarism in Japan and, with its territory as war base and its people as cannon fodder, to make Japan a tool of the United States in continuing and expanding aggression in Korea, China and other Asian countries.

Apart from all this, the United States Government does not plan to withdraw her military occupation troops from Japan after the signing of the peace treaty; on the contrary it has already gained the unlimited right of continuing indefinitely the occupation of Japan after the signing of the peace treaty. The United States Government is attempting to legalise its unlawful occupation of Japan by United States forces in order to place Japan in a state of long-term occupation. . . .

China completely endorses the five principal aims, proposed by the Soviet Government, which should serve as a guide in the concluding of a just and fair peace treaty with Japan on the basis of the Cairo Declaration, the Potsdam Declaration and the Yalta Agreement. These are :

"(a) Japan must become a peace-loving, democratic and independent state; (b) the population of Japan must be ensured democratic rights, and the existence of such organisations, whether political, military or para-military, whose aim is to deprive the people of their democratic rights, must not be permitted, as is provided for in the peace treaty with Italy; (c) as a guarantee against the revival of Japanese militarism, the treaty must set limitations on the size of the Japanese armed forces so that they should not exceed the requirements of self-defence, as this has been established in the peace treaty with Italy; (d) no restrictions are to be imposed on Japan as regards the development of its peaceful economy; (e) all restrictions with regard to Japan's trade with other countries will be removed."

In order to ensure concretely the realisation of the above-mentioned principal aims, the Central People's Government of the People's Republic of China fully agrees to and supports the proposals put forward by the Government of the Union of Soviet Socialist Republics that the peace treaty should provide that Japan must not take part in any alliance which is aimed against any of the Allied Powers; that all occupation troops be withdrawn from Japan not later than one year after the signing of the peace treaty with Japan; that no foreign Power should maintain armed forces or military bases in Japan; and that all signatory states of the peace treaty should jointly support Japan's entry into the United Nations Organisation. . . .

The work for the conclusion of an over-all peace treaty with Japan has become a task which can no longer be put off. Therefore, the Central People's Government of the People's Republic of China fully agrees to the proposal of the Govern-

ment of the Union of Soviet Socialist Republics: To convene
in June or July 1951, a session of the Council of Foreign
Ministers composed of representatives of the United States,
China, Great Britain and the U.S.S.R. in order to commence
preparing the peace treaty with Japan, having in view to draw
into the preparatory work of drafting the peace treaty with
Japan representatives of all states that participated with their
armed forces in the war against Japan, so that the draft peace
treaty be submitted for the consideration of the peace conference.

59. Chou En-lai's Statement on the US-British Draft Peace Treaty with Japan and the San Francisco Conference, 15 August 1951 (Extracts).

The Central People's Government of the People's Republic
of China considers that the Draft Peace Treaty with Japan as
proposed by the United States and British Governments is a
draft which violates international agreements and is therefore
basically unacceptable and that the conference, sheduled to
meet on September 4 at San Francisco, under the compulsion
of the United States Government, which audaciously excludes
the People's Republic of China, is a conference which repudia-
tes international commitments and therefore basically cannot
be recoganised. . . .

Firstly, since the United States-British Draft Peace Treaty
with Japan is the product of the efforts of the United States
Government and its satellites to seek a separate peace with
Japan, it not only ignores the views set forth in a series of
statements by the Governments of the Soviet Union and China
in connection with the main objectives of a peace treaty with
Japan, but also absurdly and openly excludes the Central
People's Government of the People's Republic of China from
the ranks of the Allied Powers at war with Japan. . . .

The United States-British Draft Peace Treaty with Japan
provides that its Article concerning the disposal of the property
and rights or interests in Japan of the Allied Powers and their
nationals during the war is applicable only to the period from
December 7, 1941, to September 2, 1945, thus completely
ignoring the period before December 7, 1941, when the Chinese

people were carrying on the war against Japan single-handed.

This illegal and truculent action on the part of the United States and British Governments, which excludes the People's Republic of China and adopts a hostile attitude towards the Chinese people, can never be tolerated by the Chinese people, but will be determinedly opposed by them.

Secondly, the provisions on territory in the United States-British Draft Peace Treaty with Japan are designed entirely to suit the desire of the United States Government to extend its occupation and aggression.

On the one hand, the Draft Treaty ensures that the United States Government, in addition to the retaining of trusteeship over those Pacific islands which were formerly placed under Japanese mandate by the League of Nations, shall secure the trusteeship over the Ryukyu Islands, the Bonin Islands, the Volcano Islands, Rosario Islands, Parece Vela and Marcus Islands, thus actually retaining the right of continued occupation of these islands, whose separation from Japan has never been provided for in any previous international agreement.

On the other hand, in violation of the agreement under the Cairo Declaration, the Yalta Agreement and the Potsdam Declaration, the Draft Treaty only provides that Japan should renounce all rights to Taiwan and the Penghu Islands (the Pescadores) as well as to the Kurile Islands, the southern part of Sakhalin and all islands adjacent to it, without mentioning even one word about the agreement that Taiwan and the Pescadores be returned to the People's Republic of China and that the Kurile Islands be handed over to, and the southern part of Sakhalin and all islands adjacent to it be returned to the Soviet Union.

The purpose of the latter omission is to attempt to create tense relations with the Soviet Union in order to cover up the extension of United States occupation. The purpose of the former omission is to enable the United States Government to prolong its occupation of Taiwan, a territory of China.

The Chinese people, however, can by no means tolerate such occupation and will never give up their sacred duty of liberating Taiwan and the Pescadores.

Moreover, the Draft Treaty stipulates that Japan should renounce all rights to Nan Wei Island (Spartly Island) and

Si Sha Islands (the Paracel Islands), but again deliberately makes no mention of the problem of restoring sovereignty over them. As a matter of fact, just like all the Nan Sha Islands, Chung Sha Islands and Tung Sha Islands, Si Sha Islands (the Paracel Islands) and Nan Wei Island (Sparatly Island) have always been China's territory. Although they had been occupied by Japan for some time during the war of aggression waged by Japanese imperialism, they were all taken over by the then Chinese Government, following Japan's surrender.

The Central People's Government of the People's Republic of China hereby declares : Whether or not the United States-British Draft Treaty contains provisions on this subject and no matter how these provisions are worded, the inviolable sovereignty of the People's Republic of China over Nan Wei Island (Spartly Island) and Si Sha Islands (the Paracel Islands) will not be in any way affected.

Thirdly. . . .The Security and Political Classes of the Draft Treaty contain no limitations whatever on the armed forces of Japan, place no ban on the remnant and reviving militaristic organisations and provide no safeguard for the democratic rights of the people. As a matter of fact, the United States occupation authorities, through all the measures adopted in the past several years, have done their utmost to prevent the democratisation of Japan and to revive militarism in Japan. . . .

In order to make it easy for the United States to prolong its occupation of Japan, not to withdraw its occupation forces, and to control Japan in such a manner as to make it an out-post of the United States aggression in the Orient, the Draft Treaty further stipulates that the Allied occupation forces through an agreement with Japan, may remain in Japan for an extended period of time.

This scheme of the United States Government, which obviously violates the obligations under international agreements, has the support of the Yoshida government which is a political mainstay of the United States occupation of Japan. The United States Government and the Yoshida government are conspiring with each other to re-arm Japan, to enslave the Japanese people, and to drive Japan once again on to the path of aggression, which had led Japan to the brink of destruction.

It is also a path which reduces Japan to the status of a dependency and a colony, subordinate to the United States scheme of aggression, and obliged to pull the chestnuts out of the fire for the United States Government. This is a conspiracy to hinder the Japanese people from proceeding along another path which leads to peace, democracy, independence and happiness.

In accordance with the provisions of the above mentioned Draft Treaty, a United States-Japanese military agreement is now in secret negotiation. This military agreement in negotiation, just like the United States-British Draft Peace Treaty with Japan, is hostile towards China and the Soviet Union and menaces the security of those Asian states and peoples that have suffered from Japanese aggression in the past. . . .

Fourthly, for the purpose of stepping up its preparations for a new world war of aggression, the United States Government will certainly further tighten its control of Japan's economy. . .

By taking advantage of the privileges which it has already secured in Japan's economy through American corporations, and of the restrictions which it has imposed on Japan's peaceful economy, the United States Government can further adapt these Economic Clauses to its monopolistic needs. Thus, if this separate peace treaty with Japan were concluded, the colonial status of Japan's economy, its dependence on that of the United States would be worsened. Not only would Japan's war industry gear its production to the United States scheme of world war, but even industry in general would serve the United States economic aggression in Asia, while the normal trade relations between Japan and China and other neighbouring states for the purpose of developing peaceful economy and improving the people's livelihood would suffer from even more outrageous and unreasonable restrictions. . . .

Fifthly, on the question of reparation, the Central People's Government of the People's Republic of China considers it necessary to clear up the confusion purposely created by the United States Government in the United States-British Draft Peace Treaty with Japan. . . .

The United States Government does not allow other states which had suffered from Japanese aggression to claim reparation from Japan. Its secret design, which it does not wish to divulge, is precisely to preserve Japan's capacity to make reparation and to meet other obligations for further exploitation by United States monopoly capital. If Japan, as it is alleged, already lacks the capacity to make reparation and to meet other obligations, then it is the result of excessive spoliation and damage by the United States occupation authorities...

The Central People's Government of the People's Republic of China desires to see Japan capable of developing its peaceful economy in a healthy manner, and restoring and developing normal trade relations between China and Japan, so that the life of the Japanese people will be free from the menace and damage of war and the possibility of its real improvement may arise. Meanwhile, those states which were occupied by Japan, suffered great losses and have difficulties in rehabilitating themselves, should reserve their right to claim reparation.

The above-mentioned facts furnish sufficient proof that the United States-British Draft Peace Treaty with Japan completely violates international agreements, damages the interests of the Allied Powers at war with Japan, exhibits hostility to China and the Soviet Union, constitutes a menace to the peoples of Asia, disrupts the peace and security of the world, and is detrimental to the interests of the Japanese people.

In this Draft Peace Treaty with Japan, the United States Government together with its satellites pursues only one central objective, namely, the re-armament of Japan in order to continue and extend its war of aggression in Asia, as well as to intensify its preparations for a new world war.

This Draft Peace Treaty, therefore, is absolutely unacceptable to the Chinese people and other Asian peoples who were victims of Japanese aggression. . . .

The Central People's Government of the People's Republic of China once again declares : If there is no participation of the People's Republic of China in the preparation, drafting and signing of a peace treaty with Japan, whatever the contents and results of such a treaty, the Central People's Government considers it all illegal, and therefore null and void. . . .

60. Joint Manifesto by various Democratic Parties and People's Organizations of China on the Sixth Anniversary of V-J Day, 2 September 1951 (Extracts).

By its utilisation of occupation of Japan, oppression of the
Japanese people, release of Japanese war criminals, re-armament of Japan, the U.S. Government intends to make the
Japanese aggressive elements once again to take the risk of
encroachment upon our country and other countries of Asia.
The U.S. Government and its Camp-follower, the U.K. Government, has completely disregarded the great contribution made
by our country in the Japanese resistance war and our just
advocacy to make peace with Japan, completely violated the
international agreements entered during World War II, summo-
ned the San Francisco Peace Conference on Japan with the
exclusion of our country, and are prepared to conclude Japanese
Peace Treaty which injures the rights of our country and threatens peace in the Far East. In all these things the mean and
cruel aim of U.S. imperialism is to utilise all direct and indirect
methods so as to destroy our great PRC and to make our
country once again a colony. . .

We welcome the stand taken by USSR, India, Burma and
world peace-loving people against US-UK draft on Japanese
peace treaty. . . .

61. Chou En-lai's Statement on the San Francisco Peace Treaty, 18 September 1951 (Extracts).

1. The separate peace treaty with Japan which was concluded under U.S. Government's coercion and without the participation of the People's Republic of China at the San Francisco
Conference is not only not an over-all peace treaty but is in no
way a genuine treaty. It is only a treaty for reviving Japanese
militarism, a treaty of hostility towards China and the Soviet
Union, a menace to Asia and a preparation for a New war of
aggression. A few hours after the conclusion of the so-called
peace treaty, the U.S. Government concluded a U.S.-Japan
Bilateral Security Pact with the Yoshida government of Japan
which aims at clearing the road for the re-armament of Japan
and turning it completely into an American military base. This
Pact is unmistakable evidence that the U.S. Government is preparing for another war of aggression in Asia and the Far East
on an even bigger scale. The Central People's Government of
the People's Republic of China considers that the San

Francisco Peace Treaty with Japan and the U.S.-Japan Bilateral Security Pact made under U.S. Government's coercion constitute a serious threat to the security of the People's Republic of China and of many other countries of Asia. . . .

2. The San Francisco Conference and the separate peace treaty with Japan signed at this conference not only do not represent the views of the people of China, the Soviet Union, the people of Asia and the world, but are actually in opposition to these views. This is because the American Government dictatorially and stubbornly rejected the suggestions put forward by the Soviet, Polish and Czechoslovak delagates at the San Francisco Conference to invite the People's Republic of China to the conference, and also rejected the various basic proposals of the Soviet Union concerning the signing of the peace treaty with Japan which were made in the spirit of the international agreements. This is because the American Government ignored the will and hopes of the Asian countries and rejected the proposals of India and Burma.

The San Francisco Peace Treaty with Japan and the U.S.-Japan Bilateral Security Pact, which were manufactured by the American Government, can never bring peace to Asia and the world. They can only aggravate the present tension in Asia and the rest of the world. . . .

3. The San Francisco Peace Treaty with Japan and the U.S.-Japan Bilateral Security Pact are by no means lenient or beneficial to Japan, but are war treaties that attempt to drag Japan into a new aggressive war and to plunge the Japanese nation into ruin. In their wild effort to revive Japanese militarism, the reactionary clique in the service of American imperialism within the ruling class of Japan did not even hesitate to sell out her national independence and sovereignty, and signed the San Francisco Peace Treaty and the U.S.-Japan Bilateral Security Pact. As a result the whole of Japan is confronted with a national crisis such as she has never before experienced. This cannot but impel the Japanese people to struggle further against the aggressive policy of American imperialism and the Japanese traitorous clique. . . .

We Chinese people express our unbounded welcome and sympathy for the struggle of patriotic people of all sections of Japanese society—for their struggle against the traitorous San

Francisco Treaty and their efforts to gain an early end to the
state of war between China and Japan and to ensure peaceful
co-existence. . . .

4. The Central People's Government of the People's Republic of China states once again that because the San Francisco
Peace Treaty with Japan was prepared, drafted and signed
without the participation of the People's Republic of China,
the Central People's Government considers it illegal and invalid
and thus cannot recognise it in any way.

**62. Announcement by Chang Han-fu, Vice Minister for Foreign
Affairs, Denouncing the US-Yoshida Plot to Conclude a
"Peace Treaty" with the Chiang Kai-shek clique, 22 January
1952 (Extracts).**

On January 16, 1952 Tokyo an Washington simultaneously
released a letter, dated December 24, 1951 from the prime
minister of the reactionary Japanese government, Shigeru
Yoshida, to the representative of the imperialist government of
the United States, John Foster Dulles. . . .

We consider this letter to be conclusive evidence of the
collusion between the reactionary government of defeated
Japan with American imperialism in preparing a new aggressive
war against the people and the territory of China. This letter
is another provocation of the imperialist government of the
United States and the reactionary government of defeated Japan
against the People's Republic of China—the most serious and
most flagrant provocation since the conclusion of the San
Francisco "peace treaty" with Japan in September 1951. . . .

The letter addressed to the U.S. government by the Yoshida
government on December 24, 1951 giving assurances that it
was ready to conclude a "peace treaty" with the remnant
Chinese Kuomintang reactionary clique in Taiwan is in fact a
further development of the San Francisco illegal "peace treaty".
No one can fail to understand that the U.S. imperialist government is now trying, through an utterly illegal "peace treaty",
to link up the reactionary Japanese government it has fostered
with the remnant Chinese Kuomintang reactionary clique in
Taiwan, seeking thus to create a military threat to the People's
Republic of China, and in this way to prepare for a new war of

aggression in the Far East. . . .

The Yoshida government has, over a long period and a consistently increasing peace, been openly betraying the national interests of Japan. After signing the San Francisco "peace treaty" and the bilateral U.S.-Japan "security pact" last year, the Yoshida government has now promised to conclude a "peace treaty" with the remnant Chinese Kuomintang reactionary clique in Taiwan and has declared that it will continue to assist in the execution of aggressive measures adopted by American imperialism against Korea and China. In so doing, it has completely turned itself into an instrument of American imperialist aggression in Asia. . . .

The policy pursued by the British government of servility towards America is not a policy to avert war, but rather one which is, step by step, dragging the British people and the peoples within the orbit of the British Empire into the abyss of war.

Not only Britain, but any country which meekly allows itself to follow a policy of submission to the United States and to be the accomplice of the United States government, will inevitably confront its people with the threat of war.

63. Chou En-lai's Statement on the US-Japan "Peace Treaty", 5 May 1952 (Extracts).

1. In defiance of all the international agreements on the question of Japan. . . .

The U.S. government has taken the extreme step of arbitrarily announcing the coming into effect of the separate peace treaty with Japan which it manufactured alone and concluded illegally. In addition, it has autocratically and high-handedly dissolved the Far Eastern Commission and the Allied Council for Japan. Such a unilateral measure is absolutely illegal and is thoroughly devoid of reason. . . .

2. This separate peace treaty with Japan which has been manufactured by the U.S. government alone is by no means a treaty to restore sovereignty and independence to Japan or to change her status as an occupied country, on the contrary, it is a treaty for war and enslavement by which Japan is turned completely into a U.S. military base and dependency. . . .

With the coming into effect of this illegal peace treaty, the so-called "U.S.-Japanese Security Pact," and "Administrative Agreement" also came into force on April 28, The "treaty," "pact" and "agreement" are deeds of betrayal of the Japanese nation and are American contraptions for enabling overall military, economic and political domination to be imposed upon Japan. They are the means whereby, under the rule of the U.S. occupationists and their loyal lackeys, the Yoshida government, Japan becomes a U.S. Military beachhead in the Far East. . . .

The whole economy of Japan becomes an appendage to the economy of the U.S.A. and is compelled to serve this latter's war preparations. . . .

By the operation of these illegal treaties, Japan is dragged by the U.S. into a position of open antagonism to China, the Soviet Union and the other Asian states concerned, thus encompassing the isolation of Japan in Asia. . . .

3. The U.S. Government has ordered the Yoshida government of Japan to conclude a so-called "peace treaty" with the remnant Kuomintang reactianaries in Taiwan. This obvious attempt at pairing off the two servile running dogs of its own breeding by means of this so-called "peace treaty" has the preposterous object of creating a military menace to the People's Republic of China. The Yoshida government of Japan, having accepted the U.S. made separate "peace treaty" with Japan, which is directed against China and the Soviet Union and betrays Japanese national interests, now dares, on the orders of its U.S. masters, to become openly the stable-mate of the remnant Chiang Kai-shek gang in Taiwan, which has long been spurned by all the Chinese people. It has even come out with the audacious and shameless statement that this "treaty" between the two should "apply to all the territory which is now under the control of the Government of the People's Republic of China or which may come under its control in the future." Furthermore, after the conclusion of the "treaty," it at once released 88 of the most vicious Japanese war criminals, including the notorious Yasutsugu Okamura, whose hands are stained with the blood of the Chinese people. This shows that throughout the period of nearly seven years, since the end of the Second World War in 1945, the reactionary rulers of Japan have shown not the

slightest intention of atoning for their crimes. They are now determined, in the wake of American imperialism, to continue the futile plans which they have pursued since 1894 for the armed invasion of China and are preparing again to invade the mainland and revive their imperialist rule over the people of China and the rest of Asia. This means that Japan has not only failed to end the state of aggressive war against the Chinese people dating back to the September 18, 1931 incident but, on the contrary, encouraged by the U.S. government, it is menacingly preparing for a new aggressive war. . . .

Of course, these despicable activities of the reactionary Yoshida government run completely counter to the wishes of all Japanese patriots who are striving to end the state of war and resume peaceful relations with the People's Republic of China. . . .

4. The Central People's Government of the People's Republic of China considers it necessary to repeat the following statement. We insist that all occupation troops should be withdrawn from Japan; the illegal separate "peace treaty" with Japan which the U.S. has announced as coming into effect can in no way be recognised; we are firmly opposed to the Yoshida-Chiang Kai-shek "peace treaty" which is an open insult and act of hostility to the Chinese people. The announcement and conclusion of these illegal "treaties" demonstrate that the U.S. reactionaries and their lackeys have taken another step in their scheme of creating a new war in the Far East. The Chinese people, are deeply convinced that if China, the Soviet Union and all other peace-loving states in Asia as well as their peoples, including the Japanese people, unite closely together to take the cause of preserving peace into their own hands, the U.S. war schemes in the Far East can undoubtedly be checked and the peace and security of the Far East and the rest of the world safeguarded.

64. Joint Statement of the Governments of China and Japan, 29 September 1972 (Extracts).

China and Japan are neighbouring countries separated only by a strip of water, and there was a long history of traditional friendship between them. The two peoples ardently wish to end the abnormal state of affairs that has hitherto existed between the two countries. The termination of the state of war and the normalization of relations between China and Japan— the realization of such wishes of the two peoples will open a new page in the annals of relations between the two co......

The Japanese side is keenly aware of Japan's responsibility for causing enormous damages in the past to the Chinese people through war and deeply reproaches itself. The Japanese side re-affirms its position that in seeking to realise the normalisation of relations between Japan and China, it proceeds from the stand of fully understanding the three principles for the restoration of diplomatic relations put forward by the Government of the People's Republic of China. The Chinese side expresses its welcome for this.

Although the social systems of China and Japan are different, the two countries should and can establish peaceful and friendly relations. The normalization of relations and the development of good-neighbourly and friendly relations between the two countries are in the interests of the two peoples, and will also contribute to the relaxation of tension in Asia and the safeguarding of world peace.

(1) The abnormal state of affairs which has hitherto existed between the People's Republic of China and Japan is declared terminated on the date of publication of this statement.

(2) The Government of Japan recognises the Government of the People's Republic of China as the sole legal government of China.

(3) The Government of the People's Republic of China re-affirms that Taiwan is an inalienable part of the territory of the People's Republic of China. The Government of Japan fully understands and respects this stand of the Government of China and adheres to its stand of complying with Article 8 of the Potsdam Proclamation.

(4) The Government of the People's Republic of China and the Government of Japan have decided upon the establishment of diplomatic relations as from September 29, 1972. The two Governments have decided to adopt all necessary measures for the establishment and the performance of functions of embassies in each other's capitals in accordance with international law and practice and exchange ambassadors as speedily as

possible.

(5) The Government of the People's Republic of China declares that in the interest of the friendship between the peoples of China and Japan, it renounces its demand for war indemnities from Japan.

(6) The Government of the People's Republic of China and Government of Japan agree to establish durable relations of peace and friendship between the two countries on the basis of the principles of mutual respect for sovereignty and territorial integrity, mutual non-aggression, non-interference in each other's internal affairs, equality and mutual benefit and peaceful co-existence.

In keeping with the foregoing principles and the principles of the United Nations Charter, the Governments of the two countries affirm that in their mutual relations, all disputes shall be settled by peaceful means without resorting to the use or threat of force.

(7) The normalisation of relations between China and Japan is not directed against third countries. Neither of the two countries should seek hegemony in the Asia-Pacific region and each country is opposed to efforts by any other country or group of countries to establish such hegemony.

(8) To consolidate and develop the peaceful and friendly relations between the two countries, the Government of the People's Republic of China and the Government of Japan agreed to hold negotiations aimed at the conclusion of a treaty of peace and friendship.

(9) In order to further develop the relations between the two countries and broaden the exchange of China and the Government of the People's Republic of China and the Government of Japan agree to hold negotiations aimed at the conclusion of agreements on trade, navigation aviation, fishery, etc., in accordance with the needs and taking into consideration the existing non-governmental agreements.

INDIA

65. Exchange of Letters between India and Japan on the Termination of the State of War, 8-10 September 1951.

(*a*) *Letter from K.K. Chettur, Head of the Indian Mission in Tokyo, to the Japanese Acting Foreign Minister, S. Matsutani, 8 September 1951.*

In accordance with the statements made by the Prime Minister of India in regard to the Japanese Peace Treaty and the declared intention of the Government of India to terminate the state of war between India and Japan at the earliest possible date and to establish full diplomatic relations between the two countries, I have the honour to enclose herewith a Draft Notification which the Government of India propose to issue simultaneously with the coming into force of the Peace Treaty which is scheduled for signature at the Conference now in session at San Francisco.

In expressing the hope that the above proposal will be acceptable to the Government of Japan, the Government of India would be grateful for an early reply.

Draft Notification

It is hereby notified for general information that the Government of India, bearing in mind that active hostilities with Japan were ended by Japan's signature of the instrument of surrender nearly six years ago and that a Treaty of Peace with Japan has been concluded and signed at San Francisco on the 8th September 1951, by a large number of the Allied Powers, have determined that the state of war between India and Japan shall cease to exist as soon as the said Treaty of Peace comes into force for any states in accordance with the provisions contained in article 23 thereof.

The Government of India propose to conclude at the earliest practicable date a separate bilateral Treaty of Peace with Japan whereby the relations between themselves and the Government of Japan would be brought into conformity with the amity which existed between them before the declaration of war with Japan.

In that Treaty the Government of India intend to stipulate provisions which will secure to themselves and the nationals of India all the rights, privileges, indemnities and advantages, together with the right to enforce the same, which under the Treaty of San Francisco have been stipulated in favour of the Allied Powers and their nationals.

(b) Reply Letter from Matsutani to Chettur, 10 September 1951.

I have the honour to acknowledge with thanks the receipt of your letter dated 8th September, 1951, with which you enclosed a Draft Notification which the Government of India propose to issue simultaneously with the coming into force of the Japanese Peace Treaty which has just been signed at San Francisco.

On behalf of the Japanese Government I have the honour to state that the Japanese Government heartily welcomes the intention of the Government of India to terminate the state of war between Japan and India and to establish full diplomatic relations between the two countries.

66. Treaty of Peace between India and Japan, 9 June 1952.

WHEREAS the Government of India have by public notification issued on the ninth day of June, 1952, terminated the state of war between India and Japan;

AND WHEREAS the Government of India and the Government of Japan are desirous of cooperating in friendly association for the promotion of the common welfare of their peoples and the maintenance of international peace and security in conformity with the principles of the Charter of the United Nations;

The Government of India and the Government of Japan have therefore determined to conclude this Treaty of Peace, and to this end have appointed as their Plenipotentiaries. . . .

Who, having indicated to each other their respective Full Powers, and found them good and in due form, have agreed on the following Articles :

Article I

There shall be firm and perpetual peace and amity between India and Japan and their respective peoples.

Article II

(a) The Contracting Parties agree to enter into negotiations for the conclusion of treaties or agreements to place their trading, maritime, aviation and other commercial relations on a stable and friendly basis.

(b) Pending the conclusion of the relevant treaty or agreement, during a period of four years from the date of the issue of the notification by the Government of India terminating the state of war between India and Japan—

(1) the Contracting Parties shall accord to each other most-favoured-nation treatment also with respect to air traffic rights and privileges;

(2) the Contracting Parties shall accord to each other most-favoured-nation treatment also with respect to customs duties and charges of any kind and restrictions and other regulations in connection with the importation and exportation of goods or imposed on the international transfer of payments for imports or exports, and with respect to the method of levying such duties and charges and with respect to all rules and formalities in connection with importation and exportation and charges to which customs clearing operations may be subject; and any advantage, favour, privilege or immunity granted by either of the parties to any product originating in or destined for any other country shall be accorded immediately and unconditionally to the like products originating in or destined for the territory of the other Party;

(3) Japan will accord to India national treatment, to the extent that India accords Japan the same, with respect to shipping, navigation and imported goods, and with respect to natural and juridical persons and their interests—such treatment to include all matters pertaining to the levying and collection of taxes, access to the courts, the making and performance of contracts, rights to property (tangible and intangible), participation in juridical entities constituted under Japanese law, and generally the conduct of all kinds of business and professional activities:

Provided that in the application of this Article, a discriminatory measure shall not be considered to derogate from the grant of national or most-favoured-nation treatment, if such measure is based on an exception customarily provided for in the commercial treaties of the party applying it, or on the necessity of safeguarding that party's external financial position or balance of payments, or on the need to maintain its essential security interests, and provided such measure is proportionate to the circumstances and is not applied in an arbitrary or unreasonable manner :

Provided further that nothing contained in sub-paragraph (2) above shall apply to the preferences or advantages which have existed since before the 15th August, 1947, or which are accorded by India to contiguous countries.

(c) No provision of this Article shall be deemed to limit the undertakings assumed by Japan under Article V of this Treaty.

Article III

Japan agrees to enter into negotiations with India, when India so desires, for the conclusion of an agreement providing for the regulation or limitation of fishing and the conservation and development of fisheries on the high seas.

Article IV

India will return or restore in their present from all property, tangible and intangible, and rights or interests of Japan or its national which were within India at the time of the commencement of the war and are under the control of the Government of India at the time of the coming into force of this Treaty; provided that the expenses which may have been incurred for the preservation and administration of such property shall be paid by Japan or its nationals concerned. If any such property has been liquidated, the proceeds thereof shall be returned, deducting the above-mentioned expense.

Article V

Upon application made within 9 months of the coming into force of this Treaty Japan will, within 6 months of the date of such application, return the property, tangible and intangible, and all rights or interests of any kind in Japan or India and her nationals which was within Japan at any time between the

7th December 1941 and the 2nd September 1945 unless the owner has freely disposed thereof without duress or fraud.

Such property will be returned free of all encumbrances and charges to which it may have become subject because of the war, and without any charges for its return.

Property the return of which is not applied for by or on behalf of its owner or by the Government of India within the prescribed period may be disposed of by the Japanese Government in its discretion.

If any such property was with Japan on the 7th December, 1941 and cannot be returned or has suffered injury or damage as a result of the war, compensation will be made on terms not less favourable than the terms provided in the Allied Powers Property Compensation Law of Japan (Law number 164, 1951).

Article VI

(a) India waives all reparations claims against Japan.

(b) Except as otherwise provided in this Treaty, India waives all claims of India and Indian nationals arising out of action taken by Japan and its nationals in the course of the prosecution of the war as also claims of India arising from the fact that it participated in the occupation of Japan.

Article VII

Japan agrees to take the necessary measures to enable nationals of India to apply within one year of the coming into force of this Treaty to the appropriate Japanese authorities for review of any judgement given by a Japanese Court between December 7, 1941, and such coming into force, if in the proceedings in which the judgement was given any Indian national was not able to present his case adequately either as plaintiff or as defendant, Japan further agrees that where an Indian national has suffered injury by reason of any such judgement, he shall be restored to the position in which he was before the judgement was given or shall be afforded such relief as may be just and equitable in the circumstances of the case.

Article VIII

(a) The Contracting Parties recognise that the intervention of the state of war has not affected the obligation to pay pecuniary debts arising out of obligations and contracts (including those in respect of bonds) which existed and rights which were acquired before the existence of the state of war, and which are due by the Government or nationals of Japan to the Government or nationals of India, or are due by the Government or nationals of India to the Government or nationals of Japan; nor has the intervention of the state of war affected the obligation to consider on their merits claims for loss or damage to property or for personal injury or death which arose between the existence of a state of war, and which may be presented or re-presented by the Government of India to the Government of Japan or by the Government of Japan to the Government of India.

(b) Japan affirms its liability for the pre-war external debt of the Japanese State and for debts of corporate bodies subsequently declared to be liabilities of the Japanese State, and expresses its intention to enter into negotiations at an early date with its creditors with respect to the resumption of payments on these debts.

(c) The Contracting Parties will encourage negotiations in respect to other pre-war claims and obligations and facilitate the transfer of sums accordingly.

Article IX

(a) Japan waives all claims of Japan and her nationals against India and her nationals arising out of the war or out of actions taken because of the existence of a state of war, and waives all claims arising from the presence, operations or actions of forces or authorities of India in Japanese territory prior to the coming into force of this Treaty.

(b) The foregoing waiver includes any claims arising out of actions taken by India with respect to Japanese ships between September 1, 1939, and the coming into force of this Treaty, as well as any claims and debts arising in respect to Japanese prisoners of war and civilian internees in the hands of India; but does not include Japanese claims specifically recognised in the laws of India enacted since September 2, 1945.

(c) Japan recognises the validity of all acts and omissions done during the period of occupation under or in consequence of directives of the occupation authorities or authorised by Japanese law at that time, and will take no action subjecting Indian nationals to civil or criminal liability arising out of such acts or omissions.

Article X

Any dispute arising out of the interpretation or application of this Treaty or one or more of its Articles shall be settled in the first instance by negotiations, and, if no settlement is reached within a period of six months from the commencement of negotiations by arbitration in such manner as may hereafter be determined by a general or special agreement between the Contracting Parties.

Article XI

This Treaty shall be ratified and shall come into force on the date of exchange of ratifications which shall take place as soon as possible at New Delhi (or Tokyo).

IN WITNESS WHEREOF, the undersigned Plenipotentiaries have signed this Treaty;

DONE in duplicate at Tokyo this Ninth day of June, 1952 in the English language. Hindi and Japanese texts of this Treaty will be exchanged by the two Governments within a month of this date

For Japan :   *For India* :
Katsuo Okazaki   K.K. Chettur

SOUTH-EAST ASIA

BURMA

67. Treaty of Peace between Burma and Japan, 5 November 1954 (came into force on 16 April 1955).

WHEREAS the Government of the Union of Burma by a declaration terminated the state of war between Japan and the

Union of Burma on April 30, 1952; and

WHEREAS the Government of Japan and the Government of the Union of Burma are desirous of cooperating in friendly association for the promotion of the common welfare of their peoples and the maintenance of international peace and security, in conformity with the principles of the Charter of the United Nations;

The Government of Japan and the Government of the Union of Burma have therefore determined to conclude this Treaty of Peace, and have accordingly appointed as their Plenipotentiaries:

The Government of Japan: Katsuo Okazaki

The Government of the Union of Burma: U. Kyaw Nyein Who, having communicated to each other their full powers found to be in due form, have agreed on the following Articles:

Article I

There shall be firm and perpetual peace and amity between Japan and the Union of Burma and their respective peoples.

Article II

The Union of Burma, within one year of the coming into force of this Treaty, will notify Japan which of the pre-war bilateral treaties or conventions that were applicable between Japan and Burma, it wishes to continue in force or revive. Any treaties or conventions so notified shall continue in force or be revived subject only to such amendments as may be necessary to ensure conformity with this Treaty. The treaties and conventions so notified shall be considered as having been continued in force or revived three months after the date of notification and shall be registered with the Secretariat of the United Nations.

All such treaties and conventions as to which Japan is not so notified shall be regarded as abrogated.

Article III

The Contracting Parties agree to enter into negotiations for the conclusion of treaties or agreements at an earliest practicable date to place their trading, maritime, aviation and other commercial relations on a stable and friendly basis.

Article IV

Japan agrees to enter into negotiations with the Union of Burma, when the latter so desires, for the conclusion of an agreement providing for the regulation or limitation of fishing and the conservation and development of fisheries on the high seas.

Article V

I. Japan is prepared to pay reparations to the Union of Burma in order to compensate the damage and suffering caused by Japan during the war and also is willing to render cooperation in order to contribute towards the economic rehabilitation and development and the advancement of social welfare in the Union of Burma. Nevertheless it is recognized that the resources of Japan are not sufficient, if it is to maintain a viable economy, to make complete reparation for all the damage and suffering of the Union of Burma and other countries caused by Japan during the war and at the same time meet its other obligations.

Therefore,

(a) (i) Japan agrees, subject to such detailed terms as may be agreed upon, to supply the Union of Burma by way of reparations with the services of Japanese people and the products of Japan, the value of which will be on an annual average seven thousand two hundred million yen (7,200,000,000 yen), equivalent to twenty million United States of America dollars ($ 20,000,000), for the period of ten years.

(ii) Japan agrees, subject to such detailed terms as may be agreed upon, to take every possible measure to facilitate the economic cooperation wherein the services of Japanese people and the products of Japan the value of which will aggregate on an annual average one thousand eight hundred million yen (1,800,000,000 yen), equivalent to five million United States of America dollars ($ 5,000,000), will be made available to the Government or people of the Union of Burma for the period of ten years.

(iii) Japan also agrees to re-examine, at the time of the final settlement of reparations towards all other claimant countries, the Union of Burma's claim for just and equitable treatment in the light of the results of such settlement as well as the economic capacity of Japan to bear the overall burden of reparations.

(b) (i) The Union of Burma shall have the right to seize, retain, liquidate or otherwise dispose of all property, rights and interests of Japan and Japanese nationals (including juridical persons) which on the coming into force of this Treaty were subject to its jurisdiction. The property, rights and interests specified in this sub-paragraph shall include those now blocked, vested or in the possession or under the control of enemy property authorities of the Union of Burma, which belonged to, or were held or managed on behalf of, Japan or any Japanese nationals (including juridical persons) at the time such assets came under the controls of such authorities.

II. The following shall be excepted from the right specified in sub-paragraph (I) above:

(i) all real property, furniture and fixtures owned by the Government of Japan and used for diplomatic or consular purposes, and all personal furniture and furnishings and other private property not of an investment nature which was normally necessary for the carrying out of diplomatic and consular functions, owned by Japanese diplomatic and consular personnel;

(ii) property belonging to religious bodies or private charitable institutions and used exclusively for religious or charitable purposes;

(iii) property, rights and interests which have come within its jurisdiction in consequence of the resumption of trade, financial and other relations subsequent to September 2, 1945, between Japan and the Union of Burma ; and

(iv) obligations of Japan or Japanese nationals, any right, title or interest in tangible property located in Japan, interests in enterprises organized under the laws of Japan, or any paper evidence thereof; provided that this exception shall only apply to obligations of Japan and its nationals expressed in Japanese currency.

(III) Property referred to in the exceptions set forth in sub-paragraph (II) above shall be returned subject to reasonable expenses for its preservation and administration. If any such property has been liquidated, the proceeds shall be returned instead.

(IV) The right to seize, retain, liquidate or otherwise dispose of property as provided in sub-paragraph (1) above shall be exercised in accordance with the laws of the Union of Burma, and the owner shall have only such rights as may be given him by those laws.

2. Except as otherwise provided in this Treaty, the Union of Burma waives all claims of the Union of Burma and its nationals arising out of any actions taken by Japan and its nationals in the course of the prosecution of the war.

Article VI

Upon application made within nine months of the coming into force of this Treaty, Japan will, within six months of the date of such application return the property, tangible and intangible, and all rights or interests of any kind in Japan of the Union of Burma and its nationals which were within Japan at any time between December 7, 1941 and September 2, 1945 unless the owner has freely disposed thereof without duress or fraud.

Such property shall be returned free of all encumbrances and charges to which it may have become subject because of the war, and without any charges for its return.

Property the return of which is not applied for by or on behalf of its owners or by the Government of the Union of Burma within the prescribed period may be disposed of by the Goverment of Japan at its discretion.

If any such property was within Japan on December 7, 1941 and cannot be returned or has suffered injury or damage as a result of the war, compensation will be made on terms not less favourable than the terms provided for in the Allied Powers Property Compensation Law of Japan (Law No. 264, 1951).

Article VII

1. The Contracting Parties recognize that the intervention of the state of war has not affected the obligation to pay pecu-

niary debts arising out of obligations and contracts (including those in respect of bonds) which existed and rights which were acquired before the existence of a state of war, and which are due by the Government or nationals of Japan to the Government or nationals of the Union of Burma, or are due by the Government or nationals of the Union of Burma to the Government or nationals of Japan; nor has the intervention of the state of war affected the obligation to consider on their merits claims for loss or damage to property or for personal injury or death which arose before the existence of a state of war, and which may be presented or re-presented by the Government of the Union of Burma to the Government of Japan or by the Government of Japan to the Government of the Union of Burma.

2. Japan affirms its liability for the pre-war external debt of the Japanese State and for debts or corporate bodies subsequently declared to be liabilities of the Japanese State, and expresses its intention to enter into negotiations at an early date with its creditors with respect to the resumption of payments on those debts.

3. The Contracting Parties will encourage negotiations in other pre-war claims and obligations and facilitate the transfer of sums accordingly.

Article VIII

1. Japan waives all claims of Japan and its nationals against the Union of Burma and its nationals arising out of the war or out of actions taken because of the existence of a state of war.

2. The foregoing waiver includes any claims arising out of actions taken by Burma or the Union of Burma with respect to Japanese ships between September 1, 1939, and the coming into force of this Treaty, as well as any claims and debts arising in respect to Japanese prisoners of war and civilian internees in the hands of Burma or the Union of Burma, but does not include Japanese claims specifically recognized in the laws of Burma or the Union of Burma enacted since September 2, 1945.

Article IX

Any dispute arising out of the interpretation or application of this Treaty shall be settled in the first instance by negotiation, and, if no settlement is reached within a period of six months from the commencement of negotiations, the dispute shall, at the request of either Contracting Party, be referred for decision to the International Court of Jusice.

Article X

This Treaty shall be ratified and shall come into force on the date of exchange of ratifications which shall take place as soon as possible at Tokyo.

IN WITNESS WHEREOF the undersigned Plenipotentiaries have signed this Treaty and have affixed hereunto their seals.

DONE IN duplicate at Rangoon, this fifth day of November of the year one thousand nine hundred and fifty-four.

For Japan : Katsuo Okazaki
For the Union of Burma : Kyaw Nyein

68. Agreement for Reparations and Economic Cooperation, 5 November 1954.

Japan and the Union of Burma,

Desiring to conclude an agreement for implementing the provisions of Article V, paragraph 1 (a) of the Treaty of Peace between Japan and the Union of Burma signed at Rangoon on November 5, 1954 (hereinafter referred to as "the Treaty").

Have accordingly appointed their respective representatives for this purpose. Who have agreed as follows :

Article I

1. Japan shall supply the Union of Burma by way of reparations with the services of Japanese people and the products of Japan, the value of which will be on an annual average seven thousand two hundred million yen (7,200,000,000 yen), equivalent to twenty million United States of America dollars ($20,000,000), for the period of ten years from the date of coming into force of the Treaty.

2. Japan shall take every possible measure to facilitate the

economic cooperation wherein the services of Japanese people and the products of Japan, the value of which will aggregate on an annual average one thousand eight hundred million yen (1,800,000,000 yen), equivalent to five million United States of America dollers ($5,000,000), will be made available in the form of joint enterprises between Japanese people and the Government or people of the Union of Burma, for the period of ten years from the date of coming into force of the Treaty.

3. The services and products referred to in paragraphs 1 and 2 above shall be supplied or made available for the economic rehabilitation and development and the advancement of social welfare in the Union of Burma as envisaged and agreed in principle on the Annex to this Agreement. Such services and products shall be determined by agreement between the Governments of the two countries.

Article II

1. The Union of Burma shall take measures necessary for the smooth implementation of the provisions of Article 1 of this Agreement.

2. The Union of Burma shall provide such local labour, materials and equipment as may be made available in order to enable Japan to supply the services and products referred to in Article 1, paragraph 1 of this Agreement.

3. The Union of Burma undertakes that the Government or people of the Union of Burma shall so provide their due shares of capital in joint enterprises as to ensure the smooth performance of the economic cooperation referred to in Article 1, paragraph 2 of this Agreement.

4. The Union of Burma undertakes that the products of Japan supplied or made available under this Agreement shall not be re-exported from the territories of the Union of Burma except as otherwise agreed between the Governments of the two countries.

Article III

1. The proportion of ownership or shares of the Government or people of the Union of Burma in the joint enterprises referred to in Article 1 of this Agreement shall not be less than 60 per cent except as otherwise agreed.

2. The ownership or shares of Japanese people in the joint enterprises shall not be expropriated by the Government of the Union of Burma for such length of time as that Government may respectively assure those Japanese people against expropriation at the time the individual contracts concerned are made.

3. In the event that the ownership or shares of Japanese people in the joint enterprises should be expropriated by the Government of the Union of Burma after the lapse of the time of assurance referred to above, such expropriation shall be made only in accordance with the terms and conditions which shall be prescribed by that Government at the time the individual contracts referred to above are made.

4. The Government of the Union of Burma shall permit the remittance to Japan of the proceeds from the expropriation referred to above or the sale of the ownership or shares of Japanese people in the joint enterprises, and the interest and dividends derived from such ownership or shares, as well as the salaries or other earnings which Japanese people may receive from the joint enterprises, in accordance with the terms and conditions which shall be prescribed by that Government at the time the individual contracts concerned are made.

Article IV

There shall be established a joint committee to be composed of representatives of the Governments of the two countries, which shall be an organ for consultation and recommendation to the Governments of the two countries on matters concerning the implementation of this Agreement.

Article V

Details for the execution of this Agreement shall be agreed upon through consultation between the Governments of the two countries.

Article VI

1. Any dispute between the two countries concerning the interpretation and implementation of this Agreement shall primarily be settled through diplomatic channels. If the Governments of the two countries fail to reach a settlement, the dispute shall be referred for decision to a tribunal of three arbitrators,

one to be appointed by each Government and the third to be agreed upon by the two arbitrators so chosen, provided that such third arbitrator shall not be a national of either country. Each Government shall appoint an arbitrator within a period of thirty days from the date of receipt by either Government from the other Government of a not requesting arbitration of the dispute and the third arbitrator shall be agreed upon within a further period of thirty days.

2. The two countries undertake to comply with any decision given under the preceding paragraph.

Article VII

This Agreement shall be approved by each country in accordance with its legal procedures, and this Agreement shall enter into force upon the date of exchange of notes indicating such approval.

IN WITNESS WHEREOF the undersigned, being duly authorised by the respective Governments of the two countries, have signed this Agreement.

DONE in duplicate at Rangoon this fifth day of November, one thousand nine hundred and fifty-four.

For Japan : Katsuo Okazaki
For the Union of Burma : Kyaw Nyein

ANNEX

1. Construction of hydro-electric plants
2. Construction of steel plants
3. Rehabilitation of port facilities
4. Construction of hospitals and provision of medical services
5. Education in Japan of Burmese technicians and students
6. Technical training in Burma of Burmese technicians
7. Construction of fertilizer plants
8. Rehabilitation of railways
9. Construction of a shipbuilding yard
10. Manufacture of explosives and shells
11. Construction of cement factories
12. Development of salterns
13. Construction of sugar factories

14. Construction of chemical industries
15. Rehabilitation of river shipping
16. Construction of non-ferrous metal industry
17. Construction of engineering industry
18. Rehabilitation of telecommunications
19. Provision of other products and services to be agreed
    upon between the Governments of the two countries.

69. First Note from Burmese Minister for Foreign Affairs, Sao Hkun Hkio to Japanese Ambassador Saburo Ohta on the implementation of the agreement of 5 November 1954 for reparations and economic cooperation, 18 October 1955.

I have the honour to refer to the Agreement for Reparation and Economic Co-operation between the Union of Burma and Japan signed at Rangoon on November 5, 1954.

The following is the understanding of the Government of the Union of Burma pertaining to the procedure for the supply of the services of Japanese people and the products of Japan as referred to in Article 1, paragraph 1 of the Agreement:

(1) The Burma Reparations Mission (or The Government of the Union of Burma pending the establishment of the Mission) shall enter into contracts with Japanese nationals or juridical persons for services and products in accordance with the annual reparations schedule to be established by agreement between the two Governments.

(2) The contracts shall be in terms of Japanese yen and be on commercial terms and conditions.

(3) The contracts so concluded, including modifications thereof, shall be forwarded to the designated Japanese authority for verification as to whether the same are in conformity with (a) the provisions of the Agreement, (b) such arrangements which may have been agreed upon by the two Governments for the execution of the Agreement and (c) the schedule in force. The verification shall be effected within the shortest time possible

(4) The Burma Reparations Mission shall enter into arrangements with Japanese foreign exchange banks and open Reparations Accounts in its own name, authorizing such banks to receive payment from the Japanese Government, etc., and

notify the Japanese Government of the contents of such arrangements. The Reparations Accounts shall be non-interest bearing accounts.

(5) When payment falls due under the terms of a contract verified under (3) above, the Burma Reparations Mission shall forward a Payment Request to the Japanese Government intimating the amount, the name of the bank to which the payment should be made and the date on which the payment has to be made to the contractor.

(6) Upon receipt of such request the Japanese Government shall take steps to pay the requested amount by the said date to the said bank to be credited to the Reparations Account.

(7) The Japanese Government shall, upon agreement between the Governments of Japan and the Union of Burma, also take steps to make payment in the same way as provided in (6) above for the expenditure of the Burma Reparations Mission, the expenses for the education and training of Burmese technicians and students, and for such other purposes as may be agreed upon between the two Governments.

(8) The Reparations Accounts shall be credited only with the amounts paid in accordance with (6) and (7) above and shall be debited only for the purposes indicated in (5) and (7) above.

(9) By and upon making the payments in accordance with paragraphs (6) and (7) above, the Japanese Government shall be deemed to have supplied the Union of Burma with the services of Japanese people and the products of Japan equivalent in value to the amount of such payment in accordance with Article 1, paragraph 1 of the Agreement and shall be released from its reparations obligation provided for in the same paragraph to the extent of such amount.

If this also is the understanding of your Government, I have the honour to propose that the present note and Your Excellency's reply in confirmation thereof should be regarded as constituting an agreement between our two Governments in this matter.

70. Reply Note from Saburo Ohta to First Note of Sao Hkun Hkio of 18 October 1955, 18 October 1955.

I have the honour to acknowledge the receipt of Your Excellency's note of today's date, which reads as follows:

[See Note 1 above]

I have the honour to inform Your Excellency that the understanding of the Burmese Government as stated in Your Excellency's note is also the understanding of the Government of Japan. Accordingly, Your Excellency's note and the present reply shall be regarded as constituting an agreement between our two Governments in this matter.

I avail myself of this opportunity to renew to Your Excellency, Monsieur le Ministre, the assurance of my highest consideration.

AGREED MINUTES

The Minister for Foreign Affairs of the Union of Burma and the Ambassador Extraordinary and Plenipotentiary of Japan hereby record the following understandings which they have reached in relation to the exchange of notes, dated October 18, 1955, pertaining to the procedure for the supply of the services of Japanese people and the products of Japan as referred to in Article 1, paragraph 1 of the Agreement for Reparations and Economic Co-operation between the Union of Burma and Japan :

1. The Japanese Government may recommend to the Burma Reparations Mission, Japanese nationals and juridical persons qualified to enter into contracts. The Burma Reparations Mission is, however, not bound to enter into contracts only with the persons so recommended.

2. The responsibility for the performance of such contracts shall rest solely with the Burma Reparations Mission and the Japanese nationals or juridical persons who are parties to such contracts.

3. In case the transportation between Japan and the Union of Burma of products or of Japanese or Burmese nationals, the insurance for such products or for such nationals, and/or the inspection of such products are paid for under the contracts, such transportation, insurance or inspection shall be effected

by Japanese nationals or juridical persons.

4. The disputes arising out of or in connection with the contracts shall be at the request of either party referred for settlement to an arbitration board of commerce in accordance with such arrangement as may be made between the two Governments.

5. In case the whole or a part of the funds paid into a Reparations Account has not been drawn by the Burma Reparations Mission because of cancellation of contracts, etc., the unpaid amount shall be applied to the payment for the purposes indicated in (5) and (7) of the note after consultation between the two Governments.

6. In case the whole or a part of the amounts paid out of a Reparations Account has been refunded to the Burma Reparations Mission, the amounts so refunded shall be credited to the Reparations Account, notwithstanding the provisions of (8) of the note. The provisions of 5 above shall apply to these amounts.

7. (a) The computation of the fulfilment by the Japanese Government of the reparations obligation as provided for in (9) of the note shall be made by calculating the amount of such payment in terms of the United States of America dollars at the basic exchange rate of Japanese yen to the United States of America dollar officially fixed by the Japanese Government and agreed to by the International Monetary Fund which is prevailing on the date of the verification of the contract under which such payment is required.

(b) However, in case the contract is one containing any escalator clause or similar provision for modification of the terms of payment of the contract, such calculation of the amount of payment for the work or services performed after the modification of the contract shall be made at the basic exchange rate as defined above which is prevailing on the date of the verification of such modified contract.

71. Second Note from Sao Hkun Hkio to Saburo Ohta, 18 October 1955.

I have the honour to refer to Article V of the Agreement for Reparations and Economic Co-operation between the Union of Burma and Japan signed at Rangoon on November 5, 1954. In accordance with the said Article, the Government of the Union of Burma hereby proposes that a Burma Reparations Mission be established as follows :

(1) The Government of the Union of Burma will establish in Tokyo a Mission of the Government of the Union of Burma as its sole and exclusive Agent to engage in activities relating to the conclusion of contracts for the supply of products and services as reparations and the execution in Japan of such contracts. The name of the Mission shall be "Burma Reparations Mission."

(2) Such offices in Japan of the Mission as are necessary for the effective performance of its activities shall be established, provided that the places where such offices shall be located shall be agreed between the Mission and the Government of Japan and that they shall be used exclusively for the activities mentioned in paragraph 1 above.

(3) Subject to the provisions of paragraph 7, the Chief of the Mission and its senior officials who are nationals of the Union of Burma shall be accorded all diplomatic privileges and immunities:

(4) Other members of the Mission who are nationals of the Union of Burma and who are not ordinarily resident in Japan shall be exempt from Japanese taxes upon emoluments which they receive in discharge of their duties and, also from customs duties and any other charges upon property which they import for personal use, in accordance with the Japanese laws and regulations applicable to such exemption in the case of diplomats and the like.

(5) The Mission shall be accorded such administrative assistance as is usually accorded to foreign mission and as is required for the effective performance of the activities of the Mission.

(6) The Japanese Government shall take necessary steps to accord the Mission such privileges and immunities as may be accorded to missions of the same nature which may be established in Japan in future.

(7) In respect of those disputes arising out of or in connection with the contracts mentioned in paragraph 1 above which are brought to the Japanese courts, the Mission and the mem-

bers thereof shall be subject to the jurisdiction of the Japanese courts for settlement in accordance with the Japanese law, and shall waive any privileges or immunities in the legal proceedings which may be taken as to such settlement. No obligation may however be imposed upon the Chief and the members of the Mission to produce in court or elsewhere documents from the archives of the Mission or to testify to their contents unless such documents relate to the transaction in dispute. The Mission shall also be exempt from the obligation to give security for the cost of legal proceedings.

(8) In enforcement of all final court decisions, the office premises of the Mission and the movable property contained therein shall not be subject to distraint.

(9) The Government of the Union of Burma shall advise the Government of Japan from time to time of the names of the Chief and other members of the Burma Reparations Mission to be authorized to act for and on behalf of the Mission in connection with the conclusion or execution of the contracts mentioned in paragraph 1 above, and shall have the aforesaid names published in the Official Gazette of Japan. The authority of such Chief and other members of the Mission shall be deemed to continue unless and until such time as notice to the contrary is published in the said Gazette.

If the above proposal is acceptable to your Government, I have the honour to propose that the present note and Your Excellency's reply to that effect should be regarded as constituting an agreement between the Government of the Union of Burma and the Government of Japan.

72. Reply Note from Saburo Ohta to Sao Hkun Hkio's Second Note, 18 October 1955.

I have the honour to acknowledge the receipt of Your Excellency's note of today's date, which reads as follows:

[See note 2 above]

I have the honour to inform Your Excellency that the proposal as stated in Your Excellency's note is acceptable to the Government of Japan. Accordingly, Your Excellency's note and the present reply shall be regarded as constituting an agreement between our two Governments in this matter.

73. Third Note from Sao Hkun Hkio to Saburo Ohta, 18 October 1955.

With reference to the joint committee as provided in Article IV of the Agreement for Reparations and Economic Co-operation between the Union of Burma and Japan signed at Rangoon on November 5, 1954, I have the honour to inform Your Excellency that the Government of the Union of Burma proposes that the following be agreed upon between our two Governments in accordance with Article V of the said Agreement :

1. The joint committee provided for in Article IV of the Agreement shall be established in Tokyo and called the Burma-Japan Joint Committee for Reparations and Economic Co-operation (hereinafter referred to as "the Joint Committee").

2. The Government of Japan and of the Union of Burma shall respectively appoint one representative and a certain number of deputies for the Joint Committee.

3. The Joint Committee shall meet at the request of the representative of either party.

4. The functions of the Joint Committee shall be consultation and recommendation to the Governments of Japan and of the Union of Burma, on the following matters:

(a) procedure concerning contracts between the Burmese Government and Japanese nationals or juridical persons for the supply to the Union of Burma of the services of the Japanese people and the products of Japan as referred to in Article 1, paragraph 1 of the Agreement;

(b) criteria for verification by the Japanese Government of the contracts mentioned in (a) above;

(c) procedure for payment in respect of the supply to the Union of Burma of the services of the Japanese people and the products of Japan as referred to in Article 1, paragraph 1 of the Agreement;

(d) matters concerning preparation and modification of the annual schedules in accordance with which Japan shall supply the services of the Japanese people and the products of Japan as referred to in Article 1, paragraph 1 of the Agreement;

(e) matters concerning the economic co-operation as referred to in Article 1, paragraph 2 of the Agreement;

(f) preparation from time to time of remuneration standard lists for the services of Japanese people as referred to in Article I, paragraph 1 of the Agreement;

(g) review of the progress of performance of the reparations including the calculation of the total amount of such performance from time to time;

(h) matters concerning the arbitration provided for in Article VI of the Agreement; and

(i) such other matters concerning the implementation of the Agreement as the parties may by consent refer to the Joint Committee.

If the above proposal is acceptable to your Government, I have the honour to suggest that the present note and Your Excellency's reply to that effect should be regarded as constituting an agreement between our two Governments in this matter.

74. Reply Note from Saburo Ohta to Sao Hkun Hkio's Third Note, 18 October 1955.

I have the honour to acknowledge the receipt of Your Excellency's note of today's date, which reads as follows :

[See note 3 above]

I have the honour to inform Your Excellency that the proposal as stated in Your Excellency's note is acceptable to the Government of Japan. Accordingly, Your Excellency's note and the present reply shall be regarded as constituting an agreement between our two Governments in this matter.

75. Memorandum concerning the Settlement of Burmese Claim for an Increase in Reparations, 26 January 1963.

As a result of conversations held in Tokyo between the representatives of the Government of Japan headed by Mr. Massayoshi Ohira, Minister for Foreign Affairs of Japan, and the representative of the Revolutionary Government of the Union of Burma headed by Brig. Gen. Aung Gyi, Member of the Revolutionary Council and Minister for Trade Development and Industry, for the purpose of re-examining the Union of Burma's claim in accordance with the provisions of Article V, paragraph 1 (a) (III) of the Treaty of peace between Japan and the Union of Burma signed at Rangoon on November 5, 1954, the following understandings have been reached.

1. Japan shall extend to the Union of Burma assistance on a grant basis for the purpose of contributing to the economic and social development of the Union of Burma, composed of the products of Japan and the services of Jananese people, the total value of which will be so much in yen as shall be equivalent to U.S. $140,000,000 at present computed at yen 50,400,000,000, within the period of 12 years as from April 16, 1965. The supply of such products and services shall be made at an annual average of so much in yen as shall be equivalent to $11,700,000 at present computed at yen 4,212,000,000 during the period of the first 11 years, the outsanding balance to be settled in the 12th year.

2. The Government of Japan shall facilitate and expedite, within the scope of pertinent laws and regulations, the extension of loans on a commercial basis, by private firms of nationals of Japan to the Government, private firms or nationals of the Union of Burma, during the period of six years from the date of coming into force of the agreement referred to in paragraph 4 below. The amount of the above mentioned loans is expected to aggregate so much in yen as shall be equivalent to $ 30,000,000 at present computed at yen 10,800,000,000, within the period mentioned.

The union of Burma will not present hereafter to Japan any claim based on the provisions of Article V, paragraph 1(a)(III) of the Treaty of peace between Japan and the Union of Burma.

Talks will be started as soon as possible between the representatives of both Governments to conclude an agreement implementing the understandings referred to in paragraphs 1,2 and 3 above.

PHILIPPINES

76. Statement by Carlos P. Romulo at the San Francisco Conference, 7 September 1951 (Extracts).

Our postwar policy toward Japan, which was set by the President of Philippines from the very beginning, was aimed at three basic objectives: first, to make certain that Japan, through genuine political and economic reform, will never again be a menace to the Philippines and other countries; second, to obtain an early and equitable reparation of the damage caused by Japan to the Philippines and other countries; and third, to welcome, at a suitable time and under proper conditions, a democratic and non-militarist Japan as a friendly neighbor and to secure its cooperation in maintaining the peace and fostering the progress of the Pacific area and of the world as a whole.

Having this policy in mind, the Philippine Government is constrained to state that the peace treaty with Japan in its present form falls short in certain respects of what it deems to be just and necessary.

Accordingly, the Philippines would have wished to see certain arrangements made, in a manner acceptable to Japan and compatible with its sovereignty, for continuing assistance to it in the development of its political institutions and system of education. We have been told that the growth of democratic institutions among the Japanese people is nothing short of phenomenal. We shall not dispute this claim, having as it does the authority of the great soldier-statesman General Douglas MacArthur. But, surely, it is straining human credulity to believe that Japan, within a brief period of six years, has been completely and permanently transformed from the aggressive, feudal, militarist police state which it has been for centuries, into a practicing and thorough-going democracy. The all-too-human clay of which we are made does not, in the mass, yield to such miracles of transformation. . . .

This treaty is probably the only treaty of its kind which provides no explicit restrictions on the re-armament of Japan.

In the five years between the promulgation of the Japanese constitution and the signing of this treaty, there has occurred so great a shift in the power relations of Asia that Japan must now arm itself against the menace of Communist aggression.

Under conditions other than the present, the Philippines would regard as completely intolerable the unrestricted right of Japan to organize its own military force. Since the treaty contemplates the entry of Japan into collective security arrangements to which the Philippines would be a party, and since the President of the Philippines has publicly expressed the view that Japan should eventually be integrated into such a system, we are satisfied that the misgivings which we would otherwise feel in the Philippines have been set at rest. We are, therefore, able to accept the security provisions of the treaty on the basis of this consideration and on the strength of the mutual defense treaty recently concluded between the United States and the Philippines. That treaty provides for common action against armed attack, whether arising from a new source or from the renewal of Japanese aggression.

The Philippine Government is not satisfied with the provisions on reparations under Article 14 (a) I of the treaty. We are aware that it is on the strength of its compassionate provisions on reparations that the claim for the uniqueness of this treaty as a non-punitive treaty is primarily based. Yet, if it is true that this is not a punitive treaty, then one must ask why Japan is deprived under Articles 2 and 3 of all its overseas territories, including the rich island of Formosa, the restoration of which to Japan would in the long run more than offset the economic consequences of heavy reparations. Moreover, Article 14 (a) 2 authorizes the seizure by the Allied Powers of Japanese overseas assets as "war trophies". The significant fact concerning these cessions of territory and confiscations of overseas assets, which are promitted under the treaty, is that the beneficiaries are almost exclusively the Great Powers. On the other hand, the payment of reparations, which is the only form in which the smaller countries damaged and occupied by Japan may be indemnified for their losses, is severely restricted under the treaty.

In effect, therefore, one might say that while the treaty is indeed a treaty of forgiveness in respect of the claims of the smaller countries, it is plainly a punitive treaty in respect of the claims of the Great Powers.

The Philippine Government cannot accept the theory that the payment of a due amount of reparations from Japan is an act of vindictiveness. The principle of indemnification for damage willfully caused can no more be renounced in the relations between States than it can be relinquished in the relations between individuals.

We do not insist on the exaction of punitive damages from Japan. We do not even insist on the payment of actual damages by Japan. We accept the statement that the "resources of Japan are not presently sufficient, if it is to maintain a viable economy, to make complete reparation for all such damage and suffering and at the same time meet its other obligations." Further we accept the principle that any arrangements for reparations "shall avoid the imposition of additional liabilities on other Allied Powers, and, where the manufacture of raw materials is called for they shall be supplied by the Allied Powers in question so as not to throw any foreign exchange burden upon Japan."

But we cannot accept any interpretation of the right of reparations guaranteed in Article 14 (a) which would limit the payment of reparations to the services of the Japanese people in the processing of raw materials supplied by a claimant State, in salvaging and other work for the Allied Powers. The restriction of the right of reparations in this manner would render completely meaningless the statement that "the resources of Japan are not presently sufficient . . . . to make complete reparation"—an assertion which certainly means that while the present resources of Japan now permit only partial reparations, there is the possibility that those resources might increase in the future to an extent that would allow the payment of complete or as nearly complete reparations as possible.

We are not splitting hairs over a matter of words. The question of Japan's actual and potential capacity to pay reparations at a stipulated figure may be a matter of dispute. But it can hardly be disputed that the Japanese economy is improving at a remarkable rate, at a rate which justifies the estimate that the national wealth of Japan today is not far below that of the pre-war level. . . .

We have accepted the principle that the payment of reparations by Japan would at all times be subject, first, to the maintenance of a viable economy; second, to the satisfaction of its. other obligations; third, to the need of avoiding additional liabilities on other Allied Powers; and fourth, to the need of avoiding the imposition of any foreign exchange burden on Japan.

We submit that, having accepted these four specific conditions the claimant countries like the Philippines are at least entitled to the satisfaction of having a freer hand in negotiating with Japan for the payment of reparations in forms other than those stipulated under Article 14 (a) I. How can it be reasonably demanded that we foreclose the whole question and agree in advance to limit our right to the payment of reparations to services in production, salvaging and other work before the facts are known ?

Furthermore, remembering as we do the pre-war predominance of Japanese industry over the economy of the rest of Asia, our fear of becoming economically subservient to Japan ought not to be lightly dismissed. Yet, the restriction of reparations in the form of services will precisely have the effect of returning the claimant States to that condition of subservience, as mere suppliers of raw materials for the Japanese industrial machine. . . .

If Article 14 (a) I is to be interpreted as an inflexible restriction on the form of reparations which is to be the subject of bilateral negotiations between Japan and the Philippines, then I would be obliged to declare that the Philippine Government will make the following reservation :

The right of the Government of the Republic of the Philippine to negotiate and mutually agree with the Government of Japan on the kinds and forms of reparations due the former from the latter and the manner of their payment or delivery is hereby reserved, and provision of the present treaty to the contrary notwithstanding. . . .

77. Interim Agreement on Reparations concerning Salvage of Sunken Vessels, 12 March 1953.

WHEREAS the Government of Japan is ready to make available to the Government of the Philippines the services of the Japanese people in the salvaging of the sunken vessels located in the mine-cleared areas of the Philippine territorial waters, with a view to assisting to compensate the cost of repairing the damage done by Japan during the war;

THEREFORE, the Government of Japan and the Government of the Philippines, in order to define conditions for providing the said services, have agreed as follows :

Article 1

The Japanese Government shall, in accordance with the provisions of the present Agreement, provide the Philippine Government with the services of Japanese people including the necessary operating equipment and supplies for salvaging sunken vessels located in the Philippine territorial waters.

Article 2

The Philippine Government shall cooperate with the Japanese Government to the extent permitted by Philippine laws in providing such facilities as are readily available locally in performing salvage operations and in procuring ordinary minor operational supplies that may be acquired locally.

The Philippine Government shall take adequate measures for the protection of the life and property of the Japanese nationals engaged in the salvaging operation. However, these responsibilities shall not include risks arising from normal operational hazards.

Article 3

Details for the execution of the present Agreement shall be agreed upon through consultation between the two Governments.

Article 4

The present Agreement will be approved by each Government in accordance with its constitutional procedures, and the present Agreement shall enter into force upon an exchange of diplomatic notes indicating such approval.

The present Agreement shall become an integral part of final arrangements on reparations which will be concluded between the Japanese Government and the Philippine Government.

IN WITNESS WHEREOF the representatives of the two Governments, duly authorized for the purpose, have signed this Agreement.

DONE at Manila, in duplicate in the Japanese and English languages, both being equally authentic, this 12th day of March, one thousand nine hundred and fifty three.

For Japan

Toru Nakagawa,
Chief,
The Japanese Mission
in the Philippines

For the Republic of the Philippines

Felino Neri,
Under-Secretary of
Foreign Affairs

78. Reparations Agreement, 9 May 1956 (came into force on 23 July 1956).

Japan and the Republic of the Philippines,
Desiring to act in line with the provisions of the Treaty of Peace with Japan signed at the city of San Francisco on September 8, 1951,

Have decided to conclude the present Reparations Agreement and have accordingly appointed as their Plenipotentiaries. . . .

Who, having communicated to each other their full powers found to be in due form, have agreed upon the following Articles :

Article I

Japan, by way of reparations, shall supply the Republic of the Philippines with the services of the Japanese people and the products of Japan in the form of capital goods, the total value of which will be so much in yen as shall be equivalent to five hundred fifty million United States dollars ($550,000,000) at present computed at one hundred ninety-eight billion yen (198,000,000,000 yen), within the period and in the manner hereinafter prescribed.

Article II

The supply of the services and products referred to in the preceding Article shall be made on an annual average of so much in yen as shall be equivalent to twenty-five million United States dollars ($ 25,000,000) at present computed at nine billion yen (9,000,000,000 yen), during the ten-year period from the date of coming into force of the present Agreement; and on an annual average so much in yen as shall be equivalent to thirty million United States dollars ($ 30,000,000) at present computed at ten billion eight hundred million yen (10,800,000,000 yen), during the succeeding ten-year period. However, by agreement between the two Governments, this latter period may be reduced to a period shorter than ten years, provided the outstanding balance is settled in full within the remainder of the reduced period.

Article III

1. The services and products to be supplied by way of reparations shall be those requested by the Government of the Republic of the Philippines and agreed upon between the two Governments. These services and products shall consist of such items as may be needed for projects to be chosen from among those enumerated in the Annex to the present Agreement, provided that such items as may be requested by the Government of the Republic of the Philippines for projects other than those listed in the aforesaid Annex may, by agreement between the two Governments, be included in the services and products to be supplied by way of reparations.

2. The products to be supplied by way of reparations shall be capital goods. However, products other than capital goods may, by agreement between the two Governments, be supplied by Japan at the request of the Government of the Republic of the Philippines.

Article IV

1. The two Governments shall fix through consultation an annual schedule (hereinafter referred to as the "Schedule") specifying the services and products to be supplied by Japan each

year.

2. The Schedule for the first year shall be fixed within sixty days from the date of the coming into force of the present Agreement. The Schedule for each succeeding year shall, until the reparations obligation specified in Article 1 above shall have been fulfilled, be fixed prior to the beginning of that year.

Article V

1. Japan agrees that the Mission mentioned in Article VII, paragraph 1 of the present Agreement shall have the authority to conclude, in behalf of the Government of the Republic of the Philippines, contracts directly with any Japanese national or any Japanese juridical person controlled by Japanese nationals, in order to have the services and products supplied in accordance with the Schedule for each year.

2. Every such contract (including modifications thereof) shall conform with (a) the provisions of the present Agreement, (b) The provisions of such arrangements as may be made by the two Governments for the implementation of the present Agreement and (c) the Schedule then applicable. Every proposed contract shall, before it is entered into, be verified by the Government of Japan as to the conformity of the same with the above-mentioned criteria. The Government of Japan shall receive a copy of each contract from the Mission on the day following the date such contract is entered into. In case any proposed contract can not be entered into due to non-verification, such proposed contract shall be referred to the Joint Committee mentioned in Article X of the present Agreement and acted upon in accordance with the recommendation of the Joint Committee. Such recommendation shall be made within a period of thirty days following the receipt of the proposed contract by the Joint Committee. A contract which has been concluded in the manner hereinabove provided, shall hereinafter be referred to as a "Reparations Contract."

3. Every Reparations Contract shall contain a provision to the effect that disputes arising out of or in connection with such Contract shall, at the request of either party thereto, be referred for settlement to an arbitration board of commerce in accordance with such arrangement as may be made between the

two Governments.

4. Notwithstanding the provisions of paragraph 1 above, the supply of services and products as reparations may be made without Reparations Contracts, but only by agreement in each case between the two Governments.

Article VI

1. In the discharge of the reparations obligations under Article 1 of the present Agreement, the Government of Japan shall, through procedures to be determined under Article XI, make payments to cover the obligations incurred by the Mission under Reparations Contracts and the expenses for the supply of services and products referred to in Article V, paragraph 4 of the present Agreement. These payments shall be made in Japanese yen.

2. By and upon making a payment in yen under the preceding paragraph, Japan shall be deemed to have supplied the Republic of the Philippines with the services and products thus paid for and shall be released from its reparations obligation to the extent of the equivalent value in United States dollars of such yen payment in accordance with Article I and II of the payment Agreement.

Article VII

1. Japan agrees to the establishment in Japan of a Mission of the Government of the Republic of the Philippines (hereinafter referred to as "the Mission") as its sole and exclusive agent to be charged with the implementation of the present Agreement, including the conclusion and performance of Reparations Contracts.

2. Such office or offices of the Mission in Japan as are necessary for the effective performance of its functions and used exclusively for that purpose may be established at Tokyo and/or other places to be agreed upon between the two Governments.

3. The premises of the office or offices, including the archives, of the Mission in Japan shall be inviolable. The Mission shall be entitled to use cipher. The real estate which is owned by the Mission and used directly for the performance of its

functions shall be exempt from the Tax on Acquisition of Real Property and the Property Tax. The income of the Mission which may be derived from the performance of its functions shall be exempt from taxation in Japan. The property imported for the official use of the Mission shall be exempt from customs duties and other charges imposed on or in connection with importation.

4. The Mission shall be accorded such administrative assistance by the Government of Japan as other foreign missions usually enjoy and as may be required for the effective performance of its functions.

5. The Chief and two senior officials of the Mission as well as the chiefs of such offices as may be established in pursuance of paragraph 2 above, who are nationals of the Republic of the Philippines, shall be accorded diplomatic privileges and immunities generally recognized under international law and usage. If it is deemed necessary for the effective performance of the functions of the Mission, the number of such senior officials may be increased by agreement between the two Governments.

6. Other members of the staff of the Mission who are nationals of the Philippines and who are not ordinarily resident in Japan shall be exempt from taxation in Japan upon emoluments which they may receive in the discharge of their duties, and, in accordance with Japanese laws and regulations, from customs duties and any other duties and any other charges imposed on or in connection with importation of property for their personal use.

7. In the event any dispute arising out of or in connection with a Reparations Contract has not been settled by arbitration or the arbitration award rendered has not been complied with, the matter may be taken, as a last resort, to the appropriate Japanese court. In such a case and solely for the purpose of whatever judicial proceedings may be necessary, the person holding the position of Chief of the Legal Section of the Mission may sue or be sued, and accordingly he may be served with process and other pleadings at his office in the Mission. However, he shall be exempt from the obligation to give security for the costs of legal proceedings. While the Mission enjoys inviolability and immunity as provided for in paragraphs 3 and 5 above, the final decision rendered by the appropriate judicial

body in such a case will be accepted by the Mission as binding upon it.

8. In the enforcement of any final court decision, the land and buildings, as well as the movable property therein, owned by the Mission and used for the performance of its functions shall in no case be subject to execution.

Article VIII

1. The services which have already been supplied or may hereafter be supplied in accordance with the exchange of notes effected at Manila on January 24, 1953, in connection with the survey of sunken vessels in Philippine territorial waters or in accordance with the Interim Agreement on Reparations Concerning Salvage of Sunken Vessels between Japan and the Republic of the Philippines signed at Manila on March 12, 1953, shall constitute part of the reparations under Article 1 of the present Agreement.

2. The supply of the above-mentioned services after the coming into force of the present Agreement shall be subject to the provisions of the Agreement.

Article IX

1. The two Governments shall take measures necessary for the smooth and effective implementation of the present Agreement.

2. Those materials, supplies and equipment which are necessary for the projects mentioned in Article III but are not included in the Schedule will be provided by the Government of the Republic of the Philippines. No Japanese labor will be utilized in such projects as may be undertaken in the Philippines except the services of Japanese technicians. The incidental expenses in local currency for such Japanese technicians as well as the expenses for local labor shall be borne by the Government of the Republic of the Philippines.

3. Japanese nationals who may be needed in the Philippines in connection with the supply of services or products under the present Agreement shall, during the required period of their stay in the Philippines, be accorded such facilities as may be necessary for the performance of their work.

4. With respect to the income derived from the supply of services or products under the present Agreement, Japanese nationals and juridical persons shall be exempt from taxation in the Philippines.

5. The products of Japan supplied under the present Agreement shall not be re-exported from the territories of the Republic of the Philippines.

Article X

There shall be established a Joint Committee to be composed of representatives of the two Governments as an organ of consultation between them, with powers to recommend on matters concerning the implementation of the present Agreement.

Article XI

Details including procedures for the implementation of the present Agreement shall be agreed upon through consultation between the two Governments.

Article XII

1. The two Governments shall endeavor, through constant consultation, to preclude the likelihood of disputes arising out of or in connection with the implementation of the present Agreement.

2. Any dispute between the two Governments concerning the interpretation and implementation of the present Agreement shall be settled primarily through diplomatic channels. If the two Governments fail to reach a settlement, the dispute shall be referred for decision to a tribunal of three arbitrators, one to be appointed by each Government and third to be agreed upon by the two arbitrators so chosen, provided that such third arbitrator shall not be a national of either country. Each Government shall appoint an arbitrator within a period of thirty days from the date of receipt by either Government from the other Government of a note requesting arbitration of the dispute and the third arbitrator shall be agreed upon within a further period of thirty days. If, within the periods respec-

tively referred to, either Government fails to appoint an arbitrator or the third arbitrator is not agreed upon, the President of the International Court of Justice may be requested by either Government to appoint such arbitrator or the third arbitrator, as the case may be. The two Governments agree to abide by any award given under this paragraph.

Article XIII

The present Agreement shall be ratified. The Agreement shall enter into force either on the date of exchange of the instruments of ratification or on the date the Republic of the Philippines deposits its instrument of ratification to the San Francisco Peace Treaty of September 8, 1951, in accordance with Article XXIV of the said Treaty, whichever date is the later.

Article XIV

The present Agreement is written in the Japanese and English languages, both being equally authentic.

IN WITNESS WHEREOF the undersigned Plenipotentiaries have signed the present Agreement and have affixed thereunto their seals.

DONE in duplicate at the city of Manila, this ninth day of May of the year one thousand nine hundred and fifty-six, Anno Domini, corresponding to the ninth day of the fifth month of the Thirty-first year of Showa; and of the Independence of the Republic of the Philippines, the tenth.

For Japan:

(Signed) Tatsunosuke Takasaki, Takizo Matsumoto, Mikio Mizuta, Aiichiro Fujiyama, Mamoru Nagano

For the Republic of the Philippines:

(Signed) Felino Neri, J. P. Laurel, Francisco A. Delgado, Gil J. PT, Arturo M. Tolentino, Miguel Cuenco, C.T. Villareal, M. Cuaderno, Lanuza, Francisco Oritgas, Jr., Calalang, Eduardo Quintero, Vicente Fabella

ANNEX

I Agricultural and Fishery Development Projects

1. Irrigation Gates and Pumping Equipment
2. Agricultural Equipment and Machineries
3. Logging Equipment
4. Saw Mill Equipment
5. Fishing Boats
6. Floating Canneries
7. Food Processing Plants
8. Animal Feed Plants
9. Salt Making Plants
10. Coconut Processing Plants
11. Wheat Flour Mills
12. Cassava Flour Mills
13. Rice Mills
14. Ramie and Abaca Decorticating and Degumming Plants
15. Tobacco Processing Plants
16. Baking Powder Plants
17. Sugar Refineries

II. Electric Power Development Projects

1. Hydroelectric Plants
2. Steam Electric Plants
3. Diesel Electric Plants
4. Substation Equipment
5. Transmission and Distribution Lines

III. Mineral Resources Development Projects

1. Coal Mining Equipment
2. Iron, Chrome and Manganese Mining Equipment
3. Iron, Chrome and Manganese Beneficiation Plants
4. Copper Mining and Beneficiation Equipment

IV. Industrial Development Projects

1. Alcohol Plants
2. Briquetted Semi-coke Plants
3. Coke Making Plants
4. Charcoal Making Plants
5. Integrated Iron and Steel Mills

6. Ferro-alloy Plants
7. Sulphur Refinery Plants
8. Copper Smelting and Refining Plants
9. Copper Rolling and Drawing Plants
10. Soda Ash-Caustic Soda Plants
11. Sheet Class Plants
12. Calcium Carbide Plants
13. Industrial Explosives Plants
14. Munitions Plants
15. Industrial Carbon Plants
16. Portland Cement Plants
17. Industrial Lime Plants
18. Asphalt Plants
19. Cotton Textile Mills
20. Rayon Plants
21. Ramie Plants
22. Pulp and Paper Plants
23. Celluloid Plants
24. Absorbent Cotton Plants
25. Paper Products Plants
26. Building Hardware Plants
27. Wall Board Plants
28. Plywood and Hardwood Plants
29. Light Chemicals Plants
30. Pharmaceuticals Plants
31. Blood Plasma Plants
32. Insecticides Plants
33. Ceramics Plants
34. Paints, Pigments and Varnish Plants
35. Resin Processing Plants
36. Photo Film Plants
37. Synthetic Leather Plants
38. Rubber Goods Plants
39. Rubber Reclaiming Plants
40. Ammonia Plants
41. Various Chemical Fertilizer Plants
42. Fertilizer Mizing-Granulating Plants
43. Electrical Manufacturing Plants
44. Agricultural Machinery and Implement Plants
45. Bicycle Plants

46. Sewing Machine Plants
47. Ball and Roller Bearing Plants
48. Cottage Industries Equipment

V. Transportation and Communication Development Projects
1. Railroad Equipment
2. Ocean-going Ships
3. Interisland Vessels
4. Telecommunication Equipment

VI. Public Works Projects
1. Artesian Well Pipes and Equipment
2. Flood Control Gates
3. Water Supply Filters, Pipes and Equipment
4. Public Housing Equipment and Materials
5. Warehousing Equipment and Materials
6. Airfield and Airport Equipment
7. Port Equipment and Facilities
8. Construction Equipment and Materials for Public Buildings
9. Road and Bridge Construction Equipment and Materials

VII. Other Projects
1. Education, Health and Social Welfare Facilities
2. Research Laboratory and Equipment
3. Survey and Salvage of Sunken Vessels
4. Coast and Geodetic Survey Equipment
5. Reclamation of Foreshore Land and Swamps
6. Training of Flipino Technicians and Craftsman in Japan
7. Transportation, Insurance, Packing, Handling and Inspection of Reparations Machineries, Equipment, etc.

79. Agreed Minutes to the Reparations Agreement, 9 May 1956.

The Plenipotentiaries of Japan and of the Republic of the Philippines wish to record the following understanding which they have reached during the negotiations for the Reparations Agreement between Japan and the Republic of the Philippines signed today:

1. Re Article III of the Agreement :

"Agreed upon between the two Governments" or "agreement between the two Governments" as mentioned in Paragraphs 1 and 2 of this Article means fixing through consultation the Schedule as provided for in Article IV, Paragraph 1.

2. Re Article IV, Paragraph 2 of the Agreement :

The two Governments will endeavor to fix the Schedule for the second year and each year thereafter at least sixty days prior to the beginning of the year concerned. For this purpose the Government of the Republic of the Philippines will forward its proposed schedule to the Government of Japan not less than one hundred and twenty days prior to the beginning of that year.

3. Re Article V, Paragraph 2 of the Agreement :

(a) The arrangements referred to in (b) means arrangements existing at the time a Reparations Contract is verified. An arrangement will not apply retroactively to a Reparations Contract which has been dully verified prior to the conclusion of such arrangement.

(b) At least three copies of every proposed contract will be furnished by the Mission to the Government of Japan for the purpose of verification.

(c) The verification by the Government of Japan will as a rule be effected within fourteen days.

4. Re Article V, Paragraph 3 of the Agreement :

The two Governments will take measures necessary to make final and enforceable all arbitration awards duly rendered.

5. Re Article IX, Paragraphs 2, 3 and 4 of the Agreement :

It is understood that Japanese nationals who may be needed in the Philippines in connection with the supply of services or products under the Agreement will be Japanese technicians or experts only:

6. Re Article IX, Paragraph 4 of the Agreement :

The Japanese juridical persons mentioned in this Paragraph are those who undertake reparations projects in the Philippines or those who provide services under Reparations Contracts.

7. Re Chapter II Payment, Paragraph 4 of the Exchange of Notes concerning details for the implementation of the Agreement :

With respect to the expenses of the Mission and the expenses for the training of Filipino technicians and craftsmen, "upon agreement between the two Governments" means "upon the completion of necessary arrangements between the two Governments concerning the specific details" of such expenses.

INDONESIA

80. Statement by Ahmed Subardjo at the San Francisco Conference, 7 September 1951 (Extracts).

As we are confronted with the problem of how to create a situation of peace with Japan, Indonesia is most desirous to give its wholehearted contribution to that effect. It is the suggestion of my government that the restoration of sovereignty to Japan be formulated as clearly as possible in the treaty. Indonesia welcomes the restoration of Japan's place in the community of nations. . . .

The damages which Indonesia suffered during the Japanese occupation are twofold : first, the loss of life of approximately four million people; and second, material damages of billions of dollars. I shall refrain from mentioning here figures since it would be irrelevant to the purport of this Conference, but my government has the facts and figures on hand and will produce them at the proper time and proper place. My government is fully aware that Japan at present—and I wish to emphasize the phrase "at present"—is in no position to pay in cash for our reparation claims. But at the same time my government believes that in due time, in the not too distant future, Japan will regain its viability and will be able properly to discharge its responsibilities.

As you are aware, Mr. Chairman, the present provisions in the treaty concerning reparations are not satisfactory to my government. Would it have been possible to introduce amendments to the reparations clauses, my government would have, for instance, made a modification of article 14 so that it would read as follows :

"Article 14. 1. Japan recognizes its obligations to pay reparation for the damage and suffering caused by it during the war.

"2. The Allied Powers adhere to the principle that Japan should pay reparation for the said damage and suffering.

"3. However, the Allied Powers are prepared under specified conditions to assume a conciliatory attitude towards Japan with the war reparations claims, taking into consideration the viability of the Japanese economy and its other obligations ensuing from this Peace Treaty.

"4. The above-mentioned conditions are as follows :

Japan will assist the Allied Powers so deserving, whose present territories were occupied by Japanese forces and damaged as a consequence of the war, with a view to compensating these countries for the cost of repairing the damage done. For instance, (A) By making available the skills and industry of the Japanese people, for the interest of the Allied Powers in question, in manufacturing, salvaging and other services to be rendered to the Allied Powers in question. (B) By paying all expenditures incurred by the consignment of raw materials which will be made available by the Allied Powers for the manufacturing of goods as stipulated in (A). (C) By making available such goods as machinery and workshops required for the reconstruction of the Allied Powers so desiring.

"(D) By making available technicians required by the Allied Powers so desiring.

"(E) By giving opportunity for trainees to work in Japan.

"(F) In conjunction with the suffering of the nationals of the Allied Powers during the war, by making funds available to mitigate the suffering.

"The points mentioned will be arranged by separate agreements between Japan and the Allied Powers in question. Japan will promptly enter into negotiations with such Allied Powers with a view to concluding such agreements. Such arrangements should avoid the imposition of additional liabilities on the Allied Powers and, where the manufacturing of raw materials is called for, they shall be supplied by the Allied Powers in question.''

So as not to throw any foreign exchange burden upon Japan Article 14 (B) should have been amended as follows :

"Except as otherwise provided for in the present Treaty, and subject to the conclusion of satisfactory arrangements as mentioned in paragraph 4, sub. (a), the Allied Powers shall waive all reparations and other claims of the Allied Powers and of Nationals arising out of any actions taken by Japan and its nationals in the course of the prosecution of the war and claims of the Allied Powers for direct military costs of occupation.''

Likewise, my government would have proposed amendments to other articles of the treaty, especially to article 9 which, in the opinion of my government, should contain a provision to the effect that, pending the conclusion of arrangements relating to fishing and fisheries on the high seas, Japan or Japanese nationals should abstain from fishing in the seas between and surrounding the Indonesian Islands without special permission from my government. Amendments were also envisaged by my government to article 12, which should include a provision already mentioned in the preamble, to the effect that Japan in public and private trade and commerce is to conform to internationally accepted fair practices.

I do not wish to conceal the fact that my government regrets that this Conference cannot consider amendments to the text of the treaty, since in the view of my government, the treaty does not go far enough to accommodate our desires, and offers inadequate provisions to meet our position in regard to a number of matters that we consider essential. Therefore, my government wishes to obtain an assurance that, subsequent to the conclusion of the peace treaty, it will be able to conclude an agreement with Japan which will set out in greater details than is provided in the peace treaty, the terms under which Japan will pay for war damage to Indonesia, and an agreement concerning fishing and fisheries. To this end, I should like to address three questions to the Chairman of the Japanese Delegation. The replies to the questions that I have in mind will greatly influence my government in determining its position in regard to the signing of the treaty.

The questions are these :

1. Is the Japanese Government prepared to pay adequate reparation to Indonesia for damages suffered by Indonesia during the Second World War in accordance with the provisions stipulated in article 14 of the Japanese Peace Treaty ?

2. Does the Japanese Government agree that these reparations will be specified and the amount thereof fixed in a bilateral treaty between Indonesia and Japan, to be concluded as soon as possible after the signing of the peace treaty ?

3. Is the Japanese Government prepared promptly to enter into negotiations with Indonesia for the conclusion of agreements providing for the regulation or limitation of fishing and the conservation of fishing on the high seas between and surrounding the Indonesian Islands in order to safeguard the fish supply of the Indonesian people ?

Mr. Chairman, my delegation trusts that the Japanese Delegation will see its way clear to give such views on these points as will be capable of removing the main obstacles to the establishment of normal relations between Indonesia and Japan.

81. Draft Interim Reparations Agreement, 18 January 1952 (Extract).

The Government of the Republic of Indonesia and the Government of Japan,

Being equally desirous to solve the question of reparations under Article 14 (a) 1 of the Treaty of Peace with Japan signed at the city of San Francisco on the 8th day of September 1951,

Considering the difficulties to reach a final agreement on reparations at the present Conference,

Taking note of the fact that :

It is the view of the Government of the Republic of Indonesia that the determination of Japan's reparation liabilities should be based upon the following damage and suffering sustained by Indonesia :

(a) direct war damage in losses of gold and silver, including shipping and fishing craft, industries and commerce including mining and power, harbor and harbor installations, railways and communications, agriculture, buildings, equipment of private physicians and other free professions and losses sustained by the issue of Japanese currency;

(b) supplementary budgetary expenditures allocable to the war;

(c) damage in losses in income attributable to the whole-sale expropriation of industries, mining, estates, agriculture, shipping, commerce and other facilities for production;

(d) losses in income as a result of heads of families and wage earners who were killed, lost or injured;

(e) additional damage as a direct result of the occupation by the Japanese forces causing decrease in production and delay in repair and reconstruction as well as social rehabilitation.

Taking note of the fact that :

It is the view of the Government of Japan that Japan's reparation liabilities should not be measured by the damage and suffering sustained by Indonesia but by Japan's capacity to fulfil, that the provisions of Article 14 (a) 1 of the Treaty of Peace with Japan require Japan to assist to compensate claimant countries for the cost of repairing that damage done, and that the interpretation of the said damage should be as follows :

(a) the damage is that which was done during the period from December 8, 1941 to September 2, 1945;

(b) the damage is that which was done by Japan;

(c) the damage is of material nature;

(d) the damage is that which was sustained by Indonesia, and

Having agreed that both views be submitted for discussion in the next conference for the purpose of coming to an agreement.

Have decided to conclude the present Interim Agreement on Reparations.

82. Treaty of Peace between Indonesia and Japan, 20 January 1958 (came into force on 15 April 1958).

The Republic of Indonesia and Japan;

Being desirous of terminating the state of war between the two countries and of co-operating in friendly association for the promotion of the common welfare of their peoples and the maintenance of international peace and security in conformity with the principles of the Charter of the United Nations.

Have determined to conclude this Treaty and have accordingly appointed as their Plenipotentiaries :

The Republic of Indonesia:

Mr. Soebandrio, Minister for Foreign Affairs.

Japan:

Mr. Aiichiro Fujiyama, Minister for Foreign Affairs.

Who, having indicated to each other their respective Full Powers found to be in good and due form, have agreed on the following Articles :

Article 1

The state of war between the Republic of Indonesia and Japan is terminated as from the date on which this Treaty comes into force.

Article 2

There shall be firm and perpetual peace and amity between the Contracting Parties and their respective peoples.

Article 3

Both Contracting Parties are desirous of strengthening further the economic relations between them in accordance with the spirit of the decisions made at the Asian-African Conference held at Bandung from 18th to 24th April, 1955. Therefore,

(a) Both Contracting Parties shall enter into negotiations for the conclusion of treaties or agreement at the earliest practicable date to place their trading, maritime, aviation and other economic relations on a stable and friendly basis.

(b) Pending the conclusion of the relevant treaty or agreement, both Contracting Parties shall accord to each other non-discriminatory treatment as compared with that accorded to any third country in the field of trading, maritime and other economic relations between them.

Article 4

1.   Japan is prepared to pay reparations to the Republic of Indonesia in order to compensate the damage and suffering caused by Japan during the war.   Nevertheless it is recognized that the resources of Japan are not sufficient, if it is to maintain a viable economy, to make complete reparation for all the damage and suffering for the Republic of Indonesia and other countries caused by Japan during the war and the same time meet its other obligations.

Therefore,

(a)   Japan agrees to supply, in accordance with detailed terms as may be agreed upon, the Republic of Indonesia by way of reparations with the products of Japan and the services of Japanese people, the total value of which will be eighty thousand three hundred and eight million eight hundred thousand yen (80,308,800,000 yen), equivalent to two hundred and twenty-three million eighty thousand United States of America dollars ($ 223,080,000), within the period of twelve years. The supply of such products and services shall be made at an annual average of seven thousand two hundred million yen (7,200,000,000 yen), equivalent to twenty million United States of America dollars ($20,000,000) during the period of the first eleven years, the outstanding balance to be settled on the twelfth year.

(b) (I)   The Republic of Indonesia shall have the right, to seize, retain, liquidate or otherwise dispose of all property, rights and interests of Japan and Japanese nationals (including juridical persons) which on the coming into force of this Treaty were subject to its jurisdiction.

The property, rights and interests specified in this sub-paragraph shall include those now blocked, vested or in the possession or under the control of enemy property authorities of the Republic of Indonesia, which belonged to or were held or managed on behalf of, Japan or any Japanese nationals (including juridical persons) at the time such assets come under the control of such authorities.

(b) (II)   The following shall be excepted from the right specified in sub-paragraph (I) above :

(i)   all real property, furniture and fixtures owned by the Government of Japan and used for diplomatic or consular purposes, and all personal furniture and furnishings and other private property not of an investment nature which was normally necessary for the carrying out of diplomatic and consular functions, owned by Japanese diplomatic and consular personnel;

(ii)   property belonging to religious bodies or private charitable institutions and used exclusively for religious or charitable purposes;

(iii)   property, rights and interests which have come within the jurisdiction of the Republic of Indonesia in consequence of the resumption of trade, financial and other relations subsequent to September 2, 1945 between the Republic of Indonesia and Japan; and

(iv)   obligations of Japan or Japanese nationals, any rights, title or interest in tangible property located in Japan, interests in enterprises organized under the laws of Japan, or any paper evidence thereof; provided that this exception shall only apply to obligations of Japan and its nationals expressed in Japanese currency.

(b) (III)   Property referred to in exceptions set forth in sub-paragraph (II) above shall be returned subject to reasonable expenses for its preservation and administration.   If any such property has been liquidated, the proceeds shall be returned instead.

(i)   The right to seize, retain, liquidate or otherwise dispose of property as provided in sub-paragraph (I) above shall be exercised in accordance with the laws of the Republic of Indonesia, and the owner shall have only such rights as may be given him by those laws.

2.   Except as otherwise provided in the preceding paragraph, the Republic of Indonesia waives all reparations claims of the Republic of Indonesia and all other claims of the Republic of Indonesia and its nationals arising out of any actions taken by Japan and its nationals in the course of the prosecution of the war.

Article 5

1.   Japan waives all claims of Japan and its nationals against the Republic of Indonesia and its nationals arising

out of the war or out of actions taken because of the existence of a state of war.

2. The foregoing waiver includes any claims arising out of actions taken by the former Netherlands East Indies or the Republic of Indonesia with respect to Japanese ships between September 1, 1939, and September 2, 1945, as well as any claims and debts arising in respect to Japanese prisoners of war and civilian internees in the hands of the former Netherlands East Indies or the Republic of Indonesia, but does not include Japanese claims specifically recognized in the laws of the Republic of Indonesia enacted since September 2, 1945.

Article 6

Any dispute arising out of the interpretation of application of this Treaty shall be settled in the first instance by negotiation, and, if no settlement is reached within a period of six months from the commencement of negotiations, the dispute shall, at the request of either Contracting Party, be referred for decision to the International Court of Justice.

Article 7

The Treaty shall be ratified and shall come into force on the date of exchange of the instruments of ratification which shall take place as soon as possible at Tokyo.

IN WITNESS WHEREOF the undersigned Plenipotentiaries have signed this Treaty and have affixed hereinto their seals.

DONE in duplicate, in the Indonesian, Japanese and English languages, at Djakarta, this twentieth day of January of the year one thousand nine hundred and fifty-eight. In case of any divergence of interpretation, the English text shall prevail.

83. Protocol on the Settlement of Certain Claims, 20 January 1958.

The Government of the Republic of Indonesia and the Government of Japan.

Desiring to settle the claims with respect to the outstanding balances in the accounts opened in accordance with the Payments agreement between the Republic of Indonesia and Japan signed at Djakarta on August 7, 1952, and the arrangements supplementary thereto of the same date;

Have agreed as follow:

Article I

The amount of claims which Japan has against the Republic of Indonesia as the overall net balance of the balances as of January 20, 1958 in the accounts provided for in the Payments Agreement between the Republic of Indonesia and Japan signed at Djakarta on August 7, 1952; the Protocol attached to the Payments agreement, signed at Djakarta on August 7, 1952; and the Exchange of Notes concerning the disposal of balance of Old Account, effected on August 7, 1952 between the Minister for Foreign Affairs of the Republic of Indonesia and the Chief Delegate of Japan to the Trade Conference between Indonesia and Japan are confirmed to be one hundred and seventy-six million nine hundred and thirteen thousand nine hundred and fifty-eight United States of America dollars and forty-one cents ($176,913,958.41).

Article II

1. Japan waives its claims of one hundred and seventy-six million nine hundred and thirteen thousand nine hundred and fifty-eight United States of America dollars and forty-one cents ($176,913,958.41), specified in the preceding Article.

2. As a result of the foregoing, all claims of the Republic of Indonesia and Japan arising out of the accounts provided for in the agreements enumerated in the preceding Article are finally disposed of.

Article III

This Protocol shall be ratified. It shall come into force either on the date of exchange of the instruments of ratification or on the date the Treaty of Peace between the Republic of Indonesia and Japan comes into force, whichever date is the later.

IN WITNESS WHEREOF, the undersigned, being duly authorized by their respective Governments, have signed this

Protocol.

DONE in duplicate at Djakarta, this twentieth day of January of the year one thousand nine hundred and fifty-eight.

84. Japanese Note to Indonesia with respect to economic co-operation, 20 January 1956.

I have the honour to confirm the following arrangement which embodies the understanding reached between the representatives of the two Governments concerning commercial loans and investments which will be advanced by nationals (including private firms, wherevere the term is used herein) of Japan to the Government and nationals of the Republic of Indonesia with a view to assisting in the further economic development of the Republic of Indonesia :

1. Commercial investments, long-term loans or similar credit arrangements (hereinafter referred to as "loans") to such amount in yen as shall be equivalent to four hundred million United States of America dollars ($400,000,000) at present computed at one hundred fortyfour billion yen (144,000,000,000 yen) will be extended by nationals of Japan to the Government or nationals of the Republic of Indonesia through appropriate contracts that may be entered into.

2. Loans shall be extended on a commercial basis and in accordance with the applicable laws and regulations of the two countries.

The Government of the Republic of Indonesia reserves the right to determine the fields of investment and the various industries for which the loans may be contracted as well as the criteria governing the eligibility of Indonesian private firms or nationals desiring such loans.

3. The two Governments shall facilitate and expedite the extension of loans within the scope of pertinent laws and regulations. The facilitation and expedition the Government of Japan is required to offer as to loans will be similar to those which are currently provided to those loans contracted between nationals of Japan and the Government or nationals of the Republic of Indonesia and financed on an ordinary commercial basis by the Japanese banking institutions like the Export-Import Bank of Japan, within their then available funds.

The two Governments shall jointly review from time to time the progress of the conclusion and performance of the loan contracts with a view to effecting the smooth operation of the present arrangement.

4. The terms and conditions of any loan shall be as agreed upon between the parties to the contract.

The loans shall be made principally in the form of machinery and equipment as well as the services incidental thereto.

5. Dispute arising out of or in connection with any loan contract shall be settled either through arbitration by agreement between the parties to the contract or in accordance with the ordinary judicial processes of the country having jurisdiction over such disputes.

6. The present arrangement shall remain in force for a period of twenty years. However, if, after the phase of nineteen years from the coming into force of the arrangement, it appears likely that the amount mentioned in 1 above may not be reached by the end of such period, the two Governments may, upon request of either of them, enter into consultation with a view to extending the period of the present arrangements.

I have the honour to propose that the present note and Your Excellency's reply confirming the contents of the arrangement as stated therein shall be regarded as constituting an agreement between the two Governments which shall come into force on the date of exchange of the instruments of ratification of the Treaty of Peace between Japan and the Republic of Indonesia.

85. Indonesian reply to Japanese Note, 20 January 1958.

I have the honour to acknowledge receipt of your note of today's date, which reads as follows:

[Japanese Note]

I have the honour to confirm the contents of the arrangement as stated in your note under acknowledgement, and to agree that the same and the present reply shall be regarded as constituting an agreement between the two Governments which shall come into force on the date of exchange of the instruments of ratification of the Treaty of Peace between the Republic of Indonesia and Japan.

CAMBODIA

86. Statement by Phleng, Foreign Minister of Cambodia, at the San Francisco Conference, 6 September 1951 (Extract).

By reason of its geographic and strategic position, as well as by reason of its very considerable economic potential, since it is one of the main producers of grain, fish, lumber, cattle, and rubber in the Far East, our country also was one of the first to be occupied by Japan.

Because of this, it is on the list of countries which have the sad honour of having suffered the most in the war. Great damage to public as well as private property, a prolonged occupation, provisioning of Japanese expeditionary forces at the expense of our economy, mutilation of one-third of our national territory over a period of years—such in brief are the evils which befell our country.

Such damage, which is considerable in the case of a large country, is even more so, comparatively speaking, for a country like ours.

Besides, we have received no reparations since the cesation of hostilities.

So many reasons could cause us to come here today in the role of a victim, intransigently demanding reparation for the injuries suffered.

The Delegation of Cambodia, however, has come to San Francisco in a different spirit.

A country profoundly peace-loving by virtue of our standard of living and culture, we are, in addition, taught by our religion and our traditions to love freedom and respect spiritual and artistic values without which life would be only an unnecessarily fierce struggle for an unworthy existence.

We recall certain horrors of the war, some of the effects of which have unfortunately not disappeared as yet. And it is precisely because we remember these things that we wish to protect our country and the world against their repetition.

That is why we have adopted the point of view that the imposition of severe conditions upon the Japanese people as regards reparations would be an illusion and would only serve to keep alive in Japan the spirit of revenge. A peace treaty should avoid carrying with it the seeds of a new war. It is taken for granted that insofar as she is capable of doing so, Japan, taking into account the damage suffered by certain countries, will strive to make reparation to them within the framework of special agreements later to be made between her and the countries concerned, as the discharge on the part of free, alert and responsible persons of the natural obligation to make reparation for the damage caused to others.

We also hold the view that, once the peace is re-established, it should be consolidated with respect to liberty, the sovereignty of nations, and the spirit of collaboration.

These considerations tally with the principles which prevailed during the preparation of the draft treaty, upon which I consider it useless to comment further. The wording thereof can always be criticized, and one must recognize that this effort to reconcile former enemies must not be frustrated; that the successful outcome of the mutual concessions of so many states for the purpose of achieving the compromise represented by the present draft cannot fail without endangering all concerned.

That is why I can say today that Cambodia will sign this treaty.

It expects from it, on the one hand, the solid establishment of security, since Cambodia is one of the first countries destined to serve as a theater for all types of aggression as long as peace is not founded on really sound bases. On the other hand, we hope that because of the size of the damages to our country, the interest which all have in re-establishing a country with definite potential and the importance of an early recovery, and because it is relatively easy to repair the damage caused to a small state, as shall receive from Japan as appropriate and quick reparation of our damages as possible.

LAOS

87. **Economic and Technical Cooperation Agreement Between Japan and Laos, 15 October 1958 (came into force on 23 January, 1959).**

The Government of Japan and the Royal Government of Laos,

Considering that Laos has renounced all its demands in the matter of reparation against Japan and that Laos has expressed the desire to see that Japan would accord it [Laos] economic and technical aid for the economic development of Laos, are convinced of concluding the present economic and technical co-operation Agreement—the articles of which are set forth as below :

Article 1

1. Japan in view of helping Laos in its economic development, undertakes to give Laos, by right of gift and in conformity with the dispositions of the present Agreement an aid of one milliard Yen that will constitute in the supply of Japanese products and services, physical and moral, of the Japanese people. This aid will aim at realizing the works determined in a common agreement by the two Governments.

2. The duration of the aid that will be given by Japan in conformity with the dispositions of the present Agreement will be for two years as from the day on which the present Agreement will come into force, except as agreed upon to the contrary by the two Governments.

Article II

The Royal Government of Laos will establish, in agreement with the Government of Japan, programmes of execution of the works mentioned in paragraph 1 of Article 1 (henceforth mentioned as "execution programmes"). The execution programmes will have to specify the products and services which Japan will supply every year.

Article III

1. In regard to the services designated by the Royal Government of Laos, the contracts will be concluded directly with those Japanese nationals doing physical labour or those Japanese doing mental labour supervised by the Japanese in view of effecting the supply of the products and the services envisaged in para 1 of Article I.

2. The contracts mentioned in paragraph 1 of the present

Article (including their modifications) should conform (a) to the dispositions of the present Agreement, (b) in terms of the arrangements between the two Governments for the contracts shall be submitted to the two Governments for approval. The contract approved according to the dispositions of the present paragraph shall be hereafter called "Contract."

3. Notwithstanding the dispositions of paragraph 1 of the present Article, the supply of the products and the services envisaged in paragraph 1 of Article I will be effected without the conclusion of the contracts, every time as there will be an agreement to this effect between the two Governments and within the limit of ten million yens.

Article IV

1. The Government of Japan will effect, following the procedures to establish according to the dispositions of Article VII, the necessary payments to fulfil the obligations of which the services of Laos, mentioned in paragraph 1 of Article III, is liable—by virtue of the clauses of contracts and, in the cases envisaged in paragraph 3 of Article III in order to cover the expenses for the supply of the products and the services stipulated according to the dispositions of the said paragraph. These payments will be made in Japanese yen.

2. The products and the services being made the object of the payments mentioned in paragraph 1 of the present article are considered to have been supplied by Japan to Laos by virtue of these payments and at the time when these payments are effected.

Article V

The two Governments will take necessary measures for the regular and efficient implementation of the present Agreement.

Article VI

There shall be established a Mixed Commission, composed of the representatives of the two Governments, entrusted with the task of controlling the realisation of the programme of execution and the contracts to make recommendations to the two

Governments concerning the implementation of the present Agreement.

Article VII

The details concerning the application of the present Agreement will be determined by a common agreement of the two Governments.

Article VIII

The present Agreement shall be ratified. It will enter into force on the date of the exchange of the instruments of ratification. The instruments of ratification will be exchanged in Vientiane as soon as possible.

IN WITNESS THEREOF, undersigned, duly authorized to this effect by their respective Governments, have signed the present Agreement.

DONE in duplicate in Tokyo, the fifteenth October 1958.

For Japan :
Aiichiro Fujiyama

For Laos :
Tiao Khamm

SOUTH VIETNAM

88. Statement by Tran Van Huu at the San Francisco Conference, 7 September 1951 (Extract).

An independant people must be a proud people, and it is because pride is valued among us that we will never do anything which might injure the pride of Japan, which has come here to request the signature of 51 nations at the Conference in order again to begin a worthy and proud national life. Nevertheless, although this draft treaty clearly indicates the right to reparations for all who have suffered at the hands of Japan, reparations which are mainly to be given in the form of services, would not be of much use to Vietnam, which does not have any raw materials. Like Japan, Vietnam needs great contributions of capital to re-establish its economy. Therefore, to accept reparations principally in services would amount to accepting a currency which is not legal tender.

We shall thus have to ask that other more effective formulas for payment be studied and that we may particularly count, in addition to the means provided, on a normal indemnification which we hope will come soon, when the restored Japanese economy will make Japan able to fulfil its obligations.

Vietnam will be deeply unhappy if its demands are considered as based on any other sentiment than that of the necessity for our country to reach economic recovery and realize for our people real social amelioration. This objective can be reached only by the use of considerable resources which are at the present moment consecrated in great part to the defense of our liberties and the service of peace.

Thus, it seems to us, as regards our area, that a collective security system would be desirable, which would complete our efforts.

89. Reparations Agreement between Japan and the Republic of Vietnam, 30 May 1959.

Japan and the Republic of Vietnam,

Desiring and basing on the provisions of the Treaty of Peace with Japan signed in the city of San Francisco on 8 September 1951,

Have decided to conclude the present Reparations Agreement and, in consequence, have designated their Plenipotentiaries:

Japan :

Aiichiro Fujiyama, Minister of Foreign Affairs

Manichiro Kubota, Ambassador Extra-ordinary and Plenipotentiary at the Republic of Vietnam

Kogoro Uemura, Advisor to the Ministry of Foreign Affairs

The Republic of Vietnam :

Vu Van Mau, Secretary of State of the Ministry of Foreign Affairs

Bui Van Thinh, Ambassador Extra-ordinary and Plenipotentiary in Japan

Phan Dang Lam, Secretary-General of the Ministry of Foreign Affairs who, after communicating their full credentials respectively having been found in good and due form, have agreed to the following Articles :

Article 1

1. Japan will furnish to the Republic of Vietnam in reparations the products, and the services of Japanese peoples, of the total value equivalent to the U.S. dollars thirty-nine million ($ 39,000,000), calculated to the actual sum of fourteen milliard and forty million Yens (14,040,000,000 yen), during period of five years counting from the day of the entry into force of the present Agreement and in the manner prescribed hereafter.

2. The furnishing of the products and the services mentioned in the preceding paragraph will be effected, in the first three years, by the annual amount in the value of Yens equivalent of ten million dollars of the United States (U.S. $ 10,000,000), in the annual money value in Yens equivalent of three milliards and six hundred million yens (3,600,000,000 yen), and for the last two years, in the annual equivalent against the yen value of four million five hundred thousand of the United States dollars (U.S. $ 4,500,000), calculated in Yens to one milliard and six hundred and twenty million (1,620,000,000 yen).

Article 2

1. The products and services in reparations are to be demanded by the Government of the Republic of Vietnam and is to be determined by the common agreement of the two Governments. These products and services will consist of necessary items and projects to be chosen among those enumerated in the Annexe of the present Agreement.

2. A large part of the products to be provided in reparations will be capital goods. However, the products other than the capital goods, in common agreement between the two Governments, will be provided by Japan upon the demand of the Government of the Republic of Vietnam.

3. The reparations under the terms of the present Agreement will be effected in such a manner that they will not prejudice the normal course of the commerce between Japan and the Republic of Vietnam, and that they will not impose on Japan any additional charge in case of change.

Article 3

The two Governments will fix by consultations and in common agreement an annual programme of execution specifying therein the products and the services to be provided by Japan each year (hereafter mentioned as "Execution Programme").

Article 4

1. The Mission mentioned in paragraph 1 of Article 6 of the present Agreement will conclude the contracts, in the name of the Government of the Republic of Vietnam, directly with the Japanese nationals doing physical or mental labour supervised by the Japanese, for effecting the provision of the produce and services conforming to the execution programme of each year.

2. All these contracts (including their modifications) should conform (a) to the dispositions of the present agreement, (b) to the terms of the arrangements which could be concluded between the two Governments for the application of the present Agreement and (c) to the Programme of Execution applicable to the time. These contracts have to be verified and endorsed by the Government of Japan in as much as their conformity with the under mentioned criteria are concerned. The contract verified and endorsed agreeably to the dispositions of the present paragraph will be hereafter denominated "contract of Reparations."

3. Every contract of Reparations should contain a clause stipulating that the differences which could proceed from this contract or arise with regard to the contract will be upon the demand of one of the interested parties, submitted to a commission for the arbitration of commerce conforming to a settlement which would be concluded between the two Governments. The two Governments will take measures necessary to finalize for execution all arbitration duly formulated.

4. Notwithstanding the dispositions of paragraph 1 of the present Article, the providing of the product and the services to the title of reparations could be effected without the contract of Reparations, every time that there will be an agreement to this effect between the two Governments.

Article 5

1. In view of discharging the obligations of reparations stipulated in Article 1 of the present Agreement, the government of Japan will effect, abiding by the procedures to establish conformingly to the dispositions of Article 9 of the present Agreement, the payments in order to meet the obligations of which the Mission mentioned in the paragraph 1 of Article 6 of the present Agreement is found indebted by virtue of the clauses of contracts of Reparations and to meet the expenses for the providing of the products and the services effected conformably to the dispositions of paragraph 4 of the preceding article. These payments will be made in Japanese yens.

2. By the fact and at the moment of payments in yens effected conformingly to the dispositions of the foregoing paragraph, Japan will be considered as having provided to the Republic of Vietnam the products and the services forming part of these payments and as being relieved of its obligations of reparations as to the amount of the value against United States dollars arising out of these payments in yens conforming to the dispositions of Article 1 of the present Agreement.

Article 6

1. Japan gives its consent to the establishment of a mission of the Government of the Republic of Vietnam in Japan (hereafter denominated "the Mission") as its sole and exclusive agent charged with the implementation of the present Agreement including the conclusion and execution of the contracts of Reparations.

2. The Bureau of the mission will be established at Tokyo, Japan. This bureau will be used exclusively for the exercise of the functions of the mission.

3. The location of the bureau, including the archives, of the Mission in Japan will be inviolable. The Mission will admit to use the codes. The immovable properties belonging to the Mission and being utilised directly for the exercise of its functions will be exempt from taxation upon the acquisition of the immovable property and of the duty on the property. The revenue of the Mission which could proceed from the exercise of its functions will be exempt from all imposition in Japan.

The goods imported for official use of the Mission will be exempt from the customs duties and all other levies collected at the importation or on occasion of the importation.

4. The chief and two other superior members of the Mission, who are under the jurisdiction of the Republic of Vietnam, will be accorded diplomatic privileges and immunities generally recognised as customary in international law.

5. The other members of the mission who are within the jurisdiction of the Republic of Vietnam and who are in fact not the residents in Japan will be exempt from taxation in Japan on the emoluments which they will receive in the exercise of their functions, and, conforming the Japanese laws and regulations, customs duties, and all other levies collected at the importation or on the occasion of the importation of the goods destined for personal use.

6. In case where the differences prove to be of a contract of Reparations or arising apropos a contract of Reparations, would not be settled by arbitration, or by the arbitration rendered to this end would not have been executed, the question could be brought in the last result, to an appropriate Japanese court. In similar cases, and only at the end of the necessary judicial procedures, the chief of the mission and the superior members mentioned in paragraph 4 of the present Article will prosecute, or be prosecuted, and as a result, receive the summary and other documents of procedure at the office of their mission. However, they will be exempted from obligation of depositing judicial surety for the expenses of the procedures. Although the Mission enjoys the inviolability and immunity as it is foreseen in the paragraphs 3 and 4 of the present Article, the final decision pronounced in similar cases by the appropriate court will be accepted by the Mission as the binding decision.

7. In the application of the final decision of the court the portion of land and the building, as well as the movable properties which are found there, belonging to the Mission and used directly for the exercise of its functions will not in any case be the object of measures for execution.

Article 7

1. The two Governments will take measures as are necessary for the regular and efficient application of the present Agreement.

2. The Republic of Vietnam will provide the manpower and the materials and equipments locally available, in view of permitting Japan to supply the products and the services envisaged in Article 1 of the present Agreement.

3. The Japanese nationals whose presence in Vietnam will be necessary for the supply of the products and the services in terms of the present Agreement will be allowed all the necessary formalities for the accomplishment of their work during the course of the period of their stay in Vietnam.

4. In as much as the revenues arising from the supply of the products and the services in terms of the present Agreement, Japanese nationals doing physical or mental labour will be exempt from the taxation in Vietnam.

5. The Republic of Vietnam agrees that the products supplied by Japan in conformity to the dispositions of the present Agreement will not be re-exported from the territory of the Republic of Vietnam.

Article 8

There shall be created a mixed commission (Commission Mixte) composed of the representatives of the two Governments as an organ for consultations between them having the power of formulating the recommendations on the questions relative to the implementation of the present Agreement.

Article 9

The details, comprising the procedures relative to the implementation of the present Agreement, will be fixed after consultations and by a common agreement between the two Governments.

Article 10

The differences between the two Governments concerning the interpretation and the implementation of the present Agreement will be regulated in the first place through the diplomatic channel. If the two Governments do not reach or come to an agreement by this channel, the differences will be submitted for decision to a tribunal of three arbitrators, one arbitrator being nominated by each Government and the third being designated by common agreement between the first two arbitrators on the condition that this third arbitrator will not be a national of one or the other of the two countries. Each of the two Governments will nominate an arbitrator within thirty days, beginning from the date of reception by one of the two Governments a note of the other demanding the arbitration of the differences. The third arbitrator will have to be designated by common agreement on a new arbitrator within another period of thirty days. If either of the Governments has not nominated its own arbitrator within the prescribed period or if the third arbitrator has not been designated according to a common agreement within the prescribed time, either of the Governments could move the President of the International Court of Justice who will designate the arbitrator or the third arbitrator as the case may be. The two Governments will undertake to comply to the arbitration rendered in application of the disposition of the present Article.

Article II

The present Agreement will be ratified and will come into force on the date of exchange of the instruments of ratification, which will take place at Tokyo as soon as possible.

IN WITNESS THEREOF, the undersigned plenipotentiaries have signed the present Agreement and have affixed their seals.

DONE at Saigon, the thirtieth day of the month of May 1959, in duplicate, in Japanese, Vietnamese, and French languages. In case of differences of interpretation, the French text will be relied upon.

For Japan
Aiichiro Fujiyama
Kubota
K. Uemura

For the Republic of Vietnam
Vu Van Mau
Bui Van Tinh
Phan Dang Lam

ANNEX

1. Construction of a central Hydroelectric Station.
2. Equipment for a Centre for Industrial Technology.
3. Supply of other products and services determined according to a common agreement by the two Governments.

(Exchange of instruments of ratification scheduled in September 1959)

NORTH VIETNAM

90. Statement by the Foreign Minister of North Vietnam on Japan-South Vietnam War Reparations Negotiations, 26 November 1957.

During World War II, the Japanese Occupation troops in Indo-China had caused to the Vietnamese people, from the North to the South, great losses in human lives and property. The Japanese Government must bear the responsibility of compensating to the whole of the Vietnamese people for these tremendous damages. All the Vietnamese people have the right to demand that the Japanese Government compensate for the damages caused by the Japanese troops during war time.

The separate negotiations between the Japanese Government and the South Vietnam administration on the question of war compensations are unjustified. According to the Geneva Agreements, the South Vietnam administration is not qualified to represent the whole of the Vietnamese people in demanding war compensations from the Japanese Government.

The Government of the Democratic Republic of Vietnam declares that it does not recognize any agreement between the Japanese Government and the South Vietnam administration on war compensations for the whole of Vietnam. The Government of the Democratic Republic of Vietnam, for its part, always reserves for itself the right to war indemnities from the Japanese Government.

THAILAND

91. **Agreement between Japan and Thailand concerning Settlement of "Special Yen Problem", 9 July 1955.**

Japan and Thailand,

Desiring equally to establish the foundation for further strengthening the traditional friendship and for promoting economic cooperation between the two countries by settling the "Special Yen Problem" pending between them,

Have agreed as follows :

Article I

1. Japan shall pay to Thailand the amount of pounds sterling equivalent to five billion four hundred million yen in five annual installments as follows :

(1) One billion yen in the Japanese fiscal year to which the date of coming into force of this Agreement belongs.

(2) One billion one hundred million yen in each Japanese fiscal year during four years subsequent to the fiscal year referred in sub-paragraph (1) above.

2. The exchange rate to be applied in the payments referred to in paragraph 1 above shall be the foreign exchange banks' T.T. selling rate of pound sterling prevailing in Japan at the time of each of such payments.

Article II

Japan agrees to supply to Thailand, as a measure for economic cooperation and subject to such terms, conditions and modality as may be agreed upon, capital goods of Japan and services of Japanese people in the form of investments and credits up to the amount of nine billion six hundred million yen.

Article III

The Government of Thailand shall, on behalf of the Government and nationals (including juridical persons) or Thailand, waive all and any claims against the Government and nationals (including juridical persons) of Japan concerning the "Special

Yen Problem", including following claims :

(1) Claims relating to the Bank of Thailand Special Yen Account established under the Arrangement between the Bank of Japan and the Ministry of Finance of Thailand concerning the settlement of payments by means of the Special Yen, signed at Tokyo on June 18, 1942 and the Arrangement between the Bank of Japan, the Ministry of Finance of Thailand and the Bank of Thailand regarding the Royal Thai Treasury Special Yen Account, signed at Bangkok on March 19, 1943.

(2) Claims relating to the gold which should have been sold by the Government of Japan to the Government of Thailand under the following letters addressed to the Minister of Foreign Affairs of Thailand from the Japanese Ambassador to Thailand and which have not been sold :

(a) Ambassador Tsubokami's letter addressed to Nai Direk Chayanam, Minister of Foreign Affairs, No. F 86/19, dated April 7, 1944.

(b) Ambassador Yamamoto's letter addressed to Nai Sisena Sombatsiri, Minister of Foreign Affairs, No. ED 9/45, dated January 18, 1945.

(c) Ambassador Yamamoto's letter addressed to Nai Sisena Sombatsiri, Minister of Foreign Affairs, No. ED 81/45, dated July 3, 1945.

(3) Claims relating to the untransferred gold mentioned in the Acknowledgement of Delivery of Gold signed by M.R. Thuaithep Devakul, Director of Department of Economic Affairs, Ministry of Foreign Affairs of Thailand and Nai Prayad Buranasiri, Head of Central Administration, Bank of Thailand on January 4, 1950.

Article IV

There shall be established in Tokyo a joint committee to be composed of representatives of the Governments of the two countries which shall be an organ for consultation, and recommendation to the Governments of the two countries, for the purpose of securing smooth implementation of this Agreement.

Article V

This Agreement shall be approved by each country in accordance with its constitutional procedures, and shall enter into force upon the date of exchange of notes indicating such approval.

IN WITNESS WHEREOF, the undersigned, being duly authorized by their respective Governments, have signed this Agreement.

DONE in duplicate, in the English language, at Bangkok, the ninth day of July, 1955.

For Japan   Ichiro Ohta
(Signed)

For Thailand   Wan Waithayakon
(Signed)   Krommun Naradhip Bongsprabandh

NORTH KOREA

92. Foreign Minister Pak Hen Yen's Note to Soviet Foreign Minister concerning the Peace Treaty with Japan, July 1951 (Extracts).

The Government of the Korean People's Democratic Republic fully shares and upholds the Soviet Government's stand concerning the conclusion of the Peace Treaty with Japan both as regards the procedure of preparing this treaty and its goal and contents.

1. The Government of the Korean People's Democratic Republic holds that the separate preparation of the Peace Treaty with Japan, chosen by the United States Government with obviously self-seeking aims, far from bringing about a peaceful settlement in the Far East will cause further undesirable complications in relations between the countries. . . .

The Chinese People's Republic is a most important factor of peace in the Far East and no peaceful settlement can have legal or practical force without her participation. The United States attempts to debar the USSR, the Chinese People's Republic and other countries from taking part in the preparation of the Peace Treaty with Japan and to substitute the just overall treaty by separate treaty betray the efforts of the American ruling circles to consolidate their positions in occupied Japan and to convert her into the main base of American aggression in Asia. . . .

The tremendous losses suffered by the Korean people as a result of the Japanese aggression, as a result of the many-year-long underground and guerilla struggles against the Japanese invaders and lastly as a result of the Korean patriots fighting within the ranks of the armed forces of the Powers who were waging war on Japan must be taken into account while this question is being solved. Special concern of the Korean People's Democratic Republic, which is the direct neighbour of Japan, about preventing Japanese aggression and assuring the democratic development of Japan must also be taken into account.

Therefore the Government of the Korean People's Democratic Republic expresses the hope that its representative will be invited to the conference to consider the Peace Treaty with Japan on an equal footing with representatives of other states concerned.

3. Wholeheartedly supporting the Soviet Government's proposals concerning the aim and contents of the Peace Treaty with Japan, which proposals are directed towards assuring a lasting and just peace in the Far East, the Government of the Korean People's Democratic Republic would like to stress that Korea is particularly interested in having this treaty contain sufficient guarantees against a revival of Japanese militarism. . . .

Revival of Japanese militarism and fresh manifestations of its aggressiveness are results of the aggressive policy pursued by the ruling circles of the United States. Their heinous anti-popular machinations in Asia lend particular urgency to the task of preventing another recurrence of Japanese aggression by speeding up the conclusion of an overall just Peace Treaty with Japan and the inclusion of the provision of a full demilitarization and democratization of Japan in accordance with the existing international agreements therein.

The Government of the Korean People's Democratic Republic also supports the Soviet Government's proposal that under the Peace Treaty Japan shall be obligated not to enter into any coalition directed against any of the states interested in the signing of the Peace Treaty with her. Of equal importance for the Korean people is the question of the withdrawal of the American occupation troops from Japan, a question which the American draft to the Peace Treaty with Japan so carefully bypasses. . . .

Continuation of the American occupation will signify a further consolidation of Japanese reaction and militarism, which in itself constitutes a mortal threat to our country. No less threatening to our country is the presence of American armed forces in close vicinity of Korea. . . .

There is no doubt that if the United States had no strategic bases in Japan and her war potential at its disposal it would not have been able to launch intervention in Korea on such a broad scale. But as justly noted by the Soviet Government, the United States utilization of the Japanese territory, its material and manpower resources for an armed intervention in Korea is incompatible with international agreements which vested American troops with the right to occupy Japan only for taking measures to demilitarize and democratize that country.

It is but natural that waging a struggle against American intervention the Korean people are vitally interested that in future the frontiers of their state be safeguarded against the threats of armed forces of the aggressive American imperialism who have illegally settled in close vicinity.

Therefore the Government of the Korean People's Democratic Republic regards as absolutely correct the USSR Government's demand that the Peace Treaty with Japan should establish a precise time limit for the withdrawal of the occupation troops and that this treaty should stipulate that no foreign state should have troops or military bases in Japan. As regards territorial and other questions the Government of the Korean People's Democratic Republic also subscribes to the viewpoint of the Soviet Government and believes that a conscientious fulfilment of the corresponding provisions of the Cairo declaration, the Yalta agreement and the Potsdam declaration must be assured.

SOUTH KOREA

93. Treaty on Basic Relations between Japan and the Republic of Korea, 22 June 1965 (Instruments of ratification exchanged at Seoul on 18 December 1965).

Japan and the Republic of Korea,

Considering the historical background of relationship between their peoples and their mutual desire for good neighborliness and for the normalization of their relations on the basis of the principle of mutual respect for sovereignty;

Recognizing the importance of their close cooperation in conformity with the principles of the Charter of the United Nations to the promotion of their mutual welfare and common interests and to the maintenance of international peace and security;

Recalling the relevant provisions of the Treaty of Peace with Japan signed at the city of San Francisco on September 8, 1951 and the Resolution 195(III) adopted by the United Nations General Assembly on December 12, 1948;

Have resolved to conclude the present Treaty on Basic Relations and have accordingly appointed as their Plenipotentiaries;

The Government of Japan :

Etsusaburo Shiina, Minister of Foreign Affairs of Japan.

Shinichi Takasugi.

The Government of the Republic of Korea :

Dong Won Lee, Minister of Foreign Affairs of the Republic of Korea.

Dong Jo Kim, Ambassador Extraordinary and Plenipotentiary of the Republic of Korea.

Who, having communicated to each other their full powers found to be in good and due form, have agreed upon the following articles;

Article I

Diplomatic and consular relations shall be established between the High Contracting Parties. The High Contracting Parties shall exchange diplomatic envoys with Ambassadorial rank without delay. The High Contracting Parties will also establish consulates at locations to be agreed upon by the two Governments.

Article II

It is confirmed that all treaties or agreements concluded between the Empire of Japan and the Empire of Korea on or before August 22, 1910 are already null and void.

Article III

It is confirmed that the Government of the Republic of Korea is the only lawful Government in Korea as specified in the Resolution 195(III) of the United Nations General Assembly.

Article IV

(a) The High Contracting Parties will be guided by the principles of the Charter of the United Nations in their mutual relations.

(b) The High Contracting Parties will co-operate in conformity with the principles of the Charter of the United Nations in promoting their mutual welfare and common interests.

Article V

The High Contracting Parties will enter into negotiations at the earliest practicable date for the conclusion of treaties or agreements to place their trading, maritime and other commercial relations on a stable and friendly basis.

Article VI

The High Contracting Parties will enter into negotiations at the earliest practicable date for the conclusion of an agreement relating to civil air transport.

Article VII

The present Treaty shall be ratified. The instruments of ratification shall be exchanged at Seoul as soon as possible. The present Treaty shall enter into force as from the date on which the instruments of ratification are exchanged.

IN WITNESS WHEREOF, the respective Plenipotentiaries

have signed the present Treaty and have affixed thereto their seals.

DONE in duplicate at Tokyo, this twenty-second day of June of the year one thousand nine hundred and sixty-five in the Japanese, Korean, and English languages, each text being equally authentic. In case of any divergence of interpretation, the English text shall prevail.

For Japan	*For the Republic of Korea*
Etsusaburo Shiina,	Dong Won Lee,
Minister of Foreign Affairs	*Foreign Secretary of the Republic of Korea*
Shinichi Takasugi,	Dong Jo Kim,
Chief of the Japanese Delegation	*Chief of the Republic of Korea Delegation*

94. Agreement between Japan and the Republic of Korea on the Settlement of Problems concerning Property and Claims and Economic Cooperation, 22 June 1965.

(Unofficial translation of the gist of the agreement)

Japan and the Republic of Korea have entered into agreement in the hope of settling problems concerning property of the two countries and their nationals and the property claims between the two countries and their nationals as follows:

Article I

1. Japan will supply to the Republic of Korea free of charge:

(a) Japanese products and services valued at $300 million, equivalent to yen 108,000 million of present rate of exchange, over a period of 10 years from the date when this agreement comes into effect. The products and services will be supplied each year within the limit of $30 million, which is equivalent to yen 10,800 million at the present rate of exchange. If the supply does not reach the above amount, the balance will be added to the amount of products and services to be supplied in the following year. However, the amount of products and services to be supplied each year may be increased or decreased according to an agreement between the two signatory countries.

Japan will provide the ROK with long-term and low-interest

loans up to $200 million, equivalent to yen 72,000 million at the present rate of exchange over a period of 10 years from the date when this agreement comes into effect. The loans will be uesd for the procurement by South Koreans of Japanese products and services required by the ROK Government for the execution of projects that will be decided under an arrangement to be concluded in accordance with Item 3 of Article I.

The loans will be provided from the funds of Japan's Overseas Economic Cooperation Fund and the Japanese Government will take the necessary steps to enable the Overseas Economic Cooperation Fund to secure the funds required to provide the loans in an equal amount annually.

The above-mentioned supply of products, services and loans must be conducive to the economic development of South Korea.

2. The two countries will establish a joint committee, composed of representatives of the Governments of the two countries, as a consultative organ which will be authorized to make recommendations regarding the problems related to the enforcement of provisions of this article.

3. The two countries will conclude arrangements necessary for the execution of provisions of this article.

Article II

1. The two signatory countries confirm that the problems concerning the property, rights and interests between the two countries and their peoples and the property claims between the two countries and their peoples have been fully and finally settled, including those stipulated under paragraph (a) of Article IV of the Peace Treaty with Japan signed in San Francisco on Sept. 8, 1951.

2. The provisions of this article will not have effect on the following (excluding those covered by the special measures taken by the two countries upto the signing of this agreement).

(a) Property, rights and interests of nationals of either of the two signatory nations who have resided in the other signatory nation between Aug. 15, 1947 and the date when the agreement was signed.

(b) The property, rights and interests of either of the two

signatory nations and its people which have been obtained
through normal contacts after Aug. 15, 1945 or have come
under the jurisdiction of the other signatory nation.

3. No claim can be made regarding the property, rights and
interests of either of the two signatory nations and its people
which are under the jurisdiction of the other signatory nation
on the date this agreement is signed. This also applies to the
property claim held by either of the two signatory nations and
its people against the other signatory nation and its people if
such a claim is caused before the agreement is signed.

Article III

1. Any dispute between the two signatory nations concerning the interpretation and enforcement of this agreement shall
be settled first through diplomatic channels.

2. Any dispute which cannot be settled by the provisions
of Item 1 shall be referred to a mediation committee. The
committee will be organized by three mediators, one each from
the signatory nations who will be appointed by either of the
Governments of the two countries within 30 days from the date
when either of the governments of the two countries received
an official document calling for mediation in the dispute and
another mediator selected by the two mediators within 30 days
after the expiration of the first 30-day period or one who will
be appointed by the Government of a third country selected
by the two mediators within the 30-day period. However, a
third mediator shall not be a national of either of the two
signatory nations.

3. If the Government of either of the two signatory nations
fails to appoint a mediator within the specified period or if no
agreement is reached regarding the third mediator within the
specified period, mediation committee shall be composed of
three mediators, one each from two countries selected by the
signatory nations within a 30-day period and another to be
appointed by a third country selected by the two countries
through consultations.

4. The two signatory nations shall abide by the decisions
made by the mediation committee stipulated in this Article IV.
This agreement must be ratified. The ratification instru-

ments should be exchanged in Seoul as soon as possible. This agreement comes into force on the date when the ratification instruments are exchanged.

95. Agreement between Japan and the Republic of Korea on Legal Status and Treatment of South Korean Residents in Japan, 22 June 1965.

(Unofficial translation of the gist of the agreement)

Whereas, Japan and the Republic of Korea consider the long-time special contacts of Korean residents with Japanese society to have developed out of the many years of their residence in Japan;

Whereas, both parties recognize as beneficial to the furtherance of friendly relationships between the two countries or the two peoples for Japan to provide Korean residents with the means to enjoy a stable life under the Japanese social order;

Japan and the Republic of Korea have, therefore, agreed on the following provisions :

Article I

1. The Japanese Government shall grant the right of permanent residence in Japan to any Republic of Korea national meeting any of the following specifications upon application for the same right according to the prescribed procedure within five years after the present agreement goes into effect.

(a) Those who have been residing in Japan since before August 15, 1945 and have continued to do so up to the time of application.

(b) Direct decedants of Korean nationals specified in (a) who were born after August 16, 1945 or who are to be born within five years after the coming into force of the present agreement and who will have continued to reside in Japan up to the time of application.

2. The Japanese Government shall grant permanent residential rights to any offspring born in Japan more than five years after the present agreement goes into effect to Koreans already enjoying the same rights under Article I when applications are made for the same rights according to the prescribed procedure within 60 days after their birth.

Article II

1. The Japanese Government shall comply with the Republic of Korea Government's request for consultations whenever made any time within 25 years after the present agreement goes into effect regarding the residence in Japan of direct decendants of Korean nationals entitled to permanent residential rights under Article I.

Article III

Those Korean nationals entitled to the right of permanent residence in Japan under Article I shall not be subjected to deportation from Japan except when any of their acts, committed after the present agreement goes into effect, falls within the following categories.

(a) Those who have been sentenced to prison terms or subjected to any severer punitive action on charges of insurrection or for crimes relating to foreign aggression.

(Excepted are those whose sentences are suspended or those who have been convicted of any accessory role in the above specified offenses).

(b) Those who have been sentenced to imprisonment or subjected to any other severer forms of penalty for offenses affecting Japan's diplomatic interests or for criminal offenses which involve a foreign head of state, foreign diplomatic personnel or their property and are injurious to Japan's diplomatic interests.

(c) Those who have been sentenced to penal servitude or imprisonment of more than three years for the breach of any laws or ordinances controlling narcotic transactions aimed at profit making (excepting the case where such sentences are suspended) as well as those who have been convicted more than three times for the same offense.

(However, those convicted for a third time for a narcotic offense committed before the coming into force of the present agreement will become deportable if and when convicted of two additional repeated offenses).

(d) Those who have been sentenced to imprisonment or penal servitude of more than seven years for the breach of any Japanese laws or ordinances.

Article IV

The Japanese Government shall give appropriate consideration to the following matters :

(a) Matters concerning the education, livelihood protection and national health insurance coverage in Japan of those Korean nationals entitled or eligible to permanently reside in Japan under Article I.

(b) Matters concerning the taking out of Japan of properties in kind as well as in cash by any Korean nationals returning from Japan to the Republic of Korea by waiving their wish for continued residence in Japan.

JAPAN

96. Statement by Japanese Foreign Ministry on Peace Treaty, 1 June 1950 (Extracts).

On Oct. 25 of the year the war ended, the diplomatic and consular relations which Japan had continued to maintain with foreign nations were ordered suspended by order of General Headquarters. As a result, she had to forego all relations of a diplomatic nature. . . . Lacking in natural resources, Japan had relied on foreign trade to maintain her economy; but with the war's end, this vital trade came to a complete halt : There was no way either to export or import. In addition, Japan had no way to communicate with nations abroad either by ordinary letters or wireless telegraphy or even radio broadcasts, and Japanese subjects were totally forbidden to go abroad for either commercial or educational purposes as they had formerly done.

With the termination of the war, our maritime transportation, which had contributed greatly to feeding our dense population, was ordered to cease functioning. And as the few ships still in operation were placed under strict supervision, Japanese fishing vessels were not free to go out to sea to catch fish which is one of the main sources of nourishment for the Japanese people. . . . In the field of domestic industry, there was much anxiety that various facilities would be removed as reparations. Moreover, many restrictions were imposed with a view of preventing Japan from ever again becoming a militaristic state.

Such was the situation prevailing in our country immediately after the war. As a result, however, of the aid given to Japan by the Allied Powers, particularly the United States, as well as of the earnest efforts made by the Japanese people themselves, Japan has now been able to reach the stage of so-called "de facto peace." What is commonly termed "de facto peace" means a situation in which there is no peace treaty but the effects produced are as similar as possible to those actually arising from such a treaty.

Ordinarily peace is established with the termination of the war by the conclusion of a treaty; but the present situation is that the victorious powers are unable to come to agreement even on the draft of the kind of treaty they want for Japan. In order to avert the various inconveniences deriving from the absence of a peace treaty, the attainment of results similar to those which would arise from the actual conclusion of such a treaty can be considered the best alternative. As she has already fulfilled the conditions demanded of her by the Allied Powers, Japan's "de facto peace" relations are making steady progress. Without a "de facto peace" arrangement, Japan would have remained driven to the wall even to this very day; but thanks to this arrangement, her position is becoming almost like that which would constitute a return to normal status. . . . The fact that no peace treaty has been concluded is, as General MacArthur has stated, not Japan's responsibility, but due to an international situation about which Japan can do nothing. . . .

Due to the absence of a peace treaty, legally a state of war still exists between Japan and the Allied Powers. Under hitherto prevailing concepts Japan could not have even hoped to receive aid from or trade with any of the Allied Powers; nor could she have hoped to send people to such countries or have people come here from them.

In other words, things which are usually allowed after the conclusion of a formal peace treaty are now actually being permitted without one. Of course, as long as it is a "de facto peace," there can be no formal return to international society; nevertheless, a state of affairs similar to a formal return is becoming evident in various fields.

With regard to Japan's foreign relations, it is gratifying to note that Japanese Government overseas agencies have been established in five United States cities and also that many other countries are now granting or considering granting permission to set up such agencies.

Not having recovered the authority to have diplomatic relations, Japan cannot establish embassies or legations; but the present arrangement must be termed far better than having no overseas agencies at all.

With regard to overseas travel, restrictions have been substantially eased. For instance, if a Japanese trader exports goods abroad, he receives payment in the form of foreign currency and can utilize a part of such proceeds to establish agencies abroad or to go abroad himself. Although she has not yet concluded a peace treaty, Japan can how send representatives to international conferences, not only as observers but also as formal participants.

It is most important to make the foreign trade of Japan thrive if she is to have economic recovery. Since the period immediately after the war, when there was hardly any trade at all, trade has become increasingly free. By January of this year, except for a part of the hitherto existing regulations, private trade became practically free of all restrictions.

The number of trade agreements Japan has concluded, including that with the sterling area, already adds up to twenty-one. Judging from results obtained last year, these agreements are playing a great part in promoting our export trade. They accounted for approximately 70 per cent, i.e., over $300,000,000 of the total amount of our exports. . . .

Furthermore, what practically amounts to complete freedom has been permitted with regard to international mail, parcel post, telegrams, telephone and radio broadcasts.

At the outset of the occupation ordinary foreigners could not enter Japan freely but now the number of tourists, traders and other foreigners coming to this country has become remarkably large. . . . As for the operation of Japanese vessels, there had been many restrictions, but from August, 1948, voyages made by Japanese ships to foreign countries became quite numerous, some sailing to the distant Persian Gulf to load and bring back petroleum and others going to Thailand for rice.

Immediately after the war, restrictions were clamped on the

operation of fishing vessels, just as in the case of ordinary ships. . . . Due to the successive extensions. . . . Japanese fishing craft may now operate almost as far out as they did before the war. . . . In the political sphere it has been made possible for the Japanese Government to demonstrate its autonomy. In December, 1949, the Military Government teams in the various prefectures were abolished and civil affairs offices were set up at eight places, thus consolidating and contracting the system.

Looking at the field of production, we find that the ship-building industry, on which there had been various restrictions has been permitted to construct large-size oceangoing vessels: as a result the industry is becoming more and more brisk with activity.

In addition, the operations of basic industries, such as the iron, production machinery, soda, thermal power electricity, sulphuric acid, and bearing industries, were severely limited by the reparations program. But these industries have started to become active again as a result of the United States Government's interim decision of May, 1949, to suspend the removal of their facilities as reparations.

Furthermore, our textile industry has been restored up to the 4,000,000 spindle level. Before concluding, we would like to add that just as a business man needs capital to initiate a business enterprise, so does a nation need capital to rehabilitate its industries. As all the industries of our country were devastated by the war, it must look to foreign countries for capital.

In this respect, since January of last year, when permission was granted for foreigners to conduct investment activities in Japan, private foreign investment and commercial activities in this country have become quite brisk. Although Japan has had to depend on large sums of the American taxpayers' money for aid, she cannot expect such aid to continue indefinitely. That is why the induction of private foreign capital is such a welcome matter. Moreover, in view of the fact that our industrial techniques are far behind the times, we must import foreign machinery and technical methods. Otherwise, we cannot hope to compete in foreign markets.

It is unfortunate that circumstances existing among the Allied Powers have prevented the conclusion of a formal peace treaty in spite of the fact that Japan fully possesses the necessary qualifications; but as there are always two parties to a peace treaty, it cannot be expected that all developments with respect to such a treaty will be in accordance with Japan's wishes. As there are no prospects for the immediate conclusion of peace, it is desirable that arrangements similar as possible to those existing under a peace treaty be made with various countries, thereby alleviating as much as possible the impoverished conditions of our economy.

Arguments to the effect that business with foreign countries, dispatch of persons abroad and induction of foreign capital should not be undertaken until a formal peace treaty has been signed can by no means be afforded in the Japan of today. It is the hope of everyone that a so-called over-all peace will be concluded; but we cannot be so nonchalant as to assert that it would be advisable to hope for over-all peace and have the present system of control continue indefinitely. Our nation should embark on a program of steadily achieving normal international status by concluding peace treaties with nations willing to accord it independence and equality.

97. Statement by Shigeru Yoshida, Prime Minister of Japan, at the San Francisco Conference, 7 September 1951 (Extracts).

The Japanese delegation accepts the Peace Treaty before the Conference. It will restore the Japanese people to full sovereignty, equality and freedom, and reinstate us as a free and equal member in the community of nations. It is not a treaty of vengeance, but an instrument of reconciliation. This fair and generous treaty commands, I assure you, the overwhelming support of my nation. On the other hand, during these past few days in this great conference hall, criticisms and complaints have been voiced by some delegates against this treaty. It is impossible that anyone can become completely satisfied with a multilateral peace settlement at this time. Even we Japanese, who are happy to accept this treaty, find in it certain points which cause us pain and anxiety. I speak of this with diffidence, bearing in mind the treaty stands in magnanimity unparalleled in history and the position of Japan. But I would be remiss in my obligation to my own people if I failed to call your attention to these points.

In the first place, there is the matter of territorial disposition.

The Ryukyu archipelago and the Bonins may be placed under United Nations jurisdiction. The statements by the American and British Delegates on the residual sovereignty of Japan over these islands are a source of gratification to my colleagues and to all my country. I cannot but hope that the administration of these islands will be put back into Japanese hands in the not distant future with the re-establishment of world security, especially the security of Asia.

With respect to the Kuriles and South Sakhalin, the Soviet Delegate spoke the other day as though Japan had grabbed them by aggression. To state the truth, Japan's ownership of the South Kuriles was never disputed by the Czarist Government, while the exchange of South Sakhalin for the North Kuriles between Russia and Japan was agreed upon in 1875 between the two Governments through diplomatic negotiations.

It was under the Treaty of Portsmouth of 1905, concluded through the intermediary of President Theodore Roosevelt of the United States, that South Sakhalin became also Japanese territory. Both Sakhalins and the North and South Kuriles were placed under Soviet occupation as of September 20, 1945, shortly after Japan surrendered. Even the islands of Habomai and Shikotan constituting part of Hokkaido, one of Japan's four main islands, are still being occupied by Soviet forces, who landed there without authorization.

The second point is economic. Japan has lost 45 percent of her entire territory, together with its resources. Her population of almost 84 million has to be confined within the remaining areas, which are war-devastated, with their important cities bombed and blasted.

The Peace Treaty will deprive Japan of her vast overseas assets. Moreover, article 14 empowers Allied Nations which have suffered no damage from the war to seize Japanese private property in their country. There is fear as to whether Japan, reduced to such a predicamant, could ever manage to pay reparations to certain designated Allied Powers without shifting the burden upon the other Allied Powers.

However, we have undertaken the obligations of the treaty in this respect, and we mean to carry them out. I solicit the understanding and support of the governments concerned, vis-a-vis Japan's efforts toward a statisfactory solution of this prob-

DOCUMENT 97   371

lem, in the face of hugh difficulties

With her war-shattered economy salvaged through American
aid, Japan is making progress along the road to recovery. We
are determined that our nation shall cease to be a burden on
other countries, but shall contribute positively to world prosperity, while observing fully the fair trade practices in international commerce.

The present treaty opens the door to the realization of such
aspirations of Japan in the field of international economy. But
the same door may be closed by the Allied Nations at any time.
This may be an inherent feature of such a peace treaty. I only
hope that the door will be kept open by all countries as widely
as possible.

Since my speech was prepared I have heard the three
questions put to me this morning by the distinguished Foreign
Minister of Indonesia. The questions seek to resolve doubts
such as have been expressed by some others. The answer to
these questions is yes, since that means in our opinion a fair
interpretation of articles 14 and 9 of the treaty. I hope that
this answer will resolve any doubts of others as to Japan's good
intentions under the treaty.

Thirdly, there is a question of repatriation. The conclusion
of this Peace Treaty arouses afresh the anxiety of the Japanese
people regarding the state of the more than 340,000 of their
compatriots who have failed to return. In the name of humanity
I would like to appeal to all Allied Powers for continued assistance and cooperation towards speeding the repatriation of
these hapless Japanese nationals through the instrumentalities
of the United Nations or by any other means. We are thankful
that a provision relating to repatriation has been inserted in
the treaty at the final stage of drafting.

In spite of the existence of these causes for anxiety, or
rather because of it, Japan is all the more anxious to conclude
the Peace Treaty. For we expect that Japan as a sovereign and
equal power would gain wider opportunities for eliminating
anxiety as well as for dissipating the dissatisfactions, apprehensions, and misgivings on the part of other powers. I hope the
Peace Treaty will be signed by as many as possible of the
countries represented at this Conference. Japan is determined
to establish with them relations of mutual trust and under-

standing and to work together for the advancement of the cause of world democracy and world freedom.

It is with keen regret that the Japanese Delegation notices the absence of India and Burma. As an Asiatic nation, Japan is especially desirous to cultivate relations of closest friendship and cooperation with other Asiatic nations with whom we share common problems, common spiritual and cultural heritages, and common aspirations and ideals.

We hope Japan may become a good member of the world community by being first a good member of the immediate neighbourhood by contributing her full share towards its prosperity and progress.

As regards China, I confine my remarks to two points. The first point is that, like others, we regret the disunity of that country which prevents China from being here. The second is that the role of China trade in Japanese economy, important as it is, has often been exaggerated, as proven by our experience of the past 6 years. Unfortunately, the sinister thoughts of totalitarian oppression and tyranny still operate throughout the globe. These forces are sweeping over half the Asiatic continent, sowing seeds of dissention, spreading unrest and confusion, and breaking out into open aggression here and there, indeed, at the very door of Japan. Being unarmed as we are, we must, in order to ward off the danger of war, seek help from a country that can and will help us.

That is why we shall conclude a security pact with the United States under which American troops will be retained in Japan temporarily until the danger is past, or international peace and security will have been assured under the United Nations' auspices or a collective security arrangement. Japan was exposed once to the menace of Communist imperialism from the north. Today it is the Communist menace that threatens her from the same direction. When the Allied troops are withdrawn from our country with the conclusion of peace, producing a state of vacuum in the country, it is as clear as day that this tide of aggression will beat down upon our shores. It is imperative for the sake of our very existence that we take an adequate security measure. This should not raise a bugbear of Japanese peril. Japan, beaten and battered, dispossessed of her overseas possessions and resources, is absolutely incapable of equipping herself for modern warfare to such an extent as to make her a military menace to neighbours. For that she has not the material, she has not the means, she has not the will. . . .

We have listened to the delegates who have recalled the terrible human sufferings and the great material destruction of the late war in the Pacific. It is with feelings of sorrow that we recall the part played in that catastrophic human experience by the old Japan. I speak of the old Japan because out of the ashes of the old Japan there has arisen a new Japan. My people have been among those who suffered greatly from the destruction and devastation of the recent war. Purged by that suffering of all untoward ambition, of all desire for the path of military conquest, my people burn now with a passionate desire to live at peace with their neighbours in the Far East and in the entire world and to rebuild their society so that it will in ever greater fullness yield better life for all.

98. Agreement for the settlement of disputes arising under Article 15(a) of the [San Francisco] Treaty of Peace with Japan, 12 June 1952.*

The Governments of the Allied Powers signatory to this Agreement and the Japanese Government desiring, in accordance with Article 22 of the Treaty of Peace with Japan signed at San Francisco on September 8, 1951, to establish procedures for the settlement of disputes concerning the interpretation and execution of Article 15 (a) of the Treaty have agreed as follows :

---

* In accordance with Article VIII, the Agreement came into force between Japan and each of the following States on the dates indicated:

Australia	12 Aug 1952	Mexico	11 Aug 1952
Belgium	22 Aug 1952	New Zealand	19 Jun 1952
Cambodia	13 Aug 1952	Norway	9 Sep 1952
Canada	13 Jun 1952	Pakistan	16 Jul 1952
Ceylon	16 Jun 1952	Turkey	24 Jul 1952
Cuba	15 Aug 1952	United Kingdom	14 Jul 1952
Dominican Republic	12 Jun 1952	USA	19 Jun 1952
France	24 Jul 1952		

Article I

In any case where an application for the return of property, rights, or interests has been filled in accordance with the provisions of Article 15 (a) of the Treaty of Peace, the Japanese Government shall within six months from the date of such application, inform the Government of the Allied Power of the action taken with respect to such application. In any case where a claim for compensation has been submitted by the Government of an Allied Power to the Government of Japan in accordance with the provisions of Article 15 (a) of the Treaty and the Allied Powers Property Compensation Law (Japanese Law No. 264, 1951), the Japanese Government shall inform the Government of the Allied Power of its action with respect to such claim within eighteen months from the date of submission of the claim. If the Government of an Allied Power is not satisfied with the action taken by the Japanese Government with respect to an application for the return of property, rights, or interests, or with respect to a claim for compensation, the Government of the Allied Power, within six months after it has been advised by the Japanese Government of such action, may refer such claim or application for final determination to a commission appointed as hereinafter provided.

Article II

A commission for the purpose of this Agreement shall be appointed upon request to the Japanese Government made in writing by the Government of an Allied Power and shall be composed of three members; one, appointed by the Government of the Allied Power, one, appointed by the Japanese Government, and the third, appointed by mutual agreement of the two Governments. Each commission shall be known as the (name of the Allied Power concerned)—Japanese Property Commission.

Article III

The Japanese Government may appoint the same person to serve on two or more commissions; Provided, however, that if, in the opinion of the Government of the Allied Power, the service of the Japanese member on another commission or commissions unduly delays the work of the commission, the Japanese Government shall upon the request of the Government of the Allied Power appoint a new member. The Government of an Allied Power and the Japanese Government may agree to appoint as a third member, a person serving as a third member on other commissions; Provided, however, that if, in the opinion of either the Government of the Allied Power or the Japanese Government, the service of the third member on another commission or commissions unduly delays the work or the commission, either party may require that a new third member be appointed by agreement of the Government of the Allied Power and the Japanese Government.

Article IV

If the Japanese Government or the Government of the Allied Power fails to appoint a member within thirty days of the request referred to in Article II or, if the two Governments fail to agree on the appointment of a third member within ninety days of the request referred to in Article II, the Government which has already appointed a member in the first case, and either the Government of the Allied Power or the Japanese Government in the second case may request the President of the International Court of Justice to appoint such member or members. Any vacancy which may occur in the membership of a commission shall be filled in the manner provided in Articles II and III.

Article V

Each commission created under this Agreement shall determine its own procedure, adopting rules conforming to justice and equity.

Article VI

Each Government shall pay the remuneration of the member appointed by it. If the Japanese Government fails to appoint a member, it shall pay the remuneration of the member appointed on its behalf. The remuneration of the third member of each commission and the expenses of each commission shall be fixed by, and borne in equal shares by the Government of the Allied Power and the Japanese Government.

Article VII

The decision of the majority of the members of the commission shall be the decision of the commission, which shall be accepted as final and binding by the Government of the Allied Power and the Japanese Government.

Article VIII

This Agreement shall be open for signature by the government of any state which is a signatory to the Treaty of Peace. This Agreement shall come into force between the Government of an Allied Power and the Japanese Government upon the date of its signature by the Government of the Allied Power and the Japanese Government, or upon the date of the entry into force of the Treaty of Peace between the Allied Power whose Government is a signatory hereto and Japan, whichever is the later.

Article IX

This Agreement shall be deposited in the archives of the Government of the United States of America, which shall furnish each signatory Government with a certified copy thereof.

SOURCES OF DOCUMENTS

1. United States, Department of State, *Foreign Relations of the United States* (hereinafter cited as *Foreign Relations*), *1943, the Conferences of Cairo and Tehran* (Washington, D.C. 1961) 448-9.

2. *Ibid., the Conferences of Malta and Yalta* (Washington, D.C. 1955) 984.

3. US, *Department of State Publication*, 2671, Far Eastern Series, 17, 53.

4. *Foreign Relations*, n. 1, 1947, Vol. VI, *The Far East* (Washington, D.C., 1972) 489-90.

5. *Ibid.*, 537-8 and 540-3.

6. *Ibid.*, 1948, Vol. VI, *The Far East and Australia* (Washington, D.C., 1974) 656-60.

7. *Ibid.*, 695 and 713-6.

8. *Ibid.*, 963.

9. *Ibid.*, 964-6.

10. *Ibid.*, 989-90.

11. *Ibid.*, 858-62 and 877.

12. *Ibid.*, 1044-5.

13. US, Department of State Press Release 1180, 24 Nov 1950.

14. *Ibid.*, 1267, 28 Dec 1950.

15. *Department of State Bulletin* (12 Mar 1951) 403-7. Also Japan, Ministry of Foreign Affairs, *Collection of Official Foreign Statements on Japanese Peace Treaty*, Vol. II (Tokyo, 1951) 31-9.

16. *Collection of Official Foreign Statements on Japanese Peace Treaty*, n. 15, 55-62.

17. *Department of State Bulletin* (9 Apr 1951) 576-80.

18. *Ibid.* (28 May 1951) 852-6.
19. *Ibid.* (23 Jul 1951) 143-4.
20. *Ibid.*, 132-8.
21. *Ibid.* (17 Sep 1951) 447-50.
22. *Ibid.*, 452-9.
23. Japan, Ministry of Foreign Affairs, *Japanese Peace Conference* San Francisco, California, September 1951, Provisional Verbatim Minutes of the Conference (Tokyo, undated) 353-4.
24. *Department of State Bulletin* (27 Aug 1951) 349-54.
25. *Ibid.*, 354-5.
26. *Ibid.*, 355-7 ; Also UK, *Command Papers*, *Cmd.* 8300, Draft Peace Treaty with Japan ; Also Ceylon Treaty Series No. 1 of 1952, *Treaty of Peace with Japan* (Colombo, 1952) 15-8.
27. United States, Department of State, *United States Treaties and Other International Agreements*, Vol. 3, Part 3, 1952 (Washington, D.C., 1955) 3331-2.
28. *Ibid.*, 3300.
29. *Information Bulletin* (Embassy of Japan, New Delhi) (1 Oct 1956) 1-2.
30. *Foreign Relations*, 1947, n. 4, 532-4.
31. *Ibid.*, 410-1.
32. UK, Parliamentary Debates, House of Commons, Vol. 490 (1951) colls. 632-7.
33. *Ibid.*, Written Answers, colls. 49-51.
34. *Ibid.*, Vol. 491 (1951) colls. 478-84.
35. *Japanese Peace Conference*, n. 23, 87-98.
36. USA, Department of Press Release 1180, 24 Nov 1950.
37. *Department of State Bulletin* (28 May 1951) 856-8.
38. *Ibid.* (23 Jul 1951) 138-43.
39. *Japanese Peace Conference*, n. 23, 105-28.
40. *Information Bulletin* (15 Nov 1956) 1-3.
41. *Ibid.*, 1 Mar 1957.
42. *Contemporary Japan* (Apr 1957) 731.
43. *Foreign Relations*, 1948, n. 6, 799-800.
44. *Department of State Bulletin* (28 Jan 1952) 120.
45. *Ibid.*, 120.
46. *China Handbook 1952-53* (Taipeh, 1952) 154-6.
47. *Ibid.*, 156-7.

48. *Ibid.*, 157-9.

49. *Ibid.*, 159-60.

50. *China Digest* (4 Nov 1947) 8-11.

51. *Ibid.* (24 Feb 1948) 10-1.

52. *Ibid.* (28 Jun 1949) 14-5.

53. *China Weekly Review* (2 Jul 1949) 109.

54. *Ibid.* (9 Jul 1949) 127.

55. *Ibid.* (25 Mar 1950) 68.

56. *People's China* (Peking) (16 Dec 1950) Supplement, 17-9.

57. *Soviet Press Translations* (15 Apr 1951) 207-9.

58. *People's China.* (1 Jun 1951) Supplement, 3-5.

59. *Ibid.* (1 Sep 1951) Supplement, 3-6.

60. Shih-chieh Chih-shih Ch'u-pan-hsie, *Chung-hua Jen-min Kung-he Kuo tui-wai Kuan-hsi Wen-Chien Chi*, Vol. 2, 1951-53 (Peking, 1958) 196-8.

61. *People's China* (1 Oct 1951) 38-9.

62. *Ibid.* (1 Feb 1952) 11-2.

63. *Ib'd.* (16 May 1952) 4-6.

64. *Peking Review* (6 Oct 1972) 12-3.

65. India, Press Information Bureau, Press Release dated 10 Sep 1951.

66. India, Lok Sabha Secretariat, *Foreign Policy of India : Texts of Documents, 1947-59* (New Delhi, 1959) 71-5.

67. *Contemporary Japan*, Vol. 23 (Nos. 4-6, 1955) 424-7.

68. *Ibid.*, 427-9.

69. *United Nations Treaty Series*, Vol. 251, No. 3543, 226-32.

70. *Ibid.*

71. *Ibid.*, 234-42.

72. *Ibid.*

73. *Ibid.*

74. *Ibid.*

75. *Contemporary Japan* (Oct 1963) 795.

76. *Japanese Peace Conference*, n. 23, 258-65.

77. *Gaimusho Bulletin* (Tokyo), 12 Mar 1953.

78. *Contemporary Japan*, Vol. 24 (Nos. 4-6, 1956) 362-9.

79. *Ibid.*, 369.

80. *Japanese Peace Conference*, n. 23, 250-5.

81. Japan, Ministry of Foreign Affairs, Press Release, 31 Jan 1952.

82. Indonesia, Ministry of Information, Special Release (2),

7-13.

83. *Ibid.*, 34-5.

84. *Ibid.*, 40-3.

85. *Ibid.*

86. *Japanese Peace Conference*, n. 23, 117-9.

87. *Contemporary Japan* (Mar 1959) 718-9.

88. *Japanese Peace Conference*, n. 23, 304-5.

89. *Contemporary Japan* (Aug 1959) 185-8.

90. *Vietnam Information Bulletin* (20 Dec 1957) 2.

91. *Contemporary Japan*, Vol, 23 (Nos. 10-12, 1955) 814-5.

92. *News and Views from the Soviet Union* (30 Jul 1951) 1-6.

93. *Japan Times*, 23 Jun 1965, 257 ; Also *Contemporary Japan* (May 1966) 677-8.

94. *Japan Times*, 23 Jun 1965, 259.

95. *Ibid.*

96. *New York Times*, 2 Jun 1950.

97. *Japanese Peace Conference*, n. 23, 327-32.

98. *United Nations Treaty Series*, Vol. 138, no. 1869, 184-8.

Appendix 1

List of 49 States declaring belligerence against Japan

Country	Date of declaring belligerence	Country	Date of declaring belligerence
Argentina	27 Mar 1945	Italy	15 Jul 1945
Australia	8 Dec 1941	Lebanon	27 Feb 1945
Belgium	20 Dec 1941	Liberia	27 Jan 1944
Bolivia	7 Apr 1943	Luxembourg	8 Sep 1942
Brazil	6 Jun 1945	Mexico	22 May 1942
Canada	7 Dec 1941	Netherlands	8 Dec 1941
Chile	12 Feb 1945	New Zealand	8 Dec 1941
China	9 Dec 1941	Nicaragua	8 Dec 1941
Costa Rica	8 Dec 1941	Norway	7 Dec 1941
Cuba	9 Dec 1941	Panama	7 Dec 1941
Czechoslovakia	9 Dec 1941	Paraguay	8 Feb 1945
Dominican		Peru	11 Feb 1945
Republic	8 Dec 1941	Philippines	7 Dec 1941
Ecuador	2 Feb 1945	Poland	11 Dec 1941
Egypt	26 Feb 1945	Saudi Arabia	1 Mar 1945
El Salvador	8 Dec 1941	Syria	26 Feb 1945
Ethiopia	1 Dec 1942	Turkey	23 Feb 1945
France	Oct 1944	South Africa	8 Dec 1941
Greece	8 Dec 1941	U.K.	7 Dec 1941
Gautemala	9 Dec 1941	Uruguay	22 Feb 1945
Haiti	8 Dec 1941	Venezuela	14 Feb 1945
Honduras	8 Dec 1941	Yugoslavia	7 Dec 1941
India	7 Dec 1941	Mongolia	10 Aug 1945
Iran	28 Feb 1945	USA	7 Dec 1941
Iraq	16 Jan 1943	USSR	9 Aug 1945

Note : China, Italy and Mongolia were not invited to the San Francisco Peace Conference ; India and Yugoslavia (Burma also) declined.

the invitation to participate in the Conference and concluded separate bilateral peace treaties; Taiwan signed bilateral Treaty of Peace with Japan on 28 April 1952 but this was declared to have lost its *raison d'etre* in September 1972 when Japan normalised its relations with the People's Republic of China ; Czechoslovakia, Poland and USSR attended the San Francisco Peace Conference but did not sign the San Francisco Treaty. They normalised their relations with Japan in 1956-1957 but the formal peace treaties have not yet been concluded. With the exception of 8 states (China, Czechoslovakia, India, Italy, Poland, Yugoslavia, Mongolia and USSR) all others (41 states) in the above list of 49 states plus Cambodia, Ceylon, Colombia, Indonesia, Laos, Pakistan and South Vietnam signed the San Francisco Peace Treaty on 8 September 1951. Of these 48 states, signatories to the San Francisco Peace Treaty, Indonesia alone failed to ratify it and preferred to conclude a separate bilateral Treaty of Peace in January 1958.

Appendix 2

Members of the Far Eastern Commission

1. Australia
2. Canada
3. China
4. France
5. India
6. Netherlands
7. New Zealand
8. Philippines
9. UK
10. USA
11. USSR

Note : The above 11 countries were original members of the Far Eastern Commission. Burma and Pakistan became members of the Commission in November 1949.

SELECT BIBLIOGRAPHY

Books

Allen, G.C. *A Short Economic History of Japan.* London, 1962.
———. *Japan's Economic Expansion.* London, 1965.
Baerwald, Hans. *The Purge of Japanese Leaders under the Occupation.* Berkeley, Calif., 1959.
Ball, William M. *Japan—Enemy or Ally?* New York, 1949.
Beal, R.J. *John Foster Dulles : 1888-1957.* New York, 1957.
Beasley, W.G. *The Modern History of Japan.* London, 1973.
Bisson, T.A. *Zaibatsu Dissolution in Japan.* Berkeley, Calif., 1954.
Blakeslee, George H. *A History of the Far Eastern Commission.* Washington, 1953.
———. *The Far Eastern Commission : A Study in International Cooperation, 1945 to 1952.* Washington, D.C., 1953.
Borton, Hugh, ed. *Japan.* New York, 1950.
———. *Japan Between East and West.* New York, 1957.
———. *Japan's Modern Century.* New York, 1955.
Borton, Hugh and Pearn, B.R. *The Far East, 1942-1946.* London, 1955.
Burton, Robert J.C. *Japan's Decision to Surrender.* Stanford, Calif., 1954.
Butow, R.J.C. *Japan's Decision to Surrender.* Stanford, Calif., 1954.
———. *Tojo and the Coming of the War.* Princeton, N.J., 1961.
Byrnes, James F. *Speaking Frankly.* New York, 1947.
Cohen, Bernard C. *The Political Process and Foreign Policy : The Making of the Japanese Peace Settlement.* Princeton, N.J., 1957.

Cohen, Jerome B. *Economic Problems of Free Japan.* Princeton,. N.J., 1952.

Crowley, James B. *Japan's Quest for Autonomy.* Princeton, N.J. 1966.

Deverall, Richard, L.G. *Red Star Over Japan.* Calcutta, 1952.

Dunn, Frederick S. *Peace-Making and the Settlement with Japan.* Princeton, N.J., 1963.

Fearey, Robert A. *Occupation of Japan, Second Phase, 1948-1950.* New York, 1950.

Feis, Herbert. *Contest Over Japan.* New York, 1967.

Gross, Ernest A. *Japan Between East and West.* New York,. 1957.

Hellmann, Donald C. *Japanese Domestic Politics and Foreign Policy : The Peace Agreement with the Soviet Union.* Berkeley, Calif., 1969.

Ito, Nobufumi. *New Japan : Six Years of Democratization.* Tokyo, 1951.

Jain, J.P. *China in World Politics : A Study of Sino-British Relations. 1949-1975.* New Delhi, 1976.

Japan, Ministry of Foreign Affairs. *Documents Concerning the Allied Occupation of Japan.* Tokyo, 1949.

———. *Japan, Her Security and Mission.* Tokyo, 1950.

———. *Japanese Peace Conference, San Francisco, Provisional Verbatim Minutes.* Tokyo, undated.

———. *Nihon no Baisho* (Japan's Reparations). Tokyo, 1963.

———. *Collection of Official Foreign Statements on Japanese Peace Treaty,* 3 vols. Tokyo, 1951.

———. *Tainichi Baisho Bunshoshu.* (Documents Concerning Japanese Reparations). 3 vols. Tokyo, 1951.

———. *The Northern Islands : Background of Territorial Problems in the Japanese-Soviet Negotiations.* Tokyo, 1955.

Jones, F.C., "China and Japan," in Peter Calvocoressi. *Survey of International Affairs 1951.* London, 1954. 378-433.

Kawai, Kazuo. *Japan's American Interlude.* Chicago, 1960.

Kennan, George F. *American Diplomacy, 1900-1950.* New York, 1963.

———. *Russia and the West under Lenin and Stalin.* New York, 1962.

Kesavan, K.V. *Japan and Southeast Asia, 1952-60.* Bombay, 1972.

Latourettee, Kenneth Scott. *American Record in the Far East*. New York, 1953.

Leng Shao Chuan. *Japan and Communist China*. Kyoto, undated.

Lewe Van Aduard, Evert J. *Japan from Surrender to Peace*. The Hague, 1953.

MacArthur, Douglas. *Reminiscences*. New York, 1964.

Mallappa, Amravati. *Relations Between Japan and the United States since 1945 with special reference to the Peace Treaty and the Security Pact*. Ph.D. Thesis of Jawaharlal Nehru University, New Delhi, 1969.

Martin, Edwin M. *The Allied Occupation of Japan*. Stanford, Calif., 1948.

Maxon, Yale C. *Control of Japanese Foreign Policy*. Barkeley, Calif., 1957.

National Peace Council. *Views of Kagawa and Nehru on Japan's Future*. N.C. 5269. London, 26 Nov. 1945.

New Zealand. Department of External Affairs. *Japanese Peace Settlement*. No. 1060. Wellington, 1951.

———. *Report on British Commonwealth Conference*, Canberra, *26 August—2 September 1947*, No. 38. Wellington, 1947.

Olson, Lawrence, *Japan in Postwar Asia*, New York, 1970.

Packard, G.R. *Protest in Tokyo, The Security Treaty Crisis of 1960*. Princeton, N.J., 1966.

Pascuel, Ricardo R. and Majul, Cesar A. *Foreign Policy of the Republic of the Philippines*. Manila, 1958.

Pauley, Edwin W. *Report on Japanese Reparations to the President of the U.S., November 1945 to April 1946*. Washington, D.C., 1946.

Philippine Reparations Commission, Manila. *Report of the Reparations Commission to the President of the Philippines, the Senate, the House of Representatives, the National Economic Council for the Period from 20 September 1956 to 31 December 1958*.

———. *Report of the Reparations Commission to the President of the Republic of the Philippines, the Senate, the House of Representatives, the National Economic Council for the Period 1 January 1959 to 31 December 1959*.

Reischauer, Edwin O. *Japan : Past and Present*, 3rd ed. New York, 1964.

———. *Japan and America Today*. Stanford, Calif , 1953.

———. *The United States and Japan*. New York, 1965.

———. *Wanted A Far Eastern Policy*. New York, 1955.

Rosecrance, R.N. *Australian Diplomacy and Japan 1945-1951*. Melbourne, 1962.

Sebald, William. *With MacArthur in Japan*. New York, 1965.

Shigemitsu, Mamoru. *Japan and Her Destiny—My Struggle for Peace*. London, 1958.

Stephan, John J. *The Kurile Islands : Russo-Japanese Frontier in the Pacific*. London, 1974.

Stockurn, Arthur. *The Japanese Socialist Party and Neutralism*. London, 1968.

Sugiyama, Shigeo. *Northern Territories of Japan*. Tokyo, 1972.

Swearingen, Rodgar and Lenger, Paul. *Red Flag in Japan : International Communism in Japan*. Cambridge, 1954.

Truman, Harry S. *Memoirs : Years of Trial and Hope*. 2 vols. New York, 1956.

Tsukshira, Toshio. G. *The Postwar Evolution of Communist Strategy in Japan*. Cambridge, 1954.

United Kingdom, Ministry of Foreign Affairs. *Japan No 1, Draft Peace Treaty with Japan*. Cmd. 8300. London, 1951.

———. *Japan No. 2, Amendments to Draft Treaty of Peace with Japan*. Cmd. 8316. London, 1951.

———. *Japan No. 3, Draft Treaty of Peace with Japan as Amended 13 August 1951*. Cmd. 8341. London, 1951.

United States, Congress. *Japanese Peace Treaty and Other Treaties Relating to Security in the Pacific, Hearings Before the Senate Committee on Foreign Relations*, 82nd Congress, Second Session. Washington, D.C., 1952.

United States, Department of State. *A Decade of American Foreign Policy: Basic Documents, 1941-9*. Washington, D.C., 1950.

———. *American Foreign Policy, 1950-1955 Basic Documents*. 2 vols. Washington, D.C., 1957.

———. *Japan : Free World Ally*. Washington, D.C., 1957.

———. *Occupation of Japan, Policy and Progress*. Washington, D.C., 1957.

———. *Record of Proceedings of the Conference for the Conclusion and Signature of the Treaty of Peace with Japan*. Washington, D.C., 1951.

————. *The Conferences at Cairo and Tehran, 1943.* Washington, D.C., 1955.

————. *The Conferences at Malta and Yalta, 1945.* Washington, D.C., 1955.

————. *United States Relations with Japan, 1945-1953.* New York, 1952.

————. *United States Treaties and Other International Agreements.* Vol. 33. Part 3, 1952. Washington, 1955.

United States, Far Eastern Command, *Japan, Friend and Ally.* Tokyo, 1952.

Viswanathan, Savitri. *Normalization of Japanese-Soviet Relations 1945-1970.* Tallahasee, Florida, 1973.

Weinstein, Martin E. *Japan's Postwar Defence Policy, 1947-1968.* New York, 1971.

Whitney, Courtney. *MacArthur : His Rendezvous with History.* New York, 1956.

Willoughby, Charless A. *MacArthur, 1941-1951.* New York, 1954.

World Affairs Council of Northern California. *Peace Making with Japan, Study Group Report 2.* San Francisco, 1948.

Yoshida, Shigeru. *Japan's Decisive Century 1867-1967.* New York, 1967.

————. *Yoshida Memoirs : The Story of Japan in Crisis.* London, 1961.

Articles

Akiyama, Goro. "Tainichi Kowo o meguru kokusai tairitsu," (International Conflict Surrounding Japanese Peace Treaty) *Chuo Koron* (Sep 1951) 210-21.

Alison, John M. "Japanese Peace Treaty and Related Security Pact," *Proceedings, American Society of International Law* (Apr 1952) 35-43.

Ball, W.M. "Reflections on Japan," *Pacific Affairs* (Mar 1948) 3-19.

Ballantine, Joseph W. "The Future of the Ryukyus," *Foreign Affairs* (Jul 1953) 663-74.

Bisson, T.A. "Reparations and Reform in Japan," *Far Eastern Survey* (17 Dec 1947) 241-7.

Borton, Hugh. "United States Occupation Policies in Japan Since Surrender," *Political Science Quarterly* (Jun 1947) 250-7.

Brotherton, A. "Indonesia and the Japanese Peace Treaty," *Eastern World* (Feb 1952) 15-6.

Buck, James H., "The Japanese Self-Defense Forces," *Asian Survey* (Sep 1967) 597-613.

Buss, Claude A. "Making Peace with Japan : U.S. Policy on the Japan Treaty," *Far Eastern Survey* (Jun 1951) 113-9.

Coons, Arthur G. "Neutralism : The Problem of Japan in East-West Relations," *World Affairs Interpreter* (Winter, 1955) 385-90.

Cotton, Kenneth E., George Totten and Others. "Japan Since Recovery of Independence," *Annals of the American Academy of Political and Social Science* (Nov 1956) 1-174.

Cuenco, Jesus M. "Threat of Japanese Peace Pact to the Philippines Stressed," *Manila Chronicle* (15 Jul 1951).

Djatiasmono, Basuki. "Reparations Get Off to a Promising Start," *Japan Times* (Tokyo) (17 Aug 1959).

Dulles, John Foster. "Japan and the Philippines," *Far Eastern Survey* (13 Jun 1951) 115.

———. "Security in the Pacific," *Foreign Affairs* (Jan 1952) 175-87.

Espinosa, Emilio. "Reparations : An Appraisal," *Congressional Annual, 1958* (Manila) 54-5.

Evatt, Herbert V. "Japan is Still a Menace," *New York Times Magazine* (3 Feb 1946) 10, 46-7.

Fang, C.C. "The US Draft Peace Treaty with Japan Menaces All Asia," *People's China* (1 Sep 1951) 5-7.

Farley, Miriam S. "Japan and U.S. Post-Treaty Problems," *Far Eastern Survey* (27 Feb 1952) 33-8.

Gibson, James B. "The Occupation of Japan—Ten Years Later," *World Affairs* (1952) 1-35.

Green, Heslie C. "Making Peace with Japan," *Yearbook of World Affairs* (1952) 1-35.

Guillain, Robert. "The Resurgense of Military Elements in Japan," *Pacific Affairs* (Sep 1952) 221-5.

Hayashi, Yijiro. "The Relations Between Reparations and Foreign Trade," *Asian Affairs* (Tokyo) (Sep 1956) 260-73.

Hayden, Ralston. "China, Japan and the Philippines," *Foreign*

Affairs (Jul 1933) 711-6.

Ichikawa, Tsunezo. "Japan's Liabilities—Reparations and External Debts," *Contemporary Japan*, Vol. 24 (Nos. 4-6, 1956) 337-41.

Iguchi, Sadao. "The Place of Japan in a Resurgent Asia," *Annals of the American Academy of Political and Social Science* (Jul 1954) 8-13.

Ikeda, Hayato. "Japan's Share in Economic Cooperation," *Contemporary Japan* (Aug 1959) 22.

Imperial, Jose F. "The Philippines and Japan," *Fookien Times Yearbook 1953*, 72.

Inamura, Junzo. "In Rebuttal of Those Who Oppose Both the San Francisco Peace Treaty and Mutual Security Agreement," *Journal of Social and Political Ideas in Japan* (Apr 1965) 45-8.

Itagaki, Yoichi. "Reparations and Southeast Asia," *Japan Quarterly* (Tokyo) (Oct-Dec 1959) 410-9.

Jain, J.P. "The Legal Status of Formosa : A Study of British, Chinese and Indian Views," *American Journal of International Law* (Jan 1963) 25-45.

Kawai, Kazu. "Japanese Views on National Security," *Pacific Affairs* (Jun 1950) 115-27.

Kawakami, Kivishi Karl. "America and Japan's Permanent Neutrality," *World Affairs* (Summer 1949) 35-7.

Kennan, George F. "Japanese Security and American Policy," *Foreign Affairs* (Oct 1964) 14-28.

Kiichi, Sabeki. "The Building of Japan's Self-Defence," *Japan Quarterly* (Jan-Mar 1957) 101-10.

Lanuza, Caezar. "The Marikina Dam," *Philippine Reparations Report, 1959*, 225-8.

————. "Reparations for the Greatest Good of the Greatest Number," *Philippine Reparations Report, 1959*, 470-3.

Laurel, Jose B. "Political Motivations of the Philippine-Japan Treaty," *Fookien Times Yearbook 1961*, 67.

MacArthur, Douglas II. "The Evolution of the Japanese-American Partnership," *Department of State Bulletin* (17 Apr 1961) 556-61.

Masamichi, Royama, "The U.S. Japanese Security Treaty—A Japanese View," *Japan Quarterly* (Jan-Mar 1957) 284-95.

Mendel, Douglas H. "Japanese Attitude Toward American

Military Bases," *Far Eastern Survey* (Sep 1959) 129-34.

————. "Japanese Views of the American Alliance," *Public Opinion Quarterly* (Fall 1959) 326-42.

Menzies, Robert G. "The Pacific Settlement Seen From Australia," *Foreign Affairs* (Jan 1952) 188-96.

Metzger, Stanley D. "The Liberal Japanese Peace Treaty," *Cornell Law Quarterly* (Spring 1952) 382-402.

Morley, James W. "Japan and the U.S.S.R.," in Princeton University Conference, *The New Japan : Prospects and Promises* (Princeton, N.J., 1963) 45-53.

————. "Soviet-Japanese Peace Declaration," *Political Science Quarterly* (Sep 1957) 370-9.

Morris, I. "Japanese Foreign Policy and Neutralism," *International Affairs* (Jan 1960) 7-20.

Mukra Kawa, Toshiyuki. "Heiwa Joyaku Aoan no sho mondai," (The Problems of the Draft Peace Treaty) *Sekai* (Oct 1951) 48-61.

Nakagawa, Toru. "Japan-Philippines Relations," *Fookien Times Yearbook 1953*, 74.

Nanbara, Shigeru. "Sekaiteki kiki to Nihon no dokuritsu" (The Global Crisis and Japan's Independence) *Sekai* (Sep 1952) 18-31.

New, Felino. "Japanese Reparations—An Opportunity and a Challenge," *Commerce* (Manila) (Jun 1956) 29-30.

————. "Philippines-Japan Relations," *Progress* (Annual of *Manila Times*) (1957) 71-3.

Ohno, Takushi, "United States Policy on Japan War Reparations, 1945-1951," *Asian Studies* (Dec 1975) 23-46.

Okazaki, Katsuo. "Japan's Foreign Relations," *Annals of the American Academy of Political and Social Science* (Nov 1956) 156-66.

Patricio, Nicanor M. "Should the Philippines Ratify Treaty with Japan?" *Saturday Mirror* (Manila) (29 Aug 1964) 30-1.

Polyziodes, A. "The Japanese Peace Treaty and After," *World Affairs Interpreter* (Autumn 1951) 296-310.

Rama, Napoleon. "Reparations Vessels Going to Waste," *Philippines Free Press* (13 Aug 1960) 40-4.

Rawlings, C.H. "The Japanese Peace Treaty," *Contemporary Review* (Oct 1951) 202-5.

Recto, Claro M. "Dulles' Final Draft Gives Philippines Nothing," *Manila Chronicle* (17 Aug 1951).

Ryu. Shintaro. "The Timing of Japan's Peace Treaty," *Far Eastern Survey* (Sep 1951) 165-8.

Sakamoto, Yashikazu. "Neutralism and the Idea of Peaceful Co-Existence," *Journal of Social and Political Ideas in Japan* (April 1963) 63-7.

"Soren no kowa koser" (Soviet Union's Peace Offensive) *Chou Koron* (Oct 1951) 37-49.

Storry, Richard. "Options for Japan in the 1970s," *The World Today* (Aug 1970).

———. "The New Tensions in Japan : The American Connection and the Future," *Conflict Studies* (Aug 1974) 14-6.

Stratton, Samuel S. "Far Eastern Commission," *International Organization* (9 Feb 1948) 1-18.

Takagi, Koichi. "Indonesian Reparations," *Japan Times* (12 Jul 1957).

Vellut, J.L.L. "Japanese Reparations to the Philippines," *Asian Survey* (Oct 1963) 496-506.

Yamamoto, Noburu. "Reparations and Economic Cooperation," *Asian Affairs* (Sep 1956) 246-59.

Yoshida, Shigeru. "Japan and the Crisis in Asia," *Foreign Affairs* (Jan 1951) 171-81.

INDEX